Forecasting of Corporate Bankruptcy

Forecasting of Corporate Bankruptcy

Edited by
Mark Brooks

www.willfordpress.com

Published by Willford Press,
118-35 Queens Blvd., Suite 400,
Forest Hills, NY 11375, USA

ISBN: 978-1-64728-524-1

Cataloging-in-Publication Data

Forecasting of corporate bankruptcy / edited by Mark Brooks.
    p. cm.
Includes bibliographical references and index.
ISBN 978-1-64728-524-1
1. Bankruptcy--Forecasting. 2. Corporate reorganizations. 3. Business failures. I. Brooks, Mark.
HG3761 .F67 2023
332.75--dc23

For information on all Willford Press publications
visit our website at www.willfordpress.com

Contents

Preface

In my initial years as a student, I used to run to the library at every possible instance to grab a book and learn something new. Books were my primary source of knowledge and I would not have come such a long way without all that I learnt from them. Thus, when I was approached to edit this book; I became understandably nostalgic. It was an absolute honor to be considered worthy of guiding the current generation as well as those to come. I put all my knowledge and hard work into making this book most beneficial for its readers.

Corporate bankruptcy forecasting is a vast area of finance and accounting research that seeks to predict bankruptcy and various measures of financial distress in public firms. It is an important indicator, which assists the investors and policy makers in taking proactive measures to minimize the impact of bankruptcies. In modern economies, banks, retail investors, institutional investors and lenders keep searching for information that can forecast financial distress in public firms. Bankruptcy prediction helps in better allocation of resources. It helps in highlighting the issues in businesses to provide business managers with additional time for taking corrective measures to avoid bankruptcy. In recent years, researchers have developed machine learning algorithms, which use financial ratios for the prediction of bankruptcy. This book outlines the key concepts of bankruptcy prediction in detail. A number of latest researches have been included to keep the readers up-to-date with the global concepts in this area of study.

I wish to thank my publisher for supporting me at every step. I would also like to thank all the authors who have contributed their researches in this book. I hope this book will be a valuable contribution to the progress of the field.

Editor

Review of Research into Enterprise Bankruptcy Prediction in Selected Central and Eastern European Countries

Błażej Prusak [ID]

Faculty of Management and Economics, Gdańsk University of Technology, 80-233 Gdańsk, Poland;
blaprusa@pg.edu.pl

Abstract: In developed countries, the first studies on forecasting bankruptcy date to the early 20th century. In Central and Eastern Europe, due to, among other factors, the geopolitical situation and the introduced economic system, this issue became the subject of researcher interest only in the 1990s. Therefore, it is worthwhile to analyze whether these countries conduct bankruptcy risk assessments and what their level of advancement is. The main objective of the article is the review and assessment of the level of advancement of bankruptcy prediction research in countries of the former Eastern Bloc, in comparison to the latest global research trends in this area. For this purpose, the method of analyzing scientific literature was applied. The publications chosen as the basis for the research were mainly based on information from the Google Scholar and ResearchGate databases during the period Q4 2016–Q3 2017. According to the author's knowledge, this is the first such large-scale study involving the countries of the former Eastern Bloc—which includes the following states: Poland, Lithuania, Latvia, Estonia, Ukraine, Hungary, Russia, Slovakia, Czech Republic, Romania, Bulgaria, and Belarus. The results show that the most advanced research in this area is conducted in the Czech Republic, Poland, Slovakia, Estonia, Russia, and Hungary. Belarus Bulgaria and Latvia are on the other end. In the remaining countries, traditional approaches to predicting business insolvency are generally used.

Keywords: corporate bankruptcy prediction; bankruptcy risk; financial analysis; comparative analysis

JEL Classification: G33; G17; F37; C38

1. Introduction

Bankruptcy is an indispensable part of the functioning of enterprises in market economy conditions. On the one hand, it is normal, as competition forces the liquidation of unprofitable units and the creation of space for those using scarce resources more efficiently. On the other hand, every bankruptcy has a negative impact on many stakeholders, including creditors, employees, suppliers, consumers, and the local community. In particular, the creditors and suppliers are exposed to the risk of loss when the debtors go bankrupt. *"Failure to fulfill debt commitments by a customer may hamper the solvency of the supplier (creditors), who may become unable in turn to pay its own suppliers located in the upper level, which may lead to a chain of similar failures (domino effect) and in extreme cases result in bankruptcy avalanches"* (Battiston et al. 2007).

Therefore, it is important to conduct research into the prediction of bankruptcy risk. Early detection of signs of deteriorating financial situation may allow taking corrective actions. It can also prevent sustaining losses by current or potential capital providers. In the United States, such research has been conducted since the beginning of the 20th century, while in other developed countries it was initiated in the 70s of the previous century. In the countries of Central and Eastern Europe, however, the interest in this area began much later. It is a result of the fact that before the dissolution of the Soviet Union these countries had a centrally planned economy, which in principle did not provide for the existence of the institution of bankruptcy. It was only in the early 1990s that the transformation of economy started and first insolvency laws were introduced in the majority of the former Eastern Bloc countries, followed by first bankruptcy proceedings. It was only then that the researchers from these countries began to be interested in the issue of assessing enterprises in view of the threat of insolvency they face. The introduction of effective tools for corporate failure forecasting in these countries enables to identify potential bankruptcies and, consequently, reduce losses by avoiding cooperation with such entities. In addition, these tools can act as early warning systems against insolvency and allow to identify early stages of a crisis. As a result, these companies may take early recovery action to improve their financial standing and to continue as a going concern. Therefore, it is worthwhile to analyze whether these countries conduct bankruptcy risk assessments and what their level of advancement is.

That is why the main objective of the article is the review and assessment of the level of advancement of bankruptcy prediction research in countries of the former Eastern Bloc, in comparison to the latest global research trends in this area. For this purpose, the method of analyzing scientific literature was applied. The publications chosen as the basis for the research were mainly based on information from the Google Scholar and ResearchGate databases during the period Q4 2016–Q3 2017. According to the author's knowledge, this is the first such large-scale study involving the countries of the former Eastern Bloc—which includes the following states: Poland, Lithuania, Latvia, Estonia, Ukraine, Hungary, Russia, Slovakia, Czech Republic, Romania, Bulgaria, and Belarus. On that basis, differences in the level of advancement of research on forecasting the corporate bankruptcy in the analyzed countries were identified. The strengths and weaknesses of the models built in them were determined and on this basis the directions of changes in the countries with the lowest level of research advancement in this area were proposed. Moreover, specific factors in relation to highly developed countries, which had an impact on the effectiveness of the developed models, were presented.

Apart from the introduction, the article is divided into three parts. The first part describes the global history of research into bankruptcy prediction and the latest trends in this area. In the next section, the results of literature studies concerning individual countries are presented. Additionally, a ranking of countries in terms of the degree of advancement of bankruptcy prediction studies is proposed, as well as specific characteristics of some countries are highlighted. The last part of the article contains conclusions.

2. Global Experience—Literature Review

The interest in predicting bankruptcy dates to the beginning of the 20th century, and the first research was initiated in the United States. Originally, researchers used single indicators or financial parameters to distinguish between insolvent and solvent entities. For example, already in 1908 Rosendale (Beaver 1968) tried to evaluate the risk of insolvency of companies based on information on their current assets. In the later period, the ratio analysis in this research area was used, among others, by Ramser and Foster—1931 (Back et al. 1997), Fitzpatrick (1932), Smith and Winakor (1935), Merwin (1942, as in Back et al. 1997), as well as (Beaver 1966). The latter applied univariate discriminant analysis. Considering multiple financial measures, he defined the discriminative power of each of them separately. For this purpose, the percentage of correct and incorrect predictions in the five years preceding the bankruptcy of enterprises was calculated.

The breakthrough came, however, in 1968—after Altman's publication (Altman 1968). He considered simultaneous impact of several indicators on the financial condition of the company by combining them into a single measure (Z-score). He used the technique of the multivariate linear discriminant analysis to achieve this purpose. Altman (2015), alone or in collaboration with other scientists, developed later numerous other models, dedicated to both the American companies and companies from other countries (Altman and Narayanan 1997). He found many followers in the United States and abroad, and the multivariate linear discriminant analysis has become the most popular technique used to develop corporate bankruptcy forecasting models (Bellovary et al. 2007; Aziz and Dar 2006).

In the 1970s and early 1980s the linear multivariate discriminant analysis was criticized, which resulted in the appearance of the logit and probit anaylsis in studies in the field of forecasting corporate bankruptcy (Chesser 1974; Martin 1977; Ohlson 1980; Wiginton 1980, as in Härdle et al. 2004; Zavgren 1983; Zmijewski 1984). In the 1970s and 1980s as an alternative to the linear multivariate discriminant analysis method and the logit and probit method studies were published in which the authors used other techniques, such as linear programming, the method of recursive division, cluster analysis or classification trees (Prusak 2005).

Another significant breakthrough came in the early 1990s. The development of statistical and analytical tools enabled the use of more sophisticated techniques for analyzing larger data sets, and the race to find more and more effective methods continues today. At that time the non-parametric methods began to be used in evaluating the threat of corporate bankruptcy—in particular the artificial neural networks (Odom and Sharda 1990; Raghupathi et al. 1991, as in Jo et al. 1997; Coats and Fant 1991; Tam and Kiang 1992; Fletcher and Goss 1993; Rahimian et al. 1993; Wilson and Sharda 1994; Boritz and Kennedy 1995; Serrano-Cinca 1997). Recent years have also seen a group of new methods from the area of forecasting corporate bankruptcy, categorized as the so-called soft computing techniques (Korol 2010a, 2013). Such a direction of progress stems from the use of computer applications that enable the implementation of advanced computational processes. Apart from the above-mentioned artificial neural networks, this category of methods includes, among others, genetic algorithms (Shin and Lee 2002), the method of support vectors (Härdle et al. 2004), fuzzy logic (Michael et al. 2001), as well as recently fashionable swarm algorithms, the most popular of which in this research area is the ant colony algorithm (Zhang and Wu 2011; Martin et al. 2014). In contrast to traditional statistical techniques, such as linear multivariate discriminant analysis or logit and probit analysis, these methods cope better with imprecisely defined problems, incomplete data, inaccuracy, imprecision, and uncertainty. They process information in cases difficult to illustrate in the form of algorithms and do this in conjunction with the symbolic representation of knowledge (Korol 2010b).

At the same time, the evolution of structural models based on the option theory was observed, with the KMV model as the most popular one (Iazzolino and Fortino 2012). They mainly use market information, rather than accounting data as in the previously presented approaches, to forecast bankruptcies. Also worth mentioning are gambling models, the main advantage of which is their dynamic nature, compared to the static approach used in traditional methods (Shumway 2001).

Apart from the aforementioned concepts, belonging to the most commonly used in the field of bankruptcy forecasting, the following approaches can be found in the literature of the subject: rough set theory (Slowinski and Zopounidis 1995), cash management methods (Laitinen and Laitinen 1998), catastrophe theory (Gregory-Allen and Henderson 1991), multicriteria decision aid methodology (Zopounidis and Doumpos 1999), Case-Based Reasoning (Park and Han 2002), Data Envelopment Analysis (Premachandra et al. 2009), multidimensional scaling (Molinero and Ezzamel 1991), concepts based on the entropy theory (Bal et al. 2013), pattern recognition method (Kolari et al. 1996), the self-organizing map method (Kiviluoto 1998; Du Jardin and Séverin 2011), bankruptcy trajectories (Argenti 1976; Du Jardin and Séverin 2010) and opinions of auditors on the continuation of business activity of the surveyed companies (Carson et al. 2013).

In addition to pursuing increasingly advanced techniques, appropriate significance should be attributed to the variables used in the models being built. Initially, only financial ratios and amounts that could be derived from financial statements were used. Over time, however, other factors, such as those related to macroeconomics, business sector or corporate governance, were increasingly considered, which has affected the efficiency of models (Dyrberg 2004; Lee et al. 2003; Grunert et al. 2005).

In forecasting corporate bankruptcy, there are also two extreme approaches to building models that can be observed. On the one hand, models adapted to the specificity of the analyzed enterprises are proposed. In this case, it is suggested that models suitable for the units operating in a given country (Altman and Narayanan 1997) or sector (Altman 2000), having appropriate size (Khmerkan and Chancharat 2015) or listed or not on a stock exchange (Altman 2000) should be developed. Such models are generally characterized by higher efficiency than in the case of universal models, as they consider the specific characteristics of the examined enterprise group. However, they do not enable the comparisons of the risk of insolvency between different groups of enterprises. Therefore, the literature of the subject also presents proposals of models that are universal, i.e., based on data from companies operating in different sectors, countries, etc. The examples include models that are global (Alaminos et al. 2016) or regional, i.e., estimated based on data from companies operating in selected countries in a given area, e.g., the European Union, Central and Eastern Europe, etc. (Laitinen and Suvas 2013; Režňáková and Karas 2014; Vavřina et al. 2013; Babič et al. 2013; Novotná 2012; Klepáč and Hampel 2016).

3. Research into Business Insolvency Forecasting in Selected Central and Eastern European Countries—Results

3.1. Methodology

A critical literature analysis of the subject was used as a research method. First, the second section presents the results of research on corporate bankruptcy prediction related to highly developed countries, which reaches many years back. It depicts both the historical outline and the latest global trends in the forecasting of corporate bankruptcy. This point determines, on the one hand, an introduction to the main research and a comparative basis for the Central and Eastern European countries.

In the second stage, material was collected in the form of publications on the forecasting of corporate bankruptcy in selected Central and Eastern European countries. This group included countries which founded the CMEA (Council for Mutual Economic Assistance) or which later emerged as a result of its collapse (Poland, Lithuania, Latvia, Estonia, Ukraine, Hungary, Russia, Slovakia, Czech Republic, Romania, Bulgaria, Belarus). Information on the publications was obtained during the period of Q4 2016–Q3 2017 from Google Scholar and ResearchGate databases by entering the phrases "corporate bankruptcy prediction" or "bankruptcy prediction" in the search field. The choice of Google Scholar results from the fact that it is one of the most extensive databases, which also includes many publications indexed in Web of Science and Scopus. ResearchGate was a kind of supplement for Google Scholar and facilitated to obtain publications through, inter alia, direct contact with their authors.

3.2. Literature Review

3.2.1. Belarus

The institutions of bankruptcy in their early form, as in other post-Soviet countries, appeared in Belarus in the early 1990s. Originally, Russian bankruptcy law applied there, and the number of bankruptcies was small. It was only at the beginning of the 21st century that it increased significantly, reaching e.g., about 500 cases in 2001, and 1150 cases in 2002. This was a consequence of introducing new regulations aimed at harmonizing Belarussian insolvency law with European standards (Smolski 2006). Therefore, until the implementation of the new law interest in the problem of assessing the risk of enterprise insolvency was insignificant. The interest in these problems intensified particularly in the second half of the first decade of the 21st century, when two national models were estimated by Savitskaya. They were built using the techniques of linear multidimensional discriminatory and logit analysis and are designed to assess the risk of bankruptcy of companies in the agricultural sector. These models are rather theoretical than practical and have never been officially recognized as a tool for forecasting bankruptcy risk. This is because the Belarusian law imposes a methodology for estimating the risk of bankruptcy. It considers three indicators that refer to liquidity and funding structure (Kareleu 2015). Nevertheless, Shakun and Skrobko (2012) conducted a comparative analysis of the efficiency of foreign models (of Altman, Taffler, Tishaw,

Beaver, Fedotov, Sajfulin, Kadykov and Zaitsev) and the Savitskaya linear discriminant analysis model and compared their results to the method of calculating the risk of insolvency imposed by the Belarussian law. The research was carried out based on companies from the agricultural sector and it is, therefore, not surprising that the best results were obtained in the national model. They also coincided with the results produced by the Belarussian analytical tool provided for in the national law. Vodonosova (2012) also conducted a comparative analysis of foreign models, including Russian ones; however, the research sample was not very numerous, as it included only 9 construction companies. Nevertheless, this shows that Belarussian researchers did attempt to use foreign models to assess the risk of insolvency of domestic entities. Kareleu (2015) in his polemic article also notes that due to differentiated access to data, different economic models of countries and economic cycles foreign models cannot be simply transferred to another country, as these tools should be adapted to the prevalent national standards. In addition to traditional techniques, the Belarussian scientists also paid attention to the possibility of using more sophisticated methods, such as fuzzy logic, for predicting bankruptcy. Nevertheless, the article that drew attention to this possibility was rather a presentation than a model (Lobanova et al. 2012).

3.2.2. Bulgaria

In Bulgaria, the bankruptcy procedure is governed by the Commerce Act enacted in 1994[1]. However, insolvency proceedings basically did not take place until July 1996 (Bideleux and Jeffries 2007).

One of the first studies on the financial condition of Bulgarian public companies and investment preferences at the same time, using bankruptcy prediction models, was carried out by Popchev and Radeva (2006). They used the Altman, Fulmer, Springate, R and Voronov-Maximov models to assign the investigated business units to three groups: risky, financially secure to a satisfactory degree and having a very good financial position. In the later period Radkov and Minkova (2011); Radkov (2013) presented the possibility of applying the ASFR-asymptotic single-risk factor and Merton models to estimate the likelihood of bank failures in their country. On the other hand, Angelov (2014) used foreign models, i.e., Beaver, Altman, Fulmer, Springate, Fox and Taffler, to analyze the threat of bankruptcy of six Bulgarian public companies. More extensive research in this area was conducted by Delev (2014, 2016a). He used primarily Western models (of Taffler, Taffler and Tishaw, Springate, Lis, Zmijewski) and Polish models (Pogodzińska and Sojak, Hadasik, poznański) to assess the risk of insolvency of Bulgarian public companies. The models that proved highly efficient in Bulgarian conditions included the approaches of Taffler and Tischaw and Zmijewski, as well as all Polish models. As part of his doctoral dissertation, Delev also presented a model developed for Bulgarian conditions based on 60 non-financial companies listed on the Bulgarian stock exchange. He used linear multiple discriminant analysis (Delev 2016b) to construct his model.

3.2.3. Czech Republic

In the Czech Republic bankruptcy law was enacted on 1 October 1991, while a larger number of bankruptcy petitions appeared only in 1993 (Venyš 1997). The first attempt at developing a national bankruptcy risk assessment model was made by Neumaiers in 1995 (so-called IN95 model). In the following years, the same authors, having a larger sample of companies, built other national models—IN99, IN01 and IN05 (Divišová 2011). Then a significant number of publications on this subject appeared. The main conclusions are presented below, divided into two areas: suggestions of original national models and the proposals related to using already existing domestic and foreign models and financial measures to assess the risk of bankruptcy of Czech companies.

---

[1] See Delchev, Insolvency Law in Bulgaria, https://www.delchev-lawfirm.com/practice-areas/insolvency/ (accessed on 5 September 2017).

An interesting study in bankruptcy of Czech small and medium enterprises was conducted by Korab (2001). A fuzzy logic technique was used to assess the threat of corporate bankruptcy and, in addition, both quantitative (financial and non-financial) and qualitative (e.g., location, qualifications and skills of management team or quality of products and services) measures were applied as explanatory variables. The studies on forecasting bankruptcies of Czech companies were also conducted by Dvořáček and Sousedíková (2006), along with other authors. Originally, they used univariate discriminant analysis (Dvořáček and Sousedíková 2006), which was followed by multidimensional linear discriminant analysis, logit analysis and artificial neural networks that led to the development of several models, mainly of universal nature (Dvořáček et al. 2008, 2012a, 2012b). They used financial ratios as explanatory variables and the best results were obtained using the neural network model. Jakubík and Teplý (2011) built a logit model for predicting bankruptcy based on a large sample of non-financial Czech enterprises. What is new is that they proposed the aggregation of data derived from this model as the next step and, on this basis, they established a measure they called 'JT index', the purpose of which was to illustrate the financial condition of the non-financial sector. Hampel et al. (2012) proposed a model for forecasting the bankruptcy of enterprises from the Czech agribusiness industry sector. They used the function of production for this purpose, which is rare in this research area. The results were then compared with those obtained using the Altman model. They appeared comparable in terms of efficiency, but it should be noted that the research sample was small and the conclusions that can be drawn are not very significant. Kalouda and Vaníček (2013) proposed two national bankruptcy prediction models, CZ2 and FK, constructed using linear multidimensional discriminant analysis. They then compared their performance with the Altman and IN05 models. In particular, the CZ2 model proved superior to the remaining ones. The studies on forecasting bankruptcies of Czech companies were also conducted by Karas and Režňáková, along with other authors. At first, they verified the performance of the Altman model in Czech conditions, which turned out to be low. They then tried to adapt this model to national conditions by modifying weights and the grey zone to get better forecasts (Karas et al. 2013). Later, they built national models using linear multidimensional discriminant analysis and the boosted tree method. In a direct comparison, a model developed based on a nonparametric method was demonstrated to be more efficient (Karas and Režňáková 2013; Karas and Režňáková 2014). Also, based on a sample of manufacturing and construction companies, they conducted a comparative analysis of their own model of linear discriminant analysis (BI—bankruptcy index), another Czech model of linear multidimensional discriminant analysis IN05 and the Altman model. The models generated similar, although low (less than 60%), efficiency levels (Karas and Režňáková 2015). Kocmanová et al. (2014) proposed a measure for the assessment of Czech manufacturing companies in terms of their sustainable development, the so-called SCPI (Sustainable Corporate Performance Index). It is not a typical measure of bankruptcy prediction, as apart from the financial aspects it includes other explanatory variables of environmental, social, and corporate governance nature. Nevertheless, it is an interesting addition to the models discussed in this article. Machek et al. (2015) proposed using linear discriminant and logit analysis to create models allowing to verify the risk of bankruptcy of companies operating in the cultural sector, which is a novelty in relation to other studies. Vochozka et al. (2015a) built a highly efficient model for transportation and shipping companies using logit analysis and financial variables. Bemš et al. (2015) proposed a new solution in enterprise insolvency forecasting, namely the concept of a modified magic square which was used in macroeconomics, among others. They used financial ratios as explanatory variables and the objects were Czech companies. By comparing the models estimated using different techniques, they used the model they proposed to obtain results similar to those obtained using the logit model, artificial neural networks, evolutionary algorithms, and Bayes classifiers. As the added value of this model in relation to others, they recognized the possibility of presenting the results of the financial condition of a company together with the impact of particular explanatory variables graphically. Vochozka et al. (2015b, 2016) developed models for predicting the bankruptcy of Czech manufacturing and construction companies using artificial neural networks having the accuracy of over 90%. On the other hand, Němec and Pavlík (2016) built a logit model for the Czech conditions and then compared its efficiency with other Czech and foreign models based on a validation test. It turned out that their model generated the highest efficiency of 83.97%.

Research using both financial ratios and domestic and foreign models to assess the risk of bankruptcy of Czech companies from different sectors and of different sizes was conducted among others by: Klecka and Scholleova (2010); Divišová (2011); Pitrová (2011); Kubíčková (2011, 2015); Cámská (2012, 2013, 2016); Čámská and Hájek (2012); Šlégr (2013); Mičudová (2013a, 2013b); Kubecová and Vrchota (2014); Machek (2014); Rudolfova and Skerlíkova (2014); Dolejšová (2014, 2015); Hajdíková et al. (2015); Daniela et al. (2016). In addition, Kubíčková and Nulicek (2016) proposed potential indicators that act as predictors of enterprise bankruptcy under Czech conditions. Kubíčková (2011) came to interesting conclusions. She determined the values of the financial measures necessary to calculate the value of the Altman function for selected Czech companies based on the financial statements drawn up in accordance with the Czech accounting standards and in accordance with the International Accounting Standards. It turned out that both the values of the indicators and the Altman model parameters differed and, in some cases, generated contradictory predictions regarding the risk of bankruptcy.

3.2.4. Estonia

In Estonia, as in other post-Soviet countries, the problem of corporate insolvency emerged in the early 1990s, when the country regained its independence. The bankruptcy law was passed on 10 June 1992 and entered into force on 1 September 1992 (Varul 1999).

The first studies on the prediction of business insolvency using the appropriate models appeared, however, only at the end of the 20th century. In 1999, Künnapas (as in Männasoo 2007) built a model for forecasting the bankruptcy of Latvian manufacturing companies using linear multidimensional discriminative analysis, and seven years later Lukason proposed national models (for Estonian conditions) that were estimated using the following techniques: linear multidimensional discriminant analysis, logit analysis, artificial neural networks, and recursive division methods. Männasoo (2007) applied the survival analysis for this purpose. Later, Grünberg and Lukason (2014) developed two models of forecasting bankruptcy of production companies using, respectively, the logit analysis and artificial neural networks. Data of 11,542 sound enterprises and 58 bankruptcies from the years 2005–2008 were used to estimate these figures. As the explanatory variables for the model the financial ratios, the size of the company measured by the level of assets and the age of the company were chosen. Model testing was performed on a validation sample for two periods, i.e., the period of economic growth (2005–2008) and the years of recession (2009–2010). The results can be considered unsatisfactory as far as the efficiency of the forecasts is concerned. In particular, the first type accuracy proved to be low. In the case of one-year time advance, the logit model for the growth period yielded 72% efficiency, while during the recession it amounted to 51%. For a model developed using artificial neural networks, the results were as follows: 84% and 65%. For two- and three-year advance for the economic growth period, the logit model generated first type accuracy close to 40%, while the artificial neural network model achieved efficiency close to 60%. Generally, the predictive results obtained using the artificial neural network model were slightly better than in the case of the logit model. These studies also show that models developed based on data from the period of economic growth do not work well for predicting the bankruptcy of companies that occurred during the recession. Other studies on forecasting the bankruptcy of Estonian companies were carried out by Käsper (2016). He focused exclusively on forecasting the bankruptcy of micro-enterprises which obtained grants for starting up business in the period 2004–2009. Using the logit method, he estimated his own model with financial indicators as the explanatory variables and then compared its performance with

Stahlman[2] and Altman[3] models. The efficiency of all models for the period of one year and two years preceding the bankruptcy proved to be very low—it did not exceed 60%. Only in the case of two-year advance the Käsper model allowed for reaching 67.9% of correct classifications. It is also worth noting that in the case of each of the models there were significant differences between first- and second-type accuracies. These analyses show that traditional bankruptcy prediction models failed to predict the financial condition of small businesses. The same author, in cooperation with Lukason (Lukason and Käsper 2017), expanded his research in the field of forecasting bankruptcy risk by considering all start-ups that received government grants in the period 2004–2013. Upon selection, data were collected for 417 companies, based on which models were built using logistic regression. However, they generated low efficiency, which is why the concept of trajectory, called 'financial patterns' by the authors, was also used in the research.

3.2.5. Hungary

In Hungary, as in other post-Soviet countries, the problem of corporate insolvency emerged in the early 1990s[4]. The first models of bankruptcy risk prediction for the Hungarian market were developed by Hajdu and Virág (2001). To this end, they selected a sample of 154 companies, of which half were insolvent. As explanatory variables, the indicators based on the financial statements of 1990–1991 were used. The models were constructed based on linear discriminant analysis and logistic regression. Later, in 1996, they developed several industry models using the same methods (they presented in their publication 26 industries). In 2005, Virág and Kristóf (2005) published a paper in which, based on the same data from 1990–1991 used to build previous models, they built another model using artificial neural networks. Compared to earlier models, it was characterized by higher efficiency, which confirmed the superiority of artificial neural network techniques over linear multidimensional discriminant analysis and logistic regression in predicting the risk of insolvency of enterprises. A similar research was conducted on another sample of companies by Bozsik (2010). He built models using linear multidimensional discriminant analysis and artificial neural networks and compared their efficiency on a validation sample. The results were comparable to those obtained by Virág and Kristóf, i.e., models of neural networks proved to be better, and among them the one with two layers was exceptionally superior. In subsequent studies, using the same learning sample from the years 1990–1991, Virág and Kristóf (2014) built models using the techniques of support vector machines and rough set theory. Based on the validation sample it was found that both models generated efficiencies similar to the one of the model developed using artificial neural networks.

Very extensive research on the forecasting of bankruptcy of Hungarian small and medium-sized enterprises was conducted by Kristóf and Koloszár (2014). They estimated their own models using the following techniques: linear discriminant analysis, logit analysis, classification trees and artificial neural networks, and then compared the efficiencies of these models with the efficiencies of other Hungarian (Virág-Hajdú discriminant and logistic models) and foreign (Altman, Springate, Comerford, Ohlson, Zmijewski) models both on the learning sample and on the validation sample. What is not surprising is that for the learning sample the models estimated by them were highly efficient—their efficiency was much higher than in the case of other models. Out of these, the best models were estimated using classification trees and artificial neural networks. The results obtained for the validation sample were much worse, as the best model built by the authors achieved an overall error of 26.7%. The other models were characterized by significantly higher errors. This means that under no circumstances should foreign models be used to predict the bankruptcy of Hungarian companies and national models can only serve as supplementary tools for assessing the risk of bankruptcy of units from

---

[2] The Stahlman logit model is based on the financial data derived from the micro and small companies (Käsper 2016).
[3] In these studies, the author used the Altman logistic model from 2014 (Altman et al. 2017).
[4] Act XLIX of 1991 on Bankruptcy Proceedings and Liquidation Proceedings, http://matraholding.hu/images/userfiles/files/Legislation.pdf (accessed on 10 March 2017).

the SME sector. In the same year the results of the financial analysis of Hungarian dairy companies were published by Andrea (2014). She used the ratio analysis and the Altman and Springate models. The Altman, Springate, Comerford and Virág-Hajdú models were also used for assessing the risk of bankruptcy of Hungarian companies in studies of Dorgai et al. (2016). As part of these analyses, Altman and Springate models proved to be the best, but it should be noted that the sample was not very large. Finally, Bauer and Edrész (2016), based on data from 1996–2014, built a probit model for predicting the insolvency of private Hungarian companies. One of the distinguishing features of their research was the inclusion of, apart from typical explanatory variables such as financial indicators, also macroeconomic variables (GDP growth, cost of borrowing and the rate of total bank loan volume growth) and qualitative variables (company size, age, ownership structure, industry, exporter status etc.).

3.2.6. Latvia

In Latvia, the first bankruptcy law was introduced in the same year in which the country regained its independence, i.e., in 1991. Later amendments were made, and new regulations were introduced (Klauberg and Gebhardt 2007; Draba 2012).

Probably the first model adapted to local conditions was developed by Šorins and Voronova (as in Sneidere and Bruna 2011) and published in 1998. The next study results available to the author come from the end of the first and the beginning of the second decade of the 21st century and concern mainly the use of foreign models for forecasting the risk of bankruptcy of Latvian companies. In 2009 Koleda and Lace (2009) presented a tool to assess the risk of bankruptcy of Latvian enterprises from the SME sector. It was based on combining the concepts of four foreign models, i.e., the two-factor model, the models of Altman and Tafler, as well as the R-model into one measure, and each of them was given different weights. Two years later Sneidere and Bruna (2011) published the results of a study on assessing the risk of insolvency of Latvian companies from four sectors: services, manufacturing, trade, and construction. They used foreign models of Altman, Fulmer and Zmijewski, as well as the national model of Šorins and Voronova. Based on them, different accuracy scores were obtained depending on the type of sector, while only the Altman and Fulmer models accounted for over 80% of accurate forecasts in the complete validation sample. In the same year, Genriha et al. (2011) proposed a national logit tri-factor bankruptcy risk assessment model and compared its efficiency with ten foreign models. It turned out to have the highest level of accuracy. The publication of Voronova (2012), which presents various concepts of bankruptcy risk measurement, is also worth noting. Based on the conducted literature research Voronova showed that the Altman models had been used to assess bankruptcy risk in many Central and Eastern European countries (Belarus, Estonia, Czech Republic, Poland, Latvia, Lithuania, Romania, Russia, Ukraine). She suggested that in the case of the SME sector during the early stage of risk management system creation companies used simple methods, such as the Kraliček test and the Duran technique.

3.2.7. Lithuania

In the period after the Second World War the Lithuanian bankruptcy law in Lithuania it was adopted on 15 October 1992, while the first cases of corporate bankruptcies appeared only in 1993[5]. Probably the first national model built in 2003 by Grigaravičius (2003). To do this, he used the logit method with a sample of 88 entities. The estimates of other models dedicated to the Lithuanian market were provided by Purvinis et al. (2005a, 2005b). They used the technique of linear multivariate discriminant analysis and artificial neural networks with the learning sample consisting of only 13 companies. In 2008, the same authors presented hybrid models combining the technologies of artificial

---

[5]   See Republic of Lithuania, Law of Enterprise Bankruptcy, http://www.litlex.lt/litlex/eng/frames/laws/Documents/21. HTM (accessed on 20 July 2016) and Spaičienė (2008).

neural networks and fuzzy logic (Purvinis et al. 2008). In this case, the study sample was more numerous and comprised of 30 sound and 200 bankrupt companies. Their best performance model allowed them to obtain, based on a validation sample, the first type accuracy of slightly more than 80%, which still was higher by 7 percentage points than the result obtained using the Altman's model. In 2006, based on 56 companies, Stundžienė and Boguslauskas (2006) developed a model for assessing the risk of bankruptcy using cluster analysis. It provided higher efficiency in relation to the Altman's one. In the same period Merkevicius et al. (2006) modified, by using the technique of self-organizing maps, the weights in Altman's model to better adapt it to the conditions prevalent in Lithuania. Four years ago, Butkus et al. (2014) built several models using the logit method. It is noteworthy that they had a sectoral nature (related to construction, commercial and industrial companies) and were supplemented by additional models estimated for enterprises of various sizes. The last of the available models was developed by Šlefendorfas (2016). The author used a sample of 145 enterprises for this purpose and the linear multivariate discriminant analysis method. The efficiency determined for learning sample was 89%.

Similar to other countries, Lithuanian scientists have also used foreign models to assess the risk of enterprise insolvency. The first studies with their use were conducted at the end of the 20th century, and a detailed review of the literature in this area was presented by Kanapickiene and Marcinkevicius (2014). It showed that native researchers often used foreign models to assess the threat of insolvency of Lithuanian companies—they employed the models of Altman, Taffler and Tishaw, Springate, Zavgren, Lis and Chesser. Their efficiency in different studies was varied. This means that none of these systems can be considered to work best in conditions prevalent in Lithuania. It should also be noted that these studies were carried out based on companies from different sectors and the sample size in some cases was very small.

3.2.8. Poland

In Poland in the postwar period bankruptcy and reorganization law was in force, supplemented by appropriate ministerial ordinances[6]. Due to the economic system, however, it was dead. Only upon the commencement of economic transformation did it start to be actually applied, and the first corporate bankruptcies took place in 1990. In 2003, the new bankruptcy law was introduced, which, with later amendments, is still in force[7]. On 1 January 2016, it was supplemented by new restructuring law[8].

The problems of forecasting corporate bankruptcies in Poland have been of interest to the researchers only since mid-1990s, although it must be said that since then the studies dealing with this issue have been numerous. For this reason, only an overview of the most important literature on this topic is presented below. The pioneering research was aimed at using foreign models, particularly the Altman model, to predict bankruptcies of Polish enterprises (Mączyńska 1994; Gasza 1997; Łukaszewski and Dąbroś (1998a, 1998b); Bławat 1999; Zdyb 2001). Zdyb (2001) proposed, among other things, adjusting the cutoff point in Altman's model to Polish conditions, so that it generates more efficiency. In the similar period the Polish researchers also started using the ratio analysis (Wędzki 2000; Stępień and Strąk 2003; Michaluk 2003; Kniewski 2004; Prusak 2005), as well as building first national models allowing for predicting corporate bankruptcies (Pogodzińska and Sojak 1995; Gajdka and Stos 1996; Hadasik 1998; Wierzba 2000). Due to the limited access to or scarcity of data, these models were created using small samples and based on multivariate linear discriminant analysis. Later, several other models were created using the same statistical technique and the sizes of learning samples were mostly higher (Hołda 2001; Sojak and Stawicki 2000; Mączyńska 2004; Appenzeller and Szarzec 2004; Korol 2004; Hamrol et al. 2004; Prusak 2005;

Siudek 2005; Jagiełło 2013; Juszczyk and Balina 2014). As in the developed countries, newer statistical techniques also began to be used, such as the logit method (Gruszczyński 2003; Michaluk 2003; Wędzki 2004; Stępień and Strąk 2004; Prusak and Więckowska 2007; Jagiełło 2013; Pisula et al. 2013; Pociecha et al. 2014; Karbownik 2017), artificial neural networks, genetic algorithms, classification trees or survival analysis using the Cox model (Michaluk 2003; Korol 2004; Pisula et al. 2013; Pociecha et al. 2014; Pisula et al. 2015; Gąska 2016; Ptak-Chmielewska 2016), a naive Bayesian classifier, a method indirectly based on the logit model, the k-nearest neighbors method, potential functions, kernel classifiers, random forests, Bayesian networks and methods for combining classifiers into an aggregate model (Gąska 2016). Korol (2010b) also applied the method of support vectors and fuzzy logic. This concept was also used by Pisula et al. (2015). It is worth noting that in addition to universal models, many sectoral models were created, dedicated to, among others:

- companies from the logistics sector (Brożyna et al. 2016; Karbownik 2017),
- companies dealing with: wholesale trade in food, beverages and tobacco products, construction of buildings or road transport of goods (Balina and Jan Bąk 2016),
- transport, construction, service, commercial and industrial companies (Jagiełło 2013; Karbownik 2017),
- forwarding companies (Juszczyk and Balina 2009; Karbownik 2017),
- or cooperative banks (Siudek 2005).

Apart from sectoral models, systems of bankruptcy risk assessment considering the criterion of enterprise size were developed (Jagiełło 2013). It is also worth mentioning that Polish researchers used not only financial ratios but also macroeconomic measures (Korol 2010a) as explanatory variables to construct the models of enterprise bankruptcy risk assessment. In addition, Pociecha and Pawełek (2011) based on the conducted research showed that the risk of bankruptcy depends on the economic cycle and therefore suggested that enterprise bankruptcy forecasting models should consider measures showing changes in economic conditions.

3.2.9. Romania

In Romania the bankruptcy regulations had been in operation since 1887 and were included in the Commercial Code. Because of economic and political changes, they lost their significance in 1948. After the fall of the Soviet bloc and the introduction of market mechanisms, new law on restructuring and liquidation was adopted in 1995 (Branch et al. 2010).

Already in the second half of the 1990s several national models of enterprise insolvency forecasting have been developed (Manecuta and Nicolae—model for metallurgical enterprises in 1996, Bailesteanu model in 1998, Ivonciu model in 1998). These proposals were mainly based on ratio analysis and univariate discriminant analysis. Research in this area was continued in the 21st century (models: Anghel—2002—linear multidimensional discriminant analysis, Siminica—2005, Robu-Mironiuc ZRM—2012—linear multidimensional discriminant analysis, an aggregated index of financial condition of construction companies in Galati County developed by Barbuta-Misu—2012, Armeanu et al.—2012) (Barbuta-Misu 2012; Robua et al. 2014; Dinca and Bociu 2015). Most of these models were estimated using linear discriminant analysis. Other techniques were also considered. For example, Robua et al. (2013) used survival analysis and the Cox regression model to predict the bankruptcy of Romanian companies listed on a stock exchange. A very extensive study for Timis county was carried out by Brîndescu-Olariu and Goleț (2013a, 2013b), who, based on a sample of 26,980 companies first developed a linear multidimensional discriminant analysis model and then based on a more homogeneous sample of 4327 units estimated also a logit model. A logit and probit model for large and medium companies was developed by Megan and Circa (2014). On the other hand, Ioan-Bogdan Robua et al. (2014) used such statistical techniques as: analysis of variance (ANOVA), linear regression and analysis of covariance (ANCOVA) models for assessing the risk of insolvency of Romanian companies listed on the Bucharest Stock Exchange (BSE). These models were built based on

70 companies and their purpose was to support the decision to buy/sell shares. They connected the risk of insolvency calculated using the Robu-MironiucRM model with stock return rates. It turned out that companies with high/low risk of default generated negative/positive returns, which confirmed the correlation between the risk of default and the rate of return on shares.

Romanian scientists also used foreign models to assess the risk of insolvency, for example: Burja and Burja (2013) used the revised Altman Z-score model to assess the financial condition of BSE-listed Romanian companies from the agricultural sector; Barbuta-Misu together with Codreanu (Barbuta-Misu and Codreanu 2014) and Stroe (Barbuta-Misu and Stroe 2010) used the Altman and Conan-Holder models to assess the risk of bankruptcy of construction companies. The same models were recognized as efficient in the research on insolvency risk of companies from mining and energy sectors conducted by Catalin and Ion (2016). On the other hand, Crăciun et al. (2013) and Dinca and Bociu (2015) used the Altman model and Romanian Anghel model for bankruptcy forecasting.

3.2.10. Russia

After the dissolution of the Soviet Union bankruptcy law was passed in Russia on 19 November 1992 and entered into force on 1 March 1993. In the first two years of its existence, the number of bankruptcies was insignificant and reached slightly over 100 in 1993 and 240 in 1994 (Vitryansky 1999). Therefore, as in other Central and Eastern European countries, interest in the problem of predicting bankruptcy of enterprises appeared relatively late compared to developed countries.

The first Russian models were built using mainly linear multidimensional discriminant analysis in the mid-1990s by Sayfulin-Kadykov, Zaytseva, Davydova and Bielikov. Fedorova et al. (2013) compared the performance of these models with the results obtained using models created in developed countries (by Altman, Springate, Taffler and Zmijewski) and it unexpectedly appeared that the latter were better at predicting the bankruptcies of Russian manufacturing companies. Later, these authors built national models using the following techniques: linear multidimensional discriminant analysis, logit method, classification trees and neural networks. The best classification results were obtained using neural networks—their overall accuracy reached 88.8%. Moreover, the studies included the indicators recommended by the Russian legislation for investigating the threat of bankruptcy of enterprises. It turned out that only 1 out of 13 of these measures was statistically significant and exhibited discriminatory power. In another publication, Fedorova et al. (2016) proposed a change of thresholds to obtain the highest efficiencies for domestic and foreign models in the various sectors. Foreign models allowed for achieving higher efficiencies and the best of them was Zmijewski's model. Moreover, these authors built their own model using logit analysis, based on a sample of Russian large and medium enterprises. In addition to the above-mentioned models, national models for assessing enterprise insolvency risk using linear multidimensional discriminant analysis were also built by: Fedotova—1995, Lugovskaya—2010—model for small and medium enterprises (Voronova 2012) and Burganova and Salahieva (2015)—model for the forecasting the bankruptcy of manufacturers of building materials based in the Tatarstan Republic. One novelty of the latter model was the fact that the authors considered as variables the average annual rates of change of certain financial ratios, which to a certain extent allowed them to dynamize the model. The researchers who assessed national models of insolvency risk using techniques other than multidimensional linear discriminant analysis include, among others, Evrostopova, who built a logit model (Makeeva and Neretina 2013a, 2013b), and Makeeva and Neretina (2013a, 2013b), who applied logit and probit approaches in addition to the aforementioned multidimensional linear discriminant analysis. Models developed by the latter of the above-mentioned authors are dedicated to the companies in the construction sector. A slightly different approach to predicting bankruptcy risk was presented by Shirinkina and Valiullina (2015). In the first place, they selected the most commonly used metrics in different foreign and domestic models. Next, they examined their impact on the risk of bankruptcy and proposed a simplified model in the form of a pyramid of insolvency risk.

Apart from assessing the risk of bankruptcy of enterprises from different sectors, due to the banking crisis in Russia in 1998 research into forecasting bankruptcies of banks has been very popular. Studies were performed by both Russian and foreign researchers. For example, Peresetsky et al. (2004, 2011) applied cluster analysis and showed that the use of macroeconomic variables (export-to-import rate and ruble/dollar exchange rate) in a model increases its efficiency. Lanine and Vennet (2006) used logit analysis and the trait recognition approach. Both methods yielded satisfactory results and the latter one was slightly better. On the other hand, Kaminsky et al. (2012) used a logit model. They selected measures using the CAMEL (capital adequacy, asset quality, management, earnings, liquidity) model and considered also macroeconomic and institutional variables, among which the consumer price index (positive correlation) and the monopolistic power (negative correlation) proved to have a significant impact on the probability of bank bankruptcies.

3.2.11. Slovakia

In Slovakia, the bankruptcy regulations were introduced in 1993, when the division of Czechoslovakia took place (Janda and Rakicova 2014).

Chrastinová (Chrastinová 1998) and Gurčík (Gurčík 2002) belonged to the first researchers who developed models for the Slovak conditions—they were based on using linear multivariate discriminant analysis. Both concerned business units from the agricultural sector. In the second half of the first decade of the 21st century Hiadlovský and Král' (Bod'a 2009) developed several national models using such techniques as factor analysis, discriminant analysis, logit analysis and fuzzy (2009) theory. Gavliak (Bod'a 2009) also applied a linear probability model. On the other hand, Bod'a

tried to use the artificial neural network technique to predict the bankruptcy of Slovak companies. In the second decade of the 21st century Král' et al. (2014) used penalized logistic regression and random forest techniques to test whether enhancing a model with variables reflecting the changes of indicators over time can improve its efficiency for a sample of Slovak enterprises. The results of their research indicate that models that account for changes in financial indicators over time generated slightly better predictive results than models with static data. In subsequent studies, the above-mentioned authors, in cooperation with Kakaščík (Stachová et al. 2015), verified whether obtaining data from a longer period in the past may improve the efficiency of models. The results show that prolonging the time from which the data for model construction is collected leads to lower predictive errors, which confirmed their hypothesis. Bányiová et al. (2014) applied the Data Envelopment Analysis (DEA) method to predict the bankruptcy of agricultural companies operating in Slovakia. They proposed four models with low overall accuracy (between 54% and 70%). Considering previous research, these authors concluded that better forecast results can be derived from models built on such techniques as linear multidimensional discriminant analysis, logit analysis and classification trees. The DEA method was also used to forecast the bankruptcies of enterprises in Slovakia by Roháčová and Pavol (2015). In this case, however, the validation of the model was not performed. Interesting research carried out on a large sample of Slovak enterprises was conducted by Kubicová and Faltus (2014). They used measures reflecting income taxation to forecast corporate insolvency. It was shown, however, that single indicators of this kind have low discriminatory power. A logit model based on three measures related to taxation generated much better prognostic results than single measures but it failed to provide a guarantee of efficiency higher than in the case of models including other financial measures. Mihalovic (2016 two national models based on a linear multi-dimensional discriminatory analysis and logit analysis using a balanced sample of 236 bankrupt and non-bankrupt enterprises. As explanatory variables, financial indicators were used. The results obtained for a validation sample of enterprises showed the superiority of the logit model, with general efficiencies being not very high (logit model—68.64%, model based on linear multidimensional discriminative analysis—61.86%).

Researchers from Slovakia also performed comparative analyses of the efficiency of different models, including foreign ones. Delina and Packová (2013) analyzed 1560 Slovak enterprises, out of which 103 were bankrupt. The financial data of these companies came from the years 1993–2007.

Three measures of bankruptcy risk assessment were selected for the study: the Altman model, IN05 index and Bonity index. Each of them was characterized by low efficiency. Therefore, these authors proposed to create their own national model using the regression technique. In principle, this model generated better forecasts in comparison to the other three measures, but it should be noted that the efficiencies were determined based on a learning sample, which requires further verification using a validation test. Šofranková (2013) used the Altman model to assess the financial condition of 46 companies offering accommodation (hotels) and verified the relationship between the results from the Altman model and four non-financial measures, i.e., the organizational form, the number of employees, the number of beds offered and the type (class) of the hotel measured by the number of stars. Dependence between the last three measures and the Altman index was observed and on this basis the author suggested constructing an original model considering the specificity of the hotel industry. Later, Šofranková (2014) conducted similar studies but using the IN01 and IN05 models. She reached similar conclusions, namely that it would be worthwhile to include the following non-financial variables in hotel risk assessment models: the class of the hotel measured by the number of stars, the number of beds and the type of hotel ownership (state or private). On the other hand, Braunová and Jantošová (2015) used the Altman model to assess the risk of bankruptcy of hospitals in Žilina region. Adamko and Svabova (2016) verified the efficiency of three Altman logit models from 2014 on a sample of Slovak enterprises for which 2013 and 2014 data were obtained. These results were promising in comparison with the results obtained in other countries, and the AUC (area under curve) measure was between 0.8116 and 0.8835, depending on the model and years.

3.2.12. Ukraine

Ukraine gained independence in 1991, while its bankruptcy law came into force on 1 July 1992[9]. The first national models for predicting the bankruptcy of Ukrainian companies appeared in the early 21th century and were developed by Martynenko and Tereschenko (Voronova 2012). Both authors used the linear discriminative analysis technique to estimate them. Matviychuk (2010) reached interesting conclusions—he provided arguments confirming the claim that foreign models would not work in Ukrainian conditions. This is due, among other factors, to the fact that many Ukrainian companies understate their income to avoid taxation. The group of main indicators in foreign models includes profitability measures, which automatically results in underestimating their value and leads to the indication of increased risk of insolvency. That is why Matviychuk developed national models using linear discriminant analysis techniques and fuzzy logic with financial indicators as explanatory variables. The discriminatory model he developed was validated on a sample consisting of 40 bankrupt and 40 non-bankrupt companies. The overall efficiency was 80.1% and was significantly higher than in the case of the results obtained with the following models: Altman, Davydova-Bielikov and Tereschenko. What is more, the fuzzy logic model was significantly better than the discriminatory model, achieving efficiency above 90%. The comparative analysis of the efficiency of the following models: Altman, Conan and Holder, Lis, Taffler, Springate, Beaver, the universal model based on discriminant function, Chepurko, Saifullin and Kadykov and Sumy was conducted by Druzin (2013) on a sample of 15 enterprises. It turned out that the best results were achieved using the Springate, Lis and Beaver models. The author also pointed out that one of the main problems in forecasting the bankruptcy of Ukrainian companies is the low credibility of publicly available financial data. An interesting concept of enterprise bankruptcy forecasting model was proposed by Kozak et al. (2013). It combines quantitative and qualitative variables by generating causal relationships. The authors used a combination of fuzzy logic and cognitive technology to construct the model. This method is known in theory as fuzzy cognitive maps. Nevertheless, the authors apart from presenting the concept of this model did not show how it should be implemented in practice. Harafonova and Ulchenko (2014)

---

[9]   The Law of Ukraine Bankruptcy dated 14 May 1992 Vidomosti of the Supreme Rada, No. 31, item 440.

characterized in their article the Altman and Ohlson models. They presented their advantages and disadvantages, paying attention to the different accounting standards and conditions of enterprise operation in Ukraine and in the countries in which these models originated. They said that after making appropriate adjustments, these models could be used to forecast the bankruptcy of Ukrainian companies. Kornyliuk (2014) conducted a study on the key determinants enabling the identification of the risk of bankruptcy of Ukrainian banks. He tested 12 financial indicators, the most discriminating of which were the measures of profitability and the ratio of household deposits to liabilities. Among the qualitative factors, the risk of bankruptcy of Ukrainian banks was most influenced by their ownership structure. Banks with foreign capital were much less exposed to the risk of bankruptcy than those with domestic capital. Neskorodeva and Pustovgar (2015) used the Kohonen neural network and financial metrics to build a model enabling the assessment of the risk of bankruptcy of companies from the steel industry. In 2015, Kleban (2015) proposed the use of fuzzy logic for forecasting the insolvency of enterprises. He used the Takagi-Sugeno algorithm, with financial indicators and figures as explanatory variables. Lytvyn (2015) developed the models for forecasting the bankruptcies of insurers using the technique of support vehicle machine. Among the best models, overall efficiency was close to 90%. Klebanova et al. (2016) developed based on 12 bankrupt and 24 non-bankrupt enterprises a model for forecasting bankruptcy of enterprises in the agricultural sector. To this end, they applied a concept combining artificial neural networks and fuzzy logic.

3.3. Summary of Results

Based on the literature review conducted in Section 3.2, in Table 1 the most important conclusions from the research were presented. For this purpose, three most important areas have been identified, i.e., the techniques used to develop national corporate bankruptcy prediction models, types of variables and information on sectoral models.

Table 1. Summary of research on forecasting enterprise bankruptcy in Central and Eastern Europe.

Techniques Used in National Models	Variables	Sectoral Models
Belarus		
linear multiple discriminant analysis and logit technique	financial ratios	agricultural sector
Bulgaria		
linear multiple discriminant analysis	financial ratios	non-financial companies listed on the Bulgarian stock exchange
Czech Republic		
univariate discriminant analysis, linear multiple discriminant analysis, logit technique, artificial neural networks, fuzzy logic technique, function of production, boosted tree technique, Sustainable Corporate Performance Index, modified magic square, evolutionary algorithms and Bayes classifiers	quantitative (financial and non-financial—e.g., variables of environmental, social, and corporate governance nature) and qualitative (e.g., location, qualifications, and skills of management team or quality of products and services) measures	non-financial enterprises, agribusiness industry sector, manufacturing companies, cultural sector, transportation, and shipping companies
Estonia		
linear multiple discriminant analysis, logit technique, artificial neural networks, recursive division methods, survival analysis, financial patterns	financial ratios, size of the company	production companies, micro-enterprises which obtained grants for starting up business
Hungary		
linear multiple discriminant analysis, logit and probit analysis, artificial neural networks, support vector machines, rough set theory, classification trees	financial indicators, macroeconomic variables (GDP growth, cost of borrowing and the rate of total bank loan volume growth) and qualitative variables (company size, age, ownership structure, industry, exporter status etc.)	small and medium-sized enterprises, 26 different industries

Table 1. *Cont.*

Techniques Used in National Models	Variables	Sectoral Models
Latvia		
linear multiple discriminant analysis, logit technique	financial ratios	small and medium-sized enterprises
Lithuania		
linear multiple discriminant analysis, logit technique, artificial neural networks, fuzzy logic, cluster analysis	financial indicators	construction, commercial and industrial companies
Poland		
univariate and linear multiple discriminant analysis, logit analysis, artificial neural networks, fuzzy logic technique, genetic algorithms, classification trees, survival analysis using the Cox model, method of support vectors, a naive Bayesian classifier, a method indirectly based on the logit model, the k-nearest neighbors method, potential functions, kernel classifiers, random forests, Bayesian networks and methods for combining classifiers into an aggregate model	financial indicators, macroeconomic measures	small and medium-sized enterprises, logistics sector, wholesale trade in food, beverages and tobacco products, construction of buildings or road transport of goods, transport, construction, service, commercial and industrial companies, forwarding companies, public companies
Romania		
univariate and linear multiple discriminant analysis, logit technique, survival analysis and the Cox regression model, ANOVA, linear regression, ANCOVA	financial indicators	metallurgical enterprises, construction companies, public companies
Russia		
linear multiple discriminant analysis, logit and probit analysis, artificial neural networks, classification trees, pyramid of insolvency risk, cluster analysis	financial ratios, in case of banks macroeconomic and institutional indicators	small and medium-sized enterprises, manufacturers of building materials, construction sector, banks
Slovakia		
linear multiple discriminant analysis, factor analysis, logit analysis, fuzzy set theory, linear probability technique, random forest, DEA method, classification trees	financial ratios, measures reflecting income taxation	agricultural sector
Ukraine		
linear multiple discriminant analysis, fuzzy logic technique, Kohonen neural network, Takagi-Sugeno algorithm	financial ratios, in case of banks qualitative factors (e.g., ownership structure)	banks, steel industry, agricultural sector

Source: own work.

Table 1 presents that the most advanced techniques are used in the Czech Republic and Poland, while only classical methods were implemented in Bulgaria, Belarus, Romania, and Latvia. In many countries, in addition to financial ratios, other variables were applied as explanatory variables. The exceptions were Belarus, Bulgaria, Latvia, Lithuania, and Romania. In most countries, sectoral models have been developed. The exception was Bulgaria, in which only a universal model limited to companies listed on the stock market was created. The highest number of sector model proposals was recorded in Poland and Hungary.

Considering the information included in Table 1 and the literature analysis conducted in Section 3.2, the rating of the countries is proposed in terms of the state of advancement of bankruptcy forecast models in the Central and Eastern European countries (Table 2). Countries have been assigned with grades 0 to 4, with a higher score resulting in a more advanced research toolbox for forecasting corporate failure. A detailed description of the evaluation criteria is presented in Table 2.

Table 2. Comparative analysis of the level of advancement of research on forecasting enterprise bankruptcy in Central and Eastern Europe.

Country	Rating	Comment
Belarus	1.5	Mainly foreign models have been used to assess the risk of enterprise bankruptcy. National solutions have also been proposed and they are not numerous.
Bulgaria	1.5	Mainly foreign models have been used to assess the risk of enterprise bankruptcy. National solutions have also been proposed and they are not numerous.
Czech Republic	4	Numerous studies have been performed in this area. Many national and sectoral models have been evaluated using the latest statistical methods. Both financial and non-financial information has been used as explanatory variables. In addition, several new solutions have been proposed, such as the modified magic square and the Sustainable Corporate Performance Index.
Estonia	3	National models have been evaluated using the latest techniques. Models have been proposed that considered the specificity of given groups of companies (e.g., manufacturing companies or micro-enterprises obtaining grants).
Hungary	3	Many national models have been proposed, including those built using the latest statistical methods. Sectoral models and models considering business size have been also developed. Financial ratios have been used as explanatory variables, but other economic and non-financial measures were also proposed.
Latvia	2	Mainly foreign models have been used to assess the risk of bankruptcy, while several national models were estimated using basic statistical methods.
Lithuania	2.5	Foreign and national models have been used to assess the risk of bankruptcy—the latter were estimated using more sophisticated statistical methods. There have also been isolated attempts to build sectoral models.
Poland	4	Numerous studies have been performed in this area. Many national and sectoral models have been evaluated using the latest statistical methods. Both financial and non-financial information have been used as explanatory variables. Additionally, attention was paid to the impact of the economic climate on the efficiency of models for the forecasting of enterprise insolvency.
Romania	2	Foreign and national models have been used to assess the risk of bankruptcy—the latter were estimated using more traditional statistical methods. There have also been isolated attempts to build sectoral models.
Russia	3	National models have been evaluated using the latest techniques. Models have been proposed that consider the specificity of given groups of companies (e.g., the construction sector and building materials manufacturers, banks, SME sector).
Slovakia	3.5	Numerous studies have been performed in this area. Many national and sectoral models have been evaluated using the latest statistical methods. For the first time, attempts have been made to use measures that consider income taxation to assess the bankruptcy risk of companies.
Ukraine	2.5	Foreign and national models have been used to assess the risk of bankruptcy—the latter were estimated using more sophisticated statistical methods. There have also been isolated attempts to build sectoral models.

Ratings:
0—There are no studies in enterprise bankruptcy risk prediction in the given country.
1—Analyses are conducted to assess the risk of bankruptcy of enterprises using only foreign models in the country concerned.
2—Both national and foreign models are used to assess the risk of business insolvency in the country concerned, with national models being constructed using less sophisticated statistical methods, i.e., linear multidimensional discriminant analysis, logit and probit methods etc.
3—Both national and foreign models are used to assess the risk of business insolvency in the country concerned, with national models being constructed using also more advanced methods: artificial neural networks, genetic algorithms, the support vector method, fuzzy logic, etc. Moreover, national sectoral models are also estimated.
4—The most advanced methods are used in enterprise bankruptcy risk forecasting in the country concerned and the researchers propose new solutions that affect the development of this discipline.

Source: own work.

The level of experience and advancement of corporate bankruptcy prediction research is varied, but it should be added that many of the latest developments in this area were implemented in most of the countries. Among the analyzed countries, the most advanced research in the field of enterprise bankruptcy forecasting was observed in the Czech Republic, Slovakia, and Poland. Advanced statistical techniques for modelling are employed and other new solutions are proposed in these countries. At the other end were Belarus, Bulgaria and Latvia, where only attempts at constructing national models using basic statistical techniques have been made. The remaining countries are in the middle of this group, but it is worth noting that in most of them the latest statistical techniques to build national models are used and sectoral models were also proposed.

4. Conclusions

Due to the political and economic changes, the institution of bankruptcy in the countries of Central and Eastern Europe began to function in the first half of the 1990s. During this period, the first cases of bankruptcy emerged, which caused interest in the problem of forecasting the risk of insolvency of enterprises. Due to the lack of statistical material in these countries, foreign models were originally used. It was only later that more sophisticated solutions known in developed countries were introduced and national models were built.

According to literature analysis, it means that even though the institution of bankruptcy was introduced in Central and Eastern Europe relatively late, in terms of research on enterprise bankruptcy risk forecasting, some countries currently do not depart from global patterns. The literature review shows that the best world practices are reflected in the research provided in Poland, the Czech Republic and Slovakia. Advanced models have also been developed in Russia, Estonia, Hungary and, to smaller extent, Ukraine. In Romania and Lithuania, mainly classical techniques were used to create bankruptcy forecasting models, using only financial indicators. Bulgaria, Belarus, and Latvia were ranked the weakest. In these countries, there have been single attempts to develop national models using the simplest statistical techniques and applying only financial indicators as explanatory variables.

It is also worth noting that some of these countries are characterized by certain specifics which influence the development of the research area analyzed in this article. For example, in Ukraine profitability metrics have limited prognostic value because of the lowering of income by tax-avoiding enterprises. In Russia and Belarus, the methodology used to examine the risk of bankruptcy of enterprises was included in legal acts, but the efficiency of the proposed tools was not confirmed by research. Moreover, research conducted in Ukraine has shown that the probability of bankruptcy of local banks is lower for those with foreign capital. Regarding the development of bankruptcy forecasts, it is also worth mentioning the differences that may occur when applying different accounting standards. Differing results are also obtained when financial statements are prepared in accordance with national or international accounting standards.

Acknowledgments: I thank the editor and anonymous reviewers for their insightful comments.

References

Adamko, Peter, and Lucia Svabova. 2016. Prediction of the risk of bankruptcy of slovak companies. Paper presented at 8th International Scientific Conference Managing and Modelling of Financial Risks Ostrava VŠB-TU of Ostrava, Faculty of Economics, Department of Finance, Ostrava, Czech Republic, September 5–6, pp. 15–20.

Alaminos, David, Agustín del Castillo, and Manuel Ángel Fernández. 2016. A Global Model for Bankruptcy Prediction. *PLoS ONE* 11: e0166693. Available online: http://journals.plos.org/plosone/article?id=10.1371/journal.pone.0166693 (accessed on 17 July 2017). [CrossRef] [PubMed]

Altman, Edward I. 1968. Financial ratios, discriminant analysis and the prediction of corporate bankruptcy. *The Journal of Finance* 23: 589–609. [CrossRef]

Altman, Edward I. 2000. Predicting Financial Distress of Companies: Revisiting The Z-score and ZETA®Models. Available online: http://pages.stern.nyu.edu/~ealtman/Zscores.pdf (accessed on 17 July 2017).

Altman, Edward I. 2015. *Edward I. 2015 Honorary Doctor of SGH. Selected Articles.* Warsaw: Warsaw School of Economic Press.

Altman, Edward I., and Paul Narayanan. 1997. An international survey of business failure classification models. *Financial Markets, Institutions & Instruments* 6: 1–57. [CrossRef]

Altman, Edward, Malgorzata Iwanicz-Drozdowska, Erkki Laitinen, and Arto Suvas. 2017. Financial Distress Prediction in an International Context: A Review and Empirical Analysis of Altman's Z-Score Model. *Journal of International Financial Managament & Accounting* 28: 131–71. [CrossRef]

Andrea, Rózsa. 2014. Financial Performance Analysis and Bankruptcy Prediction in Hungarian Dairy Sector. *The Annals of the University of Oradea. Economic Sciences* XXIII: 936–45.

Angelov, George. 2014. Options for modelling the financial viability of Sofix companies in the post-crisis years. *Економічний вісник Донбасу* 4: 102–8. [CrossRef]

Appenzeller, Dorota, and Katarzyna Szarzec. 2004. Forecasting the bankruptcy risk of Polish public companies. *Rynek Terminowy* 1: 120–28.

Argenti, John. 1976. *Corporate Collapse: The Causes and Symptoms*. New York: Wiley, Halsted Press.

Aziz, Adnan M., and Humayon A. Dar. 2006. Predicting corporate bankruptcy—Where we stand? *Corporate Governance Journal* 6: 18–33. [CrossRef]

Babič, František, Cecília Havrilová, and Ján Paralič. 2013. Knowledge Discovery Methods for Bankruptcy Prediction. In *Business Information Systems. BIS 2013. Lecture Notes in Business Information Processing*. Edited by Witold Abramowicz. Berlin/Heidelberg: Springer, vol. 157, pp. 151–62.

Back, Barbro, Teija Laitinen, Jukkapekka Hekanaho, and Kaisa Sere. 1997. *The Effect of Sample Size on Different Failure Prediction Methods*. TUCS Technical Report No. 155. Turku: Turku Centre for Computer Science.

Bal, Jay, Yen Cheung, and Hsu-Che Wu. 2013. Entropy for business failure prediction: An improved prediction model for the construction industry. *Advances in Decision Sciences* 2013: 1–14. [CrossRef]

Balina, Rafał, and Maksymilian Jan Bąk. 2016. *Discriminant Analysis as a Prediction Method for Corporate Bankruptcy with the Industrial Aspects*. Waleńczów: Wydawnictwo Naukowe Intellect.

Bányiová, Tatiana, Tatiana Bieliková, and Andrea Piterková. 2014. Prediction of agricultural enterprises distress using data envelopment analysis. Paper presented at 11th International Scientific Conference European Financial Systems, Lednice, Czech Republic, June 12–13; Brno: Masaryk University, pp. 18–25.

Barbuta-Misu, Nicoleta. 2012. Aggregated index for modelling the influence of financial variables on enterprise performance. *EuroEconomica* 2: 155–65.

Barbuta-Misu, Nicoleta, and Elena-Silvia Codreanu. 2014. Analysis and Prediction of the Bankruptcy Risk i Romanian Building Sector Companies. *Ekonomika* 93: 131–46.

Barbuta-Misu, Nicoleta, and Radu Stroe. 2010. The adjustment of the Conan & Holder Model to the Specifity of Romanian Enterprises—A local study for building sector. *Economic Computation and Economic Cybernetics Studies and Research/Academy of Economic Studies* 44: 123–39.

Battiston, Stefano, Domenico Delli Gatti, Mauro Gallegati, Bruce Greenwald, and Joseph E. Stiglitz. 2007. Credit chains and bankruptcy propagation in production networks. *Journal of Economic Dynamics and Control* 31: 2061–84. [CrossRef]

Bauer, Péter, and Marianna Edrész. 2016. *Modelling Bankruptcy Using Hungarian Firm-Level Data MNB Occasional Papers 122*. Budapest: Magyar Nemzeti Bank.

Beaver, William H. 1966. Financial ratios as predictors of failure. Empirical research in accounting: Selected Studies, Supplement to Vol. 5. *Journal of Accounting Research* 1967: 71–111. [CrossRef]

Beaver, William H. 1968. Alternative accounting measures as predictors of failure. *The Accounting Review* 43: 113–22.

Bellovary, Jodi L., Don E. Giacomino, and Michael D. Akers. 2007. A review of bankruptcy prediction studies: 1930 to Present. *Journal of Financial Education* 33: 1–42.

Bemš, Július, Oldřich Starý, Martin Macaš, Jan Žegklitz, and Petr Pošík. 2015. Innovative default prediction approach. *Expert Systems with Applications* 42: 6277–85. [CrossRef]

Bideleux, Robert, and Ian Jeffries. 2007. *The Balkans: A Post-Communist History*.. London and New York: Routledge.

Bławat, Fławat. 1999. Threat of bankruptcy of joint-stock companies in Poland. In *Polish Economy during the Transformation Period*. Edited by Jerzy Czesław Ossowski. Zeszyt nr 3. Gdańsk: Wydawnictwo Politechniki Gdańskiej.

Bod'a, Martin. 2009. Predicting bankruptcy of Slovak enterprises by an artificial neural network. *Forum Statisticum Slovacum* 9: 3–6.

Boritz, J. Efrim, and Duane B. Kennedy. 1995. Effectiveness of neural network types for prediction of business failure. *Expert Systems with Applications* 9: 503–12. [CrossRef]

Bozsik, József. 2010. Artificial neural networks in default forecast. Paper presented at 8th International Conference on Applied Informatics, Eger, Hungary, January 27–30; vol. 1, pp. 31–39.

Branch, Ben, Octavian Ionici, and Iuliana Ismailescu. 2010. Bankruptcy Proceedings in Romania. *Norton Journal of Bankruptcy Law and Practice* 19: 631–50.

Braunová, Mária, and Lucia Jantošová. 2015. The development prediction of financial and economic indicators of hospitals operating in Žilina Region. *Slovak Scientific Journal Management: Science and Education* 4: 12–14.

Brîndescu-Olariu, Daniel, and Ionuţ Goleţ. 2013a. Bankruptcy prediction ahead of global recession: Discriminant Analysis Applied on Romanian Companies in Timiş County. *Timisoara Journal of Economics and Business* 6: 70–94.

Brîndescu-Olariu, Daniel, and Ionuţ Goleţ. 2013b. Prediction of corporate bankruptcy through the use of logistic regression. *Annals of Faculty of Economics, University of Oradea, Faculty of Economics* 1: 976–86.

Brożyna, Jacek, Grzegorz Mentel, and Tomasz Pisula. 2016. Statistical methods of the bankruptcy prediction in the logistics sector in Poland and Slovakia. *Transformations in Business & Economics* 15: 80–96.

Burganova, R. A., and M. F. Salahieva. 2015. Z-Score for bankruptcy forecasting of the companies producing building materials. *Asian Social Science* 11: 109–14. [CrossRef]

Burja, Camelia, and Vasile Burja. 2013. Entrepreneurial Risk and Performance: Empirical Evidence of Romanian Agricultural Holdings. *Annales Universitatis Apulensis Series Oeconomica* 15: 561–69.

Butkus, Mindaugas, Sigita Žakarė, and Diana Cibulskienė. 2014. Bankroto diagnostikos modelis ir jo pritaikymas bankroto tikimybei lietuvos įmonėse prognozuoti. *Taikomoji Ekonomika: Sisteminiai Tyrimai* 8: 111–32. [CrossRef]

Cámská, Dagmar. 2012. Predicting corporate financial distress in the case of operational program environment. *Intellectual Economics* 6: 450–62.

Cámská, Dagmar. 2013. Predicting financial distress of companies operating in construction Industry. Paper presented at 8th International Conference Accounting and Management Information Systems AMIS, Bucharest, Romania, June 12–13; Bucharest: The Bucharest University of Economic Studies, pp. 51–65.

Cámská, Dagmar. 2016. Accuracy od models predicting corporate bankruptcy in a selected industry branch. *Ekonomický Časopis* 64: 353–66.

Čámská, Dagmar, and Jiří Hájek. 2012. Companies related to the glass making industry and their financial health. In *International Scientific Conference—Transaction Costs of Czech Businesses in Insolvency Proceedings, the Possibility of Their Reduction and Improvement of Statistics of Insolvency Proceedings*. Edited by Eva Kislingerová and J Jindřich Špička. Prague: University of Economics, pp. 11–16.

Carson, Elizabeth, Neil L. Fargher, Marshall A. Geiger, Clive S. Lennox, Kannan Raghunandan, and Marleen Willekens. 2013. Audit reporting for going-concern uncertainty: A Research Synthesis. *Auditing: A Journal of Practice & Theory* 32: 353–84. [CrossRef]

Catalin, Corici Marian, and Medar Lucian Ion. 2016. Analysis methods of bankruptcy risk in Romanian Energy Mining Industry. *Annals of the "Constantin Brâncuşi" University of Târgu Jiu, Economy Series* 1: 180–85.

Chesser, Delton L. 1974. Predicting loan noncompliance. *The Journal of Commercial Bank Lending* 56: 28–38.

Chrastinová, Zuzana. 1998. *Metódy Hodnotenia Ekonomickej Bonity a Predikcie Finančnej Situácie Poľnohospodárskych Podnikov*. Bratislava: VÚEPP.

Coats, Pamela K., and L. Franklin Fant. 1991. A neural network approach to forecasting financial distress. *Journal of Business Forecasting* 10: 9–12.

Crăciun, Mihaela, Crina Raţiu, Dominic Bucerzan, and Adriana Manolescu. 2013. Actuality of Bankruptcy rediction Models used in Decision Support System. *International Journal of Computers Communications & Control* 8: 375–383.

Delev, Atanas. 2014. Is there a Risk of Bankruptcy for Bulgarian Public Companies? (JPMNT) Journal of Process Management (Special Edition). New Technologies, the International Scientific Conference "New Knowledge for the New People", Ohrid, May 21–24. pp. 252–59. Available online: http://www.japmnt.com/images/SpecialEdition2014/45.%20IS%20THERE%20A%20RISK%20OF%20BANKRUPTCY%20FOR%20BULGARIAN%20PUBLIC%20COMPANIES.pdf (accessed on 9 March 2017).

Delev, Atanas. 2016a. Problems and Challenges in Assessing the Risk of Bankruptcy in Bulgarian Companies. *Икономически изследвания* 3: 118–36.

Delev, Atanas. 2016b. Българските Публични Дружества В Словията На Финансова Криза. Available online: http://rd.swu.bg/media/46177/avtoreferat.pdf (accessed on 14 March 2017).

Delina, Radoslav, and Miroslava Packová. 2013. Validacia Predikčných Bankrotových Modelov v Podmienkach SR (Prediction Bankruptcy Models Validation in Slovak Business Environment). *E&M Economic and Management* 3: 101–12.

Dinca, Gheorghita, and Madalina Bociu. 2015. Using discriminant analysis for credit decision. *Bulletin of the Transilvania University of Braşov. Series V: Economic Sciences* 8: 277–88.

Divišová, Pavla. 2011. The Use of the "IN" index for assessing the financial health of companies operating in chemical industry. Paper presented at 10th International Conference, Liberec Economic Forum, Vancouver, BC, Canada, April 27–May 1; Liberec: Faculty of Economics, Technical University of Liberec, pp. 100–9.

Dolejšová, Miroslava. 2014. Which Altman model do we actually use? *Acta Universitatis Bohemiae Meridionales* 17: 103–11.

Dolejšová, Miroslava. 2015. Is it worth comparing different bankruptcy models? *Acta Universitatis Agriculturae* et Silviculturae Mendelianae Brunensis 63: 525–31. [CrossRef]

Dorgai, Klaudia, Veronika Fenyves, and Dávid Súto. 2016. Analysis of commercial enterprises' solvency by means of different bankruptcy models. *Gradus* 3: 341–49.

Draba, Edvin. 2012. Modernising Insolvency Law in Latvia: Successes and failures. *Eurofenix* 2012/2013: 26–27.

Druzin, Ruslan Valentinovich. 2013. About possibility of usage methodological approaches to bankruptcy prediction. *Studies and Scientific Researches. Economics Edition* 18: 177–81. [CrossRef]

Du Jardin, Philippe, and Eric Séverin. 2010. Dynamic analysis of the business failure process: A study of bankruptcy trajectories. Paper presented at 6th Portuguese Finance Network Conference, Ponta Delgada, Azores, June 30–July 4; vol. 2010.

Du Jardin, Philippe, and Eric Séverin. 2011. Predicting corporate bankruptcy using a self-organizing map: An empirical study to improve the forecasting horizon of a financial failure model. *Decision Support Systems* 51: 701–11. [CrossRef]

Dvořáček, Jaroslav, and Radmila Sousedíková. 2006. Forecasting companies' future economic development. *Acta Montanistica Slovaca* 11: 283–86.

Dvořáček, Jaroslav, Radmila Sousedíková, and Lucia Domaracká. 2008. Industrial enterprises bankruptcy forecasting. *Metalurgija* 47: 33–36.

Dvořáček, Jaroslav, Radmila Sousedíková, M. Řepka, Lucia Domaracká, Pavel Barták, and M. Bartošíková. 2012a. Choosing a Method for Predicting Economic Performance of Companies. *Metalurgija* 51: 525–28.

Dvořáček, Jaroslav, Radmila Sousedíková, Pavel Barták, Jiří Štěrba, and Kamil Novák. 2012b. Forecasting Companies' Future Economic Development. *Acta Montanistica Slovaca* 17: 111–18.

Dyrberg, A. 2004. *Firms in Financial Distress: An Exploratory Analysis*. Danmarks Nationalbank Working Papers, No. 17. Copenhagen: Danmarks Nationalbank.

Fedorova, Elena, Evgenii Gilenko, and Sergey Dovzhenko. 2013. Bankruptcy prediction for Russian companies: Application of combined classifiers. *Expert Systems with Applications* 40: 7285–93. [CrossRef]

Fedorova, E. A., S. E. Dovzhenko, and F. Y. Fedorov. 2016. Bankruptcy Prediction Models for Russian Enterprises: Specific Sector-Related Characteristics. *Studies on Russian Economic Development* 27: 254–61. [CrossRef]

Fitzpatrick, Paul Joseph 1932. A Comparison of Ratios of Successful Industrial Enterprises with Those of Failed Firm. *Certified Public Accountant* 6: 727–31.

Fletcher, Desmond, and Ernie Goss. 1993. Forecasting with Neural Networks: An Application Using Bankruptcy Data. *Information & Management* 24: 159–67. [CrossRef]

Gajdka, Jerzy, and Daniel Stos. 1996. The use of discriminant analysis in assessing the financial condition of enterprises. In *Restructuring in the Process of Transformation and Development of Enterprises*. Edited by Ryszard Borowiecki. Kraków: Wydawnictwo Akademii Ekonomicznej w Krakowie.

Gąska, Damian. 2016. Predicting Bankruptcy of Enterprises with the use of Learning Methods. Ph.D. disertation, Wrocław University of Economics, Wrocław, Poland.

Gasza, R. 1997. The relationship between the results of the Altman model and the stock prices of selected listed companies in Poland. *Bank i Kredyt* 3: 59–63.

Genriha, Irina, Gaida Peterre, and Irina Voronova. 2011. Entrepreneurship insolvency risk management: A case of Latvia. *International Journal of Banking Accounting and Finance* 3: 31–46. [CrossRef]

Gregory-Allen, B. Russell, and Glenn V. Henderson Jr. 1991. A Brief Review of Catastrophe Theory and a Test in Corporate Failure Context. *Financial Review* 62: 127–55. [CrossRef]

Grigaravičius, Saulius. 2003. Corporate Failure Diagnosis: Reliability and Practice. *Organizacijų Vadyba: Sisteminiai Tyrimai* 28: 29–42.

Grünberg, Martin, and Oliver Lukason. 2014. Predicting Bankruptcy of Manufacturing Firms. *International Journal of Trade, Economics and Finance* 5: 93–97. [CrossRef]

Grunert, Jens, Lars Norden, and Martin Weber. 2005. The Role of Non-Financial Factors in Internal Credit Ratings. *Journal of Banking and Finance* 29: 509–31. [CrossRef]

Gruszczyński, Marek. 2003. *Models of microeconometrics in the analysis and forecasting of the financial risk of enterprises.* Warszawa: Zeszyty Polskiej Akademii Nauk nr 23.

Gurčík, Lubomír. 2002. G-index—The financial situation prognosis method of agricultural enterprises. *Agricultural Economics (zemědělská ekonomika)* 48: 373–78. [CrossRef]

Hadasik, Dorota. 1998. *The Bankruptcy of Enterprises in Poland and Methods of its Forecasting.* Poznań: Wydawnictwo Akademii Ekonomicznej w Poznaniu, vol. 153.

Hajdíková, Taťána, Štěpánka Ondoková, and Lenka Komárková. 2015. Financial Models in the Nonprofit Sector. In *Scientific Conference.* Brno: Masaryk University, pp. 174–80.

Hajdu, Otto, and Miklos Virág. 2001. A Hungarian Model for Predicting Financial Bankruptcy. *Society and Economy in Central and Eastern Europe* 23: 28–46.

Hampel, David, Jan Vavřina, and Jitka Janová. 2012. Predicting bankruptcy of companies based on the production function parameters. Paper presented at 30th International Conference Mathematical Methods in Economics, Karviná, Czech Republic, September 11–13; Edited by Jaroslav Ramík and Daniel Stavárek. Karviná: Silesian University in Opava, School of Business Administration, pp. 243–48.

Hamrol, Mirosław, Bartłomiej Czajka, and Maciej Piechocki. 2004. Enterprise bankruptcy—discriminant analysis model. *Przegląd Organizacji* 6: 35–39.

Harafonova, Olha, and Dmytro Ulchenko. 2014. Financial Restructuring as a Means of Financial Recovery of Enterprises. *Фінансові Ресурси: Проблеми Формування Та Використання* 4: 267–72.

Härdle, Wolfgang Karl, Rouslan A. Moro, and Dorothea Schäfer. 2004. *Rating Companies with Support Vector Machines.* German Institute for Economic Research, Discussion Papers, No. 416. Berlin: German Institute.

Hołda, Artur. 2001. Forecasting the bankruptcy of an enterprise in the conditions of the Polish economy using the discriminatory function Z_H. *Rachunkowość* 5: 306–10.

Iazzolino, Gianpaolo, and Adolfo Fortino. 2012. Credit risk analysis and the KMV Black & Scholes model: A proposal of correction and an empirical analysis. *Investment Management and Financial Innovations* 9: 167–81.

Jagiełło, Robert. 2013. *Discriminant and Logistic Analysis in the Process of Assessing the Creditworthiness of Enterprises.* Materiały i Studia, Zeszyt 286. Warszawa: NBP.

Jakubík, Petr, and Petr Teplý. 2011. The JT Index as Indicator of Financial Stability of Corporate Sector. *Praque Economic Papers* 2: 157–76. [CrossRef]

Janda, Karel, and Anna Rakicova. 2014. Corporate Bankruptcies in Czech Republic, Slovakia, Croatia and Serbia. MPRA Paper No. 54109, University of Economics, Prague, Charles University in Prague. Available online: https://mpra.ub.uni-muenchen.de/54109/1/MPRA_paper_54109.pdf (accessed on 8 September 2017).

Jo, Hongkyu, Ingoo Han, and Hoonyoung Lee. 1997. Bankruptcy Prediction Using Case-Based Reasoning, Neural Networks and Discriminant Analysis. *Expert Systems with Applications* 13: 97–108. [CrossRef]

Juszczyk, Sławomi, and Rafał Balina. 2009. Forecasting the bankruptcy of forwarding companies as a banking decision-making tool. *Zeszyty Naukowe SGGW—Ekonomika i Organizacja Gospodarki Żywnościowej* 78: 161–74.

Juszczyk, Sławomi, and Rafał Balina. 2014. Forecasting the bankruptcy risk of enterprises in selected industries. *Ekonomista* 1: 67–95.

Kalouda, František, and Roman Vaníček. 2013. Alternative bankruptcy models—First results. Paper presented at 10th International Scientific Conference European Financial Systems, Telč, Czech Republic, June 10–11; Brno: Masaryk University, pp. 164–68.

Kaminsky, Alexander, Alexander Kostrov, and Taras Murzenkov. 2012. Comparison of Default Probability Models: Russian Experience. Higher School of Economics Research Paper No. WP BRP 06/FE/2012. Available online: https://ssrn.com/abstract=2152384orhttp://dx.doi.org/10.2139/ssrn.2152384 (accessed on 8 September 2017).

Kanapickiene, Rasa, and Rosvydas Marcinkevicius. 2014. Possibilities to apply classical bankruptcy models in the construction sector in Lithuania. *Economics and Management* 19: 317–32. [CrossRef]

Karas, Michal, and Mária Režňáková. 2014. A parametric or nonparametric approach for creating a new bankruptcy prediction model: The Evidence from the Czech Republic. *International Journal of Mathematical Models and Methods in Applied Sciences* 8: 214–23.

Karas, Michal, and Mária Režňáková. 2015. Predicting bankruptcy under alternative conditions: The effect of a change in industry and time period on the accuracy of the model. *Procedia—Social and Behavioral Sciences* 213: 397–403. [CrossRef]

Karas, Michal, Maria Reznakova, Vojtech Bartos, and Marek Zinecker. 2013. Possibilities for the Application of the Altman Model within the Czech Republic. In *Recent Reserches in Law Science and Finances: Proceedings of the 4th International Conference on Finance, Accounting and Law (ICFA 13), Crete Island, Greece, August 27–29*. Edited by Kalliopi Kalampouka and Carmen Nastase. Chania: WSEAS Press, *Business and Economics Series*; vol. 11, pp. 203–208.

Karbownik, Lidia. 2017. *Methods for Assessing the Financial Risk of Enterprises in the TSI Sector in Poland*. Łódź: Wydawnictwo Uniwersytetu Łódzkiego.

Kareleu, Yury Y. 2015. "Slice of Life" Customization of Bankruptcy Models: Bielarusian Experience and Future Developmnet. *Research Papers of Wrocław University of Economics* 381: 115–31.

Käsper, Kaspar. 2016. *Permanent Insolvency Prediction Model in the Example of Estonian MicroEnterprises Financed with Start-up Grant*. Tartu: University of Tartu, Available online: https://dspace.ut.ee/bitstream/handle/10062/52390/kasper_kaspar.pdf?sequence=1&isAllowed=y (accessed on 18 September 2017).

Khmerkan, Jeeranun, and Surachai Chancharat. 2015. Performance of Minority Data in Financial Distress Prediction Models. Application of Multiple Discriminate Analysis Logit, Probit and Artificial Neural Networks. *Journal of Applied Economic Sciences* 10: 954–60.

Kiviluoto, Kimmo. 1998. Predicting bankruptcies with the self-organizing map. *Neurocomputing* 21: 191–201. [CrossRef]

Klauberg, Theis, and Alexander Gebhardt. 2007. Latvia. In *The Insolvency Law of Central and Eastern Europe. Twelve Country Screenings of the New Member and Candidate Countries of the European Union: A Comparative Analysis*. Edited by Jens Lowitzsch. Berlin: INSOL EUROPE/Inter-University Centre at the Institute for East European Studies, Free University of Berlin, pp. 251–79.

Kleban, Yuriy. 2015. Diagnosis of Companies' Bankruptcy Using Takagi-Sugeno Model. *Нейро-Нечіткі Технології Моделювання В Економіці* 4: 62–79.

Klebanova, Tamara, Lidiya Guryanova, and Vitalii Gvozdytskyi. 2016. Neural Fuzzy Models of Estimation of the Financial Condition of Corporate Systems. Available online: http://repository.hneu.edu.ua/jspui/bitstream/123456789/14947/1/ICAICTSEE-2016%20Bulgaria.pdf (accessed on 7 March 2017).

Klecka, Jiri, and Hana Scholleova. 2010. Bankruptcy Models Enuntiation for Czech Glass Making Firms. *Economics and Management* 15: 954–59.

Klepáč, Václav, and David Hampel. 2016. Prediction of Bankruptcy with SVM Classifiers among Retail Business Companies. *Acta Universitatis Agriculturae et Silviculturae Mendelianae Brunensis* 64: 627–34. [CrossRef]

Kniewski, Adam. 2004. Formula for an bankrupt. *Businessman* 10: 163–68.

Kocmanová, Alena, Marie Pavláková Dočekalová, and Petr Němeček. 2014. Sustainable Corporate Performance Index for Manufacturing Industry. Paper presented at 18th World Multi-Conference on Systemics, Cybernetics and Informatic, Orlando, FL, USA, July 15–18; Orlando: International Institute of Informatics and Systemics, pp. 1–6.

Kolari, James, Michele Caputo, and Drew Wagner. 1996. Trait Recognition: An Alternative Approach to Early Warning Systems in Commercial Banking. *Journal of Business Finance & Accounting* 23: 1415–34. [CrossRef]

Koleda, Nadezhda, and Natalja Lace. 2009. Development of Comparative-Quantitative Measures of Financial Stability for Latvian Enterprises. *Economics & Management* 14: 78–84.

Korab, Vojtech. 2001. One Approach to Small Business Bankruptcy Prediction: The Case of the Czech Republic. In *VII SIGEFF Congress New Logistics for the New Economy*. Naples: SIGEFF International Association for FUZZY SET, University Degli Studi Di Napoli, Federico II, pp. 359–68.

Kornyliuk, Roman. 2014. Early Warning Indicators of Defaults in the Banking System of Ukraine. *Journal of European Economy* 13: 333–48.

Korol, Tomasz. 2004. *Assessment of the Accuracy of the Application of Discriminatory Methods and Artificial Neural Networks for the Identification of Enterprises Threatened with Bankruptcy*. Gdańsk: Doctoral dissertation.

Korol, Tomasz. 2010a. *Early Warning Systems of Enterprises to the Risk of Bankruptcy*. Warszawa: Wolters Kluwer.

Korol, Tomasz. 2010b. Forecasting bankruptcies of companies using soft computing techniques. *Finansowy Kwartalnik Internetowy "e-Finanse"* 6: 1–14.

Korol, Tomasz. 2013. *A new Approach to Ratio Analysis in an Enterprise*. Warszawa: Wolters Kluwer Polska.

Kozak, Liudmila, Elena Bakulich, Valentin Ziuzina, and Olesia Fedoruk. 2013. The Use of Fuzzy Cognitive Models for Diagnostics of Probability of Enterprises' Bankruptcy. *Modern Management Review* 18: 73–85. [CrossRef]

Kráľ, Pavol, Mária Stachová, and Lukáš Sobíšek. 2014. Utilization of repeatedly measured financial ratios in corporate financial distress prediction in Slovakai. Paper presented at 17th Applications of Mathematics and Statistics in Economics, International Scientific Conference, Poland, August 27–31; pp. 156–63.

Kristóf, Szeverin, and László Koloszár. 2014. The Efficiency of Bankruptcy Forecast Models in the Hungarian SME Sector. *Journal of Competitiveness* 6: 56–73.

Kubecová, Jana, and Jaroslav Vrchota. 2014. The Taffler's Model and Strategic Management. *The Macrotheme Review* 3: 188–94.

Kubíčková, Dana. 2011. Model Z-score in Conditions of Transition to International Financial Reporting Standards in Czech Republic. Paper presented at Cambridge Business & Economics Conference (CBEC), Cambridge, UK, June 27–29; Cambridge: Murray Edwards College, Cambridge University. Available online: http://www.gcbe.us/2011_CBEC/data/confcd.htm (accessed on 9 June 2017).

Kubíčková, Dana. 2015. Ohlson's Model and its Prediction Ability in Comparison with Selected Bankruptcy Models in Conditions of Czech SMEs. *Acta VŠFS* 2: 155–73.

Kubíčková, Dana, and Vladimir Nulicek. 2016. Predictors of Financial Distress and Bankruptcy Model Construction. *International Journal of Management Science and Business Administration* 2: 34–42. [CrossRef]

Kubicová, Jana, and Slavomír Faltus. 2014. Tax Debt as an Indicator of Companies' Default: The Case of Slovakia. *Journal of Applied Economics and Business* 2: 59–74.

Laitinen, Erkki K., and Teija Laitinen. 1998. Cash Management Behavior and Failure Prediction. *Journal of Business Finance & Accounting* 25: 893–919. [CrossRef]

Laitinen, Erkki K., and Arto Suvas. 2013. International Applicability of Corporate Failure Risk Models Based on Financial Statement Information: Comparisons across European Countries. *Journal of Finance & Economics* 1: 1–26. [CrossRef]

Lanine, Gleb, and Rudi Vander Vennet. 2006. Failure prediction in the Russian bank sector with logit and trait recognition models. *Expert Systems with Applications* 30: 463–78. [CrossRef]

Lee, Tsun-Siou, Yin-Hua Yeh, and Rong-Tze Liu. 2003. *Can Corporate Governance Variables Enhance the Predicting Power of Accounting-Based Financial Distress Prediction Models?* Center for Economic Institutions Working Paper Series, No. 14; Kunitachi: Hitotsubashi University.

Lobanova, Elena, A. I. Zmitrovich, A. A. Voshevoz, A. V. Krivko-Krasko, and S. N. Zbarouski. 2012. Current Financial Diagnostics of Enterprises, Modeling and Simulation. Paper presented at International Conference, Minsk, Belarus, May 2–4; Minsk: Publ. Center of BSU, pp. 66–69.

Lukason, Oliver, and Kaspar Käsper. 2017. Failure Prediction of government fundeded start-up firms. *Investment Management and Financial Innovations* 2017: 296–306. [CrossRef]

Łukaszewski, K., and P. Dąbroś. 1998a. How and where to find a bankrupt? *Prawo i Gospodarka* 49.

Łukaszewski, K., and P. Dąbroś. 1998b. Altman's indicator. *Prawo i Gospodarka* 0.

Lytvyn, Anton V. 2015. Applying support vector machines to financial crisis forecasting in Ukrainian Insurance Companies. *Actual Problems of Economics* 5: 481–92.

Machek, Ondrej. 2014. Long-term Predictive Ability of Bankruptcy Models in the Czech Republic: Evidence from 2007–2012. *Central European Business Review* 3: 14–17. [CrossRef]

Machek, Ondřej, Luboš Smrčka, and Jiří Strouhal. 2015. How to predict potential default of cultural organizations. Paper presented at 7th International Scientific Conference Finance and Performance of Firms in Science, Education and Practice, Zlín, Czech Republic, April 23–24; Edited by E. Astuszková, Z. Crhová, J. Vychtilová, B. Vytrhlíková and A. Knápková. Zlín: Univerzita Tomáše Bati ve Zlíně, pp. 893–902.

Mączyńska, Elżbieta. 1994. Assessment of the condition of the enterprise. Simplified methods. *Życie Gospodarcze* 38: 42–45.

Mączyńska, Elżbieta. 2004. Early warning systems. *Nowe Życie Gospodarcze* 12: 4–9.

Makeeva, Elena, and Eaterina Neretina. 2013a. The Prediction of Bankruptcy in a Construction Industry of Russian Federation. *Journal of Modern Accounting and Auditing* 9: 256–71.

Makeeva, Elena, and Eaterina Neretina. 2013b. A Binary Model versus Discriminant Analysis Relating to Corporate Bankruptcies: The Case of Russian Construction Industry. *Journal of Accounting, Finance and Economics* 3: 65–76.

Männasoo, Kadri. 2007. *Determinants of Firm Sustainability in Estonia*. Working Paper Series 4; Tallinn: Bank of Estonia.

Martin, Daniel. 1977. Early Warning of Bank Failure: A Logit Regression Approach. *Journal of Banking and Finance* 1: 249–76. [CrossRef]

Martin, Aruldoss, Travis Miranda Lakshmi, and Venkatasamy Prasanna Venkatesan. 2014. A Framework to Develop Qualitative Bankruptcy Prediction Rules Using Swarm Intelligence. *St. Joseph's Journal of Humanities and Science* 1: 73–81.

Matviychuk, Andriy. 2010. Bankruptcy Pediction in Trasformational Economy: Discriminant Analysis and Fuzzy Logic Approaches. *Fuzzy Economic Review* 15: 21–38.

Megan, Ovidiu, and Cristina Circa. 2014. Insolvency Prediction Tools for Middle and Large Scale Romanian Enterprises. *Transformations in Business & Economics* 13: 661–75.

Merkevicius, Egidijus, Gintautas Garšva, and Stasys Girdzijauskas. 2006. A Hybrid SOM-Altman Model for Bankruptcy Prediction. Paper presented at Computational Science—ICCS 2006: 6th International Conference, Part IV, Reading, UK, May 28–31; Edited by Vassil N. Alexandrov, Geert Dick van Albada, Peter M. A. Sloot and Jack Dongarra. Berlin/Heidelberg: Springer, pp. 364–71.

Michael, Spanos, Dounias Georgios, Matsatsinis Nikolaos, and Zopounidis Constantin. 2001. A Fuzzy Knowledge-Based Decision Aiding Method for the Assessment of Financial Risks: The Case of Corporate Bankruptcy Prediction. Available online: http://citeseerx.ist.psu.edu/viewdoc/download; jsessionid=99316C2CD8D0EDD1791DCB3890D4C8B9?doi=10.1.1.21.4596&rep=rep1&type=pdf (accessed on 13 July 2017).

Michaluk, Krzysztof. 2003. Effectiveness of corporate bankruptcy models in Polish economic conditions. In *Corporate Finance in the Face of Globalization Processes*. Edited by Leszek Pawłowicz and Ryszard Wierzba. Warszawa: Wydawnictwo Gdańskiej Akademii Bankowej.

Mičudová, Kateřina. 2013a. Discriminatory Power of the Altman Z-Score Model. *Littera Scripta* 6: 95–106.

Mičudová, Kateřina. 2013b. Bankruptcy Risk—Financial Ratios of Manufacturing Firms. Paper presented at 5th International Applied Economics, Business and Development (AEBD'13), Chania, Greece, August 27–29; Edited by Pedro Lorca and Catalin Popescu. pp. 173–78.

Mihalovic, Matús. 2016. Performance Comparison of Multiple Discriminant Analysis and Logit Models in Bankruptcy Prediction. *Economics & Sociology* 9: 101–18. [CrossRef]

Molinero, C. Mar, and Mahmoud Ezzamel. 1991. Multidimensional Scaling Applied to Corporate Failure. *OMEGA International Journal of Management Science* 19: 259–74. [CrossRef]

Němec, Daniel, and Michal Pavlík. 2016. Predicting Insolvency Risk of the Czech Companies. Paper presented at International Scientific Conference Quantitative Methods in Economics (Multiple Criteria Decision Making XVIII), Bratislava, Vrátna, Slovakia, May 25–27; pp. 258–63.

Neskorodeva, Inna, and Svetlana Pustovgar. 2015. An Approach to Predicting the Insolvency of Ukrainian Steel Enterprises Based on Financial Potential. *Journal of Eastern European and Central Asian Research* 2: 1–11. [CrossRef]

Novotná, Martina. 2012. The use of different approaches for credit rating prediction and their comparison. Paper presented at 6th International Scientific Conference Managing and Modelling of Financial Risks Ostrava VŠB-TU, Ostrava, Czech Republic, September 10–11; Ostrava: Faculty of Economics, Finance Department, pp. 448–57.

Odom, Marcus D., and Ramesh Sharda. 1990. A Neural Network Model for Bankruptcy Prediction. Paper presented at IEEE International Conference on Neural Network, San Diego, CA, USA, June 17–21; vol. 2.

Ohlson, James A. 1980. Financial Ratios, and the Probabilistic Prediction of Bankruptcy. *Journal of Accounting Research* 18: 109–31. [CrossRef]

Park, Cheol-Soo, and Ingoo Han. 2002. A Case-Based Reasoning with the Feature Weights Derived by Analytic Hierarchy Process for Bankruptcy Prediction. *Expert Systems with Application* 23: 255–64. [CrossRef]

Peresetsky, Anatoly A., Alexandr A. Karminsky, and Sergei V. Golovan. 2004. Probability of Default Models of Russian Banks. BOFIT Discussion Paper No. 21/2004. Available online: https://ssrn.com/abstract= 1015451orhttp://dx.doi.org/10.2139/ssrn.1015451 (accessed on 8 September 2017).

Peresetsky, Anatoly A., Alexandr A. Karminsky, and Sergei V. Golovan. 2011. Probability of Default Models of Russian Banks. *Economic Change and Restructuring* 44: 297–334. [CrossRef]

Pisula, Tomasz, Grzegorz Mentel, and Jacek Brożyna. 2013. Predicting Bankruptcy of Companies from the Logistics Sector Operating in the Podkarpacie Region. *Modern Management Review* 18: 113–33. [CrossRef]

Pisula, Tomasz, Grzegorz Mentel, and Jacek Brożyna. 2015. Non-statistical Methods of Analyzing of Bankruptcy Risk. *Folia Oeconomica Stetinensia* 15: 7–21. [CrossRef]

Pitrová, Kateřina. 2011. Possibilities of the Altman ZETA Model Application to Czech Firms. *Ekonomika A Management* 3: 66–76.

Pociecha, Józef, and Barbara Pawełek. 2011. Bankruptcy Prediction and Business Cycle, Contemporary Problems of Transformation Process in the Central and East European Countries. Paper presented at 17th Ukrainian-Polish-Slovak Scientific Seminar, Lviv, Ukraine, September 22–24; Lviv: The Lviv Academy of Commerce, pp. 9–24.

Pociecha, Józef, Barbara Pawełek, Mateusz Baryła, and Sabina Augustyn. 2014. *Statistical Methods of Forecasting Bankruptcy in the Changing Economic Situation.* Kraków: Fundacja Uniwersytetu Ekonomicznego w Krakowie.

Pogodzińska, Marzanna, and Sławomir Sojak. 1995. *The Use of Discriminant Analysis in Predicting Bankruptcy of Enterprises.* Ekonomia XXV, Zeszyt 299. Toruń: AUNC.

Popchev, Ivan, and Irina Radeva. 2006. A Decision Support Method for Investment Preference Evaluation. *Cybernetics and Information Technologies* 6: 3–16.

Premachandra, I. M., Gurmeet Singh Bhabra, and Toshiyuki Sueyoshi. 2009. DEA as a Tool for bankruptcy assessment: A comparative study with logistic regression technique. *European Journal of Operational Research* 193: 412–24. [CrossRef]

Prusak, Błażej. 2005. *Modern Methods of Forecasting Financial Risk of Enterprises.* Warszawa: Difin.

Prusak, Błażej, and Agnieszka Więckowska. 2007. Multidimensional models of discriminant analysis in the study of the bankruptcy risk of Polish companies listed on the WSE. In *Economic and Legal Ascpects of Corporate Bankruptcy.* Edited by Błażej Prusak. Warszawa: Difin.

Ptak-Chmielewska, Aneta. 2016. Statistical Models for Corporate Credit Risk Assessment—Rating Models. *Acta Universitatis Lodziensis Folia Oeconomica* 3: 98–111. [CrossRef]

Purvinis, Ojaras, Povilas Šukys, and Rūta Virbickaitė. 2005a. Bankruptcy Prediction in Lithuanian Enterprises Using Discriminant Analysis. *Ekonomika ir vadyba: Aktualijos ir Perspektyvos* 5: 314–18.

Purvinis, Ojaras, Povilas Šukys, and Rūta Virbickaitė. 2005b. Research of Possibility of Bankruptcy Diagnostics Applying Neural Networks. *Engineering Economics* 1: 16–22.

Purvinis, Ojaras, R. Virbickaite, and Povilas Sukys. 2008. Interpretable Nonlinear Model for Enterprise Bankruptcy Prediction. *Nonlinear Analysis: Modelling and Control* 13: 61–70.

Radkov, Petar. 2013. Measuring Default Risk of Bulgarian Public Banks with Meton Model. Available online: https://www.researchgate.net/publication/264681559_Measuring_default_risk_of_Bulgarian_public_banks_with_Merton_model (accessed on 9 March 2017).

Radkov, Petar, and Leda Minkova. 2011. Assessing Bank's Default Probability Using ASFR Model. Available online: https://www.researchgate.net/publication/237020492_Assessing_bank%27s_default_probability_using_the_ASRF_model (accessed on 9 March 2017).

Rahimian, E., Sameer Singh, T. Thammachote, and R. Virmani. 1993. Bankruptcy Prediction by Neural Network. In *Neural Networks in Finance and Investing.* Edited by Robert R. Trippi and Efraim Turban. Chicago and London: Probus Publishing Company.

Karas, Michal, and Mária Režňáková. 2013. Bankruptcy Prediction Model of Industrial Enterprises in the Czech Republic. *International Journal of Mathematical Models and Methods in Applied Sciences* 5: 519–31.

Režňáková, Mária, and Michal Karas. 2014. Identifying bankruptcy prediction factors in various environments: A contribution to the discussion on the transferability of bankruptcy models. *International Journal of Mathematical Models and Methods in Applied Sciences* 8: 69–74.

Robua, Ioan-Bogdan, Mihaela-Alina Robua, and Marilena Mironiuc. 2013. Risk assessment of financial failure for Romanian Quoted companies based on the survival analysis. Paper presented at 8th International Conference Accounting and Management Information Systems AMIS, Bucharest, Romania; Bucharest: The Bucharest University of Economic Studies, pp. 51–65.

Robua, Ioan-Bogdan, Mihaela-Alina Robua, Marilena Mironiuc, and Florentina Olivia Balu. 2014. The value relevance of financial distress risk in the case of RASDAQ companies. *Accounting and Management Information Systems* 13: 623–42.

Roháčová, Viera, and Král' Pavol. 2015. Corporate Failure Prediction Using DEA: An Application to Companies in the Slovak Republic. Paper presented at 18th Applications of Mathematics and Statistics in Economics, International Scientific Conference, Jindřichuv Hradec, Czech Republic, September 2–6.

Rudolfova, Lucie, and Tatiana Skerlíkova. 2014. Discrepancy between the Default and the Financial Distress Measured by Bankruptcy Models. *Journal of Eastern European and Central Asian Research* 1: 1–12.

Daniela, Rybárová, Braunová Mária, and Jantošová Lucia. 2016. Analysis of the Construction Industry in the Slovak Republic by Bankruptcy Model. *Procedia—Social and Behavioral Sciences* 230: 298–306. [CrossRef]

Serrano-Cinca, Carlos. 1997. Feedforward Neural Networks in the Classification of Financial Information. *European Journal of Finance* 3: 183–202. [CrossRef]

Shakun, A. S., and A. V. Skrobko. 2012. Agricultural enterprise probability forecasting on the basis of discriminant multifactor models. *Problems and Prospects* 17: 169–77.

Shin, Kyung-Shik, and Yong-Joo Lee. 2002. A genetic algorithm application in bankruptcy prediction modelling. *Expert Systems with Applications* 23: 321–28. [CrossRef]

Shirinkina, Elena V., and Laisan A. Valiullina. 2015. Formalization of the Model of the Enterprise Insolvency Risk Prediction. *Actual Problems of Economics and Laws* 4: 169–80. [CrossRef]

Shumway, Tyler. 2001. Forecasting Bankruptcy More Accurately: A simple Hazard Model. *Journal of Business* 74: 101–24. [CrossRef]

Siudek, Tomasz. 2005. Forecasting the bankruptcy of cooperative banks using discriminant analysis. *Roczniki Naukowe Stowarzyszenia Ekonomistów Rolnictwa i Agrobiznesu* 7: 86–91.

Šlefendorfas, Gediminas. 2016. Bankruptcy Prediction Model for Private Limited Companies in Lithuania. *Ekonomika* 95: 134–52. [CrossRef]

Šlégr, Pavel. 2013. The Evaluation of Financial Stability of Czech Companies through the Z-Score nad the IN05 Index and their Comparison. Paper presented at 7th WSEAS International Conference on Management, Marketing and Finances (MMF '13), Cambridge, MA, USA, January 30–February 1; pp. 29–33.

Slowinski, Roman, and Constantin Zopounidis. 1995. Application of the Rough Set Approach to Evaluation of Bankruptcy risk. *Intelligent Systems in Accounting, Finance and Management* 4: 27–41. [CrossRef]

Smith, Raymond F., and Arthur H. Winakor. 1935. *Changes in Financial Structure of Unsuccessful Industrial Corporations.* Bureau of Business Research, Bulletin 51. Urbana: University of Illinois Press.

Smolski, Aliaksei P. 2006. Tendencies and Problems of Economical Insolvency (Bankruptcy) Institution Development in Belarus: 1991–2005 (No. smolski_aliaksei. 39168-b1). Socionet. Available online: http://refor.socionet.ru/files/Tendencies.doc (accessed on 9 March 2016).

Sneidere, Ruta, and Inta Bruna. 2011. Predicting Business Insolvency: The Latvian Experience. *Journal of Modern Accounting and Auditing* 7: 487–97.

Šofranková, Beáta. 2013. Analysis of Impact of Non-financial Criteria and Z-score in Accommodation Facilities in Slovakia. *Slovak Scientific Journal Management: Science and Education* 2: 72–74.

Šofranková, Beáta. 2014. Analysis of Impact of Non-financial Criteria and Z-score in Accommodation Facilities in Slovakia. CER Comparative European Research. Paper presented at Research Tracks of the 1st Biannual CER Comparative European Research Conference, London, UK, March 17–21; pp. 88–91.

Sojak, Sławomir, and Józef Stawicki. 2000. The use of taxonomic methods to assess the economic condition of enterprises. *Zeszyty Teoretyczne Rachunkowości* 3: 55–66.

Spaičienė, Jurgita. Bankruptcy Law Development in The Republic of Lithuania, Summary of the Doctoral Dissertation, Vilnius. Available online: http://www.youscribe.com/catalogue/rapports-et-theses/savoirs/bankruptcylaw-development-in-the-republic-of-lithuania-bankroto-1426976 (accessed on 20 July 2016).

Stachová, Mária, Král' Pavol, Lukáš Sobíšek, and Martin Kakaščík. 2015. Analysis of Financial Distress of Slovak Companies Using Repeated Measurements. Paper presented at Applications of Mathematics and Statistics in Economics, International Scientific Conference, Jindřichuv Hradec, Czech Republic, September 2–6.

Stępień, Paweł, and Tomasz Strąk. 2003. Signs of the threat of bankruptcy of Polish enterprises—Empirical study. In *Time for Money, t. II.* Edited by Dariusz Zarzecki. Szczecin: Wydawnictwo Uniwersytetu Szczecińskiego.

Stępień, Paweł, and Tomasz Strąk. 2004. Multidimensional logit models for assessing the risk of bankruptcy of Polish enterprises. In *Time for Money, t. I.* Edited by Dariusz Zarzecki. Szczecin: Wydawnictwo Uniwersytetu Szczecińskiego.

Stundžienė, Alina, and Vytautas Boguslauskas. 2006. Valuation of Bankruptcy Risk for Lithuanian Companies. *Engineering Economics* 4: 29–36.

Tam, Kar Yan, and Melody Y. Kiang. 1992. Managerial Applications of Neural Networks: The Case of Bank Failure Predictions. *Management Science* 38: 926–47. [CrossRef]

Varul, Paul. 1999. On the Development of Bankruptcy Law in Estonia. *Juridica International* 1: 172–78.

Vavřina, Jan, David Hampel, and Jitka Janová. 2013. New Approaches for the Financial Distress Classification in Agribusiness. *Acta Universitatis Agriculturae et Silviculturae Mendelianae Brunensis* 61: 1177–82. [CrossRef]

Venyš, Ladislav. 1997. Bankruptcy in the Czech Republic, NATO Democratic Institutions Fellowship Programme 1995–1997. Available online: http://www.nato.int/acad/fellow/95-97/venys.pdf (accessed on 7 September 2017).

Virág, Miklós, and Tamás Kristóf. 2005. Neural Neutworks in Bankruptcy Prediction—A Comparative Study on the Basis of the First Hungarian Bankruptcy Model. *Acta Oeconomica* 55: 403–25. [CrossRef]

Virág, Miklós, and Tamás Kristóf. 2014. Is there a Trade-off between the Predictive Power and the Interpretability of Bankruptcy Models? The Case of the first Hungarian Bankruptcy Model. *Acta Oeconomica* 64: 419–40. [CrossRef]

Vitryansky, Vassily V. 1999. Insolvency and Bankruptcy Law Reform in the Russian Federation. *McGill Law Journal* 44: 409–32.

Vochozka, Marek, Jarmila Straková, and Jan Váchal. 2015a. Model to Predict Survival of Transportation and Shipping Companies. *Naše More, Special Issue* 62: 109–13. [CrossRef]

Vochozka, Marek, Zuzana Rowland, and Jaromir Vrbka. 2015b. Prediction of the Future Development of Construction Companies by Means of Artificial Neural Networks on the Basis of Data from the Czech Republic. *Математичне Моделювання в Економіці* 3: 62–76.

Vochozka, Marek, Zuzana Rowland, and Jaromir Vrbka. 2016. Evaluation of Solvency of Potential Customers of a Company. *Математичне моделювання в економіці* 1: 5–18.

Vodonosova, T. 2012. Application of Crisis-Prognostic Models in Building Sector of the Republic of Bielarus. *Экономические и Юридические Науки. Финансы и Налогообложение* 13: 93–98.

Voronova, Irina. 2012. Financial Risks: Cases of Non-Financial Enterprises. In *Risk Management for the Future. Theory and Cases*. Edited by Jan Emblemsvag. InTech: pp. 435–66.

Wędzki, Dariusz. 2000. The problem of using the ratio analysis to predict the bankruptcy of Polish enterprises—Case study. *Bank i Kredyt* 5: 54–61.

Wędzki, Dariusz. 2004. Logit model of bankruptcy for the Polish economy—Conclusions from the study. In *Time for Money. Corporate finance. Financing enterprises in the EU*. Edited by Dariusz Zarzecki. Szczecin: Wydawnictwo Uniwersytetu Szczecińskiego.

Wierzba, Dariusz. 2000. *Early Detection of Enterprises Threatened with Bankruptcy Based on the Analysis of Financial Ratios—Theory and Empirical Research. Zeszyty Naukowe nr 9*. Warszawa: Wydawnictwo Wyższej Szkoły Ekonomiczno-Informatycznej w Warszawie.

Wilson, Rick L., and Ramesh Sharda. 1994. Bankruptcy Prediction Using Neural Networks. *Decision Support Systems* 11: 545–57. [CrossRef]

Zavgren, Christine. 1983. The Prediction of Corporate Failure: The State of the Art. *Journal of Accounting Literature* 2: 1–38.

Zdyb, Marek. 2001. Assessing the enterprise's risk of bankruptcy using financial synthetic indicators. *Controlling i Rachunkowość Zarządcza* 5: 36–40.

Zhang, Yu Dong, and Le Nan Wu. 2011. Bankruptcy prediction by genetic ant colony algorithm. *Advanced Materials Research* 186: 459–63. [CrossRef]

Zmijewski, Mark E. 1984. Methodological issues related to the estimation of financial distress prediction models. *Journal of Accounting Research* 20: 59–82. [CrossRef]

Zopounidis, Constantin, and Michael Doumpos. 1999. A multicriteria aid methodology for sorting decision problems: The case of financial distress. *Computational Economics* 14: 197–218. [CrossRef]

Unraveling the Bankruptcy Risk-Return Paradox across the Corporate Life Cycle

Minhas Akbar [1][ID], **Ahsan Akbar** [2,*], **Petra Maresova** [3][ID], **Minghui Yang** [2][ID]
and **Hafiz Muhammad Arshad** [1]

1. Department of Management Sciences, COMSATS University Islamabad (Sahiwal Campus), Sahiwal 57000, Pakistan; minhasakbar@cuisahiwal.edu.pk (M.A.); hmarshadphd@cuisahiwal.edu.pk (H.M.A.)
2. International Business School, Guangzhou College of South China University of Technology, Guangzhou 510080, China; yangmh@gcu.edu.cn
3. Department of Economy, Faculty of Informatics and Management, University of Hradec Kralove, Rokitanskeho 62/26, 500 03 Hradec Kralove, Czech Republic; petra.maresova@uhk.cz
* Correspondence: akbar@gcu.edu.cn

Abstract: Bankruptcy risk is a fundamental factor affecting the financial sustainability and smooth functioning of an enterprise. The corporate bankruptcy risk-return association is well founded in the literature. However, there is a dearth of empirical research on how this association prevails at different stages of the corporate life cycle. The present study aims to investigate the bankruptcy-risk relationship at different stages of corporate life cycle by employing Hierarchical Linear Mixed Model (HLMM) regression estimation on the data of listed non-financial Pakistani firms from 12 diverse industrial segments. We grouped the firms into introduction, growth, mature, shake-out, and decline stages of the life cycle using Dickinson's model. Empirical results assert that corporate risk-taking at the introduction stage yields superior financial performance in the future, while risk at the growth stage positively contributes to a firm's current performance. Moreover, because of risk-averse and non-diversified managerial behavior, bankruptcy risk at the mature stage is negatively associated with both current and future performance. Likewise, risk-taking at the decline stage has significant negative implications for firm performance as the managers of such firms undertake heavy investments in a turnaround attempt; however, owing to the risk-averse behavior, they may indulge in negative net present value (NPV) projects. The study findings imply that managers synchronize a firm's risk exposure with the corresponding life cycle stage to avoid going bankrupt. Moreover, excessive risk-taking during the mature and decline stages can considerably harm the financial sustainability of an enterprise. Hence, investors should exercise a degree of caution when investing in highly indebted later-stage (mature and decline) firms. Overall, bankruptcy risk-return resembles an inverted U-shaped relationship. Our results are robust and can apply to various econometric specifications.

Keywords: bankruptcy risk; financial sustainability; corporate life cycle; nonfinancial firms; Pakistan

1. Introduction

Sustainability is a broad concept applicable to almost every aspect of our planet since its inception. However, since the emergence of various environmental, social, and economic issues in the past few decades, sustainability has become the focal area of research among practitioners and academicians alike. In the business world, Corporate Financial Sustainability (CFS) has been considered one of the major challenges faced by financial managers. Although there is no standard definition of CFS, in general it is "being able to be there for your beneficiaries in the long term. It is the opposite of having to cease your activities simply because you have run out of money" [1]. In simple words, a firm will be considered financially sustainable if its operations do not shut down even if external funding is suspended. Therefore, it is imperative for financial managers to keep a close eye on a company's financial distress/bankruptcy risk level and its impact on corporate returns. Failing to do so may result in either a lower return on investments for shareholders or the actual bankruptcy of the firm.

The concept of the Corporate Life Cycle (CLC) has attracted considerable interest in the last few decades as a conceptual model to understanding various aspects of corporate development [1,2]. The CLC theory entails that firms pass through a sequence of development phases and that the structures and policies of the enterprise vary considerably with changes in its development stage [3,4]. Numerous empirical studies have explored the relationship between corporate life cycle stages and firm financing decisions [5], growth [6], bankruptcy risk [7], market performance [8], investment [9], and dividend payment policies [10]. Moreover, after the recent credit crunch of 2007-8, firms' bankruptcy risk has emerged as a hot topic in the corporate finance literature as it has significant ramifications for the sustainable operations of the firm [11]. Bankruptcy or insolvency risk refers to a state of business where a firm faces difficulty paying its debt obligations; if this state of financial distress gets prolonged, it may lead to actual insolvency. Studies on bankruptcy risk predominately focus on the development of models that may predict the probability of firms filing for bankruptcy. Researchers contend that insolvency risk has a significant influence on a firm's investment choices [12], stocks and bond earnings [13,14], efficiency [15], dividend disbursements [16], and operational composition [17].

The U.S. financial crisis of 2008-2009 brought about a renewed focus on bankruptcy risk as it can significantly influence the survival and growth prospects of firms. However, there is no consensus on how bankruptcy risk affects an enterprise's present and future performance. Over the years, studies on corporate risk-taking and future financial performance have provided varying outcomes. Most firms are risk-averse and do not assume more risk unless risk-taking delivers considerable expected future returns [18,19]. Aaker and Jacobson [20] revealed a positive association between risk-taking and corporate performance. Fiegenbaum and Thomas [21] observed that, in a few industrial sectors, risk and firm performance have a positive association, while in others there is a negative association. On the contrary, [22–24] found a negative relationship between risk-taking and corporate performance, mainly for below-average performers. Following his prior research, Bowman [25] explored a positive link between risk and return for 1965 to 1969. However, the period of 1970–1979 revealed a strong negative association for the risk-return paradox. After the seminal works by [22,25], which, contrary to economic theory, suggested a negative association between risk and return, a long list of researchers probed this stream of inquiry. They came up with varying rationales to vindicate this negative association. These can be broadly divided into three categories: 1) contingent events that influence managerial attitude towards risk; 2) strategic conduct that creates differences in performance; and 3) statistical artifacts [26].

However, unlike in prior studies, we argue that this risk-return puzzle could be a function of corporate life cycle stages. The entrepreneurial activity approach postulates that markets pass through continuous changes and create profit-making opportunities for organizations that are capable and responsive [27]. Likewise, organizations evolve through different stages of the life cycle and tend to adjust their entrepreneurial strategy to suit the varying market requirements in order to capitalize the profitable opportunities [28]. The evidence suggests that CLC stages can play an important role in solving the bankruptcy risk-return puzzle. So far, there is a serious lack of empirical research that examines the bankruptcy risk-return relationship through the lens of CLC stages. Therefore, the present study aspires to fill this void in the literature and unravel the role of corporate life cycle stages in influencing the bankruptcy risk-return association. To a limited extent, our study is related to the work of Henderson and Benner [29], who found that the risk-return relationship evolves from positive to negative as a firm ages.

However, the present study is distinct in a number of ways. First, Henderson and Benner [29] used firm age as a measure of its life cycle stages, which is a sequential measure. Khan and Watts [30] assumed that organizations develop sequentially throughout their life cycle, while ignoring the fact that the nature of the life cycle can be nonsequential [31]. Certainly, these sequential measures have been denounced because of their linear application and unsuitability in the real corporate scenario (see, e.g., [32]). To overcome this issue, we follow Dickinson's (2011) model to measure CLC stages. She proposes a cyclic measure of corporate life cycle grounded on the cash flow patterns of an enterprise. Second, unlike Henderson and Benner [29], who used gains and losses as a measure of risk, our focus is on the bankruptcy risk of firms. Another relevant work is by Habib and Hasan [33]. They examined the association between firm performance and firm earnings (standard deviation of ROA and returns) based on risk proxies at different stages of CLC. However, the present study centers on bankruptcy risk and the associated firm's current and future performance conditional on CLC stages. Thus, the uniqueness of the current research lies in the fact that it is the first empirical attempt to examine the association between one of the most crucial types of risk (bankruptcy risk) at various stages of CLC and firm performance.

The contribution of this research is twofold. First, we categorize firms into various stages of CLC and use HLMM regressions that can process multilevel data when observations are not completely independent. Second, we provide new evidence about the relevance of corporate life cycle model on the bankruptcy risk-return association. The empirical results reinforce the fact that the bankruptcy risk-return relationship varies at different stages of CLC. Thus, practitioners and policymakers can only devise optimal capital structure plans by taking into consideration the corresponding stage of CLC to ensure the sustainable functioning of an enterprise.

Rest of the article is organized as follows. Section 2 constitutes the literature review and hypothesis development. Section 3 outlines research design. Empirical findings and discussion are reported in Section 4, while Section 5 concludes the study.

2. Literature Review, Theoretical Underpinning, and Hypothesis Development

The literature on corporate risk-taking and firm performance yields inconsistent outcomes. While proponents of the post-Bowman paradox [22,23,25] tried to uncover the underlying factors that explain a negative risk-return association, the prospect theory of Kahneman and Tversky [34] conjectures that managerial risk-taking preferences are dynamic, so troubled firms make hasty decisions in a turnaround attempt and to recoup losses. Furthermore, Bromiley [35] posits that poorly-performing (decline stage) firms not only take more risks, but also invest in risky gambles with lower anticipated returns. Following the prospect theory, it is plausible to maintain that early-stage firms (introduction and growth stage) have more avenues to invest in positive NPV projects, and their sales grow rapidly, which contributes to firm profitability. However, once the sales level stagnates (maturity stage), managers start to invest in long shots that further deteriorate firm performance (decline stage).

Furthermore, in a more recent study, Akbar et al. [7] revealed that introductory firms face higher bankruptcy risk with heavy financing costs because of the information asymmetry. Likewise, Liao [36] suggests that new entrants usually face negative returns because of less efficient production processes and limited access to financial resources. Hence, risk-taking at the early stage of the life cycle yields poor performance [33]. However, over the course of time, younger firms learn to avoid losses [29]. Start-up firms require higher investment in plants and equipment and thus have more options to undertake investments in positive NPV projects [37]. However, heavy investment in capital assets and capacity building at the introduction stage may result in poor current performance. Once the opportunity is properly capitalized, such firms will enjoy substantial profitability in the future. This was confirmed by Navaretti et al. [38]: in a sample of firms from three European countries (France, Italy, and Spain), they found that young firms perform better than older firms.

Growth-stage firms focus on research and development, capacity building, and advertisement to distinguish their product line from competitors, which results in higher profit margins [39]. Furthermore, growth firms focus on rapid sales growth, which boosts firm performance [3]. Ultimately, a risk-reward balance could be attained between the growth and maturity stages of the life cycle [1]. Yazdanfar and

Öhman [40] used panel data from 26,721 Swedish small to medium enterprises (SMEs) for 2008–2011 and observed that firms at their introduction and growth stage perform better than mature firms.

Lester and Parnell [41] posit that, owing to the hierarchical and bureaucratic structure of mature firms, introducing structural changes becomes difficult, which increases the likelihood of poor performance during the maturity phase. Moreover, the demand for external borrowing declines as cash flows yielded from internal operations are adequate to satisfy the operational requirements. Though mature firms can borrow at lower rates [42], they face a lack of future growth prospects owing to fewer profitable investment opportunities and a higher level of retained earnings [10]. Hence, any additional borrowing may yield negative returns because of limited positive NPV investment opportunities.

The fourth stage of corporate life cycle is the "revival phase" [3], "termination stage" [43], "renewal" [41], or "shake-out stage" [1]. As suggested by these names, researchers have competing arguments regarding the shake-out stage of a firm's life cycle. Miller and Friesen [3] and Lester and Parnell [41] propose that it is the most interesting stage of CLC. Considerable product innovations take place during this stage. Firm size increases and they expand exponentially. On the contrary, Dickinson and Gort and Klepper [1,44] contend that, during this stage, product lines start to decline and the decline in sales growth leads to declining prices [45]. However, the function of the shake-out stage of CLC is still vague in theory [1]. Thus, following [7,46,47], the shake-out stage is taken as the base in our regression analysis to compare the results of the rest of the CLC stages.

During the decline stage of CLC, firms usually abstain from innovation. They face higher bankruptcy risk [7] and their product lines become outdated and unattractive, which causes a substantial decrease in product price and revenues [3,45]. As a result, managers escalate investments to regain profitability. However, due to risk-averse and nondiversified behavior, they tend to invest in negative NPV undertakings to signal to shareholders that profitable investment options are still available [48]. However, hefty borrowing-driven investments in negative NPV projects may result in poor future performance, thus endangering their financial sustainability.

Thus, in light of the above discussion, we develop the following research hypotheses:

H1: *Risk-taking at the introduction stage yields superior subsequent firm performance.*

H2: *Risk-taking at the growth stage yields superior current performance.*

H3: *Risk-taking at the mature and decline stages yields poor firm performance.*

3. Research Design

3.1. Selection and Measurement of Variables

3.1.1. Dependent Variable

Firm performance is the dependent variable, which can be measured in several ways, such as sales growth, market capitalization, market to book ratio, turnover, and financial performance. The present study uses financial performance as the dependent variable to examine the proposed relationship. Return on Assets (ROA) and Return on Equity (ROE) are the two most commonly used proxies of corporate financial performance. ROA is measured as net income, scaled by total assets, whereas ROE is measured as net income scaled by stockholders' equity. The key difference between these two proxies is that a firm can increase its ROE, at least in the short run, by generous/higher utilization of debt without improving its earnings, though this is not the case with ROA. Moreover, in the present study bankruptcy risk is our main explanatory variable, which is also a function of a firm's debt level. Therefore, to get unbiased findings we employ ROA, measured as net earnings after tax divided by total assets, as our dependent variable. Furthermore, it is evident that when firms acquire capital assets or undertake heavy investments, their debt burden and consequent bankruptcy risk escalates in that particular period. However, this increased risk pays off in the subsequent years. Therefore, to assess the impact of current year bankruptcy risk on a firm's future performance, we also employ one year forward return on assets (ROA t + 1) as our second dependent variable.

3.1.2. Explanatory Variables

A firm's bankruptcy risk and its interaction between CLC stages (CLC stage*bankruptcy risk) are the main explanatory variables in this study. Careless selection of a bankruptcy risk measure can have adverse effects on the empirical outcome. Numerous studies have tried to measure the bankruptcy risk using a single firm-level variable such as book-to-market ratio, size, leverage, age, dividend payout, debt ratings, and group membership. These variables are not the true predictors of bankruptcy risk: for example, highly-leveraged firms have the highest bankruptcy risk, but this may not be true for a well-managed firm in a flourishing industrial segment. Similar views were presented by Clearly and Griffin and Lemmon [49,50]. Therefore, in the literature, a wide range of econometric models are available to gauge a firm's bankruptcy risk. Most of the models use different financial ratios to predict bankruptcy risk; for a good overview of these models, see, e.g., [51–54]. In the context of Pakistan, studies suggest that the Altman [51] model is an effective tool to measure the financial health of nonfinancial listed firms [55–58]. The Altman Z-score remains a familiar tool for evaluating the financial health of firms in recent research [7,59–61]. Therefore, we use Altman's Z-score as our primary dependent variable. Altman [51] used five explanatory variables and developed a model called the Altman Z-score. A lower Z-score (1.8 or below) indicates that a firm is at a high risk stage, while a higher Z-score (3 or above) predicts that a firm is in a stable situation. Thus, the inverse of the Altman Z-score is employed in the regression analysis.

Table 1 shows the year-wise bankruptcy risk level for sample firms on the basis of the Altman's Z-score. The data of financial ratios to calculate Z-score has been retrieved from a Balance Sheet Analysis (BSA) published by the State Bank of Pakistan (SBP). Calculations reveal that the highest number of firms was facing default risk in 2009. Moreover, in 2008 the number of at-risk firms was slightly less than in 2009. After 2009, the number of risky firms decreased steadily until 2013.

Table 1. Year-wise distribution of firms into various levels of bankruptcy risk using Altman's model.

Year	Number of Firms with No Bankruptcy Risk	Gray Area	Number of Firms at High Level of Bankruptcy Risk	Percentage of High-Risk Firms
2005	66	45	123	52.6
2006	68	51	121	50.4
2007	72	56	141	52.4
2008	65	46	175	61.2
2009	51	47	197	66.8
2010	67	65	168	56.0
2011	69	63	164	55.4
2012	59	64	170	58.0
2013	73	80	138	47.4

Source: Authors' calculation.

Moreover, it is difficult to calculate the life cycle stage of a particular firm that is offering fairly diverse products in multiple industries [1]. Keeping this in mind, we follow the approach used by Dickinson [1] to calculate the corporate life cycle stages. She posited that a firm's cash flow is a gauge of variations in its profitability, growth, and risk. Thus, we can classify firms into various stages of corporate life cycle, such as introduction, growth, maturity, shake-out, and decline through operating cash flows (OCF), investing cash flows (ICF), and financing cash flows (FCF). The methodology to segregate the firms is elaborated below:

Introduction, if OCF is (−), ICF is (−) while FCF is (+);

Growth, if OCF is (+), ICF is (−) while FCF is (+);

Mature, if OCF is (+), ICF is (−) while FCF is (−);

Decline, if OCF is (−), ICF is (+) while FCF is (+/−);

Shake-out = any pattern other than the aforementioned categories,

where + indicates cash flows with a value that is > 0, while − shows cash flows with a value < 0.

Figure 1 is a pie diagram that shows the life cycle-wise distribution of sample firms based on Dickinson's [1] model. Cash flow data to calculate corporate life cycle stages are retrieved from the OSIRIS database. They show that 43% of the sample firms are mature, while 7% are experiencing the decline stage of the corporate life cycle. Likewise, introduction, growth, and shake-out firms have shares of 18%, 18%, and 14%, respectively.

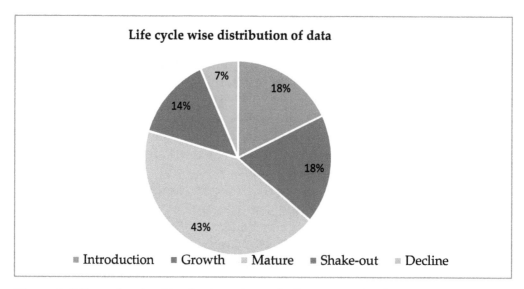

Figure 1. Life cycle-wise distribution of sample firms using Dickinson's model.

3.1.3. Firm-Level Control Variables

Firm performance is influenced by several internal factors (e.g., firm size, growth, leverage, and capital expenditure). Hence, the present study incorporates several firm-level controls that may be associated with firm profitability, as omission of these controls can give rise to unobserved heterogeneity and the correlated omitted variable issue. Comprehensive variable descriptions are presented in Appendix A.

3.1.4. Industry-Level Control Variables

We also employ control for the industry competition (INDCOM). Industry competition is calculated by using the Herfindahl index. It is a measure of firm size relative to the industry and also an indicator of the intensity of competition between firms. The Herfindahl index is calculated as the sum of the squares of the market share of firms within an industry. In such a way, the measure of industry competition will range between 0 and 10,000; a larger Herfindahl index suggests highly concentrated industry with lower competition. Following is the criteria declared by the Federal Trade Commission of America to classify an industry in any market structure using the Herfindahl index (HHI):

i.   If the HHI value is less than 1000, the industry will be considered unsaturated (competitive market);

ii.   An HHI value ranging between 1000 and 1800 means the industry is moderately saturated (monopolistic competition);

iii.   If the HHI value is more than 1800, it is a saturated market (oligopoly; if the value is > 10,000 then it is a pure monopoly).

Table 2 shows the level of concentration/competition in our sample firms within their industry using HHI scores. Stock prices data to calculate HHI for 2005 to 2013 were obtained from the business recorder group website khistocks.com. HHI scores reveal that the textile sector is the only sector that remained perfectly competitive during the study period. Chemicals, chemical products, and pharmaceuticals and motor vehicles, trailers, and auto parts were moderately saturated industries. Meanwhile, the food industry was a perfectly competitive market for 2005 to 2011. Afterwards, it was categorized as a moderately concentrated industry—except in 2012, when the HHI score reached the 1969 level. Likewise, the fuel and energy sector was found to be a moderately concentrated sector for the observed time period. The rest of the five industries were operating in an oligopolistic competition environment, except for other manufacturing, which remained concentrated during 2005 to 2007; in the subsequent period, it became a moderately concentrated industry—excluding 2011, when the HHI score was 992 (yearly scores are not reported in the table to conserve space).

Table 2. Industry wise competition/concentration using the Herfindahl index.

Industry	HHI Scores Range	Concentration	Market Structure
Textile	222 to 280	Unconcentrated	Perfect competition
Chemicals, Chemical Products, and Pharmaceuticals	1003 to 1310	Moderately concentrated	Monopolistic competition
Other Nonmetallic Mineral Products—Overall	654 to 1191	Unconcentrated + Moderately concentrated	Perfect competition+ Monopolistic competition
Other Manufacturing n.e.s.	992 to 1988	Unconcentrated + Moderately concentrated+ concentrated	Perfect competition+ Monopolistic competition+ Oligopolistic competition
Motor Vehicles, Trailers, and Auto parts	1243 to 1677	Moderately concentrated	Monopolistic competition
Food	802 to 1969	Un-concentrated+ Moderately concentrated + concentrated	Perfect competition+ Monopolistic competition+ Oligopolistic competition
Fuel and Energy	1453 to 1860	Moderately concentrated+ concentrated	Monopolistic competition+ Oligopolistic competition
Information, Comm., and Transport Services	3879 to 4317	Concentrated	Oligopolistic competition
Coke and Refined Petroleum Products	2523 to 3472	Concentrated	Oligopolistic competition
Paper, Paperboard, and Products	3206 to 4334	Concentrated	Oligopolistic competition
Other Service Activities	3242 to 5674	Concentrated	Oligopolistic competition
Electrical Machinery and Apparatus	3197 to 6488	Concentrated	Oligopolistic competition

Source: Authors' calculation.

3.1.5. Country-Level Controls

The study employed country-level economic controls in the regression analysis as these are suggested in the extant literature to have an impact on firm performance. Economic controls, industrial growth (INDGR), and GDP growth (GGDP) are included in the analysis to avoid the unobserved heterogeneity.

3.2. Sample and Data Collection

The research sample consists of all the nonfinancial listed firms in Pakistan from 2005 to 2013. The final sample includes only those firms with five consecutive years of published data available. This practice results in 295 firms with 2464 firm-year observations in 12 diverse industries. Cash flow data to calculate corporate life cycle stage were retrieved from the OSIRIS database. Stock price data were obtained from the business recorder group's website khistocks.com. To calculate bankruptcy risk proxy and control variables, the Balance Sheet Analysis (BSA) published by the State Bank of Pakistan (SBP) has been used. GDP growth data are retrieved from the World Development Index (WDI) of the World Bank. Finally, industrial growth data were obtained from the Central Intelligence Agency (CIA) World Factbook. Additionally, annual reports of the respective firm were also consulted to make up for the missing observations.

3.3. Empirical Strategy

The structure of our dataset is hierarchical in nature, consisting of 295 firms nested in 12 industries of Pakistan. From the econometric standpoint, firm-level observations are grouped under higher units (e.g., industries and countries); therefore, data analysis through OLS regressions can give rise to issues like biased estimates of standard errors or correlated error terms, and thus lead to biased interpretation of the results [62]. Moreover, it is essential to differentiate the firm-level effects from the industry- or country-level effects in order to understand the role of firm- versus industry- and country-level variables and to suitably model their interaction. Hence, the present study adopts hierarchical linear mixed models (HLMM) regression estimates, which can process multilevel data when observations are not completely independent; see [63] or [64] for an introduction to HLMM. In the present study, firms within a given industry form the base-level observations, while industries serve as higher-level observations.

There are several benefits to using a multilevel hierarchical model. First, we can test multilevel observations by simultaneously categorizing the variables at lower (firm) and higher (industry) levels without segregating the data. Second, the HLMM estimation can handle unbalanced panel data in cases where the sample size varies significantly across industries. In our study, the number of firms varies considerably across 12 diverse industrial segments. Thus, HLMM is a more suitable econometric approach for this study.

3.4. Alternate Methodology

The advantage of using panel-based models is that they help to control unobserved heterogeneity, which minimizes the possibility of getting biased results due to heterogeneity [65]. Therefore, we also apply panel fixed-effects and random-effects regressions as a robustness check. A Hausman post-estimation test was performed to choose the preferred model between fixed-effects and random-effects regressions.

3.5. Empirical Model

The following regression models were employed to empirically examine the hypotheses raised in this paper. The first model expresses the association between a firm's bankruptcy risk and current performance. The second model examines the linkage between bankruptcy risk and future corporate performance. ROA and ROA_{T+1} are the dependent variables for Equations (1) and (2), respectively. Our main variable of interest is Risk * FLCS, which is a vector of the dummy variables that symbolize corporate bankruptcy risk's interaction with firm life cycle stages, whereas $\beta 2$, $\beta 3$, $\beta 4$, and $\beta 5$ denote bankruptcy risk * introduction, bankruptcy risk * growth, bankruptcy risk * mature, and bankruptcy risk*decline, respectively. SIZE, MTB, FAGR, INDCOM, INDGR, and GGDP are control variables and represent firm size, market to book ratio, growth in fixed assets, industry competition, industrial growth, and GDP growth of the country, respectively. For variables' description and calculation, see Appendix A.

$$ROA_{i,t} = \alpha_O + \beta_1 Risk_{i,t} \sum_{k=2}^{5} \beta_k Risk_{i,t} * FLCS_{k,i,t} + \beta_6 SIZE_{i,t} + \beta_7 MTB_{i,t}$$
$$+ \beta_8 FAGR_{i,t} + \beta_9 INDCOM_{i,t} + \beta_{10} INDGR_{i,t} + \beta_{11} GGDP_{i,t} + \varepsilon_{i,t}$$

(1)

$$ROA_{i,t+1} = \alpha_O + \beta_1 Risk_{i,t} \sum_{k=2}^{5} \beta_k Risk_{i,t} * FLCS_{k,i,t} + \beta_6 SIZE_{i,t} + \beta_7 MTB_{i,t}$$
$$+\beta_8 FAGR_{i,t} + \beta_9 INDCOM_{i,t} + \beta_{10} INDGR_{i,t} + \beta_{11} GGDP_{i,t} + \varepsilon_{i,t}$$

(2)

4. Results and Discussion

4.1. Descriptive Analysis

Table 3 presents the descriptive statistics of variables. The average values of ROA, a profitability measure, shows that sample firms generate negative profits at the introduction (-0.080) and decline (-1.73) stages, while profitability is at its peak during the mature (9.41) stage of corporate life cycle. Moreover, the bankruptcy risk measure for the introduction (-1.32), growth (-1.78), and decline (-0.929) stages is higher than for the mature (-2.76) stage. FSIZE shows that firms are smaller in size at the introduction stage (12.8) and grow significantly during the growth (13.5) and mature (13.63) stages. However, they start to shrink again at the decline (12.13) stage. In line with corporate life cycle proposition, the MTB increases when the firm progresses from the introduction (0.217) to the mature (1.29) stages and declines as firms transition from the mature to the decline stage (0.839). Furthermore, fixed assets grow between the introduction and growth stages but diminish during the mature and decline stages.

Table 3. Descriptive statistics.

Variables	N	Mean	S.D.	5th percent	95th percent	Intro	Grow	Mature	Decline
ROA	2662	5.67	14.2	−13.43	30.66	−0.080	5.52	9.41	−1.73
ROA$_{+1}$	2662	5.42	14.2	−13.71	29.81	−0.525	4.44	8.98	1.02
RISK	2789	−2.16	2.99	−6.48	0.560	−1.32	−1.78	−2.76	−0.992
SIZE	2789	13.30	2.26	9.85	17.20	12.80	13.50	13.63	12.13
MTB	2789	0.958	10.80	−0.122	3.65	0.217	0.847	1.29	0.819
FAG	2789	0.293	2.17	−0.110	1.03	0.257	0.423	0.201	0.234
INCOM	2789	1179	1157	232	3983	983	1171	1207	1134
INDGR	2789	4.49	3.25	−1.90	10.70	4.76	5.09	4.21	3.76
GGDP	2789	3.79	1.87	1.60	7.70	3.74	4.33	3.70	3.25

Statistics on industry competition/concentration suggest that firms at the introduction stage are less concentrated (HHI = 983) and face a high level of competition. However, when firms advance from the introduction to the mature stage, they get much more concentrated and face less competition at the successive stages of their life cycle.

The mean values of INDGR and GGDP are 4.49 and 3.87 respectively. Life cycle-wise statistics indicate that when the values of industrial 5.09 and GDP 4.33 growth were higher, firms were at the growth stage. Contrarily, during the period of low industrial 3.76 and GDP 3.25 growth, firms switched to the decline stage.

Figure 2 depicts variations in firm bankruptcy risk and financial performance at different stages of the corporate life cycle. Whereas Return on Assets (ROA) and one-year-ahead Return on Assets (ROA+1) is used to measure corporate financial performance, the Altman z-score is deployed as a bankruptcy risk measure. It is evident that firms engaged in higher risk at the introduction stage, which gradually decreased and reached at a minimum level during the mature stage of the life cycle. However, consistent with the expectations, when firms transition from the mature to the decline stage, their bankruptcy risk tends to escalate rapidly. Interestingly, firm performance is inversely proportionate to its bankruptcy risk. Financial performance improves when firms move from the introduction to the mature stage and begins to deteriorate from the mature to the decline stage. The evidence strongly supports the notion that not only does the financial sustainability of firms vary across the corporate life cycle, but also their associated financial performance is influenced differently at each stage of CLC.

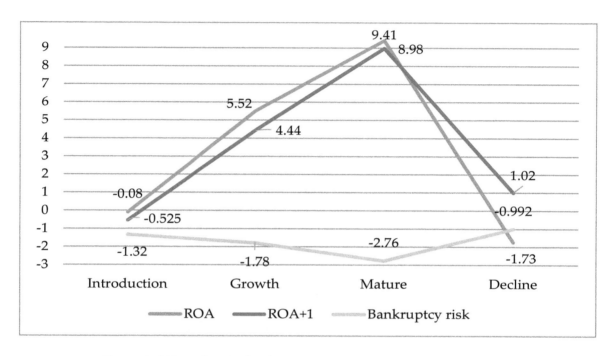

Figure 2. Life cycle-wise bankruptcy risk and return of sampled firms.

Table 4 shows the results of a pairwise correlation analysis of the baseline variables. The performance proxy ROA has a negative correlation with bankruptcy risk and fixed assets growth, but a positive association with FSIZE, MTB, INCOM, INGR, and GDPG. Firm size has a significant positive coefficient with market to book ratio, referring to the findings of Table 1, which suggests that firms at the introduction phase are smaller in size (12.8); however, their size increases as they pass through the growth (13.5) stage and is largest during the mature stage (13.63) of the life cycle. This correlation shows that, during the introduction phase of the life cycle, firms have limited information available to investors, which leads to a higher risk being associated with their stocks. However, as firms pass through different stages of the life cycle, they have more information available for stakeholders. Therefore, as compared to infant firms, investors tend to attribute more value to the stocks of growing and mature firms. Furthermore, growth in fixed assets is negatively associated with ROA, while this relationship is positive for ROA+$_1$. It reflects that investment in fixed assets yields profitability in the future.

Overall, in some cases the correlation among control variables is significant, which may give rise to a multicollinearity issue in the proposed models. Therefore, we applied Variance Inflation Factor (VIF) analysis to check if such a problem exists in our data. A VIF value of 10 or higher shows that variables have multicollinearity [66]. However, none of our variables have a VIF value greater than the prescribed limit, thus eradicating the possibility of multicollinearity in our analysis (see Appendix B).

Table 4. Correlation analysis.

	ROA	ROA+$_1$	RISK	SIZE	MTB	FAG	INCOM	INGR	GDPG
ROA	1.000								
ROA+$_1$	0.598*	1.000							
RISK	−0.579*	−0.413*	1.000						
SIZE	0.396*	0.325*	−0.37*	1.000					
MTB	0.016	0.012	0.111*	0.086*	1.000				
FAG	−0.004	0.013	−0.019	0.0339	0.003	1.000			
INCOM	0.143*	0.115*	−0.12*	0.338*	0.082*	0.019	1.000		
INGR	0.100*	0.034	−0.09*	0.077*	−0.004	−0.033	0.015	1.000	
GGDP	0.099*	0.0789*	−0.09*	0.089*	−0.013	0.025	0.0188	0.626*	1.0000

* indicates $p < 0.05$.

4.2. Regression Analysis

Table 5 reports the results of our baseline analysis, using HLMM regression to examine the association between corporate performance and bankruptcy risk at various stages of the life cycle. Robust t-statistics are in parentheses, while ***, **, and * indicate 1%, 5%, and 10% significance levels, respectively. We estimate two regression models with current ROA and one-year-ahead ROA as the dependent variables. Key variables of interest in both regression models are the interaction between corporate bankruptcy risk and life cycle stages (Risk*CLC stages), and firms' current (ROA) and future performance (ROA$_{+1}$).

The findings of Model 1 reveal that, irrespective of firm life cycle stages, ROA has a negative relationship with bankruptcy risk, inferring that escalated risk levels lead to a decline in corporate profitability. Similar findings were reported by [22,23] using different proxies of risk. RISK*Intro shows a positive yet insignificant correlation with ROA, which could be attributed to the fact that introductory firms focus on breakthrough innovations that can unleash their productivity potential and performance in the succeeding years. Likewise, RISK*Grow has a significantly ($p < 0.05$) positive association with ROA, having a coefficient of 0.479. This shows that growing firms borrow heavily through external funding sources [7]; however, high revenue growth and an emphasis on product innovation with a growing market share help to improve the firm's profitability. In line with H3, RISK*Mature has a significantly negative relationship with ROA. This suggests that, during the introduction stage, firms have more possibilities to invest in profitable avenues. Their product and process innovation will also be more attractive for customers; therefore, by assuming more risk, such firms can gain higher profitability. However, mature firms have very limited profitable investment avenues; therefore, managers may invest in negative NPV projects to give positive signals to stakeholders. Nevertheless, their innovation level also declines with stagnating sales [1,3]. Therefore, risk-taking at the mature stage generates negative future profitability. Consistent with the prospect theory, RISK*Decline has a negative and statistically significant relationship with performance, suggesting that managers of decline firms undertake hefty investments in a turnaround effort yet a risk-averse attitude may lead to investing in bad gambles, which generates poor returns.

Table 5. Panel A1: Baseline HLMM regressions of bankruptcy risk and firm performance at different life cycle stages.

	Expected Sign	Model 1 ROA	Expected Sign	Model 2 ROA+1
RISK	-	−2.182***	+?	−0.893***
		(−14.45)		(−5.22)
RISK*Intro	+	0.185	+	0.640**
		(0.74)		(2.21)
RISK*Grow	+	0.478**	+	0.287
		(2.43)		(1.26)
RISK*Mature	-	−0.865***	-	−0.892***
		(−5.63)		(−5.03)
RISK*Decline	-	−1.021***	-	−0.439
		(−3.08)		(−1.14)
SIZE	+	1.257***	+	0.861***
		(7.08)		(4.48)
MTB	+	0.0602***	+	−0.0206
		(2.81)		(−0.83)
FAG	-	0.129	+	0.106
		(1.43)		(1.01)
INCOM	+	−0.000110	+	0.000233
		(−0.32)		(0.63)
INGR	+	0.0805	+?	−0.204**
		(1.11)		(−2.40)
GGDP	+	0.123	+	0.499***
		(0.97)		(3.34)
Constant		−17.69***		−10.30***
N		2464		2464

t statistics are in parentheses; * $p < 0.1$, ** $p < 0.05$, *** $p < 0.01$.

Interestingly, the regression results of Model 2 reveal that overall bankruptcy risk has a significant negative coefficient with firms' future performance. However, the coefficients show that the average impact of bankruptcy risk is much higher on current performance as compared to the future performance of firms. This implies that firms borrow heavily to buy capital assets, which reduces their current earnings; however, as those assets start contributing to the income/value of the firm, corporate profitability increases, which helps to improve firm performance in subsequent years. Unlike in Model 1, risk-taking at the introduction stage has a significantly ($p < 0.05$) positive association with ROA_{t+1}. It strengthens the proposition that introduction firms take time to establish their business and start to generate profits. In addition, introduction firms engage in major innovation projects with a long-term strategic orientation, so risk-taking at this stage generates positive outcomes. RISK*Grow is also positively associated with future performance—though, unlike with Model 1, this association is not significant. This shows that the performance of growth firms does not respond to past risk propensities; instead, it is associated with their current level of bankruptcy risk. Similar to Model 1, RISK*Mature has a significantly ($p < 0.01$) negative association with future performance. Likewise, bankruptcy risk at the decline stage has a negative yet insignificant association with future ROA.

As with the control variables, the reported results belong to Model 1. FSIZE indicates a positive and significant relationship with firm performance, meaning that large firms intend to generate better performance. As expected, a firm's market to book ratio and sales growth contribute to its performance. Growth in fixed assets has an insignificant correlation with firm performance. This reveals that investment in fixed assets such as land and machinery is a part of long-term planning that will contribute to firm performance in the long run. Industry competition has no significant association with firm-level performance. Among country-level variables, industrial growth rates reveal a negative and significant link with future performance, while GDP growth is positively associated with a firm's future performance.

Table 6 presents the random part of our HLMM model. In this table, the observation's residual is partitioned into three parts that define its value in relation to the firm, industry, and grand means. Statistics reveal that the observations diverge from their firm mean by an average of 9.06, with a standard error of 0.144, and firm mean deviates from the respective industry mean by an average of 6.39. The industry mean of sample observations deviates from the grand mean by 0.00002. In short, this evidence strengthens our belief that the model specification is reasonable.

Table 6. (Panel-A2) Random part of this HLMM model.

Random-Effects Parameters	Standard Deviation	Standard Error
Industry	0.00002	0.00013
Firm	6.39	0.345
Residual	9.060	0.144

To check the robustness, in Table 7 we examine the similar regression models using the panel fixed effects regression estimation. Bankruptcy risk indicates a significant (0.01) and negative association with current and future firm performance. Consistent with the findings of HLMM, the coefficient for future performance is much lower than that of the current performance.

RISK*Intro is positively associated with ROA and ROA $_{t+1}$. Similarly, bankruptcy risk has a positive correlation with the performance of the growth firms; however, this association is significant only for the current performance. RISK*Mature shows a negative and statistically significant coefficient with current and future performance ($p < 0.01$). Similarly, risk-taking at the decline stage also reveals a negative coefficient. Among control variables, sales growth, market to book ratio, firm size, and growth in fixed assets have positive and statistically significant associations with corporate performance. Summing up, the findings of Table 7 are highly aligned with the findings of Table 5, which indicates that our results are robust.

Table 7. Robustness check-bankruptcy risk and corporate performance at different CLC stages using the fixed-effects model.

	Expected Sign	(Fixed-Effects) ROA	Expected Sign	(Fixed-Effects) ROA+1
RISK	-	-2.739^{***}	+?	-0.846^{***}
		(-15.14)		(-4.01)
RISK*Intro	+	0.567^{**}	+	0.620^{**}
		(2.15)		(2.01)
RISK*Grow	+	1.056^{***}	+	0.411
		(4.90)		(1.63)
RISK*Mature	-	-0.436^{***}	-	-0.527^{***}
		(-2.64)		(-2.73)
RISK*Decline	-	-0.786^{**}	-	-0.225
		(-2.30)		(-0.57)
SIZE	+	1.701^{***}	+	-0.873^{**}
		(5.25)		(-2.31)
MTB	+	0.0737^{***}	+	-0.0226
		(3.37)		(-0.89)
FAG	-	0.295^{***}	+	0.145
		(3.13)		(1.32)
INCOM	+	-0.000656	+	-0.000320
		(-0.84)		(-0.35)
INGR	+	0.0539	+	-0.153^{*}
		(0.74)		(-1.79)
GGDP	+	0.0825	+	0.555^{***}
		(0.65)		(3.72)
Constant		-22.97^{***}		13.79^{**}
		(-5.37)		(2.76)
N		2464		2464

t statistics in parentheses; * $p < 0.1$, ** $p < 0.05$, *** $p < 0.01$.

5. Conclusions

Risk is a fundamental factor affecting the financial health and smooth functioning of an enterprise. The financial crisis of 2008 and the liquidity crunch that followed have forced managers and researchers to evaluate the implications of corporate risk-taking on sustainable financial performance. This study investigates the association between a firm's bankruptcy risk and its current and future performance at various stages of the corporate life cycle. Following the entrepreneurial activity approach and prospect theory, we suppose that, at the early stages of their life cycle, firms have considerable opportunities to grow by investing in positive NPV projects; however, as firms mature, further investment in existing projects tends to cause a decline in profitability due to a nondiversified and self-serving approach, as managers may avoid investing in risky NPV undertakings. Hence, bankruptcy risk at the introduction and growth stages is positively associated with a firm's financial performance and negatively linked with the performance of mature and decline firms.

Empirical evidence suggests that, irrespective of the life cycle stages, bankruptcy risk results in negative current and future profitability. Moreover, the performance of introduction and growth firms responds positively to risk-taking. Contrarily, risk-taking during the mature and decline stages negatively correlates with firm performance, giving an inverted-U shaped pattern. This research unveils some noteworthy findings, as introduction firms have a positive but insignificant association with current performance; however, this relationship is significant for future performance, indicating that, during the start-up stage, firms mainly focus on breakthrough innovations and product development processes. Once this innovation activity is successful, it is likely to yield profitable outcomes in subsequent years. Similarly, risk-taking at the growth stage is significantly associated with current performance but insignificantly associated with the next year's performance. This indicates that the performance of these firms is quite responsive to their current capital inflows.

This study makes some important contributions to the corporate sustainability domain. First, it contributes to the enterprise management literature by directly examining the impact of firm life cycle stages on the relationship between bankruptcy risk and firm performance. Prior studies have ignored the perceived impact of life cycle stages in determining the risk-return relationship. Moreover, most earlier studies such as [20,22] report conflicting empirical findings. Second, the results of the present research suggest that managerial decisions of mature and decline firms are not aligned with the wealth maximization objective of shareholders and excessive risk-taking at these stages can considerably endanger a firm's financial sustainability. The study has practical implications for various corporate stakeholders. Managers should adjust the bankruptcy risk of their firms to be in line with the respective life cycle stage to avoid a bank run. Likewise, investors should be more cautious when investing in mature and declining firms. Furthermore, a firm's shareholders should also exert pressure on the management to align their financial decisions with the respective CLC stage to ensure the sustainable functioning of their business in crisis situations.

However, the study also has some limitations that are worth mentioning. First, the research sample is confined to listed Pakistani firms. Hence, the findings of this study can only be generalized to listed firms in developing countries with similar macroeconomic dynamics. Further studies in this area can explore how this relationship prevails in the context of advanced economies. Second, our research only takes into account the bankruptcy form of risk, ignoring other risk categories such as country risk, political risk, market risk, operational risk, etc. Therefore, future studies in this domain can explore the influence of CLC stages on the association between other risk categories and the financial performance of an enterprise.

Author Contributions: Conceptualization, M.A.; methodology, M.A.; formal analysis, M.A.; writing—original draft preparation, A.A.; writing—review and editing, P.M., H.M.A., and M.Y.; funding acquisition, P.M. All authors have read and agreed to the published version of the manuscript.

Acknowledgments: The authors thank the anonymous reviewers for their useful comments on the earlier version of this article. We also acknowledge the financial support by the University of Hradec Kralove to support the open access of this article.

Appendix A

Table A1. Variables' definition and measurement.

Variable Category and Name	Description	Calculation	Expected Sign
Dependent Variables			
Return on assets	ROA	Net income before tax, scaled by total assets at the end of fiscal year	Future performance is expected to have a negative association with the bankruptcy risk-taking of a firm
Future return on assets	ROA_{t+1}	One-year-ahead return on assets	Future corporate performance is also expected to have a negative correlation with bankruptcy risk
Independent Variables			
Bankruptcy risk-taking propensity	Risk	Inverse of Altman Z-score	An increase in bankruptcy risk is expected to decrease the future ROA
Firm life cycle stages interact with its bankruptcy risk	FLCS*Risk	Firms' different CLC stages, i.e., introduction, growth, maturity, and decline, interact with its bankruptcy risk-taking propensity	Insolvency risk propensity during the introduction and growth stages of the life cycle is expected to have a positive association with future corporate performance. However, this relationship is predicted to be negative for mature and decline firms
Firm-Level Control Variables			
Firm size	SIZE	Natural logarithm of the market value of equity of firms	A positive relationship is anticipated between firm size and its future performance
Market to book ratio	MTB	Market value of equity/book value of equity	MTB is expected to have a positive sign with future corporate performance at different CLC stages
Fixed assets growth rate	FAG	Fixed assets growth is measured as current years' fixed assets scaled by lagged fixed assets	Growth in fixed assets is expected to generate better future performance
Industry-Level Control Variable			
Industry competition	INCOM	Industry competition is measured by the Herfindahl index. It is calculated as the sum of the squares of market share of firms within a given industry. Higher value of index suggests a high market concentration and a low level of competition	An increase in competition is anticipated to have negative effects on a firm's ROA
Country-Level Control Variables			
Industrial growth rate	INGR	Annual percentage increase in industrial production of Pakistan	Increased industrial growth is expected to have a positive association with future returns on assets
Growth in Gross domestic product	GDPG	Annual GDP growth rate	GDP growth is also anticipated to have a positive relationship with future performance

Appendix B

Table A2. Variance inflation analysis.

Variable	VIF	1/VIF
GDPG	8.25	0.121252
SIZE	7.10	0.140844
RISK	5.12	0.195138
INGR	4.81	0.207937
RISK*Mature	3.51	0.284604
INCOM	2.26	0.443024
RISK*Intro	1.84	0.542774
RISK*Grow	1.75	0.571160
MTB	1.37	0.730724
RISK*Decline	1.16	0.862375
FAG	1.02	0.975757
Mean VIF	3.47	

References

Dickinson, V. Cash flow patterns as a proxy for firm life cycle. Account. Rev. 2011, 86, 1969–1994. [CrossRef]

Aghion, P.; Fally, T.; Scarpetta, S. Credit constraints as a barrier to the entry and post-entry growth of firms. Econ. Policy 2007, 22, 732–779. [CrossRef]

Miller, D.; Friesen, P.H. A longitudinal study of the corporate life cycle. Manag. Sci. 1984, 30, 1161–1183. [CrossRef]

Gray, B.; Ariss, S.S. Politics and strategic change across organizational life cycles. Acad. Manag. Rev. 1985, 10, 707–723. [CrossRef]

Canto-Cuevas, F.-J.; Palacín-Sánchez, M.-J.; Di Pietro, F. Trade Credit as a Sustainable Resource during an SME's Life Cycle. Sustainability 2019, 11, 670. [CrossRef]

Fitzsimmons, J.; Steffens, P.; Douglas, E. Growth and profitability in small and medium sized Australian firms. Growth and profitability in small and medium sized Australian firms. 2005. Available online: https://papers.ssrn.com/sol3/papers.cfm?abstract_id=1263734 (accessed on 24 April 2020).

Akbar, A.; Akbar, M.; Tang, W.; Qureshi, M.A. Is Bankruptcy Risk Tied to Corporate Life-Cycle? Evidence from Pakistan. Sustainability 2019, 11, 678. [CrossRef]

Anthony, J.H.; Ramesh, K. Association between accounting performance measures and stock prices: A test of the life cycle hypothesis. J. Account. Econ. 1992, 15, 203–227. [CrossRef]

Richardson, S. Over-investment of free cash flow. Rev. Acc. Stud. 2006, 11, 159–189. [CrossRef]

DeAngelo, H.; DeAngelo, L.; Stulz, R.M. Dividend policy and the earned/contributed capital mix: A test of the life-cycle theory. J. Financ. Econ. 2006, 81, 227–254. [CrossRef]

Oude Avenhuis, J. Testing the Generalizability of the Bankruptcy Prediction Models of Altman, Ohlson and Zmijewski for Dutch Listed and Large Non-Listed Firms; University of Twente: Enschede, The Netherlands, 2013.

Rose-Ackerman, S. Risk taking and ruin: Bankruptcy and investment choice. J. Legal Stud. 1991, 20, 277–310. [CrossRef]

Dichev, I.D. Is the risk of bankruptcy a systematic risk? J. Financ. 1998, 53, 1131–1147. [CrossRef]

Altman, E. Corporate Financial Distress and Bankruptcy; Wiley: New York, NY, USA, 1993.

Chang, H.; Feroz, E.; Bryan, D.; Fernando, G.D.; Tripathy, A. Bankruptcy risk, productivity and firm strategy. Rev. Acc. Financ. 2013, 12, 309–326.

DeAngelo, H.; DeAngelo, L. Dividend policy and financial distress: An empirical investigation of troubled NYSE firms. J. Financ. 1990, 45, 1415–1431. [CrossRef]

Sudarsanam, S.; Lai, J. Corporate financial distress and turnaround strategies: An empirical analysis. Brit. J. Manag. 2001, 12, 183–199. [CrossRef]

Armour, H.O.; Teece, D.J. Organizational structure and economic performance: A test of the multidivisional hypothesis. Bell J. Econ. 1978, 106–122. [CrossRef]

Fisher, I.N.; Hall, G.R. Risk and corporate rates of return. Q. J. Econ. 1969, 79–92. [CrossRef]

Aaker, D.A.; Jacobson, R. The role of risk in explaining differences in profitability. Acad. Manag. J. 1987, 30, 277–296.

Fiegenbaum, A.; Thomas, H. An Examination of the Structural Stability of Boman's Risk-Return Paradox; Academy of Management Proceedings, Academy of Management: New York, NY, USA, 1985; pp. 7–10.

Bowman, E.H. A Risk/Return Paradox for Strategic Management; John Wiley & Sons: Bristol, UK, 1980.

Bowman, E.H. Risk seeking by troubled firms. Sloan Manag. Rev. 1982, 23, 33.

Treacy, M.E.F. Profitability Patterns and Firm Size; Sloan School of Management: Cambridge, MA, USA, 1980.

Bowman, E.H. Content analysis of annual reports for corporate strategy and risk. Interfaces 1984, 14, 61–71. [CrossRef]

Andersen, T.J.; Denrell, J.; Bettis, R.A. Strategic responsiveness and Bowman's risk–return paradox. Strateg. Manag. J. 2007, 28, 407–429. [CrossRef]

Kirzner, I.M. Entrepreneurial discovery and the competitive market process: An Austrian approach. J. Econ. Lit. 1997, 35, 60–85.

Sørensen, J.B.; Stuart, T.E. Aging, obsolescence, and organizational innovation. Admin. Sci. Quart. 2000, 45, 81–112. [CrossRef]

Henderson, A.D.; Benner, M.J. The Evolution of Risk and Return in High-Velocity Settings; Academy of Management Best Paper Proceedings; Citeseer: New York, NY, USA, 2000.

Khan, M.; Watts, R.L. Estimation and empirical properties of a firm-year measure of accounting conservatism. Account. Econ. 2009, 48, 132–150. [CrossRef]

Amit, R.; Schoemaker, P.J. Strategic assets and organizational rent. Strateg. Manag. J. 1993, 14, 33–46. [CrossRef]

Levie, J.; Lichtenstein, B.B. A terminal assessment of stages theory: Introducing a dynamic states approach to entrepreneurship. Entrep. Theory Pract. 2010, 34, 317–350. [CrossRef]

Habib, A.; Hasan, M.M.J.A. Firm life cycle, corporate risk-taking and investor sentiment. Account. Financ. 2017, 57, 465–497. [CrossRef]

Kahneman, D.; Tversky, A. Prospect theory: An analysis of decision under risk. Econometrica 1979, 47, 363–391. [CrossRef]

Bromiley, P. Testing a causal model of corporate risk taking and performance. Acad. Manag. J. 1991, 34, 37–59.

Liao, Y. The effect of fit between organizational life cycle and human resource management control on firm performance. J. Am. Acad. Bus. 2006, 8, 192–196.

Jaafar, H.; Halim, H.A. Refining the Firm Life Cycle Classification Method: A Firm Value Perspective. J. Econ. Bus. Manag. 2016, 4, 112–119. [CrossRef]

Navaretti, G.B.; Castellani, D.; Pieri, F. Age and firm growth: Evidence from three European countries. Small Bus. Econ. 2014, 43, 823–837. [CrossRef]

Selling, T.I.; Stickney, C.P. The effects of business environment and strategy on a firm's rate of return on assets. Financ. Anal. J. 1989, 45, 43–52. [CrossRef]

Yazdanfar, D.; Öhman, P. Life cycle and performance among SMEs: Swedish empirical evidence. J. Risk Financ. 2014, 15, 555–571. [CrossRef]

Lester, D.L.; Parnell, J.A. Firm size and environmental scanning pursuits across organizational life cycle stages. J. Small Bus. Enterp. Dev. 2008, 15, 540–554. [CrossRef]

Bulan, L.; Yan, Z. The pecking order of financing in the firm's life cycle. Bank. Financ. Lett. 2009, 1, 129–140.

Chandler, A.D. Strategy and Structure; MIT Press: Cambridge, MA, USA, 1962.

Gort, M.; Klepper, S. Time paths in the diffusion of product innovations. Econ. J. 1982, 92, 630–653. [CrossRef]

Wernerfelt, B. The dynamics of prices and market shares over the product life cycle. Manag. Sci. 1985, 31, 928–939. [CrossRef]

Wang, Z.; Akbar, M.; Akbar, A. The Interplay between Working Capital Management and a Firm's Financial Performance across the Corporate Life Cycle. Sustainability 2020, 12, 1661. [CrossRef]

Hasan, M.M.; Hossain, M.; Habib, A. Corporate life cycle and cost of equity capital. J. Contemp. Account. Econ. 2015, 11, 46–60. [CrossRef]

Benmelech, E.; Kandel, E.; Veronesi, P. Stock-Based Compensation and CEO (Dis) Incentives. Q. J. Econ. 2010, 125, 1769–1820. [CrossRef]

Cleary, S. The relationship between firm investment and financial status. J. Financ. 1999, 54, 673–692. [CrossRef]

Griffin, J.M.; Lemmon, M.L. Book–to–market equity, distress risk, and stock returns. J. Financ. 2002, 57, 2317–2336. [CrossRef]

Altman, E.I. Financial ratios, discriminant analysis and the prediction of corporate bankruptcy. J. Financ. 1968, 23, 589–609. [CrossRef]

Springate, G.L. Predicting the Possibility of Failure in a Canadian Firm: A Discriminant Analysis; Simon Fraser University: Vancouver, BC, Canada, 1978.

Zmijewski, M.E. Methodological issues related to the estimation of financial distress prediction models. Account. Res. 1984, 59–82. [CrossRef]

Ohlson, J.A. Financial ratios and the probabilistic prediction of bankruptcy. J. Account. Res. 1980, 109–131. [CrossRef]

Roomi, M.S.; Ahmad, W.; Ramzan, M.; Zia-ur-Rehman, M. Bankruptcy Prediction for Non-Financial Firms of Pakistan. Int. J. Account. Financ. Rep. 2015, 5, 26–37. [CrossRef]

Hussain, F.; Ali, I.; Ullah, S.; Ali, M. Can Altman Z-score Model Predict Business Failures in Pakistan? Evidence from Textile Companies of Pakistan. J. Econ. Sustain. Dev. 2014, 5, 110–115.

Awais, M.; Hayat, F.; Mehar, N.; Ul-Hassan, W. Do Z-Score and Current Ratio have Ability to Predict Bankruptcy? Dev. Country Stud. 2015, 5, 30–36.

Ijaz, M.S.; Hunjra, A.I. Assessing the Financial Failure Using Z-Score and Current Ratio: A Case of Sugar Sector Listed Companies of Karachi Stock Exchange. World Appl. Sci. J. 2013, 23, 863–870.

Almamy, J.; Aston, J.; Ngwa, L.N. An evaluation of Altman's Z-score using cash flow ratio to predict corporate failure amid the recent financial crisis: Evidence from the UK. J. Corp. Financ. 2016, 36, 278–285. [CrossRef]

Chouhan, V.; Chandra, B.; Goswami, S. Predicting financial stability of select BSE companies revisiting Altman Z score. Int. Lett. Soc. Hum. Sci. 2014, 15, 92–105. [CrossRef]

Hoque, M.; Bhandari, S.B.; Iyer, R. Predicting business failure using cash flow statement based measures. Manag. Financ. 2013, 39, 667–676.

Garson, G.D. Hierarchical Linear Modeling: Guide and Applications; Sage: Thousand Oaks, CA, USA, 2012.

Goldstein, H. Multilevel Statistical Models; John Wiley & Sons: Bristol, UK, 2011; Volume 922.

Raudenbush, S.W.; Bryk, A.S. Hierarchical Linear Models: Applications and Data Analysis Methods; Sage: London, UK, 2002; Volume 1.

Hsiao, C. Benefits and limitations of panel data. Economet. Rev. 1985, 4, 121–174. [CrossRef]

Kennedy, P. Guide to Econometrics, 6th ed.; Wiley-Blackwell: Oxford, UK, 2008.

3

Proposing a Multidimensional Bankruptcy Prediction Model: An Approach for Sustainable Islamic Banking

Mehreen Mehreen [1],*[iD], Maran Marimuthu [1], Samsul Ariffin Abdul Karim [2][iD] and Amin Jan [1][iD]

[1] Department of Management and Humanities, Universiti Teknologi PETRONAS, Bandar Seri Iskandar, Seri Iskandar 32610, Perak, Malaysia; maran.marimuthu@utp.edu.my (M.M.); amin_17000556@utp.edu.my (A.J.)

[2] Fundamental and Applied Sciences Department and Centre for Smart Grid Energy Research (CSMER), Institute of Autonomous System, Universiti Teknologi PETRONAS, Bandar Seri Iskandar, Seri Iskandar 32610, Perak Darul Ridzuan, Malaysia; samsul_ariffin@utp.edu.my

* Correspondence: mehreen_18001045@utp.edu.my

Abstract: The main purpose of this study is to conceptualize a sustainable banking model for Islamic banking by blending three essential business aspects namely financial performance, Islamic corporate governance, and sustainability practices dimension. In the case of Islamic banking, evidence shows that a Shariah-based bankruptcy prediction model for apprehending the true bankruptcy prediction is over-sighted. This study offers an efficient Shariah-based bankruptcy prediction model by first, reviewing the previously applied conventional bankruptcy prediction models; secondly, by developing and proposing a robust, multidimensional model for predicting bankruptcy in Islamic banking. This framework may have profound implications on the existing bankruptcy evaluation structure of the Islamic banking industry and may provide a strong sustainability management guideline to the global Islamic banking industry.

Keywords: bankruptcy prediction; financial performance; Islamic banking; sustainability; Shariah governance

1. Introduction

The Islamic banking system is relatively new in the banking industry and it is still at the growing stage. Significant efforts are required for sustainability [1]. According to the Islamic Financial Services industry report 2018, Islamic banking assets retain around 76 percent share in the global Islamic financial assets. In case of any deterioration, it will affect the entire Islamic financial industry. For this purpose, the financial position of Islamic banks must be understood, therefore there is a need to understand the details of the financial attributes of Islamic banking as this may lead to financial distress. The prediction techniques used for the banking sector were developed 5 decades ago notably by [2,3]. These models contain only the financial attributes which support only the financial aspect of the firms [4]. In opposition, currently, the organizations are operating in a more complex era, where they are not only required to grow financially but also operationally and socially as well [5].

Different rating agencies also determine the rating for companies based on a combination of ratio analysis, qualitative factors, strategic decisions, and management plans, industry health. Nowadays financialists and consultants preferably utilize the blended models of financial and non-financial attributes such as considering sustainability as well instead of the more traditional models. Secondly, the traditional models used for bankruptcy prediction of banks were originally designed for manufacturing firms and were later on applied to the conventional banks with minor modifications. The same models are now used for bankruptcy prediction in Islamic banks as well. However, Islamic banks have some specific Shariah attributes that are different from conventional banks [5]. For this purpose, there is a dire need to develop a robust model that has a combination of multiple dimensions such as financial and non-financial (Shariah governance and social attributes).

The primary reason for the development of a separate Islamic based bankruptcy forecasting model lies in the deteriorations of the key performance indicators of the Islamic banking share. It is because evidence shows that the banking sector grasps a significant share in the world financial system. In case of any financial deterioration in the banking industry, the overall world financial sector will suffer. The facts show that the main key performance financial indicators of the global Islamic banking industry are deteriorating. Table 1 is providing a snapshot of the deterioration in the major financial indicators of the global Islamic banking industry.

Table 1. Deterioration of Financial indicators of the global Islamic banking industry.

Financial Indicators	Year 2013	Year 2018	Change
Capital adequacy ratio *	18.2	12.3	−5.9
Tier 1 ratio *	16.2	10.7	−5.5
Nonperforming financing to total Financing	6.0	4.9	−1.1
Return on assets	2.2	3.2	+1.0

Source: Islamic Financial Services Industry Stability Report (2019). * These Ratios are calculated differently in different countries based on the prevailing regulatory purposes.

Table 1 demonstrates the financial indicators of the Global Islamic banking industry. Capital Adequacy Ratio (CAR) and Tier 1 are considered important measures to check the position of the regulatory capital of banks. These ratios were recorded as 18.2 and 16.2 in 2013, which are decreased to 12.3 and 10.7 respectively. The main reason for this decline is the currency depreciation in Iran against the US dollar which caused a dramatic fall in the overall operational efficiency of all financial institutions in the country. Sudan faced the same depreciation during this time and affected the global Islamic banking performance. Asset quality is mostly measured through non-performing financing divided by total financing. This ratio indicates the efficiency of a bank to manage its finances. A decline of 1.1 is recorded from 2013 to 2018 but the ratio of 4.9 is still alarming and may affect the efficiency and overall rating of Islamic banking in the industry. Table 1 shows an increase in Return on Assets ROA from 2.2 to 3.2, but the increase is just marginally better which can be a hurdle in the long-term financial sustainability of the Islamic banking industry. Broadly, it alludes that, if these financial indicators are not monitored properly, it will disturb the economic sustainability of the Islamic banking industry across the world. Moreover, the top five Islamic banking counties collectively retain around 72 percent share of the global Islamic banking share (Islamic Financial Services Industry Stability Report 2019). Any deterioration in the financial indicators of these top countries may eventually affect the world Islamic banking share. Table 1 shows that the major financial indicators of the Islamic banking sector are deteriorating, against this background, the main objective of this study is to propose a bankruptcy prediction model for Islamic banks. Secondly, this study pioneered the concept of incorporating Islamic corporate governance and sustainability variables in the subjected bankruptcy prediction model. It is because the evidence supports a positive association of these variables on bankruptcy prediction [6,7]. The proposed bankruptcy prediction framework will assure the strong economic sustainability of the Islamic banks in the market-leading Islamic banking countries which accounts for almost 80 percent of the world Islamic banking assets [8]. The surveillance in a way will ensure the strong economic sustainability of the economies where the Islamic banking share is significant in the overall banking industry share of the subjected countries. Hence, achieving the objective of this study will assure sustainable Islamic banking in the market-leading Islamic banking countries.

Role of the Banking Industry in the Financial System

The financial system is considered as the backbone of any economy. It is the only systematic source of financial intermediation and facilitates the funds' circulation between the borrowers, the lenders, and investors. Therefore financial institutions play a vital role in the economic growth and development of the economy [9]. For the growth and expansion of economies, the growth of financial institutions especially the banking industry is vital. It assists the sustainable economic growth and reduces the bankruptcy risks inside the economies. To achieve this, the banking industries are required to present a clear short-term objective and long-term goals.

The banking industry is broadly responsible for financial distress due to its important intermediating role in the economy. The issue of bankruptcy forecasting came into the spotlight after the 2007–2008 financial crises [10]. Banks are required to forecast their financial status by using different prediction models and to make future plans accordingly. They can use the prediction models not only to check their own bank-level sustainability but industry level and even the overall economy as well. By doing so, the banks can foresee whether they are standing in the market, domestically and globally or not [11]? In competitive financial environments, the health of a bank is measured by its financial capacity and standing power, the ability to create cash from its running operations, its flexibility towards the financial shocks and its access to the financial markets. As a bank loses the ability to achieve the above attributes, it moves toward insolvency [12]. The regulatory authorities are required to monitor and control the financial activities of certain industries like the banking sector [13].

The failure of banks affects not only the industry but the households, government, and other stakeholders even the whole economy is directly linked and affected by the banks. One of the main aims of the central bank is to encourage an efficient financial system through the regulation and supervision of financial institutions. Some early warning systems (EWM) are used by the central banks to keep an eye on the financial position and risk of the banks [14]. However, considering the repeated bank's failures in the last two decades provides evidence that maintaining sustainability is "hard to do" and the most important task [15]. Regulatory authorities use different internal and external measures to monitor the ups and downs of the banking industry. The widely used method for monitoring is CAMELS ratings. CAMELS is used as the best monitoring method to predict bankruptcy [12]. In the case of Islamic banking, another widely used external measure is the FSB (Financial Stability Board). FSB provides surveillance to all organizations including banks and monitors their financial performance.

2. Literature Review

The banking industry is considered as a pulse of any economy and it contributes towards the economic growth and financial stability of the country significantly. Hence, monitoring its sustainability is almost as mandatory for the smooth financial operations of the economies. According to IFSB 2018, the Islamic banking industry is experiencing more complex insolvency systems as compared to their conventional rivals. The main reason for the fact is that Islamic banks have practical Shariah regulations and a specified industry different from the conventional banking sector. There are very few specific bankruptcy laws and regulatory authorities normally apply the same laws to conventional and Islamic banks.

2.1. The Emergence of Islamic Banking

According to Bank Negara Malaysia Annual report (2017), more than 75 countries are dealing with Islamic finance by running over 300 Islamic financial institutions. Details about the market-leading Islamic banking countries are presented in Table 2 below.

Table 2. Share percentage of Islamic banks globally and nationally (2018).

Countries	Global Islamic Banking Share % (Out of Total Banking Assets)	Domestic Islamic Banking Share % (Out of Total Banking Assets)
Iran	32.2	100.0
Saudi Arabia	20.2	51.5
Malaysia	10.8	26.5
UAE	9.8	20.6
Kuwait	6.3	40.6
Qatar	6.2	25.2
Turkey	2.6	5.5
Bangladesh	1.9	20.1
Indonesia	1.9	5.7
Pakistan	1.3	12.9
Sudan	0.7	100
Bahrain	0.7	14.3
Others	5.5	—

Source: Islamic Financial Services Industry Report (2019).

Table 2 shows the share of the top 10 leading Islamic banking counties ranked by global banking assets. For example, the top tier economies in Islamic banking are Iran, Saudi Arabia, Malaysia, and UAE respectively. Iran stands as the market leader in the global Islamic banking by retaining a 34 percent share in the global Islamic banking assets. Iran is followed by Saudi Arabia, Malaysia, UAE, and Kuwait having a share of 20.2 percent, 10.8 percent, 9.8 percent, and 6.3 percent respectively. Qatar, Turkey, Bangladesh, Indonesia, and Bahrain are the second tier significantly contributing countries in Islamic banking assets globally. The above 12 countries collectively account for 94.5 percent share in the global Islamic banking assets. The rest 5.5 percent share is held by the other countries. The largest shareholders are Iran, Saudi Arabia, Malaysia, UAE, Kuwait, and Qatar. In North and Sub-Saharan Africa, many countries are stepping to introduce Islamic banking in their banking industries which will boost up the current global Islamic banking assets in the future (IFSB, 2018).

2.2. Bankruptcy Forecasting

Banks and other firms use different techniques to predict bankruptcy. Kumar and Ravi [12] classified these techniques broadly into two categories, (1) statistical techniques and (ll) intelligent techniques. The prior includes used univariate analysis, multiple discriminant analysis (MDA), factor analysis, and Logit regression. The second group consisting of neural networks, self-organizing maps, decision trees, operational research techniques like data envelopment analysis (DEA), and linear programming. Literature is augmented with the use and continuous improvement of the above models for finding the bankruptcy of firms. Beaver [3] presented a pioneering study by conducting financial ratios analysis using a univariate model. Later on, [2] applied multiple discriminant analysis MDA and shortlisted liquidity, profitability, solvency, and leverage ratios as the top predictors for bankruptcy forecasting. Ohlson [16] used logistic regression on multiple ratios and found that multiple ratios have the predictive power of bankruptcy using logistic regression. Altman [17] reinvented the earlier Z-core as the ZETA model, while the Hazard model was developed by [18] using the same ratios used by [2]. The above examples support that there are many detection models for the bankruptcy of conventional banks. On the other hand, very limited studies conducted on the detection of bankruptcy for Islamic banks [19].

2.3. History of Famous Bankruptcy Forecasting Models

Many bankruptcy detections models have been developed to forecast the bankruptcy of financial and non-financial firms. Beaver [3] slogged the pioneering scope of bankruptcy by developing a univariate analysis with financial ratios. Although Beaver's model was panned by reason of its univariate nature i.e., a single variable could be studied at a time for bankruptcy prediction. Beaver's model was then revised by [2], their study introduced four additional important variables into it. This was the first-ever use of multiple discriminant analysis (MDA) for bankruptcy prediction, the study classified the sample into bankrupt and non-bankrupt groups. The model got great fame because of its accuracy and simplicity i.e., 94 percent accuracy in predicting bankruptcy. Moreover, the model was only developed for public manufacturing firms. Deakin [20] took the same variables which were used by [3], but their study conceptualized a multivariate perspective to achieve higher accuracy and got expected results [21]. Altman et al. [22] introduced a new "Zeta model" for bankruptcy prediction. The researchers used seven important financial ratios in the model on a set of fifty-three failed and fifty-eight non-bankrupt firms. The new Zeta model showed more than 95 percent accuracy overall. Moreover, the Z-score model of [2] and the Zeta model of [22] were also criticized for their limited application in the manufacturing industry only.

Springate [23] developed a bankruptcy evaluation model using multiple discriminant analysis (MDA) techniques famously known as the Springate model. The Springate model was more or less the same as that of the initial model of [2]. However, the cut-off points for the Springate model were difficult from that of Altman's. This model could divide the firm performance into two zones, bankrupt and non-bankrupt. While Altman's model could divide the bank's performance into three zones i.e., bankrupt, non-bankrupt, and safe zone. Ohlson [16] attempted to overcome the confines of the [2,3] and that of [22] by presenting the Logit regression model for bankruptcy prediction. Moreover, Ohlson analyzed the model by considering a sample of 105 insolvent and 2058 sustainable firms. Altman [24], revised the initial bankruptcy model of Altman 1968 by introducing private companies to the prediction model. By doing this, Altman increased the scope of the earlier bankruptcy model from public firms to private firms as well. In this new model, Altman changed the market value of equity to book value of equity, because the market value of private firms is not reliable [11]. Izan [25] carried out pioneering work for developing a bankruptcy model in Australia. The study took ten financial ratios from the Sydney stock exchange. The model was designed in such a way that it can be applied to many sectors. In the University of Quebec Montreal under the supervisor of Jean Legault in the year, 1987 developed a bankruptcy prediction model using MDA techniques. A sample of 173 manufacturing businesses was taken for the purpose. Aziz, et al. [26], developed a cash flow bankruptcy model, which was famously called the CFBM model. The study compared the model with previous models like that of the Zeta model by Altman et.al and reported that the CFBM model had higher accuracy in reporting financial distress 3-5 five years prior to actual bankruptcy. In general, the higher CFBM score means worse performance and vice versa. Some of the above-discussed models were applied in the banking industries over the period. The above-mentioned bankruptcy prediction models designed for conventional banks are applied to the Islamic banking market with minor modifications. Nonetheless, the Islamic banking system has some specific attributes other than conventional banks. These attributes are called Shariah Compliant principles [6]. Against that background, there is a need for a separate and specifically designed model for the Islamic banking industry [5]. Anwar and Ali [27] stated that the best effort is essential to resolve the falling financial condition of Islamic banks. Bankruptcy is not only a step to systematic and financial risk but it is a threat to the reputation of Islamic banking law. Jan, et al. [7] alluded that developing a bankruptcy prediction model using the key performance indicators blended with latest techniques is much needed for Islamic banking. Table 3 shows summary of the studies that applied the famous bankruptcy forecasting model on the banking industry. Details are shown below.

Table 3. Studies on bankruptcy forecasting models from the banking industry.

Author/Year	Objective	Variables	Method	Sample	Findings
Martin [28]	Bankruptcy prediction of banks	Asset risk, liquidity, capital adequacy, and earnings	Ratios analysis, Logistic regression, Discriminant analysis	1974 included 23 subsequently failed banks	Found the accuracies of the models almost similar but suggested discriminant analysis better for bankruptcy prediction
Doukas [29]	Comparison of Altman and Springate models	Working capital, EBIT, Sales, Total assets, Total equity, EBT, retained earnings, Total debt, Current liabilities	MDA, Altman, and Springate	25 Canadian chartered banks, counting five large banks, five more indigenous banks, and some foreign-controlled banks	Both Springate and Altman models are not the best predictors as the results gave low prediction accuracy
Čihák and Hesse [30]	Comparative analysis of bankruptcy in Islamic and conventional banks	Loans/Assets, Cost/income ratio, Income diversity, Assets in billion USD	Altman Z-score	77 Islamic banks 397 commercial banks 1993–2004	The results of Z-score supports the stability of Islamic banks more than the conventional ones
Hanif, et al. [9]	Performance comparison of Islamic and conventional banks	Profitability, liquidity, credit, risk, and solvency	Bank-o-meter	5 Islamic banks 22 conventional banks 2005–2009	Performance of Islamic banking is better than the conventional one which shows the reliability of the Islamic Banking sector in Pakistan
Husna and Rahman [19]	Bankruptcy prediction of Islamic and conventional banks	Multiple accounting ratios	Logit regression	Malaysia	Islamic banks are more liquid and less risky than conventional banks, but they have to monitor their performance regularly
Bourkhis and Nabi [31]	To check the consequence of the financial crisis on Islamic and conventional banks	Capital adequacy, Profitability, Asset quality, Earnings and, efficiency	Nonparametric analysis, parametric analysis (MDA)	34 Islamic banks and 34 conventional Banks taken from 16 countries	Soundness found similar in Islamic and conventional banks during financial crises
Jan and Marimuthu [32]	Bankruptcy forecasting from the top five Islamic banking countries	WC/TA, retained earnings/total assets, EBIT/TA, BV of Equity/BV of Total Liabilities	ANOVA and Altman Z score	Sample of 25 Islamic banks from the leading five Islamic banking countries	The difference in performance indicators is the basic reason for the difference in bankruptcy level
Jan and Marimuthu [5]	Bankruptcy forecasting from the five leading Islamic banking states	Profitability, liquidity, insolvency, productivity	ANOVA and Regression	25 banks From Iran Saudi Arabia, UAE, Malaysia, and Kuwait	Banking activities are linked with the success of the financial system. economic sustainability of Islamic banking industry can be efficiently measured by the Altman model developed for the services industry
Jan and Marimuthu [8]	Bankruptcy forecasting from the five leading Islamic banking states	Liquidity, profitability, productivity, solvency ratios	Altman Z score, MDA	Top 5 Islamic banking countries	Saudi Arabian Islamic banks are highly sustainable while Malaysian Islamic banks have the lowest sustainability

Table 3. *Cont.*

Author/Year	Objective	Variables	Method	Sample	Findings
Jan and Marimuthu [33]	Bankruptcy forecasting for the foreign and domestic Islamic banks in Malaysia	WC/TA, retained earnings/total assets, EBIT/TA, BV of Equity/BV of Total Liabilities	ANOVA and Altman Z score	Foreign and domestic Islamic banks in Malaysia (2009–2013)	Domestic Islamic banks in Malaysia are more at risk while foreign Islamic banks in the country are sustainable overall
Laila and Widihadnanto [34]	Bankruptcy prediction between Islamic and Conventional	Capital to Asset Ratio, Capital Adequacy Ratio, Cost to Income Ratio, Loans to Asset Ratio, Equity to Asset Ratio, Non-Performing Loan Ratio	Bank-o meter S-score	4 full-fledged Islamic banks and 10 conventional banks in Indonesia 2011–2014	No significant difference found in financial distress prediction between Islamic banks and conventional banks.
Halteh, et al. [35]	Comparison between different bankruptcy prediction models with some new variables	(TA), ROE, ROA, Operating income/TA, WC/TA, RE/TA, EBIT, MVE/TL, Revenue/TA, Debt ratio, Current ratio, ROR, Asset turnover, Efficiency ratio, TE/TA, Equity ratio, Total debt/Total equity	Altman Z-Score, and the Standardized Profits	A sample comprising 101 foreign Islamic banks	The used variables are important indicators for predicting bankruptcy accurately
Anwar and Ali [27]	Predicting bankruptcy using a nonparametric technique	Different financial ratios	Artificial Neural Networks	22 Islamic windows and 12 full-fledged Islamic Banks in Indonesia	Artificial Neural Network is suitable for bankruptcy prediction in Indonesian Islamic banks
Affes and Hentati-Kaffel [36]	To model the relationship between ratios and bankruptcy in US banks	Capital Adequacy Liquidity Earnings ability Asset quality	Classification and regression trees (CART) and multivariate adaptive regression splines (MARS)	410 non-active and 1205 active US banks 2008–2013	The nonparametric model gives more accuracy in terms of bankruptcy prediction of US banks
Jan, et al. [14]	Bankruptcy prediction of Islamic and conventional banks in Malaysia	Liquidity, profitability, productivity, solvency ratios	MDA	14 conventional and 14 Islamic banks in Malaysia 2008–2013	Islamic banks are more towards bankruptcy as compared to conventional banks. Profitability is the best measure for bankruptcy prediction.

Table 3 shows the history of famous bankruptcy prediction models from the banking industry in general. Broadly it shows that the extensive bankruptcy forecasting work is carried out on the conventional banking industry with limited studies on the Islamic banking industry. Secondly, it shows that most of the models were developed based on financial ratios. Hence, the literature left a gape to develop bankruptcy forecasting models for the Islamic banks with a more diverse combination of financial ratios and non-financial indicators such as governance and corporate sustainability variables. The subsequent section shows the theoretical review and proposition of this study. It shows the theoretical link of the independent variables with the dependent variable (bankruptcy) in association with different theories. The subsequent section also explains the link of the newly proposed variables (corporate governance and corporate sustainability), which this study is using in the proposed dynamic bankruptcy prediction model for sustainable Islamic banking.

2.4. Theoretical Framework and Proposition Development

The following section shows the theoretical link between the independent and dependent variables in the context of different theories. The model of this study is based on three strands of variables that is financial ratios, corporate governance, and corporate sustainability. Details about each strand in the context of theories are elaborated below. The next sections show the list of journals from which articles were selected for each strand of variables. The articles from these journals were selected on the base of their relevance with the current study i.e., bankruptcy forecasting.

Table 4 shows a list of those journals from which articles were selected for developing a new bankruptcy forecasting model. Overall it shows that the majority of the journals are impact factor journals. The articles related to bankruptcy forecasting were selected starting from 1968 until 2019. It is because the pioneer work on bankruptcy was started in 1968. Over the period, those studies were selected which were relevant to this current study i.e., related to bankruptcy prediction. The subsequent section shows the shortlisting of variables for each strand.

Table 4. List of journals selected for each strand of variables.

SN	Journal Name	Rank	No. of Papers Selected from Each Journal
01	Journal of Banking & Finance	Q1/IF 2.2	7
02	International Journal of Islamic and Middle Eastern Finance and Management	Q4/IF 0.75	2
03	Journal of Finance	Q1/IF 6.20	1
04	Journal of Accounting Research	Q1/IF 4.89	3
05	Journal of Credit Risk	Q4/IF 0.41	1
06	Journal of Business Ethics	Q1/IF 3.79	3
07	Journal of Cleaner Production	Q1/IF 6.39	1
08	Managerial Auditing Journal	Q4/IF 1.06	1
09	African Journal of Business Management	Q3/IF 1.10	1
10	Sustainability	Q2/IF 2.59	1
11	International Research Journal of Finance & Economics	Scopus/Q4	1
12	International Journal of Business and Management	ERA	3
13	Economic Change and Restructuring	ISI/ESCI	1
14	Omega	Q1/IF 5.34	1
15	Journal of Management Studies,	Q1/IF 5.83	1
16	Applied economics	Q3/IF 0.96	1
17	Journal of Financial Services Research	Q2/IF 1.66	2
18	Review of Financial Economics	Q1/IF 2.26	1
19	International Journal of Economics & Management	Scopus/Q3	1
20	Managerial Finance	Scopus/Q3	1
21	Annals of Operations Research,	Q2/IF 2.28	1
22	Journal of Accounting, Auditing & Finance	ISI/ESCI	1
23	The Quarterly Review of Economics and Finance	Q4/IF 0.10	1
24	Economic Systems	Q2/IF 1.32	1
25	Journal of Economics and Behavioral Studies	ProQuest	1
26	Journal of Behavioral Finance	Q3/IF 0.77	1
27	Journal of Accounting Research	Q1/IF 4.89	1
28	Academy of Management journal 2	Q1/IF 7.19	2
29	Journal of General Management	ISI/ESCI	1
30	Journal of Financial Economics	Q1/IF 4.6	3
31	Asian Social Science	Scopus/Q3	1
32	Corporate Governance the International Journal of Business in Society	ISI/ESCI	1
33	International Business & Economics Research	ProQuest	1
34	Journal of Financial Reporting and Accounting	ISI/ESCI	1
35	Journal of Islamic Accounting and Business Research	ISI/ESCI	1
36	Global Business & Management Research	ERA	1
37	International Journal of Economics and Finance	ERA	2
38	The journal of business	Jstor	1
39	International Journal of Trade, Economics and Finance	ProQuest	1

2.4.1. Nexus of Financial Ratios and Bankruptcy Forecasting: In the Context of the Financial Ratios Theory

In order to choose the top financial ratios used for predicting bankruptcy, the subsequent section is showing the frequency distribution of the top 6 ratios that were used for predicting bankruptcy.

Table 5 shows the frequency distribution of famous ratios that were used for measuring bankruptcy forecasting in the Islamic banking industry. The frequency distribution shows that the top tier ratios used in the past for predicting bankruptcy in the Islamic banks are as follow subsequently. Liquidity ratio with 78 percent, profitability ratio with 67 percent, solvency ratio with 63 percent, productivity ratio with 44 percent, asset quality with 37 percent and capital adequacy ratio was used by 26 percent studies. In line with that, this study selected those variables in which frequency distribution was above 25 percent.

Table 5. Top ratios used for bankruptcy forecasting.

Liquidity	Profitability	Solvency	Productivity	Asset Quality	Capital Adequacy
Martin [28] Ohlson [16] Doukas [29] Altman [17] Hanif, et al. [9] Husna and Rahman [19] Darrat, et al. [37] Bourkhis and Nabi [31] Jan and Marimuthu [8] Jan and Marimuthu [32] Jan and Marimuthu [33] Anwar and Ali [27] Affes and Hentati-Kaffel [36] Lassoued [38] Halteh, et al. [35]	Ohlson [16] Doukas [29] Altman [17] Hanif, et al. [9] Darrat, et al. [37] Bourkhis and Nabi [31] Jan and Marimuthu [8] Jan and Marimuthu [32] Mollah and Zaman [39] Jan and Marimuthu [33] Halteh, et al. [35] Affes and Hentati-Kaffel [36] Alqahtani and Mayes [40] Lassoued [38] Ogechukwu and John [41] Gandhi, et al. [42] Jan, et al. [14]	Ohlson [16] Doukas [29] Altman [17] Čihák and Hesse [30] Darrat, et al. [37] Bourkhis and Nabi [31] Jan and Marimuthu [8] Jan and Marimuthu [32] Jan and Marimuthu [33] Laila and Widihadnanto [34] Halteh, et al. [35] Alqahtani and Mayes [40] Lassoued [38] Ogechukwu and John [41] Gandhi, et al. [42]	Martin [28] Doukas [29] Altman [17] Halteh, et al. [35] Anwar and Ali [27] Lassoued [38] Ogechukwu and John [41] Halteh, et al. [35]	Martin [28] Čihák and Hesse [30] Hanif, et al. [9] Husna and Rahman [19] Bourkhis and Nabi [31] Laila and Widihadnanto [34] Halteh, et al. [35] Affes and Hentati-Kaffel [36] Alqahtani and Mayes [40] Lassoued [38] Ogechukwu and John [41]	Martin [28] Husna and Rahman [19] Bourkhis and Nabi [31] Mollah and Zaman [39] Laila and Widihadnanto [34] Halteh, et al. [35] Affes and Hentati-Kaffel [36] Gandhi, et al. [42]
78 percent	67 percent	63 percent	44 percent	37 percent	26 percent

The author [43] presented the theory of financial ratios as predictors of defaults. This theory states that financial ratios are the best predictors of the firms' financial position. Firms' financial condition can be best identified by looking at the changes in the financial statements. As ratios are derived from the financial statements and are being used to predict the firms' financial position from the pioneering study in the 1960s [3] till present. Financial ratios give a signal to the management of the firm about deteriorations in the firms' financial position [44]. Hence, ratios are the best predictors of financial distress of any firm. This study is consistent with the theory of financial ratios for the first strand of variables that is financial ratios. Moreover, as [2] was the foremost scholar which used ratios in multiple discriminant analyses for predicting bankruptcy and proved that ratios are the best predictors. Hence, the following proposition is developed.

Hypothesis 1 (H1). *There is a significant association between financial ratios and bankruptcy prediction.*

2.4.2. Nexus of Corporate Governance and Bankruptcy Forecasting: In the Context of the Agency Theory

Table 6 shows the frequency distribution of corporate governance variables used in Islamic banking. It shows that the variable of board size was used in 80 percent studies, director's independence by 53 percent studies, CEO-duality by 60 percent studies, ownership structure by 40 percent studies, while SSB was used by 27 percent studies. Consistent with the selection criteria of this study only selected those variables in which frequency distribution was above 25 percent.

Table 6. Top governance variables used for bankruptcy forecasting.

Board Size	Director Independence/Composition	CEO-Duality	Ownership Structure	Shariah Supervisory Board (SSB)
Daily and Dalton [45] Lajili and Zéghal [46] Wintoki, et al. [47] Fallatah and Dickins [48] Li, et al. [49] Naushad and Malik [50] Mollah and Zaman [39] Bansal and Sharma [51] Nawaz [52] Ogechukwu and John [41]	Daily and Dalton [45] Lajili and Zéghal [46] Wintoki, et al. [47] Li, et al. [49] Naushad and Malik [50] Mollah and Zaman [39] Bansal and Sharma [51] Nawaz [52] Anginer, et al. [53] Ogechukwu and John [41]	Daily and Dalton [45] Lajili and Zéghal [46] Wintoki, et al. [47] Fallatah and Dickins [48] Li, et al. [49] Naushad and Malik [50] Mollah and Zaman [39] Bansal and Sharma [51] Nawaz [52]	Zouari and Taktak [54] Jan, et al. [55] Li, et al. [49] Ogechukwu and John [41] Jan, et al. [7]	Li, et al. [49] Nawaz [52] Jan, et al. [55] Jan, et al. [7]
80 percent	53 percent	60 percent	40 percent	27 percent

The second class of variables taken in this study for bankruptcy forecasting deals with corporate governance mechanisms. Agency theory tends to address this issue. Agency theory explains the relationship between the principal and the agent working on behalf of the principle. The main focus of agency theory is to reduce agency costs raised due to the conflict of interest and potential goal between the shareholders and managers [56]. Agency theory highlights the monitoring and controlling role of the board of directors against management using external and internal governance mechanisms. Literature suggests that compared to healthy firms the financially distressed firms have shorter tenure of outside directors and higher director turnover [46]. The strong governance structure includes more effective monitoring which plugs in the loopholes and as a result, the firm performance is improved and subsequently, it reduces the chances of bankruptcy. This study is supported by agency theory for the second strand of variables that is corporate governance variables. Hence, it is alluding that corporate governance tools have a substantial positive influence on bankruptcy prediction. Against that background, the following proposition is developed.

Hypothesis 2 (H2). *There is a significant association between corporate governance and bankruptcy prediction.*

2.4.3. Nexus of Sustainability and Bankruptcy Forecasting: In the Context of the Stakeholders' Theory

Table 7 shows the shortlisted sustainability items that were used in the Islamic banking context. This study first divided the items used in the indexes of the Islamic banks into broader themes. Then under each theme, those items were selected which were related to Islamic banking and Shariah principles specifically. The conventional sustainability items used in the previous indexes were ignored by this study. Then with the help of Maqasid-Al-Shariah theory, the items were segregated into the three dimensions of sustainability. A total of 13 Islamic banking sustainability items were shortlisted and then placed into the three dimensions of sustainability.

Table 7. Shortlisted sustainability items from the Islamic banking industry.

Economic	Environmental	Social
1. Sadaqah, charity, Qard-e-Hassan.	1. Funding to organizations that are not harming the environment	1. Islamic Training and Education to the Staff
2. Disclosure of Earnings Prohibited by Shariah	2. Amount of donation in environmental awareness	2. Offering Scholarships, Conducting Islamic conferences
3. Shariah Screening During the Investment	3. Introduction of green Products	3. Offering New Product and Services (Approved by the Shariah Committee)
4. Allocation of Profit Based on Shariah Principles		
5. Zakat Payment		
6. Charity/Sadaqah		
7. Qard-e-Hassan (benevolent funds)		

References		
Dusuki [57]	Dusuki [57]	Dusuki [57]
Othman and Thani [58]	Amran, et al. [60]	Aribi and Gao [59]
Aribi and Gao [59]	Maali, et al. [61]	Amran, et al. [60]
Amran, et al. [60]	Hassan and Harahap [62]	Maali, et al. [61]
Maali, et al. [61]		Hassan and Harahap [62]
Hassan and Harahap [62]		Rahman, et al. [63]
Rahman, et al. [63]		Aribi and Arun [65]
Farook, et al. [64]		Haniffa and Hudaib [66]
Aribi and Arun [65]		Platonova, et al. [67]
Haniffa and Hudaib [66]		
Platonova, et al. [67]		

Literature is enriched with the association of sustainability practices and firm performance. Sustainability is reported under three heads i.e., economic sustainability, environmental sustainability, and social sustainability. This group of variables is consistent with the stakeholders' theory as the theory suggests that the value of the firm increases when multiple stakeholders of the company are addressed and satisfied. The stakeholders of the company may include those individuals or groups which are affected by the actions of the company. Generally, it includes its employees, customers, creditors, suppliers, government, regulators, political groups, and public, etc. [68]. According to stakeholder theory, sustainability practices have a positive association with firm performance. Generally, it is assumed that firms with better firm performance are less bankrupt, and firms with inefficient financial performance have higher chances to go bankrupt. Against this background, and in the context of the stakeholders' theory, it is assumed that better sustainability practices will reduce the chances of bankruptcy. Hence, hypothetically sustainability practices are assumed to have a positive significant impact on bankruptcy prediction. Hence, the following proposition is developed.

Hypothesis 3 (H3). *There is a significant association between Islamic banks sustainability practices and bankruptcy forecasting.*

After the detailed theoretical review, the conceptual framework of this study is presented in Figure 1 below.

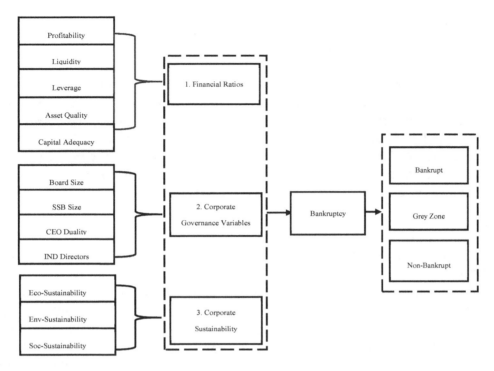

Figure 1. Conceptual framework of the study (Graphical Abstract).

2.4.4. Conceptual Framework

Figure 1 shows the detailed conceptual framework of this study. Broadly it shows the association of three strands of independent variables with the dependent variable (bankruptcy forecasting). For the purpose, top financial ratios that were used by past studies for bankruptcy forecasting are selected under the strand of financial ratios. Similarly, the most appropriate ratios comprised of Islamic and conventional corporate governance mechanisms are selected under the strand of corporate governance. Finally, under the third strand of corporate sustainability, appropriate sustainability items were selected (refer to Tables 5–7). This study claims novelty by adding two new dimensions of (corporate governance and corporate sustainability) to be the part of a bankruptcy prediction model (see Sections 2.4.2 and 2.4.3) for bankruptcy forecasting this study is proposing insolvency ratio as a proxy for bankruptcy prediction. The fuzzy technique will split the value of the dependent variable (insolvency) into three zones i.e., bankrupt, grey, and the safe zone. It will illuminate the Islamic banks from different countries whether they are in the safe zone, grey zone, or the bankrupt zone. Hence, the proposed framework is equipped with the latest parameters and measures for predicting bankruptcy instead of the past bankruptcy forecasting models which only used financial ratios for predicting bankruptcy.

Consistent with the past studies of Jan, et al. [69] this study is using a weighted content analysis technique to measure corporate governance and corporate sustainability variables. The dependent variable of this study is bankruptcy. While the nature of the subjected dependent variable (bankruptcy) is of categorical nature i.e., either a bank can be bankrupt or non-bankrupt. In the first stage of the analysis, the solvency ratio will be used to investigate the overall financial health of Islamic banks. As the solvency ratio measures the ability to meet a firm's long-term liabilities, accordingly a higher ratio indicates a greater degree of financial risk, following by bankruptcy.

3. Methodology

3.1. Population, Sampling, and Data Collection

The population of this study is the Islamic banking industry of the world. The sample of this study is the top five Islamic banking countries ranked by global banking assets. The top five Islamic banking countries ranked by global banking assets were identified from the Islamic Financial Services Industry Stability Report (2018). Five Islamic banks were selected from each country for the decade of (2009–2018) based on their total assets. Data using DataStream/Bloomberg database were cross-referenced with the annual reports of the Islamic banks operating in the top five Islamic banking countries ranked by global Islamic banking assets.

3.2. Model Development

This study followed the following steps for model development. In the first stage, this study will collect a time series data for the insolvency ratio for the selected sample. In the second step, the fuzzy technique will be applied to the insolvency ratios to create two zones that are bankrupt and non-bankrupt. Against those two zones, multinomial Logit regression will be applied using financial ratios, corporate governance, and corporate sustainability as the independent variables. The dependent variable for Logit regression will be categorical variables of 0, 1, and 2. Whereas "0" denote bankrupt zone, "1" represents a grey zone, while "2" represents a non-bankrupt zone. In this case, the independent variables of financial ratios, corporate governance, and corporate sustainability will illuminate its role in assigning the zones of 0, 1, and 2 as discussed above. The flow chart of the proposed model is shown in Figure 2.

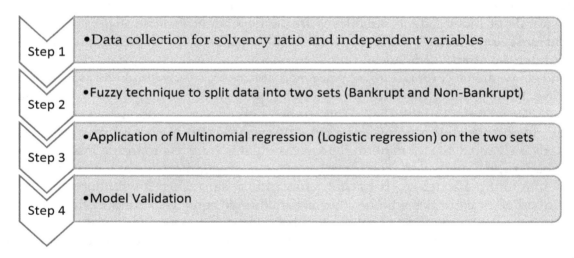

Figure 2. Flowchart of the proposed model.

The statistical representation of the model is shown below.

$$\text{Insolvency} = \alpha + \beta1 \text{ Prof } it + \beta2 \text{ Liq } it + \beta3 Lev \text{ } it + \beta4 \text{ } AQ \text{ } it + \beta5 \text{ } BS \text{ } it + \beta6 \text{ } SSB \text{ } it + \beta7 \atop IND \text{ } it + \beta8 \text{ } Duality \text{ } it + \beta9 \text{ } Eco\text{-}sus \text{ } it + \beta10 \text{ } Env\text{-}sus \text{ } it + \beta11 \text{ } Soc\text{-}sus \text{ } it + \varepsilon t \tag{1}$$

where as,

Insolvency: Categorical variable for measuring bankruptcy
Prof = Profitability
Liq = Liquidity
Lev = Leverage
AQ = Assets Quality

BS = Board Size
SSB = Shariah Supervisory Board
IND = Independent Directors
Duality = CEO Duality
Eco-sus = Economic Sustainability
Env-sus = Environmental Sustainability
Soc-sus = Social Sustainability

The newly proposed dynamic bankruptcy forecasting model (see Equation (1)) is equipped with the latest parameters and measures for predicting bankruptcy instead of the past bankruptcy forecasting frameworks which only used financial ratios for predicting bankruptcy. Therefore, it is anticipated that the proposed model will depict the true default risks of Islamic banks. It is because the previous models were mostly developed in the production era, and during that time the focus of organizations mostly revolved around maximizing productivity and profitability. The current era follows the social system theory and because of that, the previous models are obsoleted. This social system theory assures sustainability attributes and efficient teamwork through compliant governance practices in the business model along with profitability.

4. Conclusions

This study by proposing bankruptcy forecasting models for the Islamic banking industry will first help the five leading Islamic banking countries ranked by global banking assets to witness their true bankruptcy profile. Outcomes of this study will provide policy insights to the practitioners and policymakers of Islamic banks to achieve higher business sustainability by reducing the chances of bankruptcy through efficient bankruptcy estimations. It will eventually help the Islamic banks to expand internationally, which will holistically contribute towards the stability of the global financial system. Hence, the completion of this study has some serious implications on domestic as well as to the international financial system. Evidence shows that the banking industry holds a central position in the economic system. For the smooth continuation of the economic system, the proper working of its banking industries and strong surveillance models are required. In the case of Islamic banking, evidence shows that a Shariah-based bankruptcy forecasting model for apprehending the true bankruptcy position is over sighted. It can lead to a financial crisis in the countries where Islamic banking is in domination. Hence, an efficient Shariah-based bankruptcy prediction model may reduce this risk.

4.1. Significance of the Study

- Theoretical Contribution

With the execution of this research, the contemporary subject of Islamic banks bankruptcy forecasting will enrich the present body of knowledge. This study added to the theory of financial ratios by using it as a base for incorporating Islamic financial ratios in a proposed bankruptcy prediction model. This study claims novelty by adding two new dimensions of (corporate governance and corporate sustainability) to be the part of bankruptcy perdition model in the case of Islamic banks, whereas the past models only used financial ratios for apprehending bankruptcy. In a way, this study illuminated and established the link for using the stakeholders' theory in the Islamic bankruptcy forecasting studies. Subsequently, by using agency theory this study established the link of Islamic corporate governance variables in evaluating bankruptcy.

- Methodological Contribution

This study by developing and proposing a new bankruptcy prediction model aided with the latest bankruptcy techniques i.e., incorporating new dimensions of corporate governance and corporate sustainability will serve as a methodological base for future bankruptcy prediction models. Future studies by following the proposed steps can add new (governance and sustainability) variables into their bankruptcy perdition model, which will improve the precision level of their models.

- Practical Contribution Results of this study will support different matters in the following streaks

    1. It will help Islamic banks of the selected countries not only to forecast but to prevent their bankruptcy threats, and to maintain a strong sustainable Islamic banking sector industry.

    2. The bankruptcy forecasting model for Islamic banks will aid the smooth growing financial system in the selected region.

    3. This research will provide guidelines to managers and practitioners for surveillance of their subject areas and will support to keep strong economic sustainability.

    4. It will provide a ground to customers, depositors, investors, and other stakeholders about choosing more sustainable Islamic bank

4.2. Future Work

This study encourages future studies to empirically test the proposed bankruptcy prediction model in different countries to generalize the concept.

Author Contributions: Conceptualization, M.M. (Mehreen Mehreen) and M.M. (Maran Marimuthu); methodology, M.M. (Mehreen Mehreen) and M.M. (Maran Marimuthu); software, A.J.; validation, M.M. (Maran Marimuthu) and S.A.A.K.; writing—original draft preparation, M.M. (Mehreen Mehreen); writing—review and editing, A.J.; supervision, M.M. (Maran Marimuthu) and S.A.A.K. All authors have read and agreed to the published version of the manuscript.

Acknowledgments: Thank you to Universiti Teknologi PETRONAS for financial support.

References

Khan, I.; Khan, M.; Tahir, M. Performance comparison of Islamic and conventional banks: Empirical evidence from Pakistan. Int. J. Islamic Middle East. Financ. Manag. 2017, 10, 419–433. [CrossRef]

Altman, E. Financial ratios, discriminant analysis and the prediction of corporate bankruptcy. J. Financ. 1968, 23, 589–609. [CrossRef]

Beaver, W.H. Financial Ratios as Predictors of Failure. J. Account. Res. 1966, 5, 71–111. [CrossRef]

Altman, E.I. A fifty-year retrospective on credit risk models, the Altman Z-score family of models and their applications to financial markets and managerial strategies. J. Credit Risk 2018, 14. [CrossRef]

Jan, A.; Marimuthu, M. Bankruptcy and Sustainability: A Conceptual Review on Islamic Banking Industry. Glob. Bus. Manag. Res. 2015, 7, 109–138.

Jan, A.; Marimuthu, M.; Bin Mohd, M.P.; Isa, M.; Shad, M.K. Bankruptcy Forecasting and Economic Sustainability Profile of the Market Leading Islamic Banking Countries. Int. J. Asian Bus. Inf. Manag. (IJABIM) 2019, 10, 73–90. [CrossRef]

Jan, A.; Marimuthu, M.; Hassan, R. Sustainable Business Practices and Firm's Financial Performance in Islamic Banking: Under the Moderating Role of Islamic Corporate Governance. Sustainability 2019, 11, 6606. [CrossRef]

Jan, A.; Marimuthu, M. Sustainability profile of islamic banking industry: Evidence from world top five islamic banking countries. Int. J. Econ. Financ. 2015, 7, 125. [CrossRef]

Hanif, M.; Tariq, M.; Tahir, A.; Momeneen, W.U. Comparative performance study of conventional and islamic banking in Pakistan. Int. Res. J. Financ. Econ. 2012, 83, 1450–2887.

Mendicino, C.; Clerc, L.; Derviz, A.; Moyen, S.; Nikolov, K.; Stracca, L.; Suarez, J.; Vardulakis, A. Capital Regulation in a Macroeconomic Model with Three Layers of Default. 2014. Available online: https://ssrn.com/abstract=2544607 (accessed on 1 March 2020). [CrossRef]

Lin, H. Default Prediction Model for SME's: Evidence from UK Market Using Financial Ratios. Int. J. Bus. Manag. 2015, 10, 81. [CrossRef]

Ravi Kumar, P.; Ravi, V. Bankruptcy prediction in banks and firms via statistical and intelligent techniques—A review. Eur. J. Oper. Res. 2007, 180, 1–28. [CrossRef]

Rashid, M.; Nishat, A. Disparity of Performance Indicators of Islamic Banks: Study on Bangladesh. Int. J. Bus. Manag. 2009, 4, 52. [CrossRef]

Jan, A.; Marimuthu, M.; Shad, M.K.; Zahid, M.; Jan, A.A. Bankruptcy profile of the Islamic and conventional banks in Malaysia: A post-crisis period analysis. Econ. Chang. Restruct. 2019, 52, 67–87. [CrossRef]

Demyanyk, Y.; Hasan, I. Financial crises and bank failures: A review of prediction methods. Omega 2010, 38, 315–324. [CrossRef]

Ohlson, J.A. Financial ratios and the probabilistic prediction of bankruptcy. J. Account. Res. 1980, 18, 109–131. [CrossRef]

Altman, E.I. Predicting financial distress of companies: Revisiting the Z-score and ZETA models. Stern Sch. Bus. N.Y. Univ. 2000, 13, 9–12.

Shumway, T. Forecasting bankruptcy more accurately: A simple hazard model. J. Bus. 1999, 74, 101–124. [CrossRef]

Husna, H.N.; Rahman, R.A. Financial distress-Detection model for Islamic banks. Int. J. Trade Econ. Financ. 2012, 3, 158. [CrossRef]

Deakin, E.B. A discriminant analysis of predictors of business failure. J. Account. Res. 1972, 10, 167–179. [CrossRef]

Kyriazopoulos Georgios, M. The Edward I. Altman's Model of Bankruptcy and the implementation of it on the Greek cooperative banks. In Proceedings of the 9th Annual MIBES International Conference, Cambridge, MA, USA, 14–18 May 2005; pp. 423–436.

Altman, E.I.; Haldeman, R.G.; Narayanan, P. ZETATM analysis A new model to identify bankruptcy risk of corporations. J. Bank. Financ. 1977, 1, 29–54. [CrossRef]

Springate, G.L. Predicting the Possibility of Failure in a Canadian Firm: A Discriminant Analysis; Simon Fraser University: Burnaby, BC, Canada; Surrey, BC, Canada; Downtown Vancouver, BC, Canada, 1978.

Altman, E.I. The success of business failure prediction models: An international survey. J. Bank. Financ. 1984, 8, 171–198. [CrossRef]

Izan, H. Corporate distress in Australia. J. Bank. Financ. 1984, 8, 303–320. [CrossRef]

Aziz, A.; Emanuel, D.C.; Lawson, G.H. Bankruptcy prediction-an investigation of cash flow based models [1]. J. Manag. Stud. 1988, 25, 419–437. [CrossRef]

Anwar, S.; Ali, A.H. ANNs-Based Early Warning System for Indonesian Islamic Banks. Bull. Monet. Econ. Bank. 2018, 20, 1–18. [CrossRef]

Martin, D. EARLY WARNING OF BANK FAILURE A iogit regression approach. J. Bank. Financ. 1977, 1, 249–276. [CrossRef]

Doukas, J. Bankers versus bankruptcy prediction models: An empirical investigation, 1979–82. Appl. Econ. 1986, 18, 479–493. [CrossRef]

C□ ihák, M.; Hesse, H. Islamic Banks and Financial Stability: An Empirical Analysis. J. Financ. Serv. Res. 2010, 38, 95–113. [CrossRef]

Bourkhis, K.; Nabi, M.S. Islamic and conventional banks' soundness during the 2007–2008 financial crisis. Rev. Financ. Econ. 2013, 22, 68–77. [CrossRef]

Jan, A.; Marimuthu, M. Altman model and bankruptcy profile of islamic banking industry: A comparative analysis on financial performance. Int. J. Bus. Manag. 2015, 10, 110–119. [CrossRef]

Jan, A.; Marimuthu, M. Bankruptcy profile of foreign vs. domestic islamic banks of malaysia: A post crisis period analysis. Int. J. Econ. Financ. Issues 2016, 6, 332–346.

Laila, N.; Widihadnanto, F. Financial Distress Prediction Using Bankometer Model on Islamic and Conventional Banks: Evidence from Indonesia. Int. J. Econ. Manag. 2017, 11, 169–181.

Halteh, K.; Kumar, K.; Gepp, A. Financial distress prediction of Islamic banks using tree-based stochastic techniques. Manag. Financ. 2018, 44, 759–773. [CrossRef]

Affes, Z.; Hentati-Kaffel, R. Forecast bankruptcy using a blend of clustering and MARS model: Case of US banks. Ann. Oper. Res. 2018, 281, 27–64. [CrossRef]

Darrat, A.F.; Gray, S.; Park, J.C.; Wu, Y. Corporate Governance and Bankruptcy Risk. J. Account. Audit. Financ. 2014, 31, 163–202. [CrossRef]

Lassoued, M. Comparative study on credit risk in Islamic banking institutions: The case of Malaysia. Q. Rev. Econ. Financ. 2018, 70, 267–278. [CrossRef]

Mollah, S.; Zaman, M. Shari'ah supervision, corporate governance and performance: Conventional vs. Islamic banks. J. Bank. Financ. 2015, 58, 418–435. [CrossRef]

Alqahtani, F.; Mayes, D.G. Financial stability of Islamic banking and the global financial crisis: Evidence from the Gulf Cooperation Council. Econ. Syst. 2018, 42, 346–360. [CrossRef]

Ogechukwu, O.L.; John, A.T. Corporate Governance and Financial Distress in the Banking Industry: Nigerian Experience. J. Econ. Behav. Stud. 2018, 10, 182–193. [CrossRef]

Gandhi, P.; Loughran, T.; McDonald, B. Using Annual Report Sentiment as a Proxy for Financial Distress in U.S. Banks. J. Behav. Financ. 2019, 20, 1–13. [CrossRef]

Wilcox, J.W. A simple theory of financial ratios as predictors of failure. J. Account. Res. 1971, 9, 389–395. [CrossRef]

Othman, J. Analysing Financial Distress in Malaysian Islamic Banks: Exploring Integrative Predictive Methods; Durham University: Durham, UK, 2013.

Daily, C.M.; Dalton, D.R. Bankruptcy and corporate governance: The impact of board composition and structure. Acad. Manag. J. 1994, 37, 1603–1617.

Lajili, K.; Zéghal, D. Corporate governance and bankruptcy filing decisions. J. Gen. Manag. 2010, 35, 3–26. [CrossRef]

Wintoki, M.B.; Linck, J.S.; Netter, J.M. Endogeneity and the dynamics of internal corporate governance. J. Financ. Econ. 2012, 105, 581–606. [CrossRef]

Fallatah, Y.; Dickins, D. Corporate governance and firm performance and value in Saudi Arabia. Afr. J. Bus. Manag. 2012, 6, 10025–10034. [CrossRef]

Li, Y.; Armstrong, A.; Clarke, A. Relationships of corporate governance mechanisms and financial performance in Islamic banks: A meta-analysis. J. Bus. Syst. Gov. Ethics 2014, 9, 50–63. [CrossRef]

Naushad, M.; Malik, S.A. Corporate governance and bank performance: A study of selected banks in GCC region. Asian Soc. Sci. 2015, 11, 226. [CrossRef]

Bansal, N.; Sharma, A.K. Audit committee, corporate governance and firm performance: Empirical evidence from India. Int. J. Econ. Financ. 2016, 8, 103. [CrossRef]

Nawaz, T. Momentum investment strategies, corporate governance and firm performance: An analysis of Islamic banks. Corp. Gov. Int. J. Bus. Soc. 2017, 17, 192–211. [CrossRef]

Anginer, D.; Demirguc-Kunt, A.; Huizinga, H.; Ma, K. Corporate governance of banks and financial stability. J. Financ. Econ. 2018, 130, 327–346. [CrossRef]

Zouari, S.B.S.; Taktak, N.B. Ownership structure and financial performance in Islamic banks: Does bank ownership matter? In Proceedings of the Economic Research Forum, Cairo, Egypt, 25–27 March 2012.

Jan, A.; Marimuthu, M.; Mohd, M.P.b.; Isa, M. Sustainability Practices and Banks Financial Performance: A Conceptual Review from the Islamic Banking Industry in Malaysia. Int. J. Bus. Manag. 2018, 13, 61. [CrossRef]

Jensen, M.C.; Meckling, W.H. Theory of the firm: Managerial behavior, agency costs and ownership structure. Financ. Econ. 1976, 3, 305–360. [CrossRef]

Dusuki, A.W. Corporate Social Responsibility of Islamic banks in Malaysia: A synthesis of Islamic and Stakeholders' Perspectives; Loughborough University: Loughborough, UK, 2005.

Othman, R.; Thani, A.M. Islamic social reporting of listed companies in Malaysia. Int. Bus. Econ. Res. J. (IBER) 2010, 9, 99–115. [CrossRef]

Aribi, Z.A.; Gao, S.S. Narrative disclosure of corporate social responsibility in Islamic financial institutions. Manag. Audit. J. 2011, 27, 199–222. [CrossRef]

Amran, A.; Fauzi, H.; Purwanto, Y.; Darus, F.; Yusoff, H.; Zain, M.M.; Naim, D.M.A.; Nejati, M. Social responsibility disclosure in Islamic banks: A comparative study of Indonesia and Malaysia. J. Financ. Report. Account. 2017, 15, 99–115. [CrossRef]

Maali, B.; Casson, P.; Napier, C. Social reporting by Islamic banks. Abacus 2006, 42, 266–289. [CrossRef]

Hassan, A.; Harahap, S.S. Exploring corporate social responsibility disclosure: The case of Islamic banks. Int. J. Islamic Middle East. Financ. Manag. 2010, 3, 203–227. [CrossRef]

Rahman, A.A.; Hashim, M.; Bakar, F.A. Corporate social reporting: A preliminary study of Bank Islam Malaysia Berhad (BIMB). Issues Soc. Environ. Account. 2010, 4, 18–39. [CrossRef]

Farook, S.; Hassan, M.K.; Lanis, R. Determinants of corporate social responsibility disclosure: The case of Islamic banks. J. Islamic Account. Bus. Res. 2011, 2, 114–141. [CrossRef]

Aribi, Z.A.; Arun, T. Corporate social responsibility and Islamic financial institutions (IFIs): Management perceptions from IFIs in Bahrain. J. Bus. Ethics 2015, 129, 785–794. [CrossRef]

Haniffa, R.; Hudaib, M. Exploring the ethical identity of Islamic banks via communication in annual reports. Bus. Ethics 2007, 76, 97–116. [CrossRef]

Platonova, E.; Asutay, M.; Dixon, R.; Mohammad, S. The impact of corporate social responsibility disclosure on financial performance: Evidence from the GCC Islamic banking sector. J. Bus. Ethics 2018, 151, 451–471. [CrossRef]

Harrison, J.S.; Freeman, R.E. Stakeholders, social responsibility, and performance: Empirical evidence and theoretical perspectives. Acad. Manag. J. 1999, 42, 479–485.

WJan, A.; Marimuthu, M.; Mat Isa, M.P.b.M. The nexus of sustainability practices and financial performance: From the perspective of Islamic banking. J. Clean. Prod. 2019, 228, 703–717. [CrossRef]

4

Dynamic Bankruptcy Prediction Models for European Enterprises

Tomasz Korol

Faculty of Management and Economics, Gdansk University of Technology, Narutowicza 11/12, 80-233 Gdansk, Poland; tomasz.korol@zie.pg.gda.pl

Abstract: This manuscript is devoted to the issue of forecasting corporate bankruptcy. Determining a firm's bankruptcy risk is one of the most interesting topics for investors and decision-makers. The aim of the paper is to develop and to evaluate dynamic bankruptcy prediction models for European enterprises. To conduct this objective, four forecasting models are developed with the use of four different methods—fuzzy sets, recurrent and multilayer artificial neural network, and decision trees. Such a research approach will answer the question of whether changes in indicators are relevant predictors of a company's coming financial crisis because declines or increases in values do not immediately indicate that the company's economic situation is deteriorating. The research relies on two samples of firms—the learning sample of 50 bankrupt and 50 non-bankrupt enterprises and the testing sample of 250 bankrupt and 250 non-bankrupt firms.

Keywords: corporate bankruptcy; forecasting; fuzzy sets; artificial neural networks; decision trees

1. Introduction

The measurement of corporate bankruptcy risk is one of the major challenges of modern economic and financial research. Nowadays, with increased financial globalization, faster economic changes, and a new dimension of increased financial risk in the context of the global financial crisis that arose since 2007, we should focus on increasing the reliability of the forecasting model and on prolonging the forecasting horizon to even 10 years prior to announcement of bankruptcy.

The consequences of financial failure are enormous for financial creditors, managers, shareholders, investors, employees, and even a country's economy. That is why during the past five decades, predicting corporate bankruptcy has become a significant concern for the various stakeholders in firms. Accurate bankruptcy prediction usually leads to many benefits, such as cost reduction in credit analysis, better monitoring, and an increased debt-collection rate. Thus, bankruptcy forecasting has become of major interest and is gaining much more importance currently. Today, the question is not if we should use bankruptcy forecasting models, but how to increase the effectiveness of forecasting models.

Though the first law on bankruptcy was already written in 1542 in England during the reign of King Henry VIII, the first studies on forecasting bankruptcies took place in the 1960s, started by Beaver (1966) and Altman (1968). There are two main distinct strands of models that have been used to predict bankruptcy—statistical and artificial intelligence models.

Since the estimation of the pioneering model of multivariate discriminant analysis by Altman, numerous research studies have been carried out with the use of a wide variety of statistical methods (e.g., Alaka et al. 2018; Bandyopadhyay 2006; Barboza et al. 2017; Delen et al. 2013; Giannopoulos and Sigbjornsen 2019; Ho et al. 2013; Hosmer et al. 2013; Jackson and Wood 2013; Kieschnick et al. 2013; Kumar and Ravi 2007; Laitinen 2007; Lukason and Hoffman 2014; Lyandres and Zhdanov 2013; Mihalovic 2016; Orsenigo and Vercellis 2013; Psillaki et al. 2010). The most popular statistical techniques as noted by Balcaen and Ooghe (2006) are multivariate discriminant analysis and logistic regression models.

Although the statistical techniques have become the most commonly used in bankruptcy prediction, they are characterized by many disadvantages regarding statistical assumptions, such as linearity, normality, and independence among variables, which have been identified in many studies (e.g., Altman 2018; Balcaen and Ooghe 2006; Jardin and Severin 2011; Tian and Yu 2017; Jayasekera 2018). That is why in the last two decades, popularity of bankruptcy prediction methods has shifted from statistical to intelligent ones such as neural networks, genetic algorithms, vector support machines, fuzzy logic (e.g., Acosta-González and Fernández-Rodríguez 2014; Ahn et al. 2000; Andres et al. 2005; Atiya 2001; Brabazon and O'Neil 2004; Callejon et al. 2013; Dong et al. 2018; Garcia et al. 2019; Hosaka 2019; Jardin 2015; Jardin 2018; Kim and Kang 2010; Lensberg et al. 2006; Lin et al. 2014; Min and Lee 2005; Ptak-Chmielewska 2019; Ravisankar and Ravi 2010; Succurro et al. 2019; Sun et al. 2014; Tam 1991; Tsai 2014; Wu et al. 2010; Zapranis and Ginoglou 2000; Xiao et al. 2012). The most popular method, which has been in use since the 1990s, is neural networks.

A detailed analysis of the literature on bankruptcy prediction shows that since the first studies, the main concern in the literature was to assess which method was the most effective in making predictions. Though many novel sophisticated techniques have been proposed for effective prediction, the majority of models ensure optimal predictive ability when the forecasting horizon is short, and their accuracy decreases severely beyond three years. Regardless of the modeling technique (linear or non-linear, regression or classification), most models are based on a static snapshot of financial situation that is static values of financial ratios for a given moment of time (usually at the end of the year). These models lack a dynamic approach to indicators. The question arises whether changes in indicators are relevant predictors of a company's coming financial crisis because declines or increases in values do not immediately indicate that the company's economic situation is deteriorating. Nevertheless, by observing changes, we can distinguish between a company that has low financial ratios that improve each year and a company that has similarly low ratios that worsen each year. Static models will not detect the difference between such companies. Dynamic models can add an element that differentiates companies with a poor financial situation from companies that have a weak financial situation but are improving.

To answer this research question, the main objective of this study is to develop dynamic bankruptcy prediction models for European enterprises with the use of four methods—fuzzy sets, artificial neural networks (multilayer and recurrent), and decision trees. This paper, therefore, makes three major contributions to the bankruptcy prediction literature. First, it implements a dynamic approach to financial ratios describing the economic situation of enterprises. Second, it verifies the influence of the dynamic approach on effectiveness of models developed with the use of four different forecasting techniques. Third, it allows the analysis of which method has the smallest decrease in effectiveness in extending the forecast horizon from one to 10 years. Very few studies in the literature focus on this crucial aspect. By evaluating and identifying the predictive properties of models in longer forecasting periods, we can build a decision-support model that will give managers more time in the decision-making process and thus prevent bankruptcies.

The paper consists of five sections. In the Introduction, the author justifies the topic, the study objectives, and the contributions and innovations to the literature. Section 2 presents an overview of the limitations of bankruptcy prediction models. Section 3 introduces this study's assumptions. In Section 4, the author presents four bankruptcy prediction models and discusses the results of effectiveness tests. Section 5 concludes the paper.

2. Literature Review

A thoughtful review on limitations of bankruptcy prediction models is useful to help readers understand the research and the appropriate process of estimation of forecasting models.

The first discussion point is the definition of financial distress. The purpose of bankruptcy forecasting models should be early recognition that the company will be threatened with bankruptcy. From a methodological point of view, it is important to define the term "bankruptcy". In the literature, there are various definitions. The most common interpretation of "bankruptcy" is the criterion of the insolvency of the company. The insolvency is understood as the inability to pay debts (e.g., Crone and Finlay 2012; Deakin 1972; Foster 1986; Jardin 2017). If a company is not able to honor its short-term debt, it is considered to be technically insolvent. Technical insolvency indicates a lack of liquidity but does not yet determine the bankruptcy of the company. Lack of ability to pay current liabilities may be temporary and can be remedied by appropriate action of company management. Altman, a world authority on bankruptcy issues, finds that insolvency understood as a cause of bankruptcy is a long-term state in which the business is found if its total debt exceeds the value of all assets held (Altman 1968). In the studies of Doumpos and Zopounidis (Doumpos and Zopounidis 1999), financial distress not only contains inability to repay important obligatory payments, but also includes the situation of negative net asset value, which means an enterprise's total liabilities exceed its total assets from the view of accounting.

On the other hand, Berryman (1992) suggests a profitability criterion to define a company at risk of bankruptcy. According to him, "a company at risk of bankruptcy" is characterized by a lower long-term return on equity from the level of profitability possible to obtain in similar companies. However, such a wide interpretation of the term "bankruptcy" seems to be too broad. Even more so since research conducted by Davies (1997) on the fallen companies in the UK and France has revealed that most failed companies had positive financial results in the period preceding their bankruptcy.

An equally broad and controversial interpretation of the concept of corporate bankruptcies was presented by Watson and Everett (1999), who stated that a simple change of the owners of the company is a form of failure. In literature, the term "financial failure" is often used interchangeably with the term "bankruptcy". The criterion of continuity of ownership in the company seems to be a too far-fetched over-interpretation of the term "bankruptcy".

The second issue concerns an assessment of the effectiveness of the statistical bankruptcy prediction models such as the multivariate discriminant analysis and the logit and probit models. The allegation concerns the ability to manipulate the thresholds of these models in order to maximize the results of the classification of models. This objection is raised by Nwogugu (2007), according to whom statistical methods do not provide reliable results due to the ease of manual adjustment of the threshold so as to increase the effectiveness of the model. Such manipulation, of course, will not increase the effectiveness of the model in the general population of companies after implementation of the model, e.g., in a bank, but only in the given testing sample of the author of the model.

Another shortcoming of traditional forecasting models is their stationarity (e.g., Balcaen and Ooghe 2006; Grice and Dugan 2001; Liang et al. 2016; Mensah 1984). Bankruptcy models are usually estimated with the use financial ratios calculated with data from balance sheets and income statements. The use of ratios is as much due to their predictive power as to their availability and standardization (Jardin 2016). They generally allow for good discrimination between failed and non-failed firms. However, the way they are designed is one of their main weaknesses. The majority of the models are developed based on static values of financial ratios for a given moment of time, but bankruptcy has multiple causes and symptoms, and a model with variables that are solely measured over a single period would probably not be able to embody such diversity. The financial crisis in enterprise is a dynamic process, and it does not depend on the sole situation of a firm at a given period but is the result of many factors that often overlap. The ability of a model to capture the whole variety of negative situations is a key factor of its performance. As mentioned before, this raises the question of whether changes in the indicators are relevant predictors of the upcoming financial crisis in the company. The dynamic approach to financial ratios could help to introduce an additional element discriminating companies at risk of bankruptcy from enterprises that are in bad financial condition but improving, that is distancing them from the risk of going bankrupt. These considerations are part of the empirical analysis in next sections of the paper.

The next accusation against bankruptcy forecasting models is the issue of their obsolescence with the passage of time since their development. In the literature, it is assumed that the bankruptcy risk prediction models are working well for four to six years, after which it is necessary to modify and update them (e.g., Agarwal and Taffler 2007; Altman and Rijken 2006; Li and Faff 2019; Tian et al. 2015). It should be noted, however, that the model life cycle shown in Figure 1 is a matter of agreement. There are no strict rules that accurately define when the life of the model comes to an end. Common sense should be demonstrated in this regard. Models become outdated as a result of, for example, changes in the business cycle and changes in economic conditions, due to which mean values of economic and financial indicators are subject to change. Adding a dynamic perspective to the model could enhance the validity period of the models.

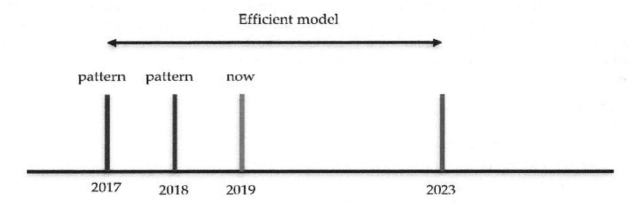

Figure 1. The life cycle of bankruptcy forecasting model. Source: Based on own studies.

Another issue arises in relation to statistical methods. As was mentioned before, there are strict assumptions regarding normal distribution of values of financial ratios used in estimating forecasting models (e.g., multivariate discriminant analysis). This assumption is usually not fulfilled due to the fact that only a few variables used in this type of model are characterized by such a distribution. However, the desire to meet this target would significantly limit the number of financial ratios that accurately reflect the economic situation of the enterprises, and thus would result in deterioration of the effectiveness of such models (e.g., Balcaen and Ooghe 2006; Kumar and Ravi 2007; Mcleay and Omar 2000).

The last important topic to consider in developing bankruptcy forecasting models is the structure of enterprises in research sample regarding their age and type of industry they operate in. In the literature, studies of individual authors (e.g., Cressy 2006) confirm the assumptions of the theoretical model developed by Jovanovic (1982). He reveals the effect of company age on the risk of bankruptcy is in the form of an inverted U shape (Figure 2).

Jovanovic suggests that after entering the market, the company begins to learn to recognize its earning potential, competitiveness, and efficiency. Research by Pakes and Ericsson (1998) has shown that the company needs time to gain that knowledge and experience to manage crisis situations. The studies of Bradley and Rubach (2002) also showed that the second and third year of existence has the highest risk of bankruptcy (52% of cases). The studies of Doyle et al. (2007) confirm that the older the company, the more established its market position but also internal financial control.

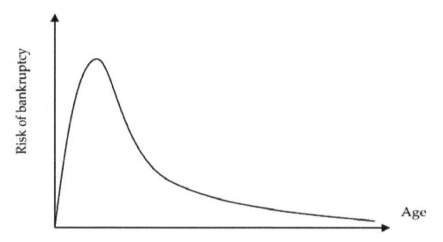

Figure 2. Age of company and the risk of bankruptcy. Source: Based on own studies.

The second demographic factor influencing the susceptibility of a company to risk of bankruptcy is the type of industry in which the company operates. According to the director of the international rating agency Standard & Poor's, the type of industry affects the risk of deterioration in financial situation of companies by such factors as (Ganguin and Bilardello 2005):

- Intensity of competition,
- Life cycle of products,
- The demand,
- Changes in consumer preferences,
- Technological change,
- Reducing entry barriers into the industry,
- Susceptibility of the industry to business cycle.

Ganguin and Bilardello (2005) emphasize that each industry has different risk parameters. In the 21st century, in an era of intense globalization, product life cycles in some industries are getting much shorter, often with increasing intensity of competition by reducing entry barriers into the industry. These authors rank industries into three risk levels:

- Riskiest sectors—industry: Metal, mining, automotive, aerospace, housing, paper,
- Medium risk industries—restaurants, retail, medical sector, tourism, transport,
- Least risky sectors—journalistic, military, pharmaceutical industry, and agriculture.

Chava and Jarrow (2004) in their studies also have demonstrated the impact of the type of industry on the bankruptcy of enterprises. They divided the population of 1461 bankrupt American joint-stock companies into 10 types of industries. Using bankruptcy prediction models by Altman, Shumway, and Żmijewski, they proved that the type of industry affects the correct coefficients in each model.

3. Data, Samples, and Modeling Methods

To address all the issues in forecasting corporate bankruptcy risk described in the previous section, the author of the paper in developing learning and the testing sample:

- Has chosen a clear definition of "bankrupt" enterprises. The enterprises at risk of bankruptcy were chosen based on the following three criteria: Information from the firm's authorities about the risk of financial failure, court judgments declaring bankruptcy, and liquidation of the company;
- Has chosen four prediction methods that do not allow manipulation of thresholds—multilayer neural network, recurrent neural network, fuzzy sets, and decision trees;
- Has calculated 20 financial ratios (Figure 3) for all the enterprises (bankrupt and non-bankrupt) for whole analyzed period of 10 years prior to bankruptcy and the dynamics for all ratios. The

assumption was to build the models with at least two variables representing the change of value of financial ratio to avoid stationarity of the created models;

- Has selected enterprises that were operating in the market for at least 10 years (to avoid the selection of new, young companies characterized with higher bankruptcy risk).

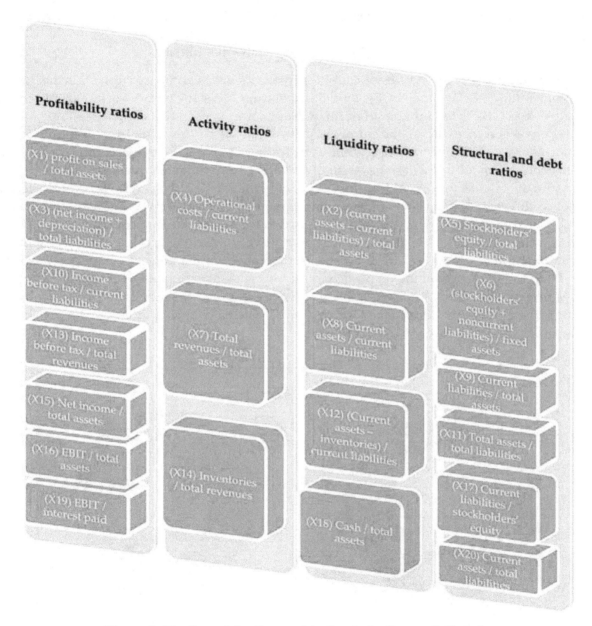

Figure 3. The financial ratios used in the study. Source: Self-study.

The forecasting horizon for all enterprises and all models comprises 10 periods: From one year to 10 years prior to bankruptcy. Such a research approach allows the identification of which model characterizes the forecast with the smallest decrease of effectiveness along the increasing horizon and verifies the influence of implementing dynamic elements to the models on its effectiveness. Depending on the enterprise, the 10-year financial statements taken for analysis covered the period from 2004 to 2017.

The learning and testing samples comprise enterprises from European countries (Germany, France, UK, Spain, Finland, Italy, Poland, Sweden, Denmark). Each testing sample includes 250 bankrupt and 250 non-bankrupt enterprises, while each learning sample includes 50 bankrupt and 50 non-bankrupt firms. Both samples consist of companies that are publicly traded, due to better availability of financial data of firms in case of such a long-term forecasting horizon (10 years prior to bankruptcy). The research contains the firms of all sizes (small, medium, and large) keeping the principle of pairing the same size and sector of bankrupt firms to non-bankrupt ones.

To assess the effectiveness of the created models, three evaluation metrics were calculated for each testing sample: Overall effectiveness and Type I and Type II errors. Overall effectiveness is calculated based on how many enterprises are correctly classified by the forecasting model in a given testing sample:

$$S = \{1 - [(D1 + D2)/(BR + NBR)]\} * 100\%$$

where D1 is the number of bankrupt firms classified by the model as non-bankrupt, D2 is the number of non-bankrupt enterprises classified by the model as bankrupt, BR is the number of bankrupt companies in the sample, and NBR is the number of non-bankrupt companies in the sample.

Type I error is a measure of the number of firms in which the model incorrectly classifies a bankrupt firm into a non-bankrupt class, while Type II error is a measure that accounts for the number of firms classified as bankrupt when they actually belong to a non-bankrupt class.

To ensure the reliable process of learning and testing the models, the enterprises were selected for both samples while maintaining very similar structure of belonging to sectors of industry. From Figure 4 it can be seen that the biggest number of enterprises was for manufacturing companies (58% and 60% of all firms in the learning and testing datasets, respectively). Although the automotive industry is part of manufacturing sector, it was distinguished separately from manufacturing industry as in many countries it has big influence on the whole economy, indirectly affecting also the financial situation of enterprises from other sectors. The second biggest share accounted for service companies—18% of all firms in learning and 20% of all firms in testing sample. Such a balanced number of sectors between the two samples should ensure the reliability of results.

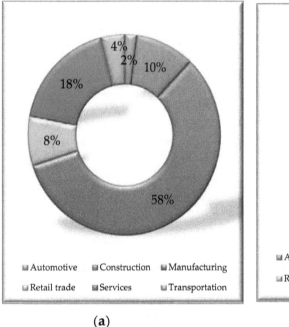
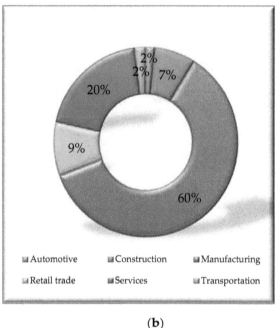

(a)   (b)

Figure 4. The sector structure of: (a) learning sample and (b) testing sample of enterprises. Source: Based on own studies.

4. Results and Discussion

In the first stage of research, the author developed two artificial neural network models—multilayer and recurrent. Inputs to the models were chosen based on the correlation matrix by choosing only the features that were poorly correlated with each other and strongly correlated with the grouping variable, representing the information about the risk of bankruptcy. This approach ensured the selection of such features, which do not duplicate information provided by other financial ratios, while being good representatives of the ratios not selected as diagnostic. The following financial ratios were set (the formulas are given in Figure 3): X1 (profitability ratio), X6 (structural ratio), X7 (activity ratio), X8 (liquidity ratio), DX1 (dynamics of ratio X1), DX8 (dynamics of ratio X8). It can be seen that each ratio belongs to a different field of financial analysis.

The multilayer neural network is the network in which the signal flow is only in one direction, from the input (financial ratios) through the hidden layer, where the main processing of neural signals takes place, to the output, where the network provides a forecast (bankrupt/non-bankrupt). The architecture of the developed multilayer network is shown in Figure 5. At the entry layer there are six neurons, in the first hidden layer there are 12 neurons (double the number of neurons as entry ones), in the second hidden layer there are four neurons and then one single output neuron where the forecast is generated.

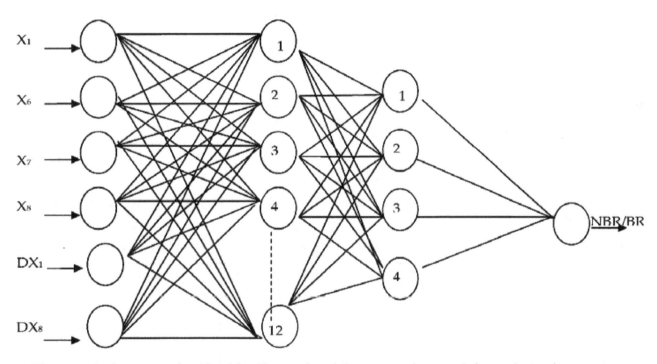

Figure 5. Architecture of artificial feedforward multilayer neural network for analysis of enterprises. Source: Based on own studies.

In topology of recurrent networks, it is acceptable to use reverse connections. The output from any neuron can be passed also to its input. Neuron state is therefore dependent not only on the value of the input signal (financial ratio), but also on the past state of any neuron, not excluding this particular neuron. The network response to specific input takes in this case an iterative character. The created architecture of the recurrent neural network for predicting risk of bankruptcy for European companies is shown in Figure 6. The developed recurrent model has the same entry layer as the previous model, but it consists of only one hidden layer with 12 neurons as the reverse connections between neurons support higher computing properties.

The next developed model was fuzzy sets model. This model requires no assumptions about the learning process and is developed based on expert knowledge and experience. The decision-making center of the fuzzy logic model is the base of rules in the form: IF-THEN, written by the author of this paper. The output of the model is a variable representing the forecast of the financial situation of the audited company. This variable has a value from 0 to 1, and it was assumed that the threshold dividing companies into at risk and not at risk of bankruptcy is 0.5. For each input, that is the financial ratio, the author defined critical value (Table 1). The fuzzy sets model consists the same entry variables as both created neural networks.

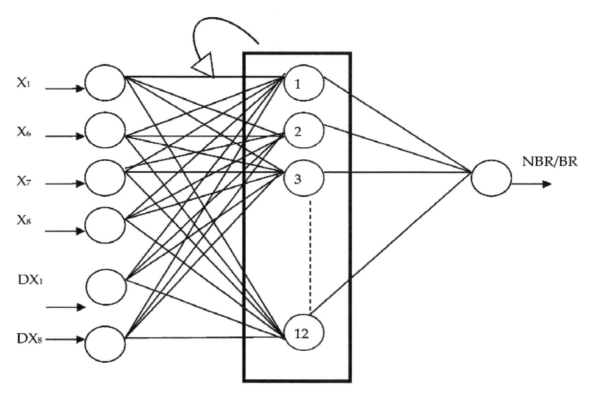

Figure 6. Architecture of artificial recurrent neural network for analysis of enterprises. Source: Based on own studies.

Table 1. Critical values of financial ratios used in the fuzzy sets model. Source: Based on own studies.

Indicator Symbol	Critical Value in Fuzzy Sets Model
X_1	0.015
X_6	0.9
X_7	0.82
X_8	1.05
DX_1	70.0%
DX_8	85.0%

To explain more how the fuzzy sets model functions, below is an example of fuzzy sets defined using membership functions for the ratio X8 (Figure 7).

For ratio X8, shown in Figure 7 (this ratio represents current liquidity of firms), the threshold between a positive and negative situation is the value of 1.05. All values less than 0.7 are strictly negative, i.e., they belong to the fuzzy subset "LOW" with the degree of membership of 1 and to a subset "HIGH" with the degree of membership equal to 0. All values greater than 1.3 are strictly positive and, therefore, belong to the fuzzy subset "LOW" with the degree of membership of 0 and to the subset "HIGH" with the degree of membership equal to 1. Values contained in the range from 0.7 to 1.3 belong to both fuzzy subsets with different values of membership functions, e.g., for values of X8 equal to 1.05, the value of the function of membership in the "LOW" set is 0.5 and for the "HIGH" set is 0.5. With such defined subsets, the boundary between the values considered positive or negative is fuzzificated—a certain ratio value is "partially high" and "partially low". There is no such possibility in the case of classical logic, which is bivalent and in which the value of the ratio is "high" or "low". Therefore, the use of classical logic in assessing the financial situation of enterprises negatively affects the effectiveness of forecasts. This is true particularly for values close to the border of subsets, where a slight excess in the critical values of the ratio determines the final assessment (as completely positive or negative), which is not true because both values of the ratio reflect almost the same situation in the firm.

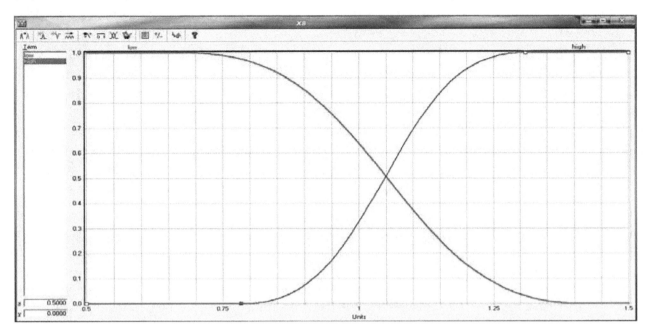

Figure 7. Fuzzy sets for ratio X8 with membership functions. Source: Own studies conducted in MATLAB.

The author has developed the following 36 decision-making "IF-THEN" rules for the fuzzy sets model:

1. If $X_1 <= 0.015$ and $X_6 <= 0.9$ and $X_7 <= 0.82$ and $X_8 <= 1.05$ and $DX_1 <= 70$ and $DX_8 <= 85$ then 0
2. If $X_1 <= 0.015$ and $X_6 <= 0.9$ and $X_7 <= 0.82$ and $X_8 <= 1.05$ and $DX_1 > 70$ and $DX_8 <= 85$ then 0
3. If $X_1 <= 0.015$ and $X_6 <= 0.9$ and $X_7 <= 0.82$ and $X_8 > 1.05$ and $DX_1 > 70$ and $DX_8 <= 85$ then 0
4. If $X_1 <= 0.015$ and $X_6 <= 0.9$ and $X_7 > 0.82$ and $X_8 > 1.05$ and $DX_1 > 70$ and $DX_8 <= 85$ then 1
5. If $X_1 <= 0.015$ and $X_6 > 0.9$ and $X_7 > 0.82$ and $X_8 > 1.05$ and $DX_1 > 70$ and $DX_8 <= 85$ then 1
6. If $X_1 > 0.015$ and $X_6 > 0.9$ and $X_7 > 0.82$ and $X_8 > 1.05$ and $DX_1 > 70$ and $DX_8 <= 85$ then 1
7. If $X_1 <= 0.015$ and $X_6 <= 0.9$ and $X_7 > 0.82$ and $X_8 <= 1.05$ and $DX_1 > 70$ and $DX_8 <= 85$ then 0
8. If $X_1 <= 0.015$ and $X_6 > 0.9$ and $X_7 <= 0.82$ and $X_8 <= 1.05$ and $DX_1 > 70$ and $DX_8 <= 85$ then 0
9. If $X_1 > 0.015$ and $X_6 <= 0.9$ and $X_7 <= 0.82$ and $X_8 <= 1.05$ and $DX_1 > 70$ and $DX_8 <= 85$ then 0
10. If $X_1 <= 0.015$ and $X_6 <= 0.9$ and $X_7 <= 0.82$ and $X_8 > 1.05$ and $DX_1 <= 70$ and $DX_8 <= 85$ then 0
11. If $X_1 <= 0.015$ and $X_6 <= 0.9$ and $X_7 > 0.82$ and $X_8 <= 1.05$ and $DX_1 <= 70$ and $DX_8 <= 85$ then 0
12. If $X_1 <= 0.015$ and $X_6 > 0.9$ and $X_7 <= 0.82$ and $X_8 <= 1.05$ and $DX_1 <= 70$ and $DX_8 <= 85$ then 0
13. If $X_1 > 0.015$ and $X_6 <= 0.9$ and $X_7 <= 0.82$ and $X_8 <= 1.05$ and $DX_1 <= 70$ and $DX_8 <= 85$ then 0
14. If $X_1 <= 0.015$ and $X_6 > 0.9$ and $X_7 > 0.82$ and $X_8 > 1.05$ and $DX_1 <= 70$ and $DX_8 <= 85$ then 1
15. If $X_1 <= 0.015$ and $X_6 <= 0.9$ and $X_7 > 0.82$ and $X_8 > 1.05$ and $DX_1 <= 70$ and $DX_8 <= 85$ then 0
16. If $X_1 <= 0.015$ and $X_6 > 0.9$ and $X_7 <= 0.82$ and $X_8 > 1.05$ and $DX_1 <= 70$ and $DX_8 <= 85$ then 0
17. If $X_1 <= 0.015$ and $X_6 > 0.9$ and $X_7 > 0.82$ and $X_8 <= 1.05$ and $DX_1 <= 70$ and $DX_8 <= 85$ then 0
18. If $X_1 > 0.015$ and $X_6 <= 0.9$ and $X_7 > 0.82$ and $X_8 <= 1.05$ and $DX_1 <= 70$ and $DX_8 <= 85$ then 0
19. If $X_1 > 0.015$ and $X_6 <= 0.9$ and $X_7 <= 0.82$ and $X_8 > 1.05$ and $DX_1 <= 70$ and $DX_8 <= 85$ then 0
20. If $X_1 > 0.015$ and $X_6 <= 0.9$ and $X_7 <= 0.82$ and $X_8 > 1.05$ and $DX_1 > 70$ and $DX_8 <= 85$ then 1
21. If $X_1 > 0.015$ and $X_6 > 0.9$ and $X_7 <= 0.82$ and $X_8 > 1.05$ and $DX_1 > 70$ and $DX_8 <= 85$ then 1
22. If $X_1 > 0.015$ and $X_6 > 0.9$ and $X_7 <= 0.82$ and $X_8 <= 1.05$ and $DX_1 > 70$ and $DX_8 <= 85$ then 1
23. If $X_1 > 0.015$ and $X_6 > 0.9$ and $X_7 > 0.82$ and $X_8 <= 1.05$ and $DX_1 <= 70$ and $DX_8 <= 85$ then 1

24.   If $X_1 > 0.015$ and $X_6 > 0.9$ and $X_7 <= 0.82$ and $X_8 > 1.05$ and $DX_1 <= 70$ and $DX_8 <= 85$ then 1
25.   If $X_1 > 0.015$ and $X_6 <= 0.9$ and $X_7 > 0.82$ and $X_8 > 1.05$ and $DX_1 > 70$ and $DX_8 <= 85$ then 1
26.   If $X_1 <= 0.015$ and $X_6 <= 0.9$ and $X_7 <= 0.82$ and $X_8 <= 1.05$ and $DX_1 <= 70$ and $DX_8 > 85$ then 0
27.   If $X_1 <= 0.015$ and $X_6 <= 0.9$ and $X_7 <= 0.82$ and $X_8 <= 1.05$ and $DX_1 > 70$ and $DX_8 > 85$ then 0
28.   If $X_1 <= 0.015$ and $X_6 <= 0.9$ and $X_7 <= 0.82$ and $X_8 > 1.05$ and $DX_1 > 70$ and $DX_8 > 85$ then 1
29.   If $X_1 <= 0.015$ and $X_6 <= 0.9$ and $X_7 > 0.82$ and $X_8 > 1.05$ and $DX_1 > 70$ and $DX_8 > 85$ then 1
30.   If $X_1 <= 0.015$ and $X_6 > 0.9$ and $X_7 > 0.82$ and $X_8 > 1.05$ and $DX_1 > 70$ and $DX_8 > 85$ then 1
31.   If $X_1 > 0.015$ and $X_6 > 0.9$ and $X_7 > 0.82$ and $X_8 > 1.05$ and $DX_1 > 70$ and $DX_8 > 85$ then 1
32.   If $X_1 > 0.015$ and $X_6 <= 0.9$ and $X_7 <= 0.82$ and $X_8 <= 1.05$ and $DX_1 <= 70$ and $DX_8 > 85$ then 0
33.   If $X_1 > 0.015$ and $X_6 > 0.9$ and $X_7 <= 0.82$ and $X_8 <= 1.05$ and $DX_1 <= 70$ and $DX_8 > 85$ then 1
34.   If $X_1 <= 0.015$ and $X_6 <= 0.9$ and $X_7 > 0.82$ and $X_8 <= 1.05$ and $DX_1 > 70$ and $DX_8 > 85$ then 1
35.   If $X_1 <= 0.015$ and $X_6 > 0.9$ and $X_7 <= 0.82$ and $X_8 > 1.05$ and $DX_1 <= 70$ and $DX_8 > 85$ then 1
36.   If $X_1 > 0.015$ and $X_6 > 0.9$ and $X_7 > 0.82$ and $X_8 <= 1.05$ and $DX_1 <= 70$ and $DX_8 > 85$ then 1

In the last stage of the research, the author estimated the decision trees model. The structure of the model is presented in Figure 8. In this model, the following financial ratios were selected: X2 (liquidity ratio), X1 (profitability ratio), X6 (structural ratio), X9 (structural ratio). As can be seen in this model, none of variables representing the change of value of ratios (dynamics) were selected during estimation process of the model. This means it is the only static model in the proposed research.

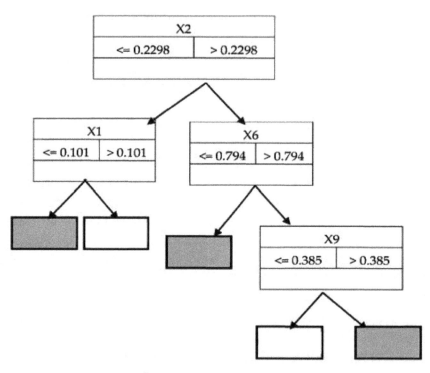

Figure 8. The structure of the Classification and Regression Tree (C&RT) model. Gray box indicates firms at risk of bankruptcy; white box, non-bankrupt firms. Source: based on own studies.

When evaluating the effectiveness of the developed models (Table 2), we can draw the following conclusions:

- During the whole analyzed period (all 10 years prior to bankruptcy) the highest effectiveness was achieved using the fuzzy sets model, with 96.2% correct classifications one year before bankruptcy, 95.4% correct classifications two years prior to financial failure, and 93.8% correct classifications three years before bankruptcy;

- The second best forecasting model is the recurrent neural network model with an effectiveness from 91.2% three years before financial crisis to up to 95.2% correct classifications one year prior to bankruptcy;
- An examination of the effectiveness of the dynamic models (fuzzy sets, multilayer and recurrent neural networks) shows that all of them stand out with very good results in the forecasting horizon of up to six years prior to bankruptcy, with an effectiveness above 80%;
- The effectiveness of the static decision tree model is smaller than the effectiveness of the dynamic models for all the analyzed years. Additionally, the model shows significantly bigger decrease of effectiveness while prolonging the period of the forecast than dynamic models;
- The fuzzy sets model as the only dynamic model maintained an effectiveness level above 70% until the eighth year prior to bankruptcy;
- Moreover, all three dynamic models have the fewest Type I errors. Such errors indicate how many bankrupt enterprises are classified as non-bankrupt firms. Type I errors, for obvious financial reasons, are far more dangerous than Type II errors.

Table 2. The results of the effectiveness of models for European firms (testing sample). Source: Based on own studies.

Years Prior to Bankruptcy	Multilayer Neural Network			Recurrent Neural Network			Fuzzy Sets			Decision Trees		
	S	E1	E2	S	E1	E2	S	E1	E2	S	E1	E2
1 year	93.4%	6.0%	7.2%	95.2%	4.0%	5.6%	96.2%	3.2%	4.4%	93.0%	8.0%	6.0%
2 years	91.8%	7.6%	8.8%	93.6%	5.6%	7.2%	95.4%	4.4%	4.8%	91.2%	10.0%	7.6%
3 years	87.4%	11.6%	13.6%	91.2%	7.6%	10.0%	93.8%	5.2%	7.2%	86.8%	14.8%	11.6%
4 years	82.8%	16.4%	18.0%	87.8%	10.4%	14.0%	90.6%	7.6%	11.2%	81.6%	19.6%	17.2%
5 years	82.4%	16.8%	18.4%	82.4%	16.8%	18.4%	87.8%	10.8%	13.6%	77.2%	24.0%	21.6%
6 years	80.8%	18.0%	20.4%	81.0%	18.4%	19.6%	82.8%	16.4%	18.0%	72.0%	30.0%	26.0%
7 years	74.2%	25.6%	26.0%	77.4%	21.6%	23.6%	80.8%	18.8%	19.6%	65.0%	35.6%	34.4%
8 years	64.4%	34.4%	36.8%	65.0%	34.4%	35.6%	71.4%	26.0%	31.2%	62.8%	38.0%	36.4%
9 years	63.4%	36.0%	37.2%	64.0%	35.2%	36.8%	67.2%	32.4%	33.2%	62.4%	38.4%	36.8%
10 years	63.0%	36.4%	37.6%	63.6%	35.6%	37.2%	65.8%	32.8%	35.6%	61.4%	39.6%	37.6%

5. Conclusions

This paper presents how to improve the effectiveness of forecasting corporate distress risk models in both the short and long horizon, exceeding five years before the announcement of bankruptcy.

The present empirical study reveals that the implementation of dynamic elements to the forecasting models positively affects the effectiveness and the stability of the forecast. The dynamic models generate a smaller number of errors, and the decrease of effectiveness of such models is smaller with extending the forecast period than in the case of static models. Additionally, this research also proved the superiority of fuzzy sets model over the other developed models, both in terms of effectiveness during all analyzed years prior to bankruptcy and in terms of the smallest decrease of predictive abilities while increasing the forecasting horizon.

The main limitation of the research is limited financial data access, especially for bankrupt enterprises (in many cases there are data available only for one to three years before the enterprise went bankrupt, which makes it difficult to conduct the research in such long horizon of 10 years prior to financial failure). That is why the studies are focused on countries with better organized financial reporting systems (EU countries). The author is going to continue the research towards the use of macroeconomic variables of selected countries in predicting the risk of bankruptcy of enterprises.

References

Acosta-González, Eduardo, and Fernando Fernández-Rodríguez. 2014. Forecasting financial failure of firms via genetic algorithms. *Computational Economics* 43: 133–57. [CrossRef]

Agarwal, Vineet, and Richard Taffler. 2007. Twenty-five years of the Taffler z-score model—Does it really have predictive ability? *Accounting and Business Research* 37: 285–300. [CrossRef]

Ahn, Byeong, Sung Cho, and Chang Kim. 2000. The integrated methodology of rough set theory and artificial neural networks for business failure prediction. *Expert Systems with Applications* 18: 65–74. [CrossRef]

Alaka, Hafiz A., Lukumon O. Oyedele, Hakeem A. Owolabi, Vikas Kumar, Saheed O. Ajayi, Olugbenga O. Akinade, and Muhammad Bilal. 2018. Systematic review of bankruptcy prediction models: Towards a framework for tool selection. *Expert Systems with Applications* 94: 164–84. [CrossRef]

Altman, Edward. 1968. Financial ratios, discriminant analysis and the prediction of corporate bankruptcy. *Journal of Finance* 23: 589–609. [CrossRef]

Altman, Edward. 2018. Applications of distress prediction models: What have we learned after 50 years from the Z-score models? *International Journal of Financial Studies* 6: 70. [CrossRef]

Altman, Edward, and Herbert Rijken. 2006. A point-in-time perspective on through-the-cycle ratings. *Financial Analysts Journal* 62: 54–70. [CrossRef]

Andres, Javier, Manuel Landajo, and Pedro Lorca. 2005. Forecasting business profitability by using classification techniques: A comparative analysis based on a Spanish case. *European Journal of Operational Research* 167: 518–42. [CrossRef]

Atiya, Amir. 2001. Bankruptcy prediction for credit risk using neural networks: A survey and new results. *IEEE Transactions on Neural Networks* 12: 929–35. [CrossRef]

Balcaen, Sofie, and Hubert Ooghe. 2006. 35 years of studies on business failure: An overview of the classic statistical methodologies and their related problems. *The British Accounting Review* 38: 63–93. [CrossRef]

Bandyopadhyay, Arindam. 2006. Predicting probability of default of Indian corporate bonds: Logistic and Z-score model approaches. *The Journal of Risk Finance* 7: 255–72. [CrossRef]

Barboza, Flavio, Herbert Kimura, and Edward Altman. 2017. Machine learning models and bankruptcy prediction. *Expert Systems with Applications* 83: 405–17. [CrossRef]

Beaver, William H. 1966. Financial ratios as predictors of failure. *Journal of Accounting Research* 4: 71–111. [CrossRef]

Berryman, John. 1992. *Small Business Bankruptcy and Failure—A Survey of the Literature*. Los Angeles: Small Business Research Institute of Industrial Economics, pp. 1–18.

Brabazon, Anthony, and Michael O'Neil. 2004. Diagnosing corporate stability using grammatical evolution. *Journal of Applied Mathematics and Computer Science* 1: 293–310.

Bradley, Don, and Michael Rubach. 2002. *Trade Credit and Small Business—A Cause of Business Failures?* Conway: University of Central Arkansas, pp. 1–7.

Callejon, A.M., A.M. Casado, Martina Fernandez, and J.I. Pelaez. 2013. A system of insolvency prediction for industrial companies using a financial alternative model with neural networks. *International Journal of Computational Intelligence Systems* 6: 29–37. [CrossRef]

Chava, Sudheer, and Robert Jarrow. 2004. Bankruptcy prediction with industry effects. *Review of Finance* 8: 537–69. [CrossRef]

Cressy, Robert. 2006. Why do most firms die young? *Small Business Economics* 26: 103–16. [CrossRef]

Crone, Sven, and Steven Finlay. 2012. Instance sampling in credit scoring: An empirical study of sample size and balancing. *International Journal of Forecasting* 28: 224–38. [CrossRef]

Davies, David. 1997. *The Art of Managing Finance*. Lincoln: McGraw-Hill Book Co.

Deakin, Edward B. 1972. A discriminant analysis of prediction of business failure. *Journal of Accounting Research* 3: 167–69. [CrossRef]

Delen, Dursun, Cemil Kuzey, and Ali Uyar. 2013. Measuring firm performance using financial ratios: A decision tree approach. *Expert Systems with Applications* 40: 3970–83. [CrossRef]

Dong, Manh Cuong, Shaonan Tian, and Cathy W.S. Chen. 2018. Predicting failure risk using financial ratios: Quantile hazard model approach. *North American Journal of Economics and Finance* 44: 204–20. [CrossRef]

Doumpos, Michalis, and Constantin Zopounidis. 1999. A multinational discrimination method for the prediction of financial distress: the case of Greece. *Multinational Finance Journal* 3: 71–101. [CrossRef]

Doyle, Jeffrey, Weili Geb, and Sarah McVay. 2007. Determinants of weaknesses in internal control over financial reporting. *Journal of Accounting and Economics* 44: 193–223. [CrossRef]

Foster, George. 1986. *Financial Statement Analysis*, 2nd ed. New York: Prentice Hall.

Ganguin, Blaise, and John Bilardello. 2005. *Fundamentals of Corporate Credit Analysis, Standard & Poor's*. New York: McGraw-Hill.

Garcia, Vincente, Ana I. Marques, J. Salvador Sanchez, and Humberto Ochoa-Dominguez. 2019. Dissimilarity-Based Linear Models for Corporate Bankruptcy Prediction. *Compotional Economics* 53: 1019–31. [CrossRef]

Giannopoulos, George, and Sindre Sigbjornsen. 2019. Prediction of bankruptcy using financial ratios in the Greek market. *Theoretical Economics Letters* 9: 1114–28. [CrossRef]

Grice, John, and Michael Dugan. 2001. The limitations of bankruptcy prediction models—Some cautions for the researcher. *Review of Quantitative Finance and Accounting* 17: 151–66. [CrossRef]

Ho, Chun-Yu, Patrick McCarthy, Yi Yang, and Xuan Ye. 2013. Bankruptcy in the pulp and paper industry: Market's reaction and prediction. *Empirical Economics* 45: 1205–32. [CrossRef]

Hosaka, Tadaaki. 2019. Bankruptcy prediction using imaged financial ratios and convolutional neural networks. *Expert Systems with Applications* 117: 287–99. [CrossRef]

Hosmer, David, Stanley Lemeshow, and Rod X. Sturdivant. 2013. *Applied Logistic Regression*. Hoboken: John Wiley & Sons.

Jackson, Richard H.G., and Anthony Wood. 2013. The performance of insolvency prediction and credit risk models in the UK: A comparative study. *The British Accounting Review* 45: 183–202. [CrossRef]

Jardin, Philippe. 2015. Bankruptcy prediction using terminal failure processes. *European Journal of Operational Research* 242: 286–303. [CrossRef]

Jardin, Philippe. 2016. A two-stage classification technique for bankruptcy prediction. *European Journal of Operational Research* 254: 236–52. [CrossRef]

Jardin, Philippe. 2017. Dynamics of firm financial evolution and bankruptcy prediction. *Expert Systems with Applications* 75: 25–43. [CrossRef]

Jardin, Philippe. 2018. Failure pattern-based ensembles applied to bankruptcy forecasting. *Decision Support Systems* 107: 64–77. [CrossRef]

Jardin, Philippe, and Eric Severin. 2011. Predicting corporate bankruptcy using a self-organizing map—An empirical study to improve the forecasting horizon of a financial failure model. *Decision Support Systems* 51: 701–11. [CrossRef]

Jayasekera, Ranadeva. 2018. Prediction of company failure: Past, present and promising directions for the future. *International Review of Financial Analysis* 55: 196–208. [CrossRef]

Jovanovic, Boyan. 1982. Selection and the evolution of industry. *Econometrica* 50: 649–70. [CrossRef]

Kieschnick, Robert, Mark La Plante, and Rabih Moussawi. 2013. Working capital management and shareholders' wealth. *Review of Finance* 17: 1827–52. [CrossRef]

Kim, Myoung-Jong, and Dae-Ki Kang. 2010. Ensemble with neural networks for bankruptcy prediction. *Expert Systems with Applications* 37: 3373–79. [CrossRef]

Kumar, Pramod, and Vadlamani Ravi. 2007. Bankruptcy prediction in banks and firms via statistical and intelligent techniques—A review. *European Journal of Operational Research* 180: 1–28. [CrossRef]

Laitinen, Erkki K. 2007. Classification accuracy and correlation—LDA in failure prediction. *European Journal of Operational Research* 183: 210–25. [CrossRef]

Lensberg, Terje, Aasmund Eilifsen, and Thomas E. McKee. 2006. Bankruptcy theory development and classification via genetic programming. *European Journal of Operational Research* 169: 677–97. [CrossRef]

Li, Leon, and Robert Faff. 2019. Predicting corporate bankruptcy: What matters? *International Review of Economics & Finance* 62: 1–19.

Liang, Deron, Chia-Chi Lu, Chih-Fong Tsai, and Guan-An Shih. 2016. Financial ratios and corporate governance indicators in bankruptcy prediction: A comprehensive study. *European Journal of Operational Research* 252: 561–72. [CrossRef]

Lin, Fengyi, Deron Liang, Ching-Chiang Yeh, and Jui-Chieh Huang. 2014. Novel feature selection methods to financial distress prediction. *Expert Systems with Applications* 41: 2472–83. [CrossRef]

Lukason, Oliver, and Richard C. Hoffman. 2014. Firm Bankruptcy Probability and Causes: An Integrated Study. *International Journal of Business and Management* 9: 80–91. [CrossRef]

Lyandres, Evgeny, and Alexei Zhdanov. 2013. Investment opportunities and bankruptcy prediction. *Journal of Financial Markets* 16: 439–76. [CrossRef]

Mcleay, Stuart, and Azmi Omar. 2000. The sensitivity of prediction models to the non-normality of bounded and unbounded financial ratios. *British Accounting Review* 32: 213–30. [CrossRef]

Mensah, Yaw. 1984. An examination of the stationarity of multivariate bankruptcy prediction models—A methodological study. *Journal of Accounting Research* 22: 380–95. [CrossRef]

Mihalovic, Matus. 2016. Performance Comparison of Multiple Discriminant Analysis and Logit Models in Bankruptcy Prediction. *Economics and Sociology* 9: 101–18. [CrossRef]

Min, Jae, and Young-Chan Lee. 2005. Bankruptcy prediction using support vector machine with optimal choice of kernel function parameters. *Expert Systems with Applications* 28: 603–14. [CrossRef]

Nwogugu, Michael. 2007. Decision-making, risk and corporate governance—A critque of methodological issues in bankruptcy/recovery prediction models. *Applied Mathematics and Computation* 185: 178–96. [CrossRef]

Orsenigo, Carlotta, and Carlo Vercellis. 2013. Linear versus nonlinear dimensionality reduction for banks credit rating prediction. *Knowledge-Based Systems* 47: 14–22. [CrossRef]

Pakes, Ariel, and Richard Ericsson. 1998. Empirical implications of alternative models of firm dynamics. *Journal of Economic Theory* 79: 1–45. [CrossRef]

Psillaki, Maria, Ioannis E. Tsolas, and Dimmitris Margaritis. 2010. Evaluation of credit risk based on firm performance. *European Journal of Operational Research* 201: 873–81. [CrossRef]

Ptak-Chmielewska, Aneta. 2019. Predicting Micro-Enterprise Failures Using Data Mining Techniques. *Journal of Risk and Financial Managament* 12: 30. [CrossRef]

Ravisankar, Pediredla, and Vadlamani Ravi. 2010. Financial distress prediction in banks using group method of data handling neural network, counter propagation neural network and fuzzy ARTMAP. *Knowledge-Based Systems* 23: 823–31. [CrossRef]

Succurro, Marianna, Giuseppe Arcuri, and Giuseppina D. Constanzo. 2019. A combined approach based on robust PCA to improve bankruptcy forecasting. *Review of Accounting and Finance* 18: 296–320. [CrossRef]

Sun, Jie, Hui Li, Qing-Hua Huang, and Kai-Yu He. 2014. Predicting financial distress and corporate failure—A review from the state-of-the-art definitions, modeling, sampling, and featuring approaches. *Knowledge-Based Systems* 57: 41–56. [CrossRef]

Tam, Kar Yan. 1991. Neural network models and the prediction of bank bankruptcy. *Omega* 19: 429–45. [CrossRef]

Tian, Shaonan, and Yan Yu. 2017. Financial ratios and bankruptcy predictions: An international evidence. *International Review of Economics and Finance* 51: 510–26. [CrossRef]

Tian, Shaonan, Yan Yu, and Hui Guo. 2015. Variable selection and corporate bankruptcy forecasts. *Journal of Banking & Finance* 52: 89–100.

Tsai, Chih-Fong. 2014. Combining cluster analysis with classifier ensembles to predict financial distress. *Information Fusion* 16: 46–58. [CrossRef]

Watson, John, and Jim Everett. 1999. Small business failure rates-choice of definition and industry effects. *International Small Business Journal* 17: 33–49. [CrossRef]

Wu, Desheng Dash, Yidong Zhang, Dexiang Wu, and David L. Olson. 2010. Fuzzy multi-objective programming for supplier selection and risk modeling: A possibility approach. *European Journal of Operational Research* 200: 774–87. [CrossRef]

Xiao, Zhi, Xianglei Yang, Ying Pang, and Xin Dang. 2012. The prediction for listed companies' financial distress by using multiple prediction methods with rough set and Dempster-Shafer evidence theory. *Knowledge-Based Systems* 26: 196–206. [CrossRef]

Zapranis, Achilleas, and Demetrios Ginoglou. 2000. Forecasting corporate failure with neural network approach: The Greek case. *Journal of Financial Management & Analysis* 13: 11–21.

5

A Comprehensive Review of Corporate Bankruptcy Prediction in Hungary

Tamás Kristóf * and Miklós Virág

Department of Enterprises Finances, Corvinus University of Budapest, Fővám tér 8, 1093 Budapest, Hungary; miklos.virag@uni-corvinus.hu

* Correspondence: tamas.kristof@uni-corvinus.hu

Abstract: The article provides a comprehensive review regarding the theoretical approaches, methodologies and empirical researches of corporate bankruptcy prediction, laying emphasis on the 30-year development history of Hungarian empirical results. In ex-socialist countries corporate bankruptcy prediction became possible more than 20 years later compared to the western countries, however, based on the historical development of corporate bankruptcy prediction after the political system change it can be argued that it has already caught up to the level of international best practice. Throughout the development history of Hungarian bankruptcy prediction, it can be tracked how the initial, small, cross-sectional sample and classic methodology-based bankruptcy prediction has evolved to today's corporate rating systems meeting the requirements of the dynamic, through-the-cycle economic capital calculation models. Contemporary methodological development is characterized by the domination of artificial intelligence, data mining, machine learning, and hybrid modelling. On the basis of empirical results, the article draws several normative proposals how to assemble a bankruptcy prediction database and select the right classification method(s) to accomplish efficient corporate bankruptcy prediction.

Keywords: bankruptcy prediction; classification; credit risk modelling; corporate failure; rating systems

---

1. Introduction

In recent years, the increasing relevance of corporate bankruptcy prediction as a research field has been corroborated also by the fact that several comprehensive reviews emerged in literature with the aim to summarise the key findings of earlier published results. Central-Eastern Europe is not an exception of global tendencies, see inter alia (Kliestik et al. 2018; Pavol et al. 2018; Popescu and Dragota 2018; Prusak 2018; Marek et al. 2019). Corporate bankruptcy prediction in ex-socialist countries became possible more than 20 years later compared to western countries, since before the political system change no bankruptcy event in today's market economy sense existed in the centrally managed planned economies. However, based on the historical development of corporate bankruptcy prediction after the political system change, it can be argued that it has already caught up to the level of international best practice regarding the examined research problems, applied methods, and empirical results.

In Hungary the legislation system was needed to be adjusted to the new socio-economic processes in a relatively short time after the political system change. The establishment of bankruptcy regulations had almost no dogmatic precedents, since the legal field of insolvency had been completely missing from the Hungarian legislative system for forty years. The Act of Bankruptcy as of 1991 qualified a company as insolvent, if its debts exceeded its assets, it did not pay obligations 60 days after maturity, the foreclosure of liabilities was resultless, and/or it cancelled the payments. The Act of Bankruptcy has been modified several times since 1991, however, the fundamental concept of insolvency has not substantially changed. In the current Hungarian legislation system legal failure can have four forms:

- Bankruptcy procedure is a process, in which the debtor initiates a payment moratorium and attempts to make a bankruptcy-agreement.
- Liquidation procedure is a process, which aims to pay off the creditors by dissolving the insolvent debtor without successor in accordance with the law.
- Winding up is a process, when an economic organization, which is in principal still solvent, decides to dissolve itself without successor and pay off the creditors.
- Compulsory strike-off is a process, which results in the dissolution of the economic organization without successor if the court decides so, in particular because of failed winding-up.

Hungary can be proud of the fact that corporate bankruptcy prediction began as early as possible, and has already achieved a 30-year development history having extensive range of results. Many of them, however, were published only in Hungarian making it difficult to analyse by international scholars, and so far no comprehensive review has been written in an international journal to evaluate them. In our opinion time has come to resolve this gap.

The article attempts to synthesize the historical development tendencies of theoretical approaches, methodologies, and empirical researches of corporate bankruptcy prediction, laying emphasis on the 30-year development history of Hungarian empirical corporate bankruptcy prediction models. Throughout the development history of Hungarian bankruptcy prediction, it can be tracked, how the initial, small, cross-sectional sample and classic methodology-based bankruptcy prediction has evolved to today's corporate rating systems meeting the requirements of the dynamic, through-the-cycle economic capital calculation models. Contemporary methodological development is characterized by the domination of artificial intelligence, data mining, machine learning and hybrid modelling.

The article evaluates the development of bankruptcy prediction methodology starting from the linear statistical methods arriving at the contemporary artificial intelligence-based machine learning procedures, providing Hungarian empirical results to the application of all methods.

The research method of completing the literature review was to collect and evaluate all theoretical, methodological and empirical publications that appeared in the field of Hungarian corporate bankruptcy prediction. Considering the fact that Hungary is a relatively small country and the research field is comparatively narrow, it has been possible to provide a review encompassing the all-inclusive set of studies. The range of studies also included the works of Hungarian researchers published abroad together with the publications of Transylvanian-Hungarian bankruptcy modellers.

In our opinion this article might serve as an instructive story for other countries being in similar shoes and for scholars interested in development histories and case studies of the professional field. Since it turned out soon that well-known international corporate bankruptcy models did not perform well in Hungary, emphasis was laid on own empirical model development efforts leading to a diverse experimentation with several approaches and techniques.

2. Theoretical Considerations

Corporate failure has been a research focus for social scientists for a long time. One of the fundamental questions of management and organisation sciences is why certain organisations survive, whereas others disappear (Virág et al. 2013). In recent decades substantial number of publications have emerged in the literature in the fields of business failure, corporate survival, bankruptcy prediction, organisational mortality, financial distress, default prediction, and credit scoring, which might seem to be at first glance different things, however, it is a mutual effort of them that they attempt to predict the occurrence of a failure event with the help of corporate descriptive variables by applying similar methods (Kristóf and Virág 2019a).

It can be concluded that bankruptcy prediction primarily supports the empirical research of corporate survival and failure by exploring the reasons for failure, and by constantly developing the multivariate classification and forecast methodology (Kristóf and Virág 2019b). Bankruptcy prediction has gone through significant progress in the recent 50 years.

In the economic system, the continuous inflow and outflow of economic organizations is a natural phenomenon. According to Schumpeter (1934), corporate failure is a necessary element of effective market economy, which enables to transform the human, physical, and financial resources to other, more productive companies.

Organizational termination has been explained by many approaches of organisational theory (Mellahi and Wilkinson 2004). Classic industrial organisation and organisational ecology emphasise on the deterministic role of environment, and scholars in this field argue that external industrial and environmental conditions leave limited freedom for the managers to make decisions, that is why it is not the managers who are responsible for corporate failure. On the other side, representatives of behaviourist, political, decision theoretic, and organisational psychologist schools pursue a voluntarist approach and blame the activities, decisions, and perceptions of managers for failure. Truth is obviously somewhere between the deterministic and voluntarist approaches.

Two tendencies might be distinguished in the research field of organisational survival (Anheier and Moulton 1999). A greater part of studies examining organisational survival/failure has been carried out at the macro level. Besides modelling financial solvency, the relevant studies survey the dynamics of organisational population, together with entrance and exit from the population. The most extensive survival-researches have been conducted by the representatives of the population ecology approach. A smaller part of studies examining the organisational survival has been performed in forms of organisation-specific analyses. Emphasis has been laid on organisational efficiency and performance criteria. From management side inter alia different behavioural characteristics, inadequate organisational structure, information asymmetry, unfounded decisions, lack of foresight and self-conceit effect might also play a role in failure (Jáki 2013a, 2013b). In the management literature organisational survival is often published in the form of 'rise and fall' of different companies (Kristóf 2008b).

On the basis of case studies and quantitative analyses, several theories were born to explain organisational survival (Virág et al. 2013). However, generalisations derived from empirical researches did not converge into a unified theory of organisational survival; they rather remained competitive and complementary streams. Under such circumstances theories are regarded as 'good', which reveal organisational survival from the most possible aspects, namely which are simultaneously able to deal with the contingency, transaction cost, principal-agent, political, life cycle, cognitive, structural, resource-based, evolutionary and decision theoretic sides of survival, and do not intend to achieve a groundlessly high level of abstraction. A deep analysis of relevant organisational theoretic schools was accomplished by Kristóf (2005b). Considering the fact that the findings of organizational theoretic schools and empirical models partially arrived at controverting results, it is not recommended to define a generic, unified theoretical-methodological framework to research organisational survival.

It raises interesting theoretical problems on how the elaborated mathematical-statistical bankruptcy prediction models can contribute to the economic theories explaining organisational survival and failure. According to Blaug (1980) it can be observed in many fields of economic sciences that different econometric studies arrive at contradicting conclusions, and taking into account the available data no best method exists, on the basis of which it could be decided which conclusion harmonizes best with reality (Scott 1981). Consequently, one might examine contradicting hypotheses throughout several decades (Westgaard 2005).

Despite the fact that as a result of enormous model development efforts a great number of appreciated relationships were found, throughout the decades-long history of bankruptcy prediction no unified consent has been achieved which explanatory variables might best predict corporate failure. The exceptionally wide range of forecast methods, together with the different modelling databases from diverse countries, industries and periods make it remarkably challenging to hypothesise what causes corporate failure and how. The lack of theoretical background to explanatory variables is a true limitation to elaborate a general comprehensive theory of bankruptcy prediction. Without a generally accepted theory, nevertheless, it might be inspiring to conclude that any empirically developed model could well operate in a different period and in a different economic environment. Accordingly, it can be argued that no bankruptcy prediction model might function independently of time, space, and economic environment (Kristóf 2008b). In this aspect Hungary is a special case even among the Central-Eastern European countries, where world-famous and widely applied models showed substantially worse performance compared to their origin and experiences gained with them in other countries (Režňáková and Karas 2015; Altman et al. 2017). No wonder that country-specific bankruptcy prediction models might significantly differ from one another although being estimated using the same modelling techniques and variables (Laitinen and Suvas 2013).

Scientific predictability problem of bankruptcy forecasting is not a unique phenomenon in the field of social sciences. Predictability in social sciences has been serving as a basis of scientific discussions for a long time (Kristóf 2006). Until the end of 1950s scientific theories were judged based on their ability to make predictions. Only in the 1970s did the evaluation of heuristic power supersede the predictive power. The possibility of exact bankruptcy prediction is to be rejected from the theoretical side, since in society and economy there are no universalities like the laws of nature, on the basis of which long-run generalizations could be formed; it is only true in the case of some trivial regularities. If it were possible to exactly predict bankruptcy and similar socio-economic events, then it would be in principal also possible to list the future economic events. However, if this list became known, it would surely inspire several actors to conduct activities, which would obstruct the occurrence of the predicted event.

Hence it is impossible to give an obvious explanation to corporate survival/failure from the viewpoint of philosophy of science. The solution to this problem is the multi-sided theory-building, concurrent observance of more approaches, and simultaneous application of more forecast methods. Theory must drive empirical model development; in addition, the examination of statistical assumptions should be carried out in theoretical context (Virág et al. 2013). To support the development of the scientific field the results of hypothesis-examinations have to be fed back to theory-formulation.

In accordance with the goals of the article, from this point, the general term 'organisation' mentioned in organisational theoretical approaches will be restricted to economic organisations (companies). Overlapping the theoretical explanations, it is worthwhile to consider which methods might be applicable to accomplish efficient corporate bankruptcy prediction.

The use of financial ratios in corporate failure prediction is based on the assumption that the failure process is characterised by a systematic deterioration in the values of the ratios (Laitinen 1991). It can be argued that different financial predictors might be efficient in the different phases of the corporate failure process (Laitinen 1993). Accordingly, firm failure processes have become more and more important concepts, since they allow considering the behaviour of failing firms in the longer perspective, leading to the breakthrough role of dynamization approaches in bankruptcy prediction (Lukason and Laitinen 2019).

3. Methodological Development in the International Literature of Corporate Bankruptcy Prediction

Corporate bankruptcy prediction has attracted substantial attention in science for many decades. According to the research of Du Jardin (2010) throughout the historical development of bankruptcy prediction, models were published worldwide by applying more than 50 different methods and 500 variables. The article encompasses the most distributed methods having the greatest impact on scientific research and practical application.

From a methodological point of view, bankruptcy prediction is a binary classification problem with the aim to differentiate between solvent and insolvent groups of companies as good as possible (Virág 2004). Bankruptcy prediction is regarded as a boundary discipline between corporate finance and statistics (data mining), which attempts to predict the future solvency of companies using financial ratios as explanatory variables applying multivariate methods (Nyitrai 2015a).

Throughout the first half of the 20th century, there were no sophisticated statistical methods and computers available to predict bankruptcy. The financial ratios of failing and non-failing companies were compared, and it was concluded that in case of bankrupt companies the most frequently used ratios behaved worse (Fitzpatrick 1932). The first methodological breakthrough came to pass when Durand (1941) published a univariate discriminant analysis (DA)-based credit scoring model. This method became worldwide spread later with the univariate DA model of Beaver (1966).

Realising that the classification of observations using one variable does not provide a reliable result, Myers and Forgy (1963) applied multivariate regression analysis and DA to elaborate a credit rating system for banking clients. In case of riskier clients multivariate DA showed better results, in particular compared to the earlier applied expert rating system, so more and more attention was given to the method. The breakthrough success was achieved by the world-famous multivariate DA model of Altman (1968), which was able to classify the companies in the sample with 95 percentage of classification accuracy. Since its first publication, the model has gone through several revisions. Despite its great number of successful applications, however, the limitations of the model have come to pass, which can be first led back to the rigorous statistical assumption system of DA, second to the application of a hard default definition as a target variable, and third the usability of the model has been reduced by the fact that it had been developed in a relatively narrow range of companies (American stock exchange corporations), thereby limiting its applicability to populations different from the modelling database.

Since the 1970s the development of the field has been dominated by the modernisation of mathematical-statistical classification methods and the IT solutions supporting them (Nyitrai 2015a). Passing through the distribution and variance assumptions of DA, logistic regression (logit) has become a more and more popular bankruptcy prediction method, which was first applied by Chesser (1974) on a credit risk database. In the global distribution of logit, the publication of Ohlson (1980) represented a milestone, which developed a logit model on a sample of 105 insolvent and 2058 solvent companies, thereby expressing that insolvent companies represent a smaller share in the population compared to the solvent ones. The application of probit regression began in the 1980s for similar methodological reasons (Zmijewski 1984).

Nonparametric methods having no statistical assumption behind appeared in bankruptcy prediction also since the 1980s. Decision trees, which are even today widespread tools to solve classification problems and to accomplish efficient data mining, were first applied for bankruptcy prediction by Frydman et al. (1985).

The 1990s brought new challenges to bankruptcy forecasting scholars and practitioners (Prusak 2005). Several critiques concerned linear or linearizable, robust models and the earlier applied methods. As a result, neural networks (NN) belonging to the family of artificial intelligence methods have been given a boost to improve the reliability of bankruptcy forecast models (Kristóf 2005a). NNs were first applied for bankruptcy prediction by Odom and Sharda (1990). The authors proved that the performance of the three-layer backpropagation networks outperformed the results of earlier methods. Since then NNs have been widely distributed, have gone through substantial developments, and represent one of the most popular methods of today.

In parallel with the spreading of NNs, modern visual clustering procedures have been gaining a wide role in bankruptcy prediction. Self-organising maps (SOM) operating on the principle of unsupervised NNs enabled to cluster databases with unknown output into solvent and insolvent classes (Kiviluoto 1998). Multidimensional scaling (MDS) visualizes the hidden relationships between data, reducing them into multidimensional coordinates (Neophytou and Molinero 2004).

The bankruptcy prediction application of neuro-fuzzy systems has become an intensively researched object since the beginning of 2000s, providing better results compared to traditional NNs (Vlachos and Tolias 2003). In parallel, the support vector machine (SVM) procedure has also been proven to achieve higher classification accuracy than earlier applied methods, which was first published based on a sample of Australian companies using twenty-fold cross-validation (Fan and Palaniswami 2000). In addition, the methods of rough set theory (RST) (Dimitras et al. 1999), k nearest neighbour (KNN) (Ardakhani et al. 2016), Bayes-networks (Sun and Shenoy 2007), genetic algorithms

(GA) (Lensberg et al. 2006), learning vector quantization (LVQ) (Neves and Vieira 2016) and case-based reasoning (CBR) (Bryant 1997) also began to spread in the 2000s.

By the 2010s ensemble methods as a special case of method-combinations have gained significance instead of individually applying certain classification methods (Marqués et al. 2012). The essence of them is multiple bootstrapping and applying classification procedures on several subsamples. The classification power of the final model is the average of that of the individual models, usually outperforming the classification power without using ensemble methods. The most frequently applied ensemble methods are boosting, bagging, random subspace, random forest, Gauss-processes and autoencoder belonging to the family of machine learning procedures (Nyitrai 2015a; Wang 2017). Today's bankruptcy prediction researches are unambiguously dominated by machine learning, data mining, artificial intelligence and hybrid modelling through creatively combining different new methods (Barboza et al. 2017). Bankruptcy prediction as a multivariate classification problem is a very popular topic in data mining competitions aiming at finding more and more reliable and contemporary algorithms, accordingly a constantly widening range of innovative solutions are becoming public day by day.

4. Empirical Development of Hungarian Corporate Bankruptcy Prediction

Under Hungarian conditions, it became possible to scientifically examine bankruptcy prediction at the beginning of 1990s by the appearance of the Bankruptcy Act regulating the cases of legally going into bankruptcy. Throughout the recent thirty years the Hungarian literature and practice of bankruptcy prediction have gone through a substantial improvement. Considering the various research goals and databases, however, the empirically measured differences between the classification powers of the elaborated models have to be interpreted in light of the range and definition of explanatory and target variables. The importance of the scientific field can be well represented by the fact that so far fourteen PhD theses in Hungary have dealt with the theoretical backgrounds, methodological challenges and/or the practical application of corporate bankruptcy prediction (Virág 1993; Arutyunjan 2002; Kiss 2003; Imre 2008; Kristóf 2008b; Oravecz 2009; Kotormán 2009; Felföldi-Szűcs 2011; Hámori 2014; Madar 2014; Nyitrai 2015a; Bozsik 2016; Fejér-Király 2016; Koroseczné Pavlin 2016). The year of 2016 was particularly strong when three PhD theses were published.

4.1. The Era of Classic DA and Logit Models

The first Hungarian corporate bankruptcy prediction study was elaborated by Péter Futó in 1989 who worked in the Industrial Economic Institution. The research used annual report data of Hungarian industrial companies from 1986–1987 and the occurrence of insolvency event in 1988 by using variance analysis (VA) and simplified DA. The definition of insolvency event was the fact the companies could not pay their obligations in at least two months throughout the first six months of 1988. The study was not published; its results were interpreted later by Virág and Hajdu (1998). Empirical results revealed that under Hungarian circumstances it became possible to examine which financial ratios might be extensively applied to predict bankruptcy.

The first published Hungarian bankruptcy models were elaborated by Miklós Virág after a 10 months long study trip in the United States using annual report data from 1990 and 1991 applying DA and logit (Virág 1993). The author applied 15 financial ratios. Within the 154 manufacturing companies involved in the research, 77 were solvent and 77 became insolvent in 1992 (in line with the novel Bankruptcy Act insolvent companies had to declare bankruptcy against themselves). The four-variate DA model had 78, and the five-variate logit model had 82 percentage of classification accuracy (Virág 1996).

Virág and Hajdu (1996) created an early warning bankruptcy model family in 1996 indicating bankruptcy dangers for different sectors and branches of the economy using DA, based on the financial data of 10,000 economic units. Altogether 41 bankruptcy models were built: one for the total economy, ten for the national economic sectors, and thirty for the branches. The accuracy of the 1996 bankruptcy model family covering national economic sectors and branches was well over the earlier models because of the details of the range of activities, namely all of them had more than 90 percent of classification accuracy. The authors drew the conclusion first time in Hungary that throughout the financial classification it was reasonable to examine how the financial situation of a company equated to companies operating in the same industry, and whether or not they became bankrupt (Hajdu and Virág 2001).

Hámori (2001) transformed the financial ratios to his logit model in a way that they could be evaluated monotonously. The author defined certain limits for the value-range of ratios, and he modified the outlier data with predefined theoretical maximum values. To avoid multicollinearity, he created four factors from the ratios. The sample consisted of 685 solvent and 72 insolvent companies. The classification accuracy of the four-factor-model was 95 percent.

Arutyunjan (2002) tested the applicability of foreign DA models on Hungarian agricultural firms. All in all, the author did not regard foreign models as reliable on the database and developed instead an own logit model achieving 92 percentage of classification accuracy.

Virág and Dóbé (2005) examined the solvency of national economic sectors applying the earlier elaborated bankruptcy model family. Input variables were considered using the sector-level aggregated ratios taking into account 30 national economic sectors and 15 financial ratios. The authors defined the average ratio values as units of analysis (centroids). It was concluded that the average picture of the majority of sectors better resembled their own surviving companies, than the bankrupt ones.

4.2. The Era of NNs and Basel II

Kiss (2003) approached the problem from the viewpoint of credit score modelling, defining a mutual comprehensive development framework between bankruptcy prediction and credit scoring. The results of his PhD thesis was the hierarchical ordering of statistical methods, in addition to the elaboration of organisational, IT and decision support framework of scoring systems.

Using the database of the first Hungarian bankruptcy model Virág and Kristóf (2005a) developed NN-based models. Experimenting with different structures a four-layer backpropagation network showed the best result outperforming the DA model by 9 percentage points, and the logit model by 5 percentage points Virág and Kristóf (2005b). The authors later performed a more complex empirical research on the same database comparing the performance of four classification procedures using the industrial mean relative ratios, and again found that NNs outperformed the traditional methods (Virág and Kristóf 2006).

Because of the fact that the Hungarian introduction of Basel II had been approaching, the Supervisory Authority of Financial Institutions launched a tender in 2006 to elaborate databases to support the application of risk management methods in financial institutions. The winner study (Info-Datax 2006) first attempted to explore the problems of statistical methods applied to probability of default (PD) prediction from the methodological side, and then used principal component analysis (PCA) for data reduction. Within the framework of empirical research, the authors compared the performance of DA, logit and decision trees on a sample of 1500 companies. All the three models showed 87–88 percentage of classification accuracy.

Certain methodological reviews of bankruptcy prediction were provided by Halas (2004); Szabadosné Németh and Dávid (2005); Oravecz (2007); Szűcs (2014); Ratting (2015); Reizinger-Ducsai (2016), however, the authors did not carry out own empirical model development. The applicability of earlier published international models were examined on small samples by Kotormán (2009) on agricultural enterprises, Rózsa (2014) on dairy firms, Pető and Rózsa (2015) on meat processing companies, Dorgai et al. (2016) on commercial enterprises and Fenyves et al. (2016) on hotels with more or less success. A small-sample model development was performed by Sütő (2018) and Ékes and Koloszár (2014).

Organisational theoretic approaches explaining corporate survival, theoretical, methodological and practical problems of bankruptcy prediction, together with the best-practice application of corporate failure models were brought together by Kristóf (2008b). Considering the industrial mean corrected variables, comparing the results of models built with and without PCA, altogether the NN models showed the best result by 84 percentage of area under receiver operating characteristic (AUROC), pursued by the logit model developed on the principal components (83 percentage), and then came the performance of decision trees developed using the original variables (81 percentage). In addition, the MDS and SOM were first time applied in Hungary for bankruptcy modelling purposes in the same study, proving the clustering and variable selection capabilities of the two methods.

Meanwhile, the bankruptcy prediction in Transylvania also attempted to catch up to international best practice. The first Transylvanian-Hungarian bankruptcy prediction models were developed by Benyovszki and Kibédi (2008) on a sample of 129 companies from Baia Mare using logit and probit, achieving 81 percent of classification accuracy with both models. The most comprehensive theoretical, methodological and empirical researches were carried out in Szeklerland in the 2010s, when different logit and NN-based models were developed on a sample of companies from Hargitha County (Fejér-Király 2015, 2016, 2017). Based on the empirical findings it can be concluded that the behaviour of Hargitha County companies is different from Hungarian experiences, since no size variable became significant in Transylvania, whereas turnover ratios showed real added value, in contrast to earlier experiences in Hungary. In addition, it was proven that applying PCA and the inclusion of macroeconomic variables provided better models.

Felföldi-Szűcs (2015) researched the predictability of buyers' non-performance derived from granting commercial loans on the sample of 905 Hungarian small and middle enterprises. The target variable was the 90 days past due event happened on behalf of the buyers. Correspondingly to banking credit risk models the author proved by logit that behavioural, non-financial variables contributed to better discriminatory power, compared to models developed using the traditional financial ratios (Felföldi-Szűcs 2011). It was an important finding in Hungary, and corroborated the results gained in other European countries, especially for small and medium enterprises (SMEs) (see i.a. Lukason and Andresson 2019).

4.3. The Challenges of Data Transformations and Method Combinations

Besides the substantial number of publications regarding comparative analytical bankruptcy prediction studies, more and more emphasis was laid on publications emphasising the importance of data preparation and data transformation procedures (Kristóf 2008a). The study of Hámori (2014) drew attention to the detection and handling of different data preparation anomalies (missing values, outliers, division by zero, double negative divisions, null per null divisions etc.) together with demonstrating a handbook-like methodological guidance and case studies to resolve the perceived problems.

Representativity of modelling sample and the problem of sampling bias were in-depth researched by Oravecz (2009). The results of her PhD thesis were the definition of missing data handling techniques together with the elaborated reject inference methods applicable in credit score modelling to manage sampling bias. The author justified on a sample of 2279 observations using logit that stronger sampling bias led to weaker model performance.

Within the framework of a small-sample empirical research Virág and Kristóf (2009) projected the dissimilarities between solvent and insolvent observations into coordinates of a lower dimensional space applying MDS, and developed a logit model on the reduced dimensional coordinates achieving outstanding classification accuracy.

The impact of relating stock balance sheet items to flow profit-and-loss statement items on the performance of bankruptcy prediction models was in-depth researched by Nyitrai (2017). The effects of handling outliers on model performance in different manners were examined by Nyitrai and Virág (2019). It was concluded that categorisation by Chi-square automatic interaction detection (CHAID) decision trees more effectively handled outliers than coercing by external percentiles or by the mean ± different standard deviations.

Examining further the favourable impact of decision trees on model performance, it was demonstrated by Kristóf and Virág (2012) on a sample of 504 Hungarian companies that the performance of logit and NN models can be further improved by applying variables discretized by CHAID decision trees compared to the application of original variables. However, PCA did not provide added value to the classification power of the models.

The efficiency of combining decision trees and NNs was proven by Bozsik (2011). The author ordered single-layer perceptron networks to the peaks of C4.5 decision trees on a sample of 250 companies using 17 variables. Both the developed brute force and fine-tuned slim models achieved 84 percentage of classification accuracy.

The impacts of company size and industry on bankruptcy models were examined by Nyitrai (2018), using the sample of annual report data from 2007–2015 of 2614 Hungarian enterprises. On the basis of the developed logit models it was proven that both company size and industry influence the design and performance of bankruptcy models.

4.4. Dynamization and Through-the-Cycle Modeling

In line with the through-the-cycle modelling requirements of Basel Capital Accord Imre (2008) applied first in Hungary time-series input variables of 2000 companies from 2002–2006, supplementing the accustomed variables by company form, county and industry. The target variable of the decision tree, logit and NN models was the occurrence of 90 days past due event. In static approach (without dynamizing the variables) the AUROC on the testing sample was 90 percentage in case of logit and NN models in contrast to the 83 percent performance of decision trees. However, by applying the dynamized variables expressing the timely change, the model performance of NN improved to 92 percentage, that of logit to 91 percentage, and that of decision trees to 84 percentage, thereby it was proven first time in Hungary that the application of dynamized variables did have a positive impact on the classification power of bankruptcy prediction models.

Insolvency prediction of 10–250 million HUF revenue Trans-Danubian companies was researched by Bareith et al. (2014) applying NNs with 1-1 hidden layers. Because of the impact of financial crisis, the database was partitioned into two economic cycles: 2002–2008 and 2009–2012. In both periods the financial ratios of three historical years were considered, filtering out the non-relevant variables with the help of a relative importance (RI) based variable selection. More dynamic variables were included in both periods. The model developed on the 2002–2008 period achieved 85 percentage of classification accuracy, compared to the 79 percentage of classification accuracy measured on the model developed using data of the 2009–2012 period. The authors performed a similar empirical research two years later on companies from Csongrád County without partitioning the period of data collection, and achieved an even higher performing neural network model (Bareith et al. 2016). Financial ratios of liquidated small enterprises were in-depth examined by Koroseczné Pavlin (2016) throughout the years before going into liquidation, showing considerable empirical results in the field.

In line with the Basel requirements, Madar (2014) elaborated a corporate rating system applying logit, which was suitable to estimate long-term PD and economic capital, using the database of a credit institution portfolio from 2007–2012 containing 78,516 observations. The author converted the original variables with the help of weight-of-evidence (WOE) transformation. The target variable was the censored default rate. The study revealed the importance of model stability and PD calibration, and proposed techniques to resolve the problems, considering the fact that in crisis periods substantially higher PD can be measured compared to the periods of economic growth.

In the field of dynamic modelling Bauer and Endrész (2016) published an outstanding study that applied a very long historical database from 1996–2014. Combining micro and macro variables the authors developed a probit model for the population of Hungarian double-entry bookkeeping companies, specifying legal failure as the target variables, handling the heterogeneity by company size. The AUROC of the model was 86 percentage.

With the aim of a Central Bank and credit institution sector research Banai et al. (2016) developed PD models for the total population of credited Hungarian SMEs by linking the database of the Central Credit Information (CCI) and financial report data, supplemented with macroeconomic variables. Data collection considered the period of 2007–2014, the target variable was the non-performing event derived from delinquent loan payment. Dynamic logit models were segmented per company size. Certain variables were categorized, lagged or discretized. The micro enterprise model had 75, the small enterprise model 79 and the middle enterprise model 84 percentage of AUROC. The model performance was less favourable than the previously developed model using legal failure as the target variable, since the non-performing event of CCI (60 days past due) is a significantly softer criterion than legal failure.

Similar research was carried out by Nyitrai and Virág (2017b) on time series financial ratios of 1542 Hungarian companies from the period of 2001–2014. Logit was applied using ten-fold cross-validation. Variables were retrospectively dynamized for all historical periods with the help of the formula earlier published by Nyitrai (2014). AUROC showed tendentiously stronger model performance when considering more and more historical years through model development. It was concluded that in case of companies younger than 10 years it was worthwhile to apply as many years as available, however, in case of companies older than 10 years the application of the last 10 years resulted in best model performance. The same authors performed similar empirical research on a different sample containing 1354 companies, which corroborated the findings (Nyitrai and Virág 2017a), which was also in compliance with the findings of an earlier modelling research performed by three different decision trees on a sample of 1082 enterprises (Virág and Nyitrai 2015).

The positive impact of dynamization on predictive power was again proven by Nyitrai (2019b) with the help of a recent Hungarian empirical research. Trends of financial ratios were expressed by indicator variables, and the minimum and maximum values of previous periods were represented as benchmarks in the models. Applying ten-fold cross-validation the developed DA, logit and decision tree models showed that dynamized variables improved classification accuracy compared to models developed from the original static variables. In addition, it was demonstrated by Nyitrai (2019a) that creating categorical variables from the number of nodes of CHAID decision trees coming from subsequent years arrived at better predictive power compared to the approach by using the original data as input variables.

To meet the requirements of IFRS-9 international accounting standards for financial instruments it became necessary to extend the one-year range of failure event to long-term. Forward-looking to the term of financial instruments Kristóf and Virág (2017) and Kristóf (2018b) developed 20-year PD forecast models for Hungarian companies applying continuous, non-homogeneous Markov chains.

4.5. Machine Learning and Data Mining

SVM was applied on a Hungarian corporate database for the first time by Virág and Nyitrai (2013) on the sample of the first bankruptcy model. Using different kernel functions the SVM model was altogether able to classify the observations 5 percentage points better than the best benchmark NN model.

Within the framework of experimenting with machine learning procedures on Hungarian companies Virág and Nyitrai (2014a) applied the RST method on the first Hungarian bankruptcy model database. In addition, the authors attempted to find answer to the question whether it was worthwhile to disregard model interpretability to achieve higher classification accuracy. Results showed that applying RST through generating easily interpretable 'if-then' rules provided similar results compared to SVM; accordingly, the trade-off between the interpretability and performance of the models became out of question.

Virág and Nyitrai (2014b) compared the performance of the two most frequently applied ensemble methods (adaboost, bagging) in the case of C4.5 decision trees using the sample of 976 Hungarian companies having financial report data for the period of 2001–2012. Model performance of the original financial ratios was compared to the model developed using the ratios after industrial mean correction, and to the model developed using dynamized ratios. To avoid sampling problems, hundred-fold cross-validation was applied. The best result was achieved by using the bagging procedure, which was underperformed by the adaboost procedure by 1 percentage point, and by 6 percentage points using the standalone C4.5. Empirical results again proved the favourable model performance impact of dynamized variables; however, industrial mean ratios did not contribute to improvement.

The KNN was applied to Hungarian bankruptcy prediction first by Nyitrai (2015b). The study examined the classification accuracy of different models developed on a balanced sample of 1000 observations using different k values, distance definitions, and variables 1, 2 and 3 years before bankruptcy and derived from multi-period variables. The best result was achieved by the model developed using the multi-period variables (80 percentage), which was followed by the model using variables 1 year before the occurrence of bankruptcy (77 percentage). Results also revealed that certain financial ratios rather give early warning indication to potential bankruptcy in the short-run, whereas others in the long-run. The author performed empirical research in the same year using CHAID decision trees and arrived at similar conclusions (Nyitrai 2015a).

CBR as a relative method to KNN was applied for Hungarian bankruptcy prediction by Kristóf (2018a) on a sample of 1,828 micro-enterprises. To make input variables orthogonal to one another the study applied PCA. The nearest neighbours were determined by the reduced dimensionality tree (RDT) method. Although the classification accuracy of the CBR model outperformed the decision trees and was similar to logit, eventually it was smaller than that of the benchmark NN model.

After carrying out the proper data preparation steps on a balanced sample of 1534 Hungarian small enterprises Boda et al. (2016) applied the component-based object comparison for objectivity (COCO) proximity analysis with different step-functions, the WizWhy data mining procedure with different layers and rule-systems, in addition logit and NN as benchmark models. Eventually COCO, logit and NN also provided 80 percent of classification accuracy, however, the WizWhy model optimised with different logics and hybrid rule systems built on already realised partial results achieved 92 percentage of classification accuracy.

Realizing the opportunities of flexible and adaptive artificial intelligence modelling Bozsik (2016) developed several hybrid artificial intelligence-based bankruptcy models by combining the advantages of different methods. From the innovative study the fuzzy system combined by SVM (FSVM) using Gauss-kernel function showed exceptional classification accuracy (93 percent). Another remarkable hybrid model was the five-layer adaptive neuro-fuzzy (ANFIS) developed by Gauss membership functions having 84 percentage of classification accuracy.

Boros (2018) experimented with several machine learning algorithms examining their impact on credit risk models using a sample of 10,000 companies. After variable selection, PCA and WOE categorisation eventually the NN model with 82 percent of AUROC became better than the SVM model (81 percent of AUROC) followed by stochastic gradient boosting (76 percent of AUROC). Initial models developed using variables without categorisation showed significantly worse performance.

4.6. Summary of Hungarian Bankruptcy Models

Evaluating the most important features and results of Hungarian corporate bankruptcy prediction, it can be argued that the country can be really proud of the rich set of empirical models and methodological development throughout the analysed period. Table 1 provides a systematic summary of the studies in a chronological order showing a comprehensive picture how development took place in time.

Table 1. Summary of Hungarian empirical corporate bankruptcy models.

Author	Year	Explanatory Variables	Target Variable	Size of Sample	Classification Method	Model Performance [1]
Miklós Virág	1993	financial ratios	legal failure	154	DA, Logit	82%
Miklós Virág and Ottó Hajdu	1996	financial ratios	legal failure	10,000 (partitioned per industry)	DA	98%
Gábor Hámori	2001	financial ratios	legal failure	757	Factor/Logit	95%
Alex Arutyunjan	2002	financial ratios	legal failure	146	DA, Logit	92%
Miklós Virág and Tamás Kristóf	2005	financial ratios	legal failure	154	DA, Logit, NN	87%
Info-Datax	2006	financial ratios	Basel II default	1500	PCA/DA, Logit, CART	88%
Miklós Virág and Tamás Kristóf	2006	industrial mean corrected financial ratios	legal failure	154	DA, Logit, CART, NN	86%
Balázs Imre	2008	dynamized financial ratios, qualitative characteristics	90+ delinquency	2000	Logit, CART, NN	92%
Tamás Kristóf	2008	industrial mean corrected financial ratios, qualitative characteristics	legal failure	504	PCA/DA, Logit, CHAID, NN	84%
Annamária Benyovszki and Kamilla Kibédi	2008	financial ratios	legal failure	129	Logit, Probit	81%
Beatrix Oravecz	2009	loan application variables	defaulted loan	2279	Reject inference/Logit	79%
Miklós Virág and Tamás Kristóf	2009	financial ratios	legal failure	100	MDS/Logit	94%
József Bozsik	2011	financial ratios	legal failure	250	C4.5/NN/brute force, fine-tuned slim	84%
Nóra Felföldi-Szűcs	2011	receivable behavioural variables, financial ratios	non-performing buyer	1398	PCA/Logit	75%
Tamás Kristóf and Miklós Virág	2012	financial ratios	legal failure	504	CHAID split/PCA/Logit, RPA, NN	95%
Miklós Virág and Tamás Nyitrai	2013	financial ratios	legal failure	154	NN, SVM	95%
Tibor Bareith, Rita Koroseczné Pavlin and György Kövér	2014	financial ratios	legal failure	8004 (partitioned per period)	RI/NN	85%
László Madar	2014	financial ratios, qualitative characteristics	legal failure, withdrawn tax number, initiated execution	78,516	WOE/Logit	72%

Table 1. *Cont.*

Author	Year	Explanatory Variables	Target Variable	Size of Sample	Classification Method	Model Performance [1]
Miklós Virág and Tamás Nyitrai	2014	financial ratios	legal failure	154	NN, SVM, RST	89%
Tamás Nyitrai	2014	dynamized financial ratios	legal failure	1000	CHAID	78%
Miklós Virág and Tamás Nyitrai	2014	dynamized financial ratios	legal failure	976	Adaboost/Bagging/C4.5	83%
Nóra Felföldi-Szűcs	2015	receivable behavioural variables, financial ratios	90+ delinquency	905	Logit	70%
Tamás Nyitrai	2015	dynamized financial ratios	legal failure	1000	KNN	80%
Tamás Nyitrai	2015	dynamized financial ratios	legal failure	1000	CHAID	78%
Miklós Virág and Tamás Nyitrai	2015	dynamized financial ratios	legal failure	1082	CART, CHAID, C4.5	81%
Tibor Bareith, Rita Koroseczné Pavlin and György Kövér	2016	financial ratios	legal failure	2483	RI/NN	96%
Dániel Boda, Martin Luptak, László Pitlik, Gábor Szűcs and István Takács	2016	financial ratios	legal failure	1534	Logit, NN, COCO, Wizwhy	92%
Péter Bauer and Marianna Endrész	2016	financial ratios, qualitative characteristics, macro variables	legal failure	1,585,663 firm-year observations	Probit	86%
Gergely Fejér-Király	2016	financial ratios, macro variables	legal failure	1075	PCA/Logit, NN	97%
József Bozsik	2016	financial ratios	legal failure	200	Gauss/FSVM, ANFIS	93%
Ádám Banai, Gyöngyi Körmendi, Péter Lang and Nikolett Vágó	2016	dynamized financial ratios, macroeconomic data	60+ delinquent payment	2,166,541 firm-year observations (partitioned per size)	Logit	84%
Tamás Nyitrai and Miklós Virág	2017	dynamized financial ratios	legal failure	1354	Logit	81%
Tamás Nyitrai and Miklós Virág	2017	dynamized financial ratios	legal failure	1542	Logit	92%
Tamás Nyitrai	2018	dynamized financial ratios, size, industry	legal failure	2614	CHAID/Logit	91%
Bence Boros	2018	financial ratios	non-performing loan	10,000	PCA/WOE/Logit, NN, SVM, gradient boosting	82%

Table 1. *Cont.*

Author	Year	Explanatory Variables	Target Variable	Size of Sample	Classification Method	Model Performance [1]
Tamás Kristóf	2018	financial ratios	legal failure	1828	PCA/Logit, CHAID, NN, RDT-CBR	87%
Tamás Nyitrai	2019	dynamized financial ratios	legal failure	3370	DA, Logit, CHAID	83%
Tamás Nyitrai	2019	dynamized financial ratios	legal failure	2098	CHAID/DA	95%
Tamás Nyitrai and Miklós Virág	2019	dynamized financial ratios	legal failure	2996	CHAID/DA, Logit, CHAID, CART, NN	87%

[1] According to classification matrix or AUROC (see the applied model performance indicator in the body text of the article for each model). The best model performance is presented, if more than one model was developed.

5. Conclusions

After the comprehensive review of relevant literature and the completely analysed 30-year of Hungarian empirical results the following normative proposals can be drawn for researchers and practitioners working in the field of corporate bankruptcy prediction.

- Considering the validity of a key theoretical finding that no bankruptcy prediction model might function independently of time, space and economic environment, it is not recommended to apply bankruptcy models on Hungarian companies that were developed on foreign corporate samples, regardless of their popularity and high citation. If it is not possible to develop an own bankruptcy model, the study revealed that a great number of Hungarian bankruptcy models were already published, which had been developed on representative Hungarian samples using diverse methods, proven to be applicable to reliably estimate the PD for Hungarian companies.

- It was also proven throughout several empirical researches in Hungary that appropriate implementation of data preparation and data transformation steps truly contribute to the predictive power of models; thereby it can be concluded that it is even more essential to professionally carry out them than to make the decision which classification method to apply. Within data transformation steps the categorisation of input variables must be emphasised, which simultaneously improve the predictive power of models, handle outliers and make models more stable in time. For this purpose, categorisation with decision trees and WOE can also be regarded as efficient.

- Studying the characteristics of bankruptcy models developed on historical databases in Hungary it can be concluded that the dynamization of input variables improve the classification accuracy of bankruptcy models. The longer historical time-series we have when dynamizing the variables, the better results we might expect. This finding is intensely true to improve model stability. At the same time, it has to be emphasised that such models can only be applicable to companies having the desired number of closed financial years, accordingly for younger companies another model has to be developed, which might have a worse classification power.

- Hungarian empirical results have also shown that in case if—beyond to the financial ratios calculated from public sources—reliable information is available about the financial behaviour of the given corporate clients/partners, including such behavioural variables to model development, better model performance can be achieved compared to model development considering only traditional financial ratios, especially when modelling the financial risks of SMEs.

- Assembling bankruptcy prediction modelling database, the problem of sampling bias has to be handled with care, otherwise it might result in a worse model performance. However, sampling problems perceived on smaller databases might be well handled by cross-validation, which provides a suitable method to prevent overtraining. At the same time, however, the definition of target variable also has a substantial impact on model performance, since the non-performing event derived from delinquent payment; represent a substantially lower criterion compared to legal failure. In addition, if large modelling sample is available, it is worthwhile to develop models separately for segments and/or industries.

- With regard to model development methodology, nowadays the two most spread techniques are the logit and NN-based bankruptcy modelling pursued by the decision trees. Considering the fact that the application of artificial intelligence and data mining-based methodologies are constantly emerging, it is recommended that at least as a benchmark model the classification power of the three most frequently applied methods must be compared to the performance of any new model. Development of innovative hybrid models are expressively supported, since they successfully combine the advantages of certain methods with others, thereby contributing to better model performance. In addition, it has to be recognised that the application of traditional bankruptcy prediction methods setting rigorous mathematical-statistical criteria (DA) might evidently raise model performance problems, which is a substantial argument against their interpretability accustomed in recent decades.

References

Altman, Edward I. 1968. Financial ratios, discriminant analysis and the prediction of corporate bankruptcy. *The Journal of Finance* 23: 589–609. [CrossRef]

Altman, Edward I., Malgorzata Iwanicz-Drozdowska, Erkii K. Laitinen, and Arto Suvas. 2017. Financial distress prediction in an international context: a review and empirical analysis of Altman's Z-score model. *Journal of International Financial Management & Accounting* 28: 131–71. [CrossRef]

Anheier, Helmut K., and Lynne Moulton. 1999. Organizational Failures, Breakdowns, and Bankruptcies. In *When Things Go Wrong. Organizational Failures and Breakdowns*. Edited by Helmut K. Anheier. Thousand Oaks: Sage Publications, pp. 3–14.

Ardakhani, Mehdi N., Vahid Zare Mehrjerdi, Mohsen Sarvi, and Elias Sarvi. 2016. A survey of the capability of k nearest neighbors in prediction of bankruptcy of companies based on selected industries. *Scinzer Journal of Accounting and Management* 2: 27–37. [CrossRef]

Arutyunjan, Alex. 2002. A mezőgazdasági vállalatok fizetésképtelenségének előrejelzése. Ph.D. thesis, Szent István Egyetem, Gödöllő, Hungary.

Banai, Ádám, Gyöngyi Körmendi, Péter Lang, and Nikolett Vágó. 2016. A magyar kis- és középvállalati szektor hitelkockázatának modellezése. In *MNB Tanulmányok 123*. Budapest: Magyar Nemzeti Bank.

Barboza, Flavio, Herbert Kimura, and Edward I. Altman. 2017. Machine learning models and bankruptcy prediction. *Expert Systems with Applications* 83: 405–17. [CrossRef]

Bareith, Tibor, Rita Koroseczné Pavlin, and György Kövér. 2014. Felszámolások vizsgálata a Nyugat-dunántúli régióban. *E-CONOM* 3: 102–24. [CrossRef]

Bareith, Tibor, Rita Koroseczné Pavlin, and György Kövér. 2016. Felszámolások előrejelzésének vizsgálata Csongrád megyei vállalkozások esetén. In *Móra Akadémia Szakkollégiumi Tanulmánykötet*. Edited by Attila Kovács and Gyöngyvér Bíró. Szeged: Szegedi Tudományegyetem Móra Ferenc Szakkollégium, pp. 11–26.

Bauer, Péter, and Marianna Endrész. 2016. Modelling bankruptcy using Hungarian firm-level data. In *MNB Occasionnal Papers 122*. Budapest: Magyar Nemzeti Bank.

Beaver, William H. 1966. Financial ratios as predictors of failure. Empirical research in accounting: selected studies. *Journal of Accounting Research* 4: 1–111. [CrossRef]

Benyovszki, Annamária, and Kamilla Kibédi. 2008. Vállalati csődelőrejelzés többváltozós statisztikai módszerrel. *Közgazdász Fórum* 11: 3–17.

Blaug, Mark. 1980. *The Methodology of Economics: or How Economists Explain*. Los Angeles: Boland.

Boda, Dániel, Martin Luptak, László Pitlik, Gábor Szűcs, and István Takács. 2016. Prediction of insolvency of Hungarian micro enterprises. In *Proceedings of the ENTRENOVA–ENTerprise Research InNOVAtion Conference, Rovinj, Croatia, September 8–9*. Zagreb: IRENET–Society for Advancing Innovation and Research in Economy, pp. 352–59.

Boros, Bence. 2018. *Artificial Intelligence and Automation in Credit Scoring*. Budapest: KPMG Tanácsadó Kft.

Bozsik, József. 2011. Decision tree combined with neural networks for financial forecast. *Periodica Polytechnica Electrical Engineering* 55: 95–101. [CrossRef]

Bozsik, József. 2016. Heurisztikus eljárások alkalmazása a csődelőrejelzésben. Ph.D. thesis, Eötvös Loránd Tudományegyetem, Budapest, Hungary.

Bryant, Stephanie M. 1997. A case-based reasoning approach to bankruptcy prediction modeling, Intelligent Systems in Accounting. *Finance and Management* 6: 195–214. [CrossRef]

Chesser, Delton L. 1974. Predicting loan noncompliance. *Journal of Commercial Bank Lending* 56: 28–38.

Dimitras, Augustinos I., Roman Slowinski, Robert Susmaga, and Constantin Zopounidis. 1999. Business failure prediction using rough sets. *European Journal of Operational Research* 114: 263–80. [CrossRef]

Dorgai, Klaudia, Veronika Fenyves, and Dávid Sütő. 2016. Analysis of Commercial Enterprises' Solvency by Means of Different Bankruptcy Models. *Gradus* 3: 341–49.

Du Jardin, Philippe. 2010. Predicting bankruptcy using neural networks and other classification methods: The influence of variable selection techniques on model accuracy. *Neurocomputing* 70: 2047–60. [CrossRef]

Durand, David. 1941. *Risk Elements in Consumer Instalment Financing.* New York: National Bureau of Economic Research.

Ékes, Szeverin Kristóf, and László Koloszár. 2014. The efficiency of bankruptcy forecast models in the Hungarian SME sector. *Journal of Competitiveness* 6: 56–73. [CrossRef]

Fan, Alan, and Marimuthu Palaniswami. 2000. Selecting Bankruptcy Predictors Using a Support Vector Machine Approach. In *Proceedings of the International Joint Conference on Neural Networks.* Neural Computing: New Challenges and Perspectives for the New Millennium, Como, Italy, July 27, pp. 354–59. [CrossRef]

Fejér-Király, Gergely. 2015. Bankruptcy Prediction: A Survey on Evolution, Critiques, and Solutions. *Acta Universitatis Sapiantiae Economics and Business* 3: 93–108. [CrossRef]

Fejér-Király, Gergely. 2016. Csődelőrejelző modellek alkalmazhatósága Hargita megyei vállalkozásoknál. Ph.D. thesis, Szent István Egyetem, Gödöllő, Hungary.

Fejér-Király, Gergely. 2017. Csődelőrejelzés a KKV-szektorban pénzügyi mutatók segítségével. *Közgazdász Fórum* 20: 3–29.

Felföldi-Szűcs, Nóra. 2011. Hitelezés vevői nemfizetés mellett. A bank és a szállító hitelezési döntése. Ph.D. thesis, Budapesti Corvinus Egyetem, Budapest, Hungary.

Felföldi-Szűcs, Nóra. 2015. A vevői nemfizetés előrejelzése viselkedési jellemzők segítségével. *Gradus* 2: 1–9.

Fenyves, Veronika, Krisztina Dajnoki, Máté Domicián, and Kata Baji-Gál. 2016. Examination of the solvency of enterprises dealing with accommodation service providing in the Northern Great Plain Region. *SEA: Practical Application of Science* 4: 197–203.

Fitzpatrick, Paul J. 1932. *A Comparison of the Ratios of Successful Industrial Enterprises with Those of Failed Companies.* Washington: The Accountants' Publishing Company.

Frydman, Halona, Edward I. Altman, and Duen-Li Kao. 1985. Introducing recursive partitioning for financial classification: The case of financial distress. *The Journal of Finance* 40: 269–91. [CrossRef]

Hajdu, Ottó, and Miklós Virág. 2001. A Hungarian model for predicting financial bankruptcy. *Society and Economy in Central and Eastern Europe* 23: 28–46.

Halas, Gábor. 2004. Hogyan mérjünk nemfizetési valószínűséget? Módszertani összehasonlítás. In *Mérés-Határ-Műhely tanulmány.* Budapest: Info-Datax Kft.

Hámori, Gábor. 2001. A fizetésképtelenség előrejelzése logit-modellel. *Bankszemle* 45: 65–87.

Hámori, Gábor. 2014. Predikciós célú klasszifikáló statisztikai modellek gyakorlati kérdései. Ph.D. thesis, Kaposvári Egyetem, Kaposvár, Hungary.

Imre, Balázs. 2008. Bázel II definíciókon alapuló nemfizetés-előrejelzési modellek magyarországi vállalati mintán (2002–2006). Ph.D. thesis, Miskolci Egyetem, Miskolc, Hungary.

Info-Datax. 2006. *Módszertani elemzés a nemfizetési valószínűség modellezéshez.* A PSZÁF "A pénzügyi szervezetek kockázatainak (partner, működési, likviditási stb.) tőkemegfelelési követelményeiből adódó, üzleti alkalmazásokat segítő módszerek kidolgozása és a módszerek működéséhez szükséges adatbázisok kiépítése" c. pályázatára készült tanulmány. Budapest: Info-Datax Kft.

Jáki, Erika. 2013a. A válság, mint negatív információ és bizonytalansági tényező–A válság hatása az egy részvényre jutó nyereség előrejelzésekre. *Közgazdasági Szemle* 60: 1357–69.

Jáki, Erika. 2013b. Szisztematikus optimizmus a válság idején. *Vezetéstudomány* 44: 37–49.

Kiss, Ferenc. 2003. A credit scoring fejlődése és alkalmazása. Ph.D. thesis, Budapesti Műszaki Egyetem, Budapest, Hungary.

Kiviluoto, Kimmo. 1998. Predicting bankruptcies with the self-organizing map. *Neurocomputing* 21: 191–201. [CrossRef]

Kliestik, Tomas, Jana Kliestikova, Maria Kovacova, Lucia Svabova, Katarina Valaskova, Marek Vochozka, and Judit Oláh. 2018. *Prediction of Financial Health of Business Entities in Transition Economies.* New York: Addleton Academic Publishers.

Koroseczné Pavlin, Rita. 2016. A felszámolási eljárás alá került hazai kisvállalkozások helyzetének elemzése. Ph.D. thesis, Kaposvári Egyetem, Kaposvár, Hungary.

Kotormán, Annamária. 2009. A mezőgazdasági vállalkozások felszámolásához vezető okok elemzése. Ph.D. thesis, Debreceni Egyetem, Debrecen, Hungary.

Kristóf, Tamás, and Miklós Virág. 2012. Data reduction and univariate splitting–Do they together provide better corporate bankruptcy prediction? *Acta Oeconomica* 62: 205–27. [CrossRef]

Kristóf, Tamás, and Miklós Virág. 2017. Lifetime probability of default modelling for Hungarian corporate debt instruments. In *ECMS 2017: 31st European Conference on Modelling and Simulation.* Edited by Zita Zoltayné Paprika. Nottingham: ECMS-European Council for Modelling and Simulation, pp. 41–46.

Kristóf, Tamás, and Miklós Virág. 2019a. A csődelőrejelzés fejlődéstörténete Magyarországon. *Vezetéstudomány* 50: 62–73. [CrossRef]

Kristóf, Tamás, and Miklós Virág. 2019b. Corporate failure prediction in Hungary–a comparative review. In *Diversity of Business Development Vol. III. Continuity and Openness.* Edited by Nikolett Deutsch. Beau Bassin: Lambert Academic Publishing, pp. 83–101.

Kristóf, Tamás. 2005a. A csődelőrejelzés sokváltozós statisztikai módszerei és empirikus vizsgálata. *Statisztikai Szemle* 83: 841–63.

Kristóf, Tamás. 2005b. Szervezetek jövőbeni fennmaradása különböző megközelítésekben. *Vezetéstudomány* 36: 15–23.

Kristóf, Tamás. 2006. Is it possible to make scientific forecasts in social sciences? *Futures* 38: 561–74. [CrossRef]

Kristóf, Tamás. 2008a. A csődelőrejelzés és a nem fizetési valószínűség számításának módszertani kérdéseiről. *Közgazdasági Szemle* 55: 441–61.

Kristóf, Tamás. 2008b. Gazdasági szervezetek fennmaradásának és fizetőképességének előrejelzése. Ph.D. thesis, Budapesti Corvinus Egyetem, Budapest, Hungary.

Kristóf, Tamás. 2018a. A case-based reasoning alkalmazása a hazai mikrovállalkozások csődelőrejelzésére. *Statisztikai Szemle* 96: 1109–28. [CrossRef]

Kristóf, Tamás. 2018b. Vállalatok hosszú távú (15-20 éves) bedőlési valószínűségének előrejelzése. In *A múltból átívelő jövő: VIII. Magyar (Jubileumi) Jövőkutatási Konferencia: 50 éves a magyar jövőkutatás, Budapest, 2018. november 14-15.* Edited by Erzsébet Nováky and Andrea S. Gubik. Győr: Palatia Nyomda és Kiadó Kft, pp. 193–205.

Laitinen, Erkki K. 1991. Financial ratios and different failure processes. *Journal of Business Finance & Accounting* 18: 649–73. [CrossRef]

Laitinen, Erkii K. 1993. Financial predictors for different phases of the failure process. *Omega* 21: 215–28. [CrossRef]

Laitinen, Erkki K., and Arto Suvas. 2013. International applicability of corporate failure risk models based on financial statement information: comparisons across European countries. *Journal of Finance & Economics* 1: 1–26. [CrossRef]

Lensberg, Terje, Aasmund Eilifsen, and Thomas E. McKee. 2006. Bankruptcy theory development and classification via genetic programming. *European Journal of Operational Research* 169: 677–97. [CrossRef]

Lukason, Oliver, and Art Andresson. 2019. Tax arrears versus financial ratios in bankruptcy prediction. *Journal of Risk and Financial Management* 12: 187–200. [CrossRef]

Lukason, Oliver, and Erkki K. Laitinen. 2019. Firm failure processes and components of failure risk: An analysis of European bankrupt firms. *Journal of Business Research* 98: 380–90. [CrossRef]

Madar, László. 2014. Scoring rendszerek hatásai a gazdasági tőkeszámítás során alkalmazott portfoliómodellek eredményeire. Ph.D. thesis, Kaposvári Egyetem, Kaposvár, Hungary.

Marek, Durica, Katarina Valaskova, and Katarina Janoskova. 2019. Logit business failure prediction in V4 countries. *Engineering Management in Production and Services* 11: 54–64. [CrossRef]

Marqués, Ana I., Vicente García, and Javier Salvador Sánchez. 2012. Exploring the behaviour of base classifiers in credit scoring ensembles. *Expert Systems with Applications* 39: 10244–50. [CrossRef]

Mellahi, Kamel, and Adrian Wilkinson. 2004. Organizational failure: a critique of recent research and a proposed integrative framework. *International Journal of Management Reviews* 5–6: 21–41. [CrossRef]

Myers, James H., and Edward W. Forgy. 1963. The development of numerical credit evaluation systems. *Journal of the American Statistical Association* 58: 799–806. [CrossRef]

Neophytou, Evi, and Cecilio Mar Molinero. 2004. Predicting Corporate Failure in the UK: A Multidimensional Scaling Approach. *Journal of Business Finance and Accounting* 31: 677–710. [CrossRef]

Neves, Joao Antunes Nuno, and Armando Vieira. 2016. Improving bankruptcy prediction with hidden layer Learning Vector Quantization. *European Accounting Review* 15: 253–71. [CrossRef]

Nyitrai, Tamás, and Miklós Virág. 2017a. A pénzügyi mutatók időbeli tendenciájának figyelembevétele logisztikus regresszióra épülő csődelőrejelző modellekben. *Statisztikai Szemle* 95: 5–28. [CrossRef]

Nyitrai, Tamás, and Miklós Virág. 2017b. Magyar vállalkozások felszámolásának előrejelzése pénzügyi mutatóik idősorai alapján. *Közgazdasági Szemle* 64: 305–24. [CrossRef]

Nyitrai, Tamás, and Miklós Virág. 2019. The effects of handling outliers on the performance of bankruptcy prediction models. *Socio-Economic Planning Sciences* 67: 34–42. [CrossRef]

Nyitrai, Tamás. 2014. Növelhető-e a csőd-előrejelző modellek előrejelző képessége az új klasszifikációs módszerek nélkül? *Közgazdasági Szemle* 66: 566–85.

Nyitrai, Tamás. 2015a. Dinamikus pénzügyi mutatószámok alkalmazása a csődelőrejelzésben. Ph.D. thesis, Budapesti Corvinus Egyetem, Budapest, Hungary.

Nyitrai, Tamás. 2015b. Hazai vállalkozások csődjének előrejelzése a csődeseményt megelőző egy, két, illetve három évvel korábbi pénzügyi beszámolók adatai alapján. *Vezetéstudomány* 46: 55–65.

Nyitrai, Tamás. 2017. Stock és flow típusú számviteli adatok alkalmazása a csődelőrejelző modellekben. *Vezetéstudomány* 48: 68–77. [CrossRef]

Nyitrai, Tamás. 2018. A vállalatok tevékenységi körének és méretének hatása a csődelőrejelző modellekre. *Statisztikai Szemle* 96: 973–1000. [CrossRef]

Nyitrai, Tamás. 2019a. CHAID alapú felülvizsgált kategorizálás a csődelőrejelzésben. *Statisztikai Szemle* 97: 656–86. [CrossRef]

Nyitrai, Tamás. 2019b. Dynamization of bankruptcy models via indicator variables. *Benchmarking: An International Journal* 26: 317–32. [CrossRef]

Odom, Marcus D., and Ramesh Sharda. 1990. A neural network model for bankruptcy prediction. Paper present at the International Joint Conference on Neural Networks, San Diego, CA, USA, June 17–21; Ann Arbor: IEEE Neural Networks Council, vol. II, pp. 163–71.

Ohlson, James A. 1980. Financial ratios and the probabilistic prediction of bankruptcy. *Journal of Accounting Research* 18: 109–31. [CrossRef]

Oravecz, Beatrix. 2007. Credit scoring modellek és teljesítményük értékelése. *Hitelintézeti Szemle* 6: 607–27.

Oravecz, Beatrix. 2009. Szelekciós torzítás és csökkentése az adósminősítési modelleknél. Ph.D. thesis, Budapesti Corvinus Egyetem, Budapest, Hungary.

Pavol, Kral, Svabova Lucia, and Durica Marek. 2018. Overview of the selected bankruptcy prediction models applied in V4 countries. *Balkans Journal of Emerging Trends in Social Sciences* 1: 70–78. [CrossRef]

Pető, Dalma, and Andrea Rózsa. 2015. Financial future prospect investigation using bankruptcy forecasting models in Hungarian meat processing industry. *Annals of the University of Oradea Economic Science* 24: 801–9.

Popescu, Madalina E., and Victor Dragota. 2018. What do post-communist countries have in common when predicting financial distress? *Prague Economic Papers* 27: 1–17. [CrossRef]

Prusak, Błażej. 2005. *Modern Methods of Predicting Financial Risk in Companies*. Warsaw: Difin.

Prusak, Błażej. 2018. Review of research into enterprise bankruptcy prediction in selected Central and Eastern European countries. *International Journal of Financial Studies* 6: 60–88. [CrossRef]

Ratting, Anita. 2015. Fizetésképtelenség-előrejelzési megközelítések. *Társadalom és Gazdaság* 7: 53–73. [CrossRef]

Reizinger-Ducsai, Anita. 2016. Bankruptcy prediction and financial statements. The reliability of a financial statement for the purpose of modeling. *Prace Naukowe Uniwersytetu Ekonomicznego We Wrocławiu* 441: 202–13. [CrossRef]

Režňáková, Mária, and Michal Karas. 2015. The prediction capabilities of bankruptcy models in different environment: an example of the Altman model under the conditions in the Visegrad Group countries. *Ekonomický časopis* 63: 617–33.

Rózsa, Andrea. 2014. Financial performance analysis and bankruptcy prediction in Hungarian dairy sector. *Annals of Faculty of Economics* 1: 938–47. [CrossRef]

Schumpeter, Joseph. 1934. *The Theory of Economic Development*. Cambridge: Harvard Business Press.

Scott, James. 1981. The probability of bankruptcy: A comparison of empirical predictions and theoretical models. *Journal of Banking & Finance* 5: 317–44. [CrossRef]

Sun, Lili, and Prakash P. Shenoy. 2007. Using Bayesian networks for bankruptcy prediction: Some methodological issues. *European Journal of Operational Research* 180: 738–53. [CrossRef]

Sütő, Dávid. 2018. Észak-alföldi élelmiszer-kiskereskedelmi vállalkozások pénzügyi helyzetének elemzése logitmodell segítségével. *Acta Carolus Robertus* 8: 223–35. [CrossRef]

Szabadosné Németh, Zsuzsanna, and László Dávid. 2005. A kis- és középvállalati szegmens mulasztási valószínűségének előrejelzése magyarországi környezetben. *Hitelintézeti Szemle* 4: 39–58.

Szűcs, Tamás. 2014. A csődmodellek és azok módozatai. *E-Controlling* 14: 1–8.

Virág, Miklós, and Ottó Hajdu. 1996. Pénzügyi mutatószámokon alapuló csődmodell-számítások. *Bankszemle* 15: 42–53.

Virág, Miklós, and Ottó Hajdu. 1998. Pénzügyi viszonyszámok és csődelőrejelzés. In *Bankról, pénzről, tőzsdéről. Válogatott előadások a Bankárképzőben 1988-1998*. Edited by Tamás Bácskai. Budapest: Nemzetközi Bankárképző, pp. 440–57.

Virág, Miklós, and Sándor Dóbé. 2005. A hazai csődmodell család alkalmazása ágazati centroidokra. *Vezetéstudomány* 36: 45–54.

Virág, Miklós, Tamás Kristóf, Attila Fiáth, and Judit Varsányi. 2013. *Pénzügyi elemzés, csődelőrejelzés, válságkezelés*. Budapest: Kossuth Kiadó.

Virág, Miklós, and Tamás Kristóf. 2005a. Az első hazai csődmodell újraszámítása neurális hálók segítségével. *Közgazdasági Szemle* 52: 144–62.

Virág, Miklós, and Tamás Kristóf. 2005b. Neural networks in bankruptcy prediction–a comparative study on the basis of the first Hungarian bankruptcy model. *Acta Oeconomica* 55: 403–25. [CrossRef]

Virág, Miklós, and Tamás Kristóf. 2006. Iparági rátákon alapuló csődelőrejelzés sokváltozós statisztikai módszerekkel. *Vezetéstudomány* 37: 25–35.

Virág, Miklós, and Tamás Kristóf. 2009. Többdimenziós skálázás a csődmodellezésben. *Vezetéstudomány* 40: 50–58.

Virág, Miklós, and Tamás Nyitrai. 2013. Application of support vector machines on the basis of the first Hungarian bankruptcy model. *Society and Economy* 35: 227–48. [CrossRef]

Virág, Miklós, and Tamás Nyitrai. 2014a. Is there a trade-off between the predictive power and the interpretability of bankruptcy models? The case of the first Hungarian bankruptcy prediction model. *Acta Oeconomica* 64: 419–40. [CrossRef]

Virág, Miklós, and Tamás Nyitrai. 2014b. Metamódszerek alkalmazása a csődelőrejelzésben. *Hitelintézeti Szemle* 13: 180–95.

Virág, Miklós, and Tamás Nyitrai. 2015. Csődelőrejelző modellek dinamizálása. In *Vezetés és szervezet társadalmi kontextusban: Tanulmányok Dobák Miklós 60. születésnapja tiszteletére*. Edited by Bakacsi Gyula, Károly Balaton and Miklós Dobák. Budapest: Akadémiai Kiadó, pp. 284–304.

Virág, Miklós. 1993. Pénzügyi viszonyszámokon alapuló teljesítmény-megítélés és csődelőrejelzés. C.Sc. thesis, Budapesti Közgazdaságtudományi Egyetem, Budapest, Hungary.

Virág, Miklós. 1996. *Pénzügyi elemzés, csődelőrejelzés*. Budapest: Kossuth Kiadó.

Virág, Miklós. 2004. A csődmodellek jellegzetességei és története. *Vezetéstudomány* 35: 24–32.

Vlachos, Dimitros, and Yannis A. Tolias. 2003. Neuro-fuzzy modeling in bankruptcy prediction. *Yugoslav Journal of Operational Research* 13: 165–74. [CrossRef]

Wang, Nanxi. 2017. Bankruptcy Prediction Using Machine Learning. *Journal of Mathematical Finance* 7: 908–18. [CrossRef]

Westgaard, Sjur. 2005. *What Can Modern Statistical and Mathematical Techniques Add to the Analysis and Prediction of Bankruptcy?* Trondheim: Department of Industrial Economics and Technology Management, Norwegian University of Science and Technology.

Zmijewski, Mark E. 1984. Methodological issues related to the estimation of financial distress prediction models. *Journal of Accounting Research* 22: 59–82. [CrossRef]

6

Support Vector Machine Methods and Artificial Neural Networks used for the Development of Bankruptcy Prediction Models and their Comparison

Jakub Horak *●, Jaromir Vrbka● and Petr Suler

School of Expertness and Valuation, Institute of Technology and Business in Ceske Budejovice, Okruzni 517/10, 37001 Ceske Budejovice, Czech Republic; vrbka@mail.vstecb.cz (J.V.); petr.suler@cez.cz (P.S.)
* Correspondence: horak@mail.vstecb.cz

Abstract: Bankruptcy prediction is always a topical issue. The activities of all business entities are directly or indirectly affected by various external and internal factors that may influence a company in insolvency and lead to bankruptcy. It is important to find a suitable tool to assess the future development of any company in the market. The objective of this paper is to create a model for predicting potential bankruptcy of companies using suitable classification methods, namely Support Vector Machine and artificial neural networks, and to evaluate the results of the methods used. The data (balance sheets and profit and loss accounts) of industrial companies operating in the Czech Republic for the last 5 marketing years were used. For the application of classification methods, TIBCO's Statistica software, version 13, is used. In total, 6 models were created and subsequently compared with each other, while the most successful one applicable in practice is the model determined by the neural structure 2.MLP 22-9-2. The model of Support Vector Machine shows a relatively high accuracy, but it is not applicable in the structure of correct classifications.

Keywords: neural networks; support vector machine; bankruptcy model; prediction; bankruptcy

1. Introduction

In financial bankruptcy analysis, the diagnosis of companies at risk for bankruptcy is crucial in preparing to hedge against any financial damage the at-risk firms stand to inflict (Kim et al. 2018). According to Rybárová et al. (2016), bankruptcy models are early warning systems based on the analysis of selected indicators able to identify a thread for financial health of a company. Kiaupaite-Grushniene (2016) states that creation of reliable models of bankruptcy prediction is essential for various decision-making processes. According to Mousavi et al. (2015), frequently used models are mainly Altman Z-Score, Taffler Z-Score, and Index IN95.

A wide number of academic researchers from all over the world have been developing corporate bankruptcy prediction models, based on various modelling techniques. Numerous statistical methods have been developed (Balcaen and Ooghe 2004). Despite the popularity of the classic statistical methods, significant problems relating to the application of these methods to corporate bankruptcy prediction remain. Problems related to statistical methods according to Balcaen and Ooghe (2004, p. 1):

1. The dichotomous dependent variable,
2. The sampling method,
3. Nonstationarity and data instability,
4. The use of annual account information,
5. The selection of the independent variables,
6. The time dimension.

For the purpose of this article, Support Vector Machines (SVM) and artificial neural networks are used. These two methods have been used by many authors to predict corporate bankruptcy, and their results suggest that these two methods are more appropriate than traditional statistical methods (Shin et al. 2005; Xu et al. 2006; Kim et al. 2018; Vochozka and Machová 2018; Machová and Vochozka 2019; Krulický 2019). SVM is sensitive to model form, parameter setting and features selection. SVM, firstly developed by Vapnik in 1995 (Vapnik 1995), is a supervised learning model with associated learning algorithms that analyze data and recognize patterns, used for classification and regression analysis (Burges 1998). According to Lu et al. (2015), compared with other algorithms, SVM has many unique advantages when applied in solving small sample, nonlinear, and high-dimensional pattern recognition problem. The concept of a neural network has been developed in biology and psychology, but its use goes to other areas, such as business and economics (Vochozka 2017). They are especially valuable where inputs are highly correlated, missing, or there are nonlinear systems and they can capture relatively complex phenomena (Enke and Thawornwong 2005). Like any method, SVM or artificial neural networks have disadvantages. Although SVM or artificial neural networks have a good performance on classification accuracy, one main disadvantage of these methods is the difficulty in interpreting the results (Härdle et al. 2009).

The aim of the paper is to develop bankruptcy prediction models and compare results of different methods using classification methods, namely Support Vector Machines and artificial neural networks (multilayer perceptron artificial neural networks—MLP and radial basis function artificial neural networks—RBF). Further to the defined goal, we will ask a research question: "Are artificial neural networks (also NN) more accurate in predicting bankruptcy than SVM?"

The article meets the formal criteria of a scientific text. In the part of literature review there are described methods for evaluation of corporate bankruptcy, attention is paid to artificial neural networks and SVM methods. The methodological part describes used data for the calculation, specifies the particular variables used and presents two above mentioned methods. In the results part there are presented the results achieved by SVM method, then the results obtained by artificial neural networks and the results of both methods are compared. The results are also compared with the results of other authors and the added value of the article is defined. The final part summarizes the results, presents the variables that have the greatest predictive power and suggests further research in this area.

2. Literature Review

Company activities are directly or indirectly influenced by various external and internal factors (Boguslauskas and Adlyte 2010). Purvinis et al. (2005) argue that unfavourable business environment, risky decisions of business managers, and unexpected and disadvantageous events may influence a company in insolvency and lead to bankruptcy. Hafiz et al. (2015) state that bankruptcy models are mainly needed by financial entities, e.g., banks. Their advantage consists especially in their ability to provide clear information about potential risks and eliminate such problems in a timely manner. They are important for current and future decision-making (López Iturriaga and Sanz 2015). Predictive models of financial bankruptcy enable to take timely strategic measures in order to avoid financial distress (Baran 2007). For other stakeholders, such as banks, effective and automated rating tools will enable to identify possible financial distress of potential clients (Gestel et al. 2006). The ability to accurately predict business failure is a very important topic in financial decision-making (Mulačová 2012).

A very useful tool to predict the development of companies going to bankrupt is by using artificial neural networks (ANNs) or Support Vector Machine (SVM). Currently, neural networks are applicable in various areas. ANNS are used for solving possible future difficulties, e.g., for predicting company bankruptcy (Pao 2008; Klieštik 2013). Sayadi et al. (2014) state that their main advantages are the ability to generalize and to learn. According to Machová and Vochozka (2019), the disadvantages of ANNs include possible illogical behaviour of networks and required high quality data. Vochozka and Machová (2018) state that ANNs are currently one of the most popular prediction methods.

The SVM method has become a powerful tool for solving problems in machine learning. Many SVM algorithms include solving of convex problems, such as linear programming, quadratic programming, as well as nonconvex and more general problems with optimization, such as integer programming, bilevel programming, etc. However, there are also certain disadvantages of SVM. An important issue that has not been solved fully is choosing the parameters of the core functions. In practical terms, the crucial problem of SVM is its high algorithmic complexity and extensive requirements for the memory of required quadratic programming in complex tasks (Tian et al. 2012).

The aim of Erdogan (2013) was to apply the SVM method in analysing bank bankruptcy. In this work, the SVM method was applied for the analysis of financial indicators. The author states that SVB is able to extract useful information from financial data and can thus be used as a part of early warning system. Chen and Chen (2011) state that the prediction of financial crisis of a company is an important and widely discussed topic. They used particle swarm optimization (PSO) to obtain optimized parameter settings for the SVM method. Moreover, they used the PSO's integrated commitment with the SVM approach to create a model of predicting financial crisis. Experimental results have shown that the approach is efficient in finding better parameter settings and significantly improves the success rate in predicting company financial crisis. Since financial indicators are independent variables, Park and Hancer (2012) applied ANNs on bankruptcy of a company operating in catering and compared the results with the results of logit model. On the basis of empirical results of these two methodologies, ANNs showed higher accuracy than logit model in sample testing. Dorneanu et al. (2011) use ANNs for predicting company bankruptcy. According to the authors, the use of ANNs for the prediction is extremely effective, since the percentage of prediction accuracy is higher than in the case of using conventional methods. The objective of Kim (2011) is to provide an optimal approach to company bankruptcy predicting and to explore functional characteristics of multivariate discriminant analysis, ANNs and the SVM method in predicting the bankruptcy of a specific company. The results have shown that ANNs and SVM are models applicable for predicting company bankruptcy and show promising results. On the basis of the information obtained, the objective of this paper can be considered relevant.

3. Materials and Methods

The Albertina database will be the source of data concerning industrial companies operating in the Czech Republic. In terms of sufficient amount of data and in particular the number of companies in liquidation and thus the relevance of the results, more fields within section C—Manufacturing of the CZ-NACE (comes from French – Czech Nomenclature statistique des Activités économiques dans la Communauté Européenne) = Classification of Economic Activities, will be used, namely in the groups 10–33:

- 10: Manufacture of food products.
- 11: Manufacture of beverages.
- 12: Manufacture of tobacco products.
- 13: Manufacture of textiles.
- 14: Manufacture of wearing apparel.
- 15: Manufacture of leather and related products.
- 16: Manufacture of wood and products of wood and cork, except furniture.
- 17: Manufacture of paper and paper products.
- 18: Printing and reproduction of recorded media.
- 19: Manufacture of coke and refined petroleum products.
- 20: Manufacture of chemicals and chemical products.
- 21: Manufacture of basic pharmaceutical products and pharmaceutical preparations.
- 22: Manufacture of rubber and plastic products.
- 23: Manufacture of other non-metallic mineral products.
- 24: Manufacture of basic metals; foundry.

- 25: Manufacture of fabricated metal products, except machinery and equipment.
- 26: Manufacture of computer, electronic and optical products.
- 27: Manufacture of electrical equipment.
- 28: Manufacture of machinery and equipment.
- 29: Manufacture of motor vehicles (except motorcycles), trailers and semi-trailers.
- 30: Manufacture of other transport equipment.
- 31: Manufacture of furniture.
- 32: Other manufacturing.
- 33: Repairs and installation of machinery and equipment.

For the same reasons, the selection of data will not be limited by the size of companies and the number of employees. The output will thus be applicable not only in specific companies, but basically in the whole economic sector.

The data series will consist of five consecutive fiscal years—for each year all the companies in liquidation will be selected and similarly, randomly selected three times the number of active enterprises. The numbers of companies for individual years are then as follows:

- Year 2013: 488 in liquidation, 1464 active,
- Year 2014: 416 in liquidation, 1248 active,
- Year 2015: 354 in liquidation, 1062 active,
- Year 2016: 287 in liquidation, 862 active,
- Year 2017: 163 in liquidation, 489 active.

The same companies will be selected for each year. Different numbers are due to the fact that some companies went bankrupt during the monitored period, ceased to be active and went into liquidation, etc. The sample starts in 2013, that is, in the period of constant economic growth following the period of economic crisis. The authors tried to avoid the results of the models to be affected by economic crisis.

Financial statements, specifically balance sheets and profit and loss statements of all the above mentioned companies will be analysed. Table 1 shows selected financial data and their averages per individual years.

Table 1. Selected financial data of data sample.

Active Companies						
Financial Data	2013	2014	2015	2016	2017	Total
Total assets	113,590.43	112,398.89	72,359.06	92,463.05	102,843.14	91,228.91
Fixed assets	51,794.64	48,418.16	32,899.65	41,244.60	49,662.11	40,808.34
Current assets	61,093.99	63,352.86	38,750.26	50,275.42	52,550.73	49,762.88
Liabilities in total	113,590.43	112,398.89	72,359.06	92,358.40	102,843.14	91,228.91
Equity	51,663.05	53,660.95	39,599.74	42,971.99	59,471.72	44,077.03
Borrowed capital	61,076.00	58,079.58	32,437.83	46,616.22	42,632.01	46,275.94
Operating result	1574.10	14,159.14	4604.23	7104.33	10,576.95	6263.25
Economic result for accounting period	1282.11	11,387.14	3168.16	5231.82	9325.24	4916.57
Companies in Liquidation						
Financial Data	2013	2014	2015	2016	2017	Total
Total assets	22,033.59	21,401.33	20,401.53	14,201.20	10,273.09	77,297.73
Fixed assets	6307.66	6768.54	5231.99	5439.59	1481.12	33,904.17
Current assets	15,615.94	14,447.03	15,116.56	8639.67	8670.90	42,801.79
Liabilities in total	22,033.23	21,390.77	20,400.42	14,201.20	10,273.09	77,254.27
Equity	5454.03	5998.58	7499.03	1768.26	2140.76	37,917.64
Borrowed capital	16,453.56	15,338.02	12,813.47	12,382.05	8064.87	38,566.51
Operating result	−1791.99	−166.49	−1219.85	214.53	284.29	7107.70
Economic result for accounting period	−1910.42	−151.22	−1492.21	116.79	141.06	5516.93

Note: all data in the Table are given in thousands of CZK. Source: own construction.

The data will be checked. Only the data that, at first sight, is not defective or intentionally distorted will be kept on the file for further analysis. This will eliminate record lines (a line represents financial statements per company and year) including:

1.   Different assets and liabilities balance,
2.   Negative assets,
3.   Negative fixed assets,
4.   Negative tangible fixed assets,
5.   Negative current assets,
6.   Negative financial assets,
7.   Negative inventories.

The input continuous variables will be:

- AKTIVACELK—Total assets resulting from past economic operations. Thus it means the future economic benefit of the company.

- STALAA—Fixed assets are long-term, fixed and noncurrent. This item includes asset components used for the company business in a long term (more than 1 year) and consumed over time.

- HIM—Intangible fixed assets will depreciate, expressed by the level of depreciation. Intangible fixed assets have a significant impact on the value of the enterprise, they maintain their value for a longer time and are not exposed to the fast operating cycle.

- OBEZNAA—Current assets characterize the operating cycle. They continuously circulate and change their form. They include cash, material, semi-finished products, work in progress, products, or receivables from customers.

- Z—Inventories are current (short-term) assets of the company. They are consumed during operation. In general, inventories include material, inventories for production of its own products and goods

- KP—Short-term receivables are payable in less than 1 year from the date when their arise and represent the creditor's right to seek fulfilment of a certain obligation from the other party, the receivable is extinguished when the obligation is paid.

- FM—Financial assets including long-term and short-term financial assets. Long-term financial assets hold their value for a longer period of time, they do not change into cash quickly. They include securities, bonds, certificates of deposit, obligations, term deposits or loans granted to companies. Short-term financial assets are used for operation, especially for payment of liabilities. Short-term assets represent high liquidity; the expected holding is less than one year. They mainly include money in bank accounts, treasury, checks, clearing notes, valuables or short-term securities and shares.

- PASIVACELK—Total liabilities—information concerning the source to cover the company's assets.

- VLASTNIJM—Equity is the internal source of finance for business assets and capital formation. It includes, in particular, contributions of the founders (owners or partners) to the capital stock and components arising from the business management.

- FTZZ—Reserve funds, undistributable reserves and other funds from profit represent the company's internal sources of finance increasing the company's equity without changing its capital stock. Reserve funds are used as internal resources to cover future losses of the company. Undistributable reserves are created by cooperatives also to cover the loss.

- HVML—Profit/loss brought forward is part of liabilities, an item of equity. These are resources created after tax in previous years. These are funds which are not transferred to funds or distributed and paid. It consists of three parts - retained earnings, loss carried forward and other profit/loss brought forward.

- HVUO—Profit and loss of the current financial period is the sum of profit and loss from operations and financial activities in the financial period and the profit before tax. For calculation, the income tax for ordinary activities is deducted.

- CIZIZDROJE—External resources are the company's debts which must be paid within a certain period of time. These are the company's payables to other entities.

- KZ—Current liabilities are payable within 1 year and used for financing (together with equity) of the normal operation of the company. In particular, they include short-term bank loans, payables to employees and institutions, debts to suppliers or delinquent tax.

- V—Production is goods and services that are used to meet the needs. They result from business activities of the company and characterize the main business activities—production.

- VS—Production consumption mainly includes the costs of consumed material, energy, travel expenses, maintenance and repairs, or low-value assets. It is a sum item which correlates with consumption of materials, services and energy.

- SPMAAEN—Material and energy consumption is an item accounting for inventories - current assets. Energy consumption rises proportionally and positively correlates with the production volume. However, material costs may decrease as the production volume increases. Material consumption is directly dependent on consumption standards and purchase prices.

- SLUZBY—Services are systematic external activities that satisfy human needs, or the business needs in their own course.

- PRIDHODN—Value added represents the sales margin, sales, stock level changes of internally produced inventories, or capitalization less production consumption. It includes the sales margin as well as production.

- MZDN—Payroll costs generally comprise of the employee's gross wages and premiums paid by the employer for each employee's social security and health insurance.

- NNSOCZAB—Employee's social security and health insurance costs.

- OHANIM—Depreciation of intangible and tangible fixed assets provides a tool for gradually assigning the value of fixed assets to expenses. Therefore, it means a gradual assignment of the fixed asset cost value to expenses. It represents depreciation of fixed assets.
The categorical output variable will be considered as:

- STAV—Identifies the situation of the company whether active or in liquidation. There will only be two possible outcomes.

The variables were chosen so that it was possible to express the main features of the company´s capital structure, sources of assets financing, corporate payment history, customers´ payment history, cost structure, and the ability to generate outcomes (sales) and realized added value. The selection of indicators is based on the analysis of the existing Altman Z-Score (Altman 1968, 2000, 2003; Altman and Hotchkiss 2006), IN (Neumaierová and Neumaier 2005, 2008), Taffler index (Taffler and Tisshaw 1977; Taffler 1983), Kralicek Quick Test (Kralicek 1993), Harry Pollak´s method (Pollak 2003), and Vochozka´s method (Vochozka 2010; Vochozka and Sheng 2016; Vochozka et al. 2017). The conditions of external environment are not considered, as all companies in the dataset operate in one market, and therefore they are all influenced equally. The output is thus analogy to certain extent. If patterns are identified (although given by a large number of input variables combinations), it is possible to observe a similar development of two companies showing just about the same combination of input variables on the basis of similarity.

The Statistica software, version 13 of TIBCO will be used to apply the classification methods.

3.1. Support Vector Machines

Machine Learning option in the Data Mining module will be used to apply SVM. The file will be divided into a train (75%) and a test (25%) data subset. Then SVM type 2 will be specified where the error function is identified as:

$$\frac{1}{2}w^T w - C\left[v\varepsilon + \frac{1}{N}\sum_{i=1}^{N}(\zeta_i + \zeta_{i\cdot})\right],\tag{1}$$

which minimizes the entity to:

$$\begin{aligned}\left[w^T\varnothing(x_1) + b\right] - y_i &\leq \varepsilon + \zeta_i\\ y_i - \left[w^T\varnothing(x_1) + b_i\right] &\leq \varepsilon + \zeta_{\cdot i}\\ \zeta_i, \zeta_{\cdot i} &\geq 0,\ i = 1,\ \ldots,\ N,\ \varepsilon \geq 0.\end{aligned}\tag{2}$$

Then the SVM (kernel function) will be selected. In this case, it will be Sigmoid that should be able to identify the extreme values:

$$K(X_i, X_j) = \tan h(\gamma X_i \cdot X_j + C),\tag{3}$$

where $K(X_i, X_j) = \varphi(X_i)\cdot\varphi(X_j)$, which means that SVM function represents an output value of input variables projected in multidimensional space using transformation φ.

The results (value 10, seed 1000) will then be cross-validated. A maximum of 10,000 iterations will be performed with a possible ending in case of the error 0.000001.

3.2. Artificial Neural Networks

Classification analysis based on multilayer perceptron neural networks and radial basis function neural networks. ANS (automatic neural network) mode will be used. In case of unsatisfactory results, the result may be corrected using the custom network designer.

The set will be divided by random into three groups of enterprises—i.e., a train file (where neural networks are trained to achieve the best results)—70% of the data, a test file (identify if the classification of trained neural structures is successful)—15% data and a validation file (used for additional verification of the result)—15% of data. Only MLP and RBF will be used in the calculation. For MLP networks, the minimum number of hidden neurons will be set to 8 and the maximum number to 25 while for RBF, the minimum will be 21 and the maximum will be 30 hidden neurons. The number of networks for training will be 10,000 whereas 5 networks with the best results will be retained. The error function will be the sum of squares:

$$E_{SOS} = \frac{1}{2N}\sum_{i=1}^{N}(y_i - t_i)^2,\tag{4}$$

where N is number of training cases, y_i is predicted target variable t_i, t_i is target variable of a i-th case.

The BFGS algorithm (Broyden–Fletcher–Goldfrarb–Shanno) will be used for calculation, for more details see Bishop (1995).

Another error function will be entropy (or, cross entropy error function):

$$E_{CE} = \sum_{i=1}^{N} t_i \ln\left(\frac{y_i}{t_i}\right),\tag{5}$$

The activation functions shown in Table 2 will be considered for NN.

Table 2. Activation functions of MLP and RBF hidden and output layer.

Function	Definition	Range
Identity	a	$(-\infty; +\infty)$
Logistic sigmoid	$\frac{1}{1+e^{-a}}$	$(0;1)$
Hyperbolic tangent	$\frac{e^a-e^{-a}}{e^a+e^{-a}}$	$(-1;+1)$
Exponential	e^{-a}	$(0; +\infty)$
Sine	$\sin(a)$	$[0; 1]$
Softmax	$\frac{\exp(a_i)}{\sum \exp(a_i)}$	$[0; 1]$
Gaussian	$\frac{1}{\sqrt{2\pi}\sigma} \exp\left[-\frac{(x-\mu)^2}{2\sigma^2}\right]$	

Source: own construction.

Neural networks work as follows: the data of a specific company are entered and subsequently, as an independent variable, the data are converted using the activation function and weights into the values of hidden neurons, which are the input variables for the second round of calculation. Here, the activation function and trained weights as used as well. The result obtained is subsequently compared at a given interval, and it is determined whether or not the company is able to survive possible financial distress.

Other settings will remain default. The result will be a bankruptcy model (the development of the company will be evaluated using two variables—survival of the company or a bankruptcy tendency—thus, the dependent variable will only take two values 0 or 1). The model development will be an iterative and recurrent process with actions to improve. The data to be analysed does not have to follow the normal distribution, the dependent variable is binary. The resulting model will have generalized characteristics—it will be applicable for prediction and the efficiency of classification into groups should be better than by chance, i.e., the efficiency of classification should be higher than 50%.

4. Results

4.1. Support Vector Machines

The defined inputs were used for calculation of a SVM model in C ++ code. The basic parameters are: 22 input continuous variables, 1 output categorical variable, classification type 2, Sigmoid function. 1162 vectors were created for active companies and 1161 vectors for companies in liquidation. The relevance of the model is examined in more detail in Table 3.

Table 3. SVM model prediction status.

	Status—Active Company	Status—In liquidation	Status—All
Total	4606	1582	6188
Correct	4578	130	4708
Incorrect	28	1452	1480
Correct (%)	99.39	8.22	76.08
Incorrect (%)	0.61	91.78	23.92

Source: own construction.

The accuracy of classifications, or predictions is more than 76%. This is certainly positive in terms of the model success. However, remember that this percentage consists of more than 99% of correct predictions of active companies and only above 8% of predictions of the companies in liquidation. Therefore, the model is not fully applicable in practice.

4.2. Artificial Neural Networks

10,000 artificial neural structures were calculated of which 5 with the best characteristics were retained (see Table 4).

Table 4. Retained neural networks.

Statistics	1	2	3	4	5
Network name	MLP 22-6-2	MLP 22-9-2	MLP 22-12-2	MLP 22-8-2	MLP 22-12-2
Training performance	81.46353	83.01016	82.2253	82.40997	83.05633
Testing performance	80.38793	81.89655	81.03448	81.25	81.14224
Validation performance	81.35776	82.65086	83.40517	82.65086	83.40517
Training algorithm	BFGS 170	BFGS 332	BFGS 56	BFGS 110	BFGS 220
Error function	Entropy	Entropy	SOS	Entropy	Entropy
Hidden activation func.	Tanh	Tanh	Identity	Logistic	Tanh
Output activation func.	Softmax	Softmax	Logistic	Softmax	Softmax

Source: own construction.

The best characteristics of generated neural structures are exclusively shown by MLP networks. NNs have 22 neurons in the input layer (based on 22 input continuous variables), 6 to 12 neurons in the hidden layer and 2 neurons in the output layer (based on one output categorical variable that can take two values). Entropy was the error function in four cases, the sum of squares in one. The identity, logistic and hyperbolic tangent functions were used to activate the hidden layer of neurons. The logistic and Softmax functions were used to activate the output layer of neurons. The performance of individual networks is always above 81% in the train data set and above 80% in the test data set and above 81% in the validation set. Thus, the performance seems very high. Table 5 shows the performance decomposition.

Table 5. Predictions of artificial neural networks.

Network	Statistics	Status—Active Company	Status—In liquidation	Status—All
1.MLP 22-6-2	Total	4606	1582	6188
	Correct	4226	804	5030
	Incorrect	380	778	1158
	Correct (%)	91.75	50.82	81.29
	Incorrect (%)	8.25	49.18	18.71
2.MLP 22-9-2	Total	4606	1582	6188
	Correct	4234	889	5123
	Incorrect	372	693	1065
	Correct (%)	91.92	56.20	82.79
	Incorrect (%)	8.08	43.81	17.21
3.MLP 22-12-2	Total	4606	1582	6188
	Correct	4315	773	5088
	Incorrect	291	809	1100
	Correct (%)	93.68	48.86	82.22
	Incorrect (%)	6.32	51.14	17.78
4.MLP 22-8-2	Total	4606	1582	6188
	Correct	4320	771	5091
	Incorrect	286	811	1097
	Correct (%)	93.79	48.74	82.27
	Incorrect (%)	6.21	51.26	17.73
5.MLP 22-12-2	Total	4606	1582	6188
	Correct	4252	873	5125
	Incorrect	354	709	1063
	Correct (%)	92.31	55.18	82.82
	Incorrect (%)	7.69	44.82	17.18

Source: own construction.

Ideally, we are looking for a neural structure which shows the highest number of correctly classified cases. However, it is very important for NN to be able to predict (classify) both active companies (i.e., businesses capable of surviving a potential crunch) and companies in liquidation (i.e., businesses in bankruptcy). In this respect, 2.MLP 22-9-2 and 5.MLP 22-12-2 networks appear to be the most successful. There is a minimum difference between them. But a higher number of correct predictions of bankruptcy for 2.MLP 22-9-2 network is more advantageous. The dominance of both networks is illustrated by the chart in Figure 1.

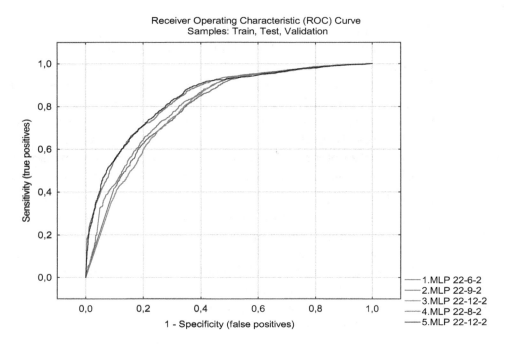

Figure 1. Threshold operating characteristics of neural network classification. Source: own construction.

Ideally, the characteristics are close to (0,1). The 2.MLP 22-9-2 and 5.MLP 22-12-2 networks are closest to this point.

4.3. SVM/NN Comparison

It is obvious from the results that the SVM model has a quite high level of reliability. However, the structure of correct classifications, i.e., 99% of correct predictions of active companies and only above 8% of predictions of companies in liquidation, makes this model inapplicable.

On the contrary, five NN models were retained by applying the methodology for creating NN. In all cases, those are MLPs that are applicable in practice. There are minimum differences between networks. Still we can identify the best neural network which is NN 2.MLP 22-9-2 without any doubt: very closely followed by NN 5.MLP 22-12-2. There is just a minimum difference between them.

This answers our research question. In this case, the answer is very simple. Artificial neural networks are much more accurate than SVM in predicting possible bankruptcy. Unlike SVM all retained NNs are well applicable in practice.

It is a bankruptcy model. We thus define a tool to identify the companies unlikely to survive a possible financial distress. In particular, we examine the ability of the tool to identify a company that can be expected to face financial distress in the future. The SVM model showed a great ability to predict the second opposite situation at first glance, that is, the ability of the company to survive a possible financial distress. In this case, the prediction of the model is correct in 99.39% of cases. However, the ability to predict bankruptcy is at the 8.22% level. In general, the SVM model predicts the future development of the company with 76.08% accuracy, which could be considered a good result. However, the problem is that the model would achieve the same or almost the same predictive power even if it did not predict any company that is going to bankrupt. In fact, the SVM method did not meet the requirements, although it shows a rather interesting result. The SVM model is thus nonapplicable.

As the confusion matrix in Table 5 indicates, artificial neural networks show higher prediction power—nearly up to 83%, but what is even more important, they have greater ability to predict companies that are going to bankrupt. Taking into account the most successful neural structure, 2.MLP 22-9-2, its accuracy is 82.79%. It is able to predict correctly 91.92% of companies that are able to survive a potential financial distress, and 56.2% of companies that are going to bankrupt. The prediction is thus applicable in practice.

Now the task is to find a generally acceptable model able to predict a potential financial distress. The Altman Z-Score (Altman 1968, 2000, 2003; Altman and Hotchkiss 2006) and many other models (Neumaierová and Neumaier 2005, 2008; Taffler and Tisshaw 1977; Taffler 1983; Kralicek 1993; Pollak 2003) were based on the data that are not relevant for the current corporate environment (small data volume, data more than 50 years old, etc.). Although the Altman Z-Score is still being used, corporate practice is well aware of their weaknesses. The paper aimed to find an alternative that respect the time lag and which would be easily applicable and showing an appropriate level of accuracy. Very often, it is about being able to detect a potential risk associated with a particular company. Subsequently, we would be able to analyse such a company in more detail, assessing whether the risk is real or not.

This requirement is definitely met by the generated neural networks, in particular 2.MLP 22-9-2. It is based on the current data in the environment where the resulting model of neural networks will be applied. As stated above, it is the first indication of possible problems used as an impulse for a more detailed analysis. The resulting model is interesting from another aspect. Despite its easy applicability, the artificial neural network assesses the future development on the basis of 22 variables characterizing the amount of company assets, structure of its financing, payment history of the company and the customers, cost structure, and the ability to generate sales (as a quantified output of core business). The individual indicators are described in Data and Methods.

Since 2000, many authors have tried to predict company bankruptcy using the models of neural networks. As an example, we can mention Becerra et al. (2002), who analysed the use of linear models and the models of neural networks for the classification of financial distress. Their calculation included 60 British companies from the period between 1997 and 2000. Zheng and Jiang (2007) used the data of Chinese listed companies between 2003 and 2005. All similarly created models are rather outdated, as they use the data that were up to date before the world financial crisis. This paper shows an up-to-date and simple model (most existing studies create relatively complex hybrid models—e.g., Xu et al. 2019), which can be gradually updated using new data, and thus even become more accurate (due to neural networks learning).

5. Discussion and Conclusions

Bankruptcy prediction is always a topical issue. This is due to very complicated business relationships between entrepreneurs and competition in the current business environment. It is characterized by instability, perhaps even turbulence. All the more important is to find a low-input tool that can evaluate future development of any company in the market.

The aim of this paper was to develop bankruptcy prediction models and evaluate the results obtained from classification methods, namely Support Vector Machines and artificial neural networks (multilayer perceptron artificial neural networks—MLP and radial basis function artificial neural networks—RBF).

In total, six models were created: 1 SVM, 5 NN. Consequently, a comparison was made between them. NN 2.MLP 22-9-2 appears to be the most successful model that is applicable in practice (NN code C++ forms). The financial variables with the highest bankruptcy predictive power are presented in Table 6.

Table 6. Sensitivity analysis.

Variables	1.MLP 22-6-2	2.MLP 22-9-2	3.MLP 22-12-2	4.MLP 22-8-2	5.MLP 22-12-2	Average
OHANIM	1.307736	8.298830	1.623772	1.197549	1.143286	2.714235
PRIDHODN	1.302244	4.395480	1.584667	2.339157	2.748509	2.474011
VS	1.319040	2.663396	1.602347	3.742576	2.887139	2.442900
HVML	1.269237	2.125292	1.520003	1.517179	3.173511	1.921044
MZDN	1.294799	2.563237	1.561902	1.494294	2.231695	1.829185
OBEZNAA	1.274424	2.737114	1.627830	1.209418	2.123338	1.794425
SPMAAEN	1.324918	2.146751	1.295759	1.266527	2.599045	1.726600
STALAA	1.173915	2.153740	1.231161	1.038480	2.572654	1.633990
Z	1.289484	2.095527	1.494067	1.115624	1.585507	1.516042
V	1.315965	2.092471	1.608308	1.113233	1.146686	1.455333
FTZZ	1.278720	1.379155	1.539660	1.668709	1.389535	1.451156
CIZIZDROJE	1.527338	1.269488	1.853573	1.073045	1.487208	1.442131
SLUZBY	1.422673	1.335220	2.002430	1.127664	1.204212	1.418440
FM	1.076257	1.418978	1.601751	1.185785	1.525021	1.361559
HVUO	1.298108	1.459786	1.454034	1.219113	1.350517	1.356312
KZ	1.258229	1.441923	1.204971	1.326370	1.334837	1.313266
HIM	1.095701	1.904764	1.004551	1.328013	1.228624	1.312330
VLASTNIJM	1.288897	1.338126	1.526678	1.225678	1.160983	1.308072
KP	1.280438	1.581155	1.337826	1.034392	1.196151	1.285992
NNSOCZAB	1.016164	1.991251	1.058640	1.060163	1.284383	1.282120
AKTIVACELK	1.274310	1.452314	1.154554	1.014583	1.388433	1.256839
PASIVACELK	1.274334	1.446461	1.154320	1.014663	1.368253	1.251606

Source: own construction.

The highest bankruptcy predictive power have "Depreciation of intangible and tangible fixed assets", "Value added" and "Production consumption". All three items are logical for the manufacturing industry.

The existing models (Altman index, Neumaier index and many others) are based on the standard statistical methods. Their deficiencies were identified by Balcaen and Ooghe (2004):

- Dependent variable dichotomy,
- Sampling method,
- Stationarity and data instability,
- Selection of variables,
- Using information from financial statements, and
- Time dimension.

Neural networks can resolve some of the defined problems. It is primarily the time dimension. For all the existing models, the previous development of the company, consequently evaluated as Active or in Liquidation, cannot be taken into account. Neural networks are able to handle large data volumes. Therefore, the values of variables of selection do not need to be restricted. It may appear that the dataset will be a limit when application for another period and different market (especially when used abroad). However, it is not the case, as we identified a structure with a relatively strong prediction power. Although it was trained and subsequently validated twice on a selected sample, the neural network can be quickly adapted to the specificities of a different market. Artificial neural network can adapt to a new environment by retraining it on a dataset sample of a given market. Due its ability to meet the requirement for changing the setting of its internal parameters, neural network can thus be considered flexible and widely applicable.

The future focus should to collect data other than information from financial statements. It will also be necessary to define the company status other than just Active or in Liquidation. However, the data problem may not be resolved.

Author Contributions: Conceptualization, J.H. and J.V.; methodology, J.H. and J.V.; software, P.S.; validation, J.H., J.V. and P.S.; formal analysis, J.H.; investigation, J.V. and P.S.; resources, J.H.; data curation, J.H.; writing—original draft preparation, J.H. and J.V.; writing—review and editing, P.S.; visualization, J.H. and J.V.; supervision, P.S. All authors have read and agreed to the published version of the manuscript.

References

Altman, Edward I. 1968. Financial Ratios, Discriminant Analysis and the Prediction of Corporate Bankruptcy. *The Journal of Finance* 23: 589–609. [CrossRef]

Altman, Edward I. 2000. Predicting Financial Distress of Companies: Revisiting the Z-Score and Zeta Models. Working Paper, New York University, New York, NY, USA.

Altman, Edward I. 2003. *The Use of Credit Scoring Models and the Importance of a Credit Culture.* Stern School of Business, New York University. Available online: http://pages.stern.nyu.edu/~ealtman/3-%20CopCrScoringModels.pdf (accessed on 25 January 2020).

Altman, Edward I., and Edith Hotchkiss. 2006. *Corporate Financial Distress and Bankruptcy: Predict and Avoid Bankruptcy, Analyze and Invest in Distressed Debt.* Hoboken: John Wiley & Sons, 368p.

Balcaen, Sofie, and Hubert Ooghe. 2004. *35 Years of Studies on Business Failure: An Overview of the Classical Statistical Methodologies and their Related Problems.* Working paper. Ghent, Belgium: Universiteit Gent, 56p.

Baran, Dušan. 2007. System approach to the stated policy of controlling the company. *Ekonomicko-Manažerské Spektrum* 1: 2–9.

Becerra, Victor Manuel, Roberto Kawakami Harrop Galvao, and Magda Abou-Seada. 2002. On the utility of input selection and pruning for financial distress prediction models. Paper presented at the 2002 International Joint Conference on Neural Networks, Honolulu, HI, USA, May 12–17; pp. 1328–33. [CrossRef]

Bishop, Christopher M. 1995. *Neural Networks for Pattern Recognition.* New York: Oxford University Press.

Boguslauskas, Vytautas, and Ruta Adlyte. 2010. Evaluation of criteria for the classification of enterprises. *Inzinerine Ekonomika-Engineering Economics* 21: 119–27.

Burges, Christopher J. C. 1998. A tutorial on support vector machines for pattern recognition. *Data Mining and Knowledge Discovery* 2: 121–67. [CrossRef]

Chen, Bo-Tsuen, and Mu-Yen Chen. 2011. Applying particles swarm optimization for Support Vector Machines on predicting company financial crisis. Paper presented at International Conference on Business and Economics Research, Kuala Lumpur, Malaysia, November 26–28; pp. 301–5.

Dorneanu, Liliana, Mircea Untaru, Doina Darvasi, Vasile Rotarescu, and Cernescu Lavinia. 2011. Using artificial neural networks in financial optimization. Paper presented at International Conference on Business Administration, Puerto Morelos, Mexico, January 29–30; pp. 93–96.

Enke, David, and Suraphan Thawornwong. 2005. The use of data mining and neural networks for forecasting stock market returns. *Expert Systems with Applications* 29: 927–40. [CrossRef]

Erdogan, Birsen Eygi. 2013. Prediction of bankruptcy using Support Vector Machines: An application to bank bankruptcy. *Journal of Statistical Computation and Simulation* 83: 1543–55. [CrossRef]

Gestel, Tony Van, Bart Baesens, Johan A. K. Suykens, Dirk Van den Poel, Dirk Emma Baestaens, and Marleen Willekens. 2006. Bayesian Kernel based classification for financial distress detection. *European Journal of Operational Research* 172: 979–1003. [CrossRef]

Hafiz, Alaka, Oyedele Lukumon, Bilal Muhammad, Akinade Olugbenga, Owolabi Hakeem, and Ajayi Saheed. 2015. Bankruptcy prediction of construction businesses: Towards a big data analytics approach. Paper presented at 2015 IEEE 1st International Conference on Big Data Computing Service and Applications, BigDataService 2015, San Francisco, CA, USA, March 30–April 3; pp. 347–52. [CrossRef]

Härdle, Wolfgang, Yuh-Jye Lee, Dorothea Schäfer, and Yi-Ren Yeh. 2009. Variable selection and oversampling in the use of smooth Support Vector Machines for predicting the default risk of companies. *Journal of Forecasting* 25: 512–34. [CrossRef]

Kiaupaite-Grushniene, Vaiva. 2016. Altman Z-Score model for bankruptcy forecasting of the listed Lithuanian agricultural companies. Paper presented at 5th International Conference on Accounting, Auditing, and Taxation, Tallinn, Estonia, December 8–9; pp. 222–16. [CrossRef]

Kim, Soo Y. 2011. Prediction of hotel bankruptcy using Support Vector Machine, artificial neural network, logistic regression, and multivariate discriminant analysis. *Service Industries Journal* 31: 441–68. [CrossRef]

Kim, Sungdo, Byeong Min Mun, and Suk Joo Bae. 2018. Data depth based support vector machines for predicting corporate bankruptcy. *Applied Intelligence* 48: 791–804. [CrossRef]

Kliestik, Tomáš. 2013. Models of Autoregression Conditional Heteroskedasticity Garch and Arch as a tool for modeling the volatility of financial time series. *Ekonomicko-Manažerské Spektrum* 7: 2–10.

Kralicek, Peter. 1993. *Základy Finančního Hospodaření [Basics of Financial Management]*. Prague: Linde, 110p.

Krulický, Tomáš. 2019. Using Kohonen networks in the analysis of transport companies in the Czech Republic. Paper presented at SHS Web of Conferences: Innovative Economic Symposium 2018—Milestones and Trends of World Economy, Beijing, China, November 8–9, article number 01010.

López Iturriaga, Félix J., and Iván Pastor Sanz. 2015. Bankruptcy visualization and prediction using neural networks: A study of U.S. commercial banks. *Expert Systems with Applications* 42: 2857–69. [CrossRef]

Lu, Yang, Nianyin Zeng, Xiaohui Liu, and Shujuan Yi. 2015. A new hybrid algorithm for bankruptcy prediction using switching particle swarm optimization and Support Vector Machines. *Discrete Dynamics in Nature and Society* 2015: 1–7. [CrossRef]

Machová, Veronika, and Marek Vochozka. 2019. Analysis of business companies based on artificial neural networks. Paper presented at SHS Web of Conferences: Innovative Economic Symposium 2018—Milestones and Trends of World Economy, Beijing, China, November 8–9, article number 01013.

Mousavi, Mohammad M., Jamal Ouenniche, and Bing Xu. 2015. Performance evaluation of bankruptcy prediction models: An orientation-free super-efficiency DEA-based framework. *International Review of Financial Analysis* 42: 64–75. [CrossRef]

Mulačová, Věra. 2012. The financial and economic crisis and SMEs. *Littera Scripta* 5: 95–103.

Neumaierová, Inka, and Ivan Neumaier. 2005. Index IN05. In *Evropské Finanční Systémy [European Financial Systems]*. Edited by Petr Červinek. Brno: Masaryk University, pp. 143–48.

Neumaierová, Inka, and Ivan Neumaier. 2008. Proč se ujal index IN a nikoli pyramidový systém ukazatelů INFA [Why took the IN index and not the pyramid system of INFA indicators]. *Ekonomika a management* 2: 1–10.

Pao, Hsiao Tien. 2008. A comparison of neural network and multiple regression analysis in modeling capital structure. *Expert Systems with Applications* 35: 720–27. [CrossRef]

Park, Soo Seon, and Murat Hancer. 2012. A comparative study of logit and artificial neural networks in predicting bankruptcy in the hospitality industry. *Tourism Economics* 18: 311–38. [CrossRef]

Pollak, Harry. 2003. *Jak Obnovit Životaschopnost Upadajících Podniků [How to Restore the Viability of Failure Businesses]*. Prague: C. H. Beck, 122p.

Purvinis, Ojaras, Povilas Šukys, and Ruta Virbickaité. 2005. Research of possibility of bankruptcy diagnostics applying neural network. *Inzinerine Ekonomika-Engineering Economics* 41: 16–22.

Rybárová, Daniela, Mária Braunová, and Lucia Jantošová. 2016. Analysis of the construction industry in the Slovak Republic by bankruptcy model. *Procedia—Social and Behavioral Sciences* 230: 298–306. [CrossRef]

Sayadi, Ahmad Reza, Seyyed Mohammad Tavassoli, Masoud Monjezi, and Mohammad Rezaei. 2014. Application of neural networks to predict net present value in mining projects. *Arabian Journal of Geosciences* 7: 1067–72. [CrossRef]

Shin, Kyung-Shik, Taik Soo Lee, and Hyun-Jung Kim. 2005. An application of Support Vector Machines in bankruptcy prediction model. *Expert Systems with Applications* 28: 127–35. [CrossRef]

Taffler, Richard J. 1983. The assessment of company solvency and performance using a statistical model—A comparative UK-based study. *Accounting and Business Research* 13: 295–308. [CrossRef]

Taffler, Richard J., and Howard Tisshaw. 1977. Going, going, gone—Four factors which predict. *Accountancy* 88: 50–54.

Tian, Yingjie, Yong Shi, and Xiaohui Liu. 2012. Recent advances on support vector machines research. *Technological and Economic Development of Economy* 18: 5–33. [CrossRef]

Vapnik, Vladimir N. 1995. *The Nature of Statistical Learning Theory*. New York: Springer.

Vochozka, Marek. 2010. Development of methods for comprehensive evaluation of business performance. *Politická Ekonomie* 58: 675–88. [CrossRef]

Vochozka, Marek. 2017. Effect of the economic outturn on the cost of debt of an industrial enterprise. Paper presented at SHS Web of Conferences: Innovative Economic Symposium 2017—Strategic Partnership in International Trade, České Budějovice, Czech Republic, October 19, article number 01028.

Vochozka, Marek, and Veronika Machová. 2018. Determination of value drivers for transport companies in the Czech Republic. *Nase More* 65: 197–201. [CrossRef]

Vochozka, Marek, and Penfei Sheng. 2016. The application of artificial neural networks on the prediction of the future financial development of transport companies. *Communications: Scientific Letters of the University of Žilina* 18: 62–67.

Vochozka, Marek, Jan Jelínek, Jan Váchal, Jarmila Straková, and Vojtěch Stehel. 2017. *Využití Neuronových sítí při Komplexním Hodnocení Podniků [Use of Neural Networks in Complex Business Evaluation]*. Prague: C. H. Beck, 234p.

Xu, Xiao-Si, Ying Chen, and Ruo-En Ren. 2006. Studying on forecasting the enterprise bankruptcy based on SVM. Paper presented at the 2006 International Conference on Management Science & Engineering, Lille, France, October 5–7; pp. 1041–45.

Xu, Wei, Hongyong Fu, and Yuchen Pan. 2019. A novel soft ensemble model for financial distress prediction with different sample sized. *Mathematical Problems in Engineering* 2019: 1–12. [CrossRef]

Zheng, Qin, and Yanhui Jiang. 2007. Financial distress prediction based on decision tree models. Paper presented at the 2007 International Conference on Service Operations and Logistics, and Informatics, Philadelphia, PA, USA, August 27–29; pp. 426–31.

7

ISA 701 and Materiality Disclosure as Methods to Minimize the Audit Expectation Gap

Tomasz Iwanowicz *[ID] and **Bartłomiej Iwanowicz**

Department of Accounting, Akademia Leona Koźmińskiego, Jagiellońska 57/59, 03-301 Warsaw, Poland; biwanowicz@kozminski.edu.pl
* Correspondence: tiwanowicz@kozminski.edu.pl

Abstract: Purpose: The main purpose of this paper is to determine how particular audit firms deal with ISA 701 requirements and the society expectations towards reporting the materiality levels. Additionally, the aim of this paper is to range the assertions in terms of the frequency of their occurrence. Design/methodology/approach: The tested sample consisted of 317 companies listed on Warsaw (158 companies) or London (159 companies) stock exchange. The analysis was divided into companies from the following ten market indexes (WIGs): construction, IT, real estate, food, media, oil and gas, mining, energy, automotive and chemicals. The research was executed based on the analysis of annual consolidated financial statements (annual reports) and independent auditor reports that were published by in-scope entities for the latest twelve-months period available as at the date of the research (mostly periods ended on 31 December 2017 and 31 March 2018). All values were denominated to euro (EUR) with use of average exchange rates published by the National Bank of Poland. All performed analyses and developed charts were supported by Microsoft Power BI data analysis tool. Findings: The general conclusion, which may be drawn from this research, is that implementation of ISA 701 and materiality disclosure limited the audit expectation gap. Detailed observations are described throughout the paper and summarized in the conclusions section. Originality/value: This study extends the prior research by providing various dimensions of the analysed matters. It contributes to understanding of the audit expectation gap and investigates on methods of minimizing it.

Keywords: ISA 701; audit expectation gap; key audit matters; materiality; Poland

---

"Capitalism without bankruptcy is like Christianity without hell"

Frank Borman—American astronaut

1. Introduction

The International Auditing and Assurance Standards Board (IAASB) is a global independent standard-setting body that serves the public interest by setting high-quality international standards, which are generally accepted worldwide. The IAASB sets its standards in the public interest with advice from the IAASB Consultative Advisory Group (CAG) and under the oversight of the Public Interest Oversight Board. Changing expectations and public confidence in audits is one of the most significant environmental drivers that have shaped the IAASB's strategy for 2020–2023 (IFAC 2019, p. 7).

There is decreasing confidence and declining trust in audits, arising from continuing high levels of reported poor results of external inspections and recent high profile corporate failures in some jurisdictions. Stakeholders' expectations are also changing about what the standards should require the auditor to do, e.g., in relation to the detection and reporting of fraud, and the consideration of going concern issues.

It has already been proved that public misperceptions are a major cause of the legal liability crisis facing the accounting profession. There is a concern that auditors and the public hold different beliefs about the auditors' duties and responsibilities and the messages conveyed by audit reports (Koh and Woo 1998). This has been named as the "auditing expectation gap" which refers to the difference between (1) what the public and other financial statement users perceive auditors' responsibilities to be and (2) what auditors believe their responsibilities entail (McEnroe and Martens 2001, pp. 345–58). This gap can be divided into three elements (ICAEW 2006):

- reasonableness gap[1] (element 'A'),
- deficient standards gap[2] (element 'B'),
- deficient performance gap[3] (element 'C').

These elements can be split down further into the following key areas:

- reporting (area '1'),
- assurance being provided (area '2'),
- regulation and liability (area '3'),
- audit independence (area '4').

The auditing expectation gap is illustrated in Figure 1 below.

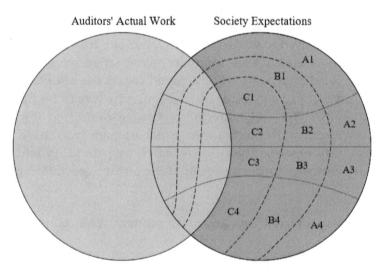

Figure 1. Auditing expectation gap divided into three elements and four key areas. Source: own elaboration based on analysed literature.

In 2015, the IAASB issued amendments to its standards. The goal of this shift was to enhance the independent auditor's reporting by making it more informative and insightful, and therefore valuable, to investors and other users of financial statements. The IAASB implemented a new International Standard on Auditing (ISA) 701, which introduced the auditor's responsibility to report on Key Audit Matters (KAM). The standard is applicable to the audit of all listed entities for periods ending on or after 15 December 2016.

Communicating key audit matters is expected to assist the users of financial statements in understanding topics, which according to the auditor were of utmost importance in the audited

---

[1]   Referring to what society expects of auditors and what can reasonably be expected of auditors to accomplish.
[2]   The gap between the responsibilities that society reasonably expects auditors to perform and auditors' actual responsibilities under statute.
[3]   The difference between the expected standard of performance of auditors and the actual performance of responsibilities by auditors.

period. Key audit matters are those matters that, in the auditor's professional judgment, were of most significance in the audit of the financial statements of the current period (IAASB 2016a, ISA 701, para. 8). At the same time, ISA 701 does not define any number of key audit matters, which ought to be identified by the auditor. The standard requires that the auditor uses his professional judgement in order to prioritize what is to be communicated within the KAM section. An attempt to determine the degree of implementation of changes in auditors' reporting for the largest companies (based on the example of the Polish market) was made in 2019 (Kutera 2019, pp. 79–94). The reports from the audit of the consolidated financial statements of the 30 largest companies listed on the Warsaw Stock Exchange for the years 2014–2016 were analyzed. The results of the analysis showed that the key audit matters mainly include estimating the impairment of assets (including deferred tax assets), revenue recognition and contingent liabilities disclosures.

Furthermore, in some jurisdictions, the auditor's report may comprise additional information going beyond the requirements of the ISA including the determination of materiality (Deloitte 2016, p. 15). The concept of materiality has received a lot of attention in recent years as high-profile accounting scandals have plagued financial reporting. ISA requires that early in an audit engagement the auditor establishes a preliminary level of materiality. This monetary value is used to determine the extent of audit testing that is to be performed. It can be changed as the audit progresses and key financial statement numbers change (Kearns 2007). Under current standards neither the preliminary nor final materiality value must be disclosed. In Poland and United Kingdom, it is permitted to disclose such additional information and therefore audit firms can decide whether or not to present this information.

The main purpose of this paper is to determine how particular audit firms deal with ISA 701 requirements and the society expectations towards reporting of the materiality levels. It compares and contrasts auditors' extent of such reporting (both KAM and materiality section) separately with regard to entities listed on Warsaw and London stock exchange and separately for analysed market indexes. Additionally, the aim of this paper is to range the assertions in terms of the frequency of their occurrence.

This study extends the prior research by providing various dimensions of the analysed matters. The article consists of an introduction, three chapters, and a summary and conclusions. The first chapter was devoted to the review of literature on the auditing expectation gap. The second chapter presents the research methodology, while the third chapter presents the results of the research.

2. Literature Review

Business failures are connected with the financial situation and non-financial factors (Ptak-Chmielewska 2019). Financial scandals have not only resulted in the loss of trust in the capital market but have also caused a crisis of credibility of auditors (Whittington and Pany 2004). There is a need to increase the usefulness of the information provided by the statutory auditors upon examination of the financial statements (Szczepankiewicz 2011). Many regulators currently debate how to increase effectiveness of supervision of public companies (Szczepankiewicz 2012, p. 25). Public expectations should go much beyond the watchdog function. The public awaits an audit to assure as to discovery of all frauds and irregularities (Gupta 2005). Absolute objectivity cannot be guaranteed since "materiality" and "material significance" are auditors' subjective concepts (Ojo 2006). A review of auditing literature shows how the auditing profession has responded to this problematic issue—including coining the phrase "audit expectation gap" (Lee et al. 2009). The expectation gap is the evolutionary development of audit responsibilities (Ebimobowei 2010, p. 129).

The audit expectation gap is a fundamental issue in every society in the world and that perception of users of financial statements as the responsibilities of auditors and the audit objective is the major cause of the gap. The gap can be addressed through (Schelluch and Gay 2006):

- emphasing the need to educate the public and reassure them about the exaggerated public outcries over isolated audit failures,
- codifying existing practices to legitimize them,

- attempting to control the audit expectation gap debate and repeatedly propounding the views of the profession,
- emphasing an awareness of the objective of the audit,
- readiness to extend the scope of an audit.

Audit definition is subject to challenges and changes according to social, economic and political developments (Jedidi and Richard 2009). Audit rules and regulations contain terms, like "reasonable", "material", and "professional scepticism" whose meanings vary in the minds of different auditors (Zikmund 2008). Independence is crucial to the reliability of auditors' reports (Salehi 2009). The literature reveals that educating the public about the objects of audit and auditors' responsibilities will help minimize the audit gap (Salehi and Rostami 2009).

The previous wording of the audit opinion no longer meets the expectations of the business community (Kutera 2018). The expanded audit report appeared to change users' perceptions about the responsibilities of management and auditors that mean users found expanded reports more useful and understandable than short-form audit reports (Aljaaidi 2009, p. 52). The professional bodies should set up new standards and renew existing ones as one of the remedies to the expectations gap (Akinbuli 2010). A common response in order to reduce the gap is to set out more auditing and accounting standards (Saeidi 2012, p. 7032). Accelerated by waves of financial crises the authorities have introduced a variety of measures to enhance the effectiveness of companies supervision (Kiedrowska and Szczepankiewicz 2011).

The IAASB implemented new ISA 701, which introduced the auditor's responsibility to report on KAM. Communicating KAMs is expected to assist the stakeholders in understanding the most important topics that occurred in the period presented in the financial statements. While determining key audit matters the auditor should consider i.a.:

- areas of higher risk of material misstatement or in which significant risks were identified (IAASB 2009e, ISA 315),
- financial statement areas, which involve substantial management judgment (e.g., accounting estimates),
- effects of significant events or transactions, which occurred during the audited period.

It must be noted that any matter giving rise to a qualified or adverse opinion (as per IAASB 2009d, ISA 705), or the existence of material uncertainty that may question the entity's ability to continue as a going concern (IAASB 2016b, ISA 570) is by its nature a KAM. However, such matters should be reported in line with applicable ISAs and the auditor should not include them in the KAM section of the report. In case when the auditor does not determine any key audit matters, he shall:

- discuss this with the engagement quality control reviewer (if appointed),
- explain in the report that there are no KAM to be reported, including the rationale for such a conclusion (IAASB 2009c, ISA 230),
- communicate this with those charged with governance.

The audit committee helps in narrowing the audit expectation gap since it is independent and non-executive and it aims to settle disputes and to reinforce external and internal audit performance. If audit committees do not play their role not more than just window dressing, then the audit expectation gap will be widened (Shbeilat et al. 2017).

An external audit of financial statements provides reasonable assurance as to whether the audited financial statements as a whole are prepared, in all material respects, in accordance with an identifiable financial reporting framework. Thus, the auditor is only responsible to detect misstatements that are material to the financial statements as a whole (IAASB 2009a, ISA 200). Misstatements, including omissions, are considered to be material if they, individually or in the aggregate, could reasonably be expected to influence the economic decisions of users taken on the basis of the financial statements

(IAASB 2009b, ISA 320, para. 2). This definition appears to be simple, however, the auditor has to distinguish between omissions and misstatements that would affect the users of financial statements and those that would not affect such users (Vorhies 2005). Additionally, there is a range of users, which makes such assessment more complex since materiality is likely to be unique to each user (Doxey 2013).

Materiality disclosures are not mandatory in Polish statutory auditing. Several foreign studies have shown that materiality disclosures in the audit report could have beneficial effects, while other studies have raised concerns about potential drawbacks. Research from a users' perspective seems to conclude that materiality should be disclosed, whilst research from the auditors' perspective is still in its fledgling stages, although it seems that auditors are rather apprehensive about disclosing materiality. This lack of consensus with regards to materiality disclosures is part of a much larger audit reporting debate that has been going on for many decades (Baldacchino et al. 2017).

3. Research Methodology

The tested sample, which was subject to the research, consisted of 317 companies listed on Warsaw (158 companies) or London (159 companies) stock exchange. The analysis was divided into companies from the following ten market indexes (WIGs): construction, IT, real estate, food, media, oil and gas, mining, energy, automotive and chemicals. The dispersion of the analyzed organizations in terms of represented WIG is illustrated in Figure 2 below.

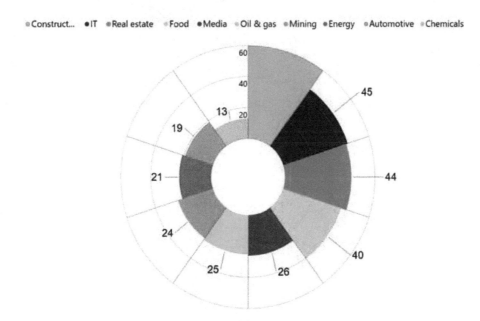

Figure 2. Tested sample by WIG. Source: own elaboration based on analyzed data.

The research was executed based on the analysis of:

- annual consolidated financial statements (annual reports)[4],
- independent auditor reports,

published by in-scope entities for the latest twelve-months period available as at the date of the research (mostly these were twelve-months periods ended on 31 December 2017 and 31 March 2018). All values were denominated to euro (EUR) with the use of average exchange rates published by the National Bank of Poland.

---

[4] The research was executed based on the analysis of the annual consolidated financial statements or standalone financial statements in situations where there was no capital group. The tested sample consisted of 317 financial statements (both consolidated and standalone).

All enterprises within the tested sample were public interest entities (PIE) listed on Warsaw or London stock exchange. Analyzed companies listed on the Warsaw stock exchange (158 companies) represented the entire population of PIE operating within the tested WIGs. Firms from the United Kingdom were randomly selected from respective WIGs to "mirror" the Polish ventures. The structure of the tested sample in terms of WIGs and the auditors is presented in Figure 3 below.

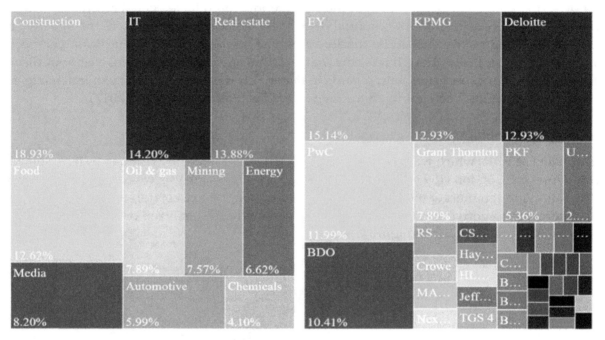

Figure 3. Structure of the tested sample in terms of WIGs and the auditors (in %). Source: own elaboration based on analyzed data.

Analyzed corporations were subject to the obligatory audits of their financial statements. The coverage of the tested sample by auditors is demonstrated in Figure 4 below.

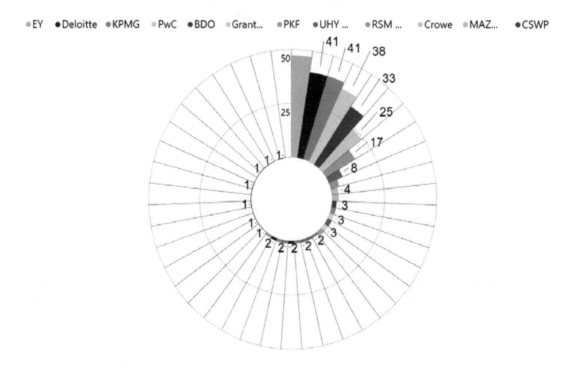

Figure 4. Structure of the tested sample in terms of the auditors. Source: own elaboration based on analyzed data.

168 of tested companies (53%) entrusted their audits to so-called "Big 4" auditing firms while the remaining (149, i.e., 47%) selected 1 of 39 other audit service providers. In the tested sample, 20 auditors (47%) were represented by a single client.

Apart from the Big 4, the auditors with the biggest share in the tested sample were:

- BDO (33, i.e., 10%);
- Grant Thornton (25, i.e., 8%);
- PKF (17, i.e., 5%).

A combined simplified balance sheet and profit and loss for the tested sample is presented in Table 1 below.

Table 1. Combined simplified balance sheet and profit and loss for the tested sample (in million EUR).

Balance Sheet	
Fixed assets	**1570**
Intangible assets	270
Tangible assets	985
Long-term receivables	36
Long-term investments	231
Long-term prepayments	48
Current assets	**641**
Inventory	168
Short-term receivables	228
Short-term investments	218
Short-term prepayments	27
Total assets	**2211**
Equity	**1013**
Provisions for liabi. and accruals	44
Long-term liabilities	701
Short-term liabilities	453
Total equity and liabilities	**2211**
Profit and Loss	
Net revenues from sales	1570
Operating expenses, incl.	1407
Amortization and depreciation	90
Other operating income	14
Other operating expenses	9
Financial income	9
Financial expenses	23
Gross profit (loss)	154
Net profit (loss)	106

Source: own elaboration based on analyzed data.

Based on the information provided in tested annual consolidated financial statements and independent auditor reports, there was a database created which contained:

- values of selected financial statements line items;
- detailed description of all KAMs reported;
- overall materiality levels and applied calculation methods.

Auditors of 317 companies, that were subjected to this test, identified a total of 793 unique KAMs. Based on their detailed descriptions they were then segmented into 36 categories (including category 'none') and finally mapped with a total of 2094 assertions from 7 types[5].

All performed analyses and developed charts were supported by Microsoft Power BI data analysis tool. With regards to presented 'sankey' type of charts, that illustrate interconnections between auditors, KAMs, assertions, WIGs, overall materiality, benchmark and Overall Materiality Rule of Thumb (OM RoT), the weights of ribbons presented were defined as number/average value of KAMs/assertions/overall materiality respectively.

4. Presentation of Research Results

In Figures 5 and 6, the KAMs' number and frequency of use and KAMs' mapping to assertions are presented, respectively. For the relationships between auditors, KAMs, assertions, and WIGs please refer to Figures 7 and 8.

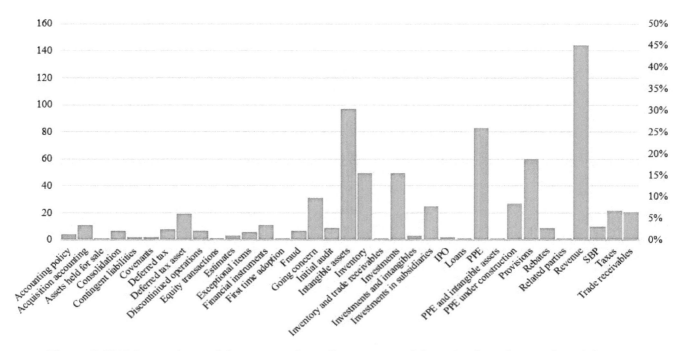

Figure 5. KAM—number and frequency of use. Source: own elaboration based on analyzed data.

---

[5]   The following types of assertions were defined and analysed: C—completeness; A—accuracy; V—valuation; CO—cut-off; PD—presentation and disclosures; E—existence; RO—rights and obligations.

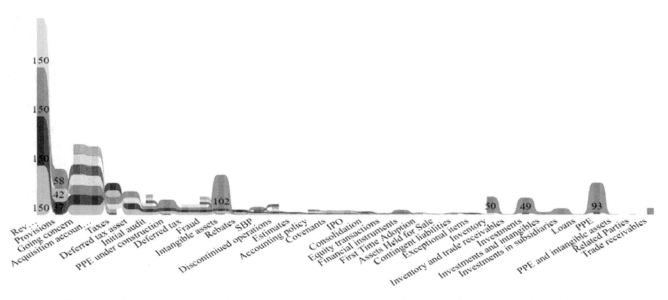

Figure 6. KAM—mapping to assertions. Source: own elaboration based on analyzed data.

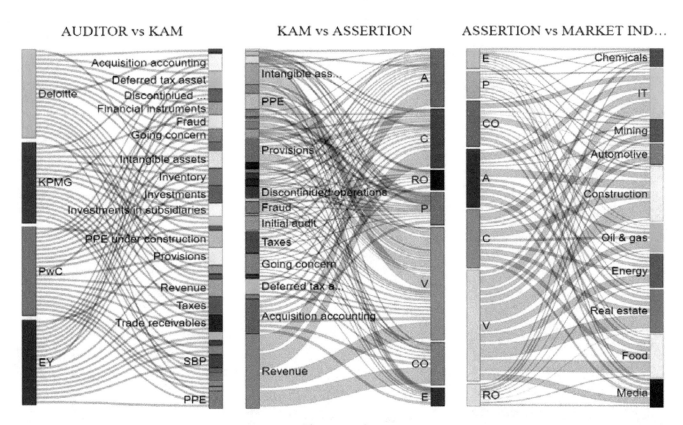

Figure 7. *Cont.*

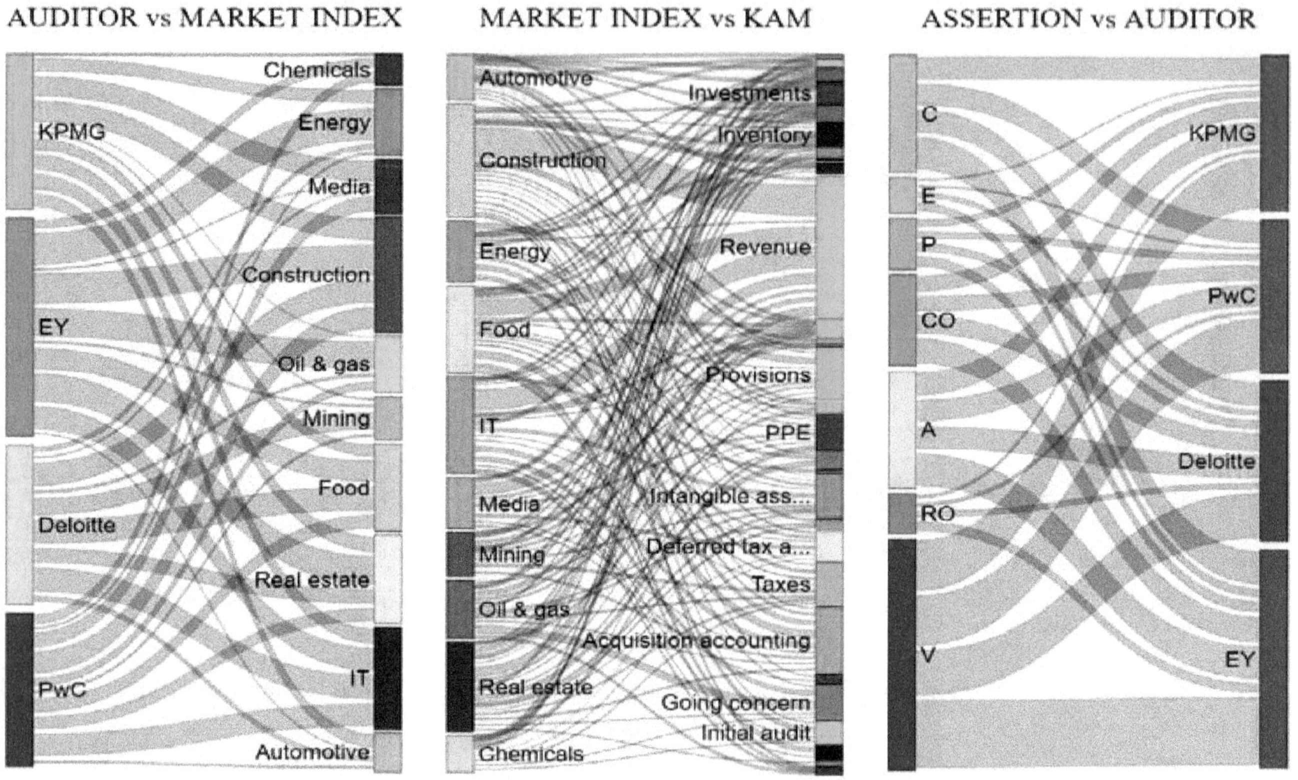

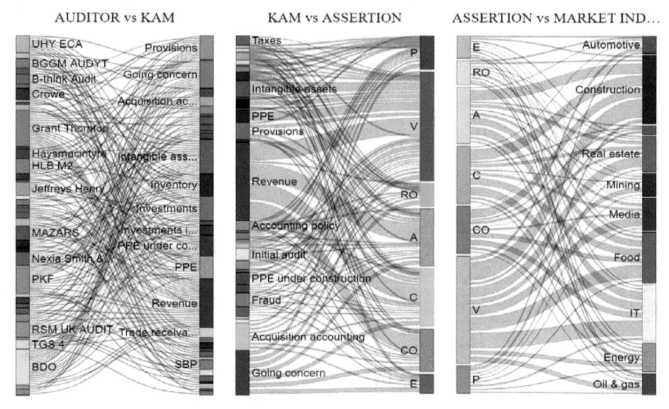

Figure 7. Relationships between auditors, KAMs, assertions, and WIGs—for Big 4 auditing firms. Source: own elaboration based on analyzed data.

Figure 8. *Cont.*

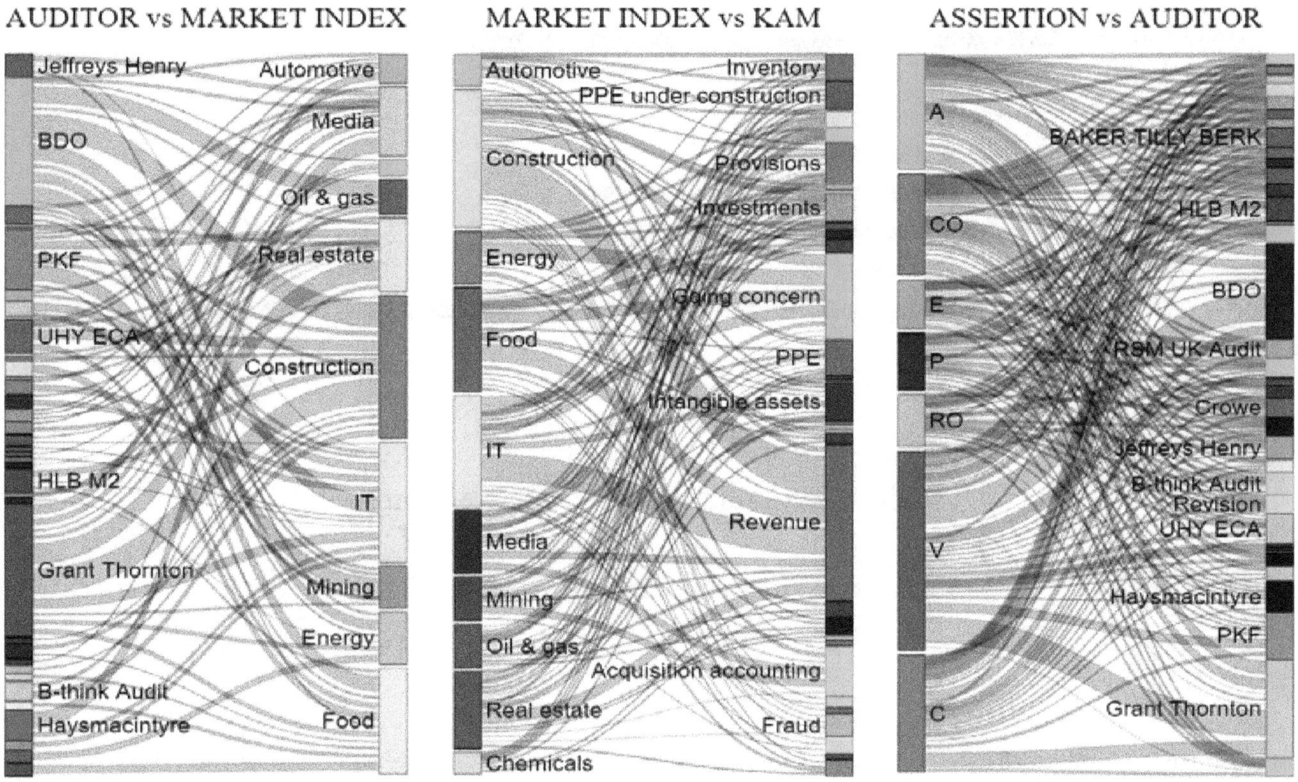

Figure 8. Relationships between auditors, KAMs, assertions, and WIGs—for non-Big 4 auditing firms. Source: own elaboration based on analyzed data.

As presented in Figures 5–8:

- for five businesses (1.6% of the tested sample) no KAMs were reported by the auditors,

- revenue is the most vastly used as a KAM category (45.3% of auditors' reports contained this KAM),

- the following 9 KAMs referred to all seven assertions: accounting policy, acquisition accounting, covenants, discontinued operations, first time adoption, fraud, going concern, initial audit and initial public offering (IPO),

- the valuation was the most frequently appearing assertion (745 items from a total of 2094, 35.6%);

- there is no clear differentiation in terms of presented patterns between Big 4 and non-Big 4 audit firms.

In Figure 9, the companies listed on the Warsaw stock exchange for which materiality levels were disclosed by auditors are presented. For the relationships between auditors, benchmarks, OM RoT, and WIGs please refer to Figures 10 and 11.

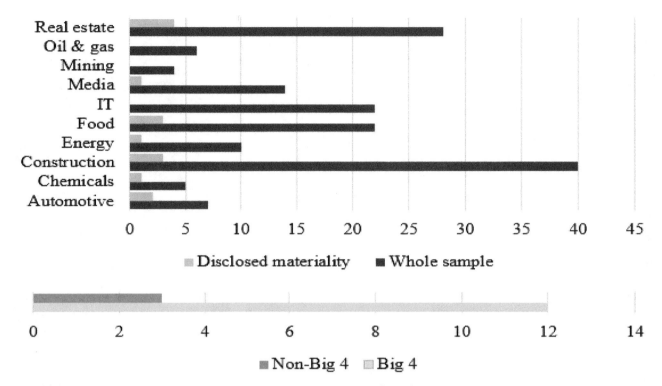

Figure 9. Companies listed on the Warsaw stock exchange for which materiality levels were disclosed by auditors—by WIG and non-Big/Big 4 auditors. Source: own elaboration based on analyzed data.

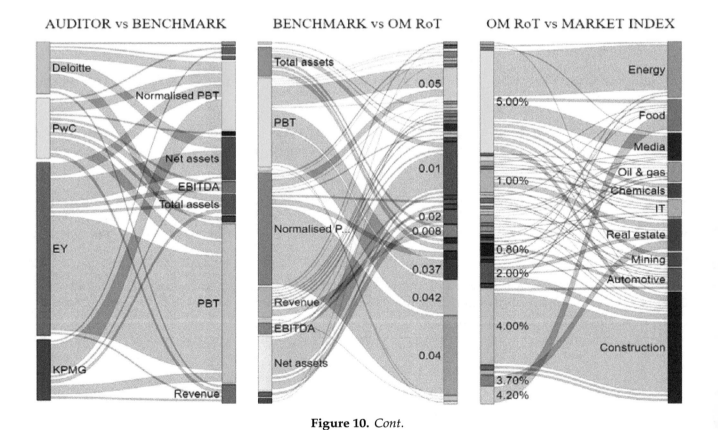

Figure 10. *Cont.*

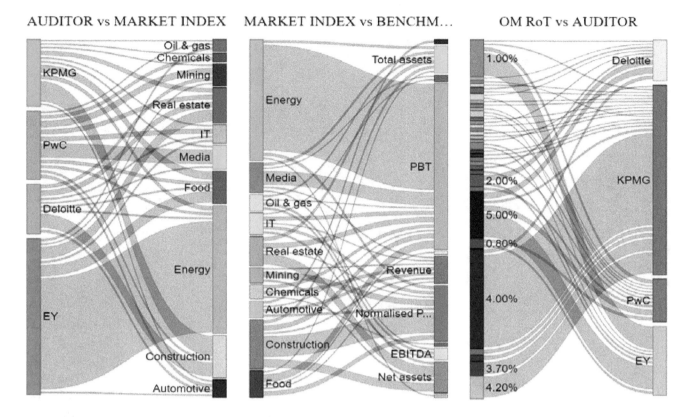

Figure 10. Relationships between auditors, benchmarks, OM RoT and WIGs—for Big 4 auditing firms. Source: own elaboration based on analyzed data.

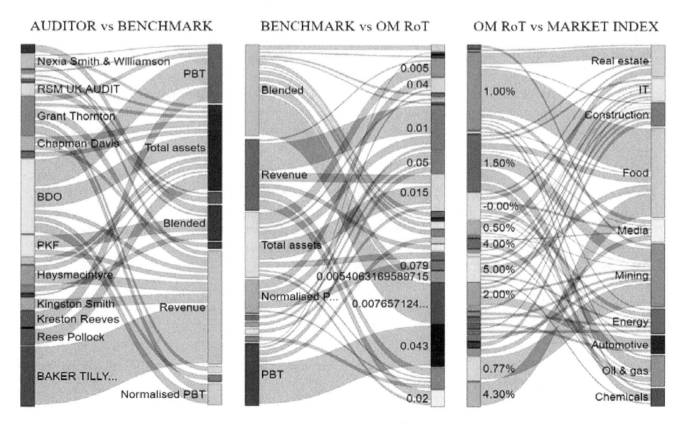

Figure 11. *Cont.*

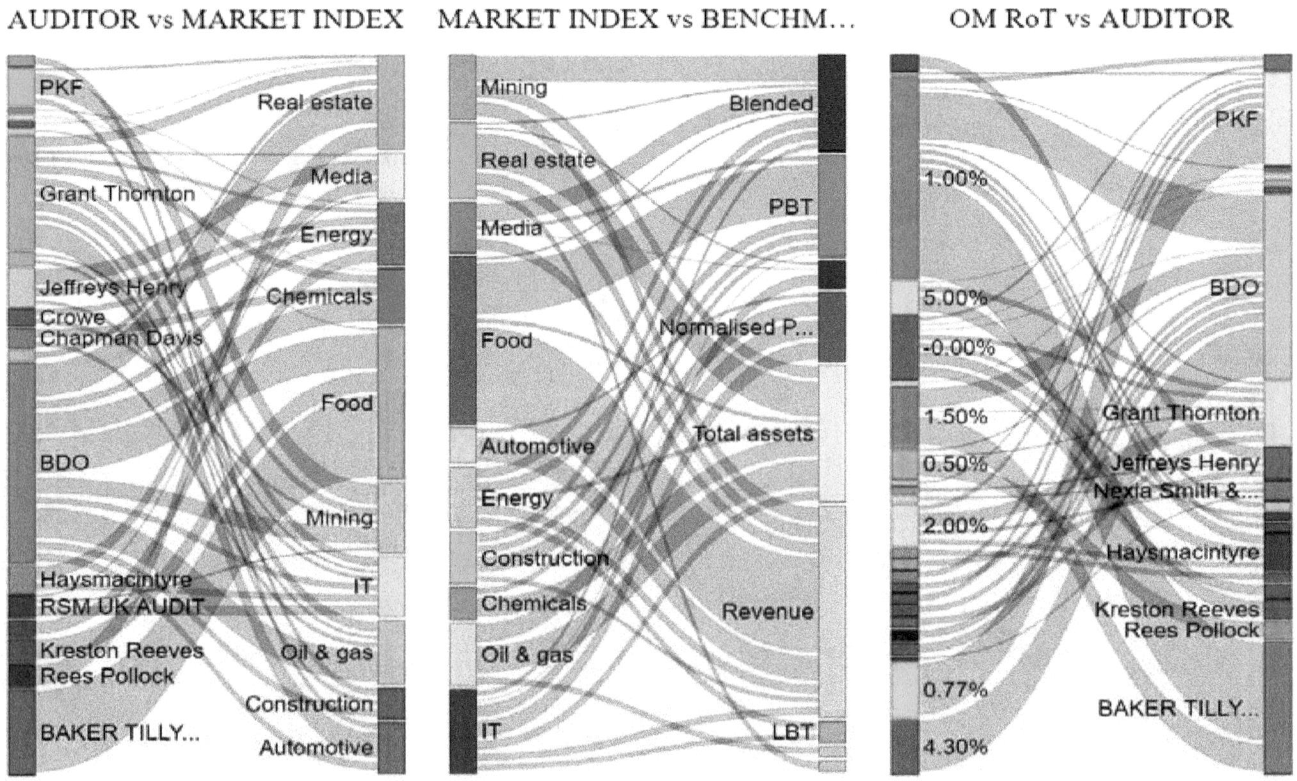

AUDITOR vs MARKET INDEX   MARKET INDEX vs BENCHM...   OM RoT vs AUDITOR

Figure 11. Relationships between auditors, benchmarks, OM RoT and WIGs—for non-Big 4 auditing firms. Source: own elaboration based on analyzed data.

All auditors of companies listed on the London stock exchange reported on the materiality levels, which they utilized for audit purposes. The information was fairly comprehensive and included: benchmark, OM RoT, overall materiality level, and de minimis materiality level. Some auditors provided also additional details about haircut and performance materiality.

As presented in Figure 9, this statistic was substantially lower for entities listed on the Warsaw stock exchange. Materiality levels were reported for 15 PIEs, which represented 9.5% of the whole population of companies operating within 10 specific industries (the Polish tested sample). It was observed that 80% of all reported materiality levels were announced by Big 4 auditors (by PwC in 11 out of 12 cases).

As presented in Figures 10 and 11:

- coverage of sectors by Big 4 representatives was fairly even, with the exception of the energy, which was dominated by EY,
- specialization of auditors may be observed (Baker Tilly's portfolio comprises mostly of food WIG) but no concentration over any particular auditor is visible within any sector,
- the most broadly used OM RoT was 4%, which was applied primarily:

  - by KPMG,
  - for normalized PBT,
  - in construction WIG;

- relatively, among Big 4, EY has the least differentiated benchmarks, with PBT being the main variable used to determine materiality,
- among Big 4, profit before tax (PBT) was the most commonly used benchmark, followed by normalized PBT, while among non-Big 4 it was revenue and total assets respectively,
- there was no other clear differentiation in terms of presented patterns between Big 4 and non-Big 4 audit firms.

The exact level of the OM is not imposed on auditors by any governing body. Its calculation is at the auditor's discretion. The auditor's determination of materiality is a matter of professional judgment and is affected by the auditor's perception of the financial information needs of users of the financial statements (ISA 320, para. 4). Determining a percentage to be applied to a chosen benchmark involves the exercise of professional judgment. There is a relationship between the percentage and the chosen benchmark, such that a percentage applied to profit before tax from continuing operations will normally be higher than a percentage applied to total revenue. For example, the auditor may consider five percent of profit before tax from continuing operations to be appropriate for a profit-oriented entity in the manufacturing industry, while the auditor may consider one percent of total revenue or total expenses to be appropriate for a not-for-profit entity (ISA 320, para. A7). The Figure below presents the OM used by Big 4 auditors in relation to those thresholds.

As presented in Figure 12, on average:

- for PBT, KPMG is 28.6% and PwC is 12.5% below the bottom threshold of 5% PBT, which means that they are even more detailed and conservative than as per the example presented in ISA 320, EY keeps it almost in the middle between the lower and upper limits, while Deloitte maintains its OM 27.3% over this base,

- for EBITDA, Deloitte stands out from the competition by getting close to the upper limit of the threshold, while the remainders keep it in the middle of the scale,

- for revenue, all Big 4 auditors except for Deloitte set up their OM below 1% revenue as per the example presented in ISA 320,

- finally, the situation for total assets is akin to the one for the revenue.

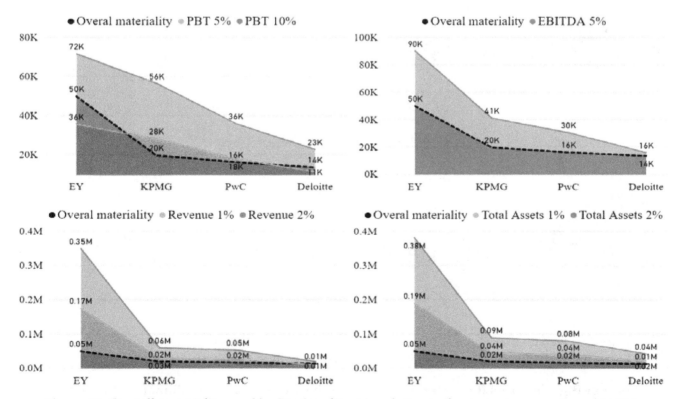

Figure 12. Overall materiality used by Big 4 auditors in relation to the percentage mentioned in ISA 320 and literature. Source: own elaboration based on analyzed data.

The Figure 13 below presents the OM used by non-Big 4 auditors in relation to those thresholds.

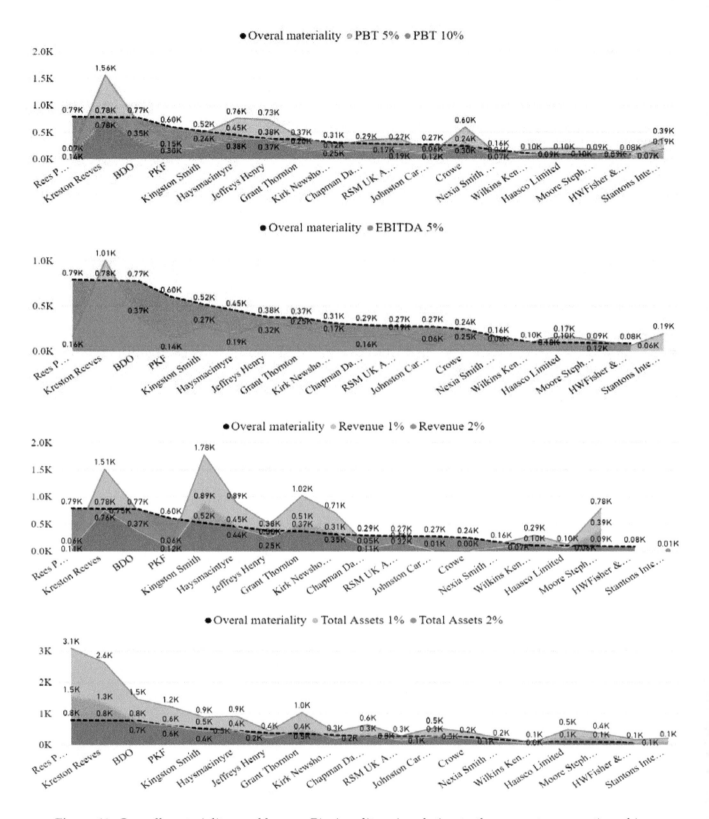

Figure 13. Overall materiality used by non-Big 4 auditors in relation to the percentage mentioned in ISA 320 and literature. Source: own elaboration based on analyzed data.

For non-Big 4 auditors it may be observed that the levels of the overall materiality, which they apply, are in general at higher stakes and in many cases, they exceed the upper thresholds as per examples presented in ISA 320.

On Figures 14 and 15 there are presented other operating income (OOI), other operating expenses (OOE), financial income (FI), and financial expenses (FE) which in some cases on average were below the OM and therefore were not audited, while they seem meaningful and vivid to the business.

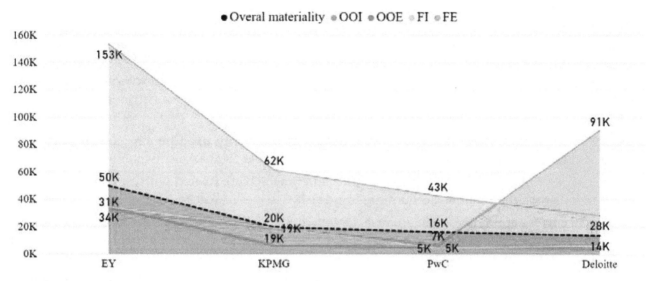

Figure 14. Average values of operating income (OOI), other operating expenses (OOE), financial income (FI), and financial expenses (FE) in relation to the OM—for Big 4 auditing firms. Source: own elaboration based on analyzed data.

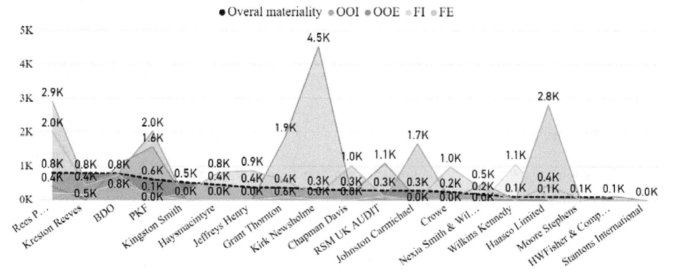

Figure 15. Average values of OOI, OOE, FI, and FE in relation to the OM—for non-Big 4 auditing firms. Source: own elaboration based on analyzed data.

As presented in Figure 14, Big 4 representatives on average do not audit OOI (except for Deloitte), OOE, and FI. The same dependencies, but for non-Big 4 auditors, are demonstrated in Figure 15, however the situation in this view is more diversified and varies by auditor. Nonetheless, it seems that there is no common approach on the market and in many cases OOI, FI, and FE are not subject to the audit of the financial statement.

5. Summary and Conclusions

Investors expect that after auditors inspect financial statements of public companies, they are complete, accurate and reliable in every significant aspect. Furthermore, as mentioned in chapter 1, investors expect that based on the auditor's reporting they will be capable of evaluating whether to invest in the entity or not. The aim of introducing ISA 701 was to further build up this confidence by ensuring that auditors, apart from "crunching numbers", also identify and pay special attention to the matters, which were the most noteworthy in the audited period and required dedicated treatment.

The performed research is the continuation of the market-wide studies conducted in this field after the implementation of the standards related to reporting on Key Audit Matters. The analysis depicted in this paper explores and re-discovers the landscape of auditing services provided to public companies in relation to the examination of their financial statements.

The general conclusion, which may be drawn from this research, is that implementation of ISA 701 and materiality disclosure limited the audit expectation gap. The study illustrates that:

- among Big 4, profit before tax (PBT) was the most commonly used benchmark, followed by normalized PBT, while among non-Big 4 it was revenue and total assets respectively,
- there were identified the following Key Audit Matters which are related with all assertions: going concern, business combination accounting, fraud risk, first-year audit and discontinued operations,
- under the current approach, some financial statement items, such as other operating expenses, are not audited at all, it should be noted that this particular category is quite capacious and can easily hide undesirable "surprises",
- although many individual Key Audit Matters were identified by auditors, they were fairly little differentiated, key categories, applied to most of the companies, were the same as benchmarks used for calculation of overall materiality,
- valuation stands out as the assertion, which is of utmost significance to the auditors, what clearly drives the way in which audit procedures are designed and performed,
- the extent of caution applied by non-Big 4 auditors, expressed by the level of overall materiality and its relation to relevant guidelines, is, in general, lower than the one exercised by their Big 4 colleagues, this means that audits performed by lesser firms may be less diligent than the ones conducted by market leaders.

The above indicates that, in general, and on average, some audits are truly commodity-like and focus only on revenues, total assets, and valuation, while other areas are not thoroughly investigated. This is especially true with regard to audit engagements performed by smaller players.

On one hand, being a commodity service is in line with the substance and the nature of the audit, which is a standardized service. On the other hand, regulators and market makers do their best to strengthen the confidence of business transactions by improving the value, which auditors create and provide to investors. In order to achieve that goal, it is necessary to re-imagine the way in which audit services are designed and delivered.

Presented results also underline the necessity to continue the discussion on the involvement of advanced tools and techniques, e.g., data analytics and visualization, machine learning (ML), blockchain, robotic process automation (RPA), and artificial intelligence (AI), to facilitate the implementation of such concepts in audit services. This idea is to be further explored in the detailed studies, which are planned to be performed following this paper. Academicians, practitioners, and regulators shall have an important insight into the current subject matter from this work. Future researchers shall also get a good base of scholarly work from this study. The proposed direction of further research is to extend the scope of the audit by including public companies listed on another European stock exchange, followed by an analysis for the next 12-month reporting periods.

Author Contributions: Conceptualization, Methodology, Software, Validation, Formal Analysis, Investigation, Resources, Data Curation, Writing-Original Draft Preparation, Writing-Review & Editing, Visualization, Supervision, Project Administration, T.I. and B.I.

References

Akinbuli, Sylvester F. 2010. The effect of audit expectation gap on the work of auditors, the profession and users of financial information. *The Nigerian Accountants* 43: 37–40.

Aljaaidi, Khaled. 2009. Reviewing the Audit Expectation Gap Literature from 1974 to 2007. *International Postgraduate Business Journal (IPBJ)* 1: 41–75.

Baldacchino, Peter J., Norbert Tabone, and Ryan Demanuele. 2017. Materiality Disclosures in Statutory Auditing: A Maltese Perspective. *Journal of Accounting, Finance and Auditing Studies* 3: 116–57.

Deloitte. 2016. Benchmarking the New Auditor's Report. Key Audit Matters and Other Additional Information. Available online: https://www2.deloitte.com/content/dam/Deloitte/ch/Documents/audit/ch-en-audit-benchmarking-auditors-report.pdf (accessed on 15 March 2019).

Doxey, Marcus M. 2013. *The Effect of Increased Audit Disclosure on Investors' Perceptions of Management, Auditors, and Financial Reporting: An Experimental Investigation.* Lexington: University of Kentucky, Available online: http://uknowledge.uky.edu/accountancy_etds/2 (accessed on 22 March 2019).

Ebimobowei, Appah. 2010. An evaluation of audit expectation gap: Issues and challenges. *International Journal of Economic Development Research and Investment* 1: 129–41.

Gupta, Kamal. 2005. *Contemporary Auditing*, 6th ed. New Delhi: Tata McGraw Hill.

International Auditing and Assurance Standards Board (IAASB). 2009a. *ISA 200 Overall Objectives of the Independent Auditor and the Conduct of an Audit in Accordance with International Standards on Auditing.* New York: The International Federation of Accountants (IFAC).

International Auditing and Assurance Standards Board (IAASB). 2009b. *ISA 320 Materiality in Planning and Performing and Audit.* New York: The International Federation of Accountants (IFAC).

International Auditing and Assurance Standards Board (IAASB). 2009c. *ISA 230 Audit Documentation.* New York: The International Federation of Accountants (IFAC).

International Auditing and Assurance Standards Board (IAASB). 2009d. *ISA 705 Modifications to the Opinion in the Independent Auditor's Report.* New York: The International Federation of Accountants (IFAC).

International Auditing and Assurance Standards Board (IAASB). 2009e. *ISA 315 Identifying and Assessing the Risks of Material Misstatement through Understanding the Entity and Its Environment.* New York: The International Federation of Accountants (IFAC).

International Auditing and Assurance Standards Board (IAASB). 2016a. *ISA 701 Communicating Key Audit Matters in the Independent Auditor's Report.* New York: The International Federation of Accountants (IFAC).

International Auditing and Assurance Standards Board (IAASB). 2016b. *ISA 570 (Revised) Going Concern.* New York: The International Federation of Accountants (IFAC).

Institute of Chartered Accountants in England and Wales (ICAEW). 2006. *Expectation Gaps.* London: Audit and Assurance Faculty, Available online: https://www.icaew.com/-/media/corporate/files/technical/audit-andassurance/audit-quality/audit-quality-forum/expectation-gaps.ashx (accessed on 22 March 2019).

The International Federation of Accountants (IFAC). 2019. Proposed Strategy for 2020–2023 and Work Plan for 2020–2021. p. 7. Available online: http://www.ifac.org/publications-resources/proposed-strategy-2020-2023-and-work-plan-2020-2021 (accessed on 8 March 2019).

Jedidi, Imen, and Chrystelle Richard. 2009. *The Social Construction of the Audit Expectation Gap: The Market of Excuses.* Strasbourg: La place de la dimension europeenne dans la Comptabillite controle Audit.

Kearns, Francis. 2007. Materiality & the Audit Report: It's Time for Disclosure. Available online: https://scholarworks.rit.edu/other/640 (accessed on 1 March 2019).

Kiedrowska, Maria, and Elżbieta Izabela Szczepankiewicz. 2011. Internal Control in the Concept of Integrated Enterprise Risk Management (ERM) System in Insurance Undertakings. *Finanse, Rynki Finansowe, Ubezpieczenia* 640: 695–706.

Chye Koh, Hian, and E-Sah Woo. 1998. The expectation gap in auditing. *Managerial Auditing Journal* 13: 147–54. [CrossRef]

Kutera, Małgorzata. 2018. Nowy raport biegłego rewidenta—Implementacja przy audycie spółek WIG-20. *Prace Naukowe Uniwersytetu Ekonomicznego We Wrocławiu* 503: 281–92. [CrossRef]

Kutera, Małgorzata. 2019. Kluczowe kwestie badania—Nowy element w raportowaniu biegłych rewidentów. *Zeszyty Teoretyczne Rachunkowości* 101: 79–94. [CrossRef]

Lee, Teck Heang, Azham Md. Ali, and Juergen Dieter Gloeck. 2009. The Audit Expectation Gap in Malaysia: An Investigation into its Causes and Remedies. *South African Journal of Accountability and Auditing Research* 9: 57–88.

McEnroe, John, and Stanley C. Martens. 2001. Auditors' and Investors' Perceptions of the "Expectation Gap". *Accounting Horizons* 15: 345–58. [CrossRef]

Ojo, Marianne. 2006. Eliminating the Audit Expectations Gap: Myth or Reality? Available online: https://mpra.ub.uni-muenchen.de/232/1/MPRA_paper_232.pdf (accessed on 15 March 2019).

Ptak-Chmielewska, Aneta. 2019. Predicting Micro-Enterprise Failures Using Data Mining Techniques. *Journal of Risk and Financial Management* 12: 6. [CrossRef]

Saeidi, Fatemeh. 2012. Audit expectations gap and corporate fraud: Empirical evidence from Iran. *African Journal of Business Management* 6: 7031–41.

Salehi, Mahdi. 2009. Audit Independence and Expectation Gap: Empirical Evidences from Iran. *Journal of Economics and Finance* 1: 165. [CrossRef]

Salehi, Mahdi, and Vahab Rostami. 2009. Audit Expectation Gap: International Evidence. *International Journal of Academic Research* 1: 140–46.

Schelluch, Peter, and Grant Gay. 2006. Assurance provided by auditors' reports on prospective financial information: Implications for the expectation Gap. *Accounting and Finance* 46: 653–76. [CrossRef]

Shbeilat, Mohammad, Waleed Abdel-Qader, and Donald Ross. 2017. The Audit Expectation gap: Does Accountability Matter? *International Journal of Management and Applied Science* 3: 75–84.

Szczepankiewicz, Elżbieta Izabela. 2011. The Role of the Audit Committee, the Internal Auditor and the Statutory Auditor as the Bodies Supporting Effective Corporate Governance in Banks. *Finanse, Rynki Finansowe, Ubezpieczenia* 640: 885–97.

Szczepankiewicz, Elżbieta Izabela. 2012. The role and tasks of the Internal Audit and Audit Committee as bodies supporting effective Corporate Governance in Insurance Sector Institutions in Poland. *Oeconomia Copernicana* 4: 23–39. [CrossRef]

Vorhies, James Brady. 2005. The New Importance of Materiality: CPAs Can Use This Familiar Concept to Identify Key Control Exceptions. *Journal of Accountancy* 199: 53.

Whittington, Ray O., and Kurt Pany. 2004. *Principles of Auditing and Other Assurance Services*, 14th ed. New York: McGraw-Hill Education.

Zikmund, Paul E. 2008. Reducing the Expectation Gap. *CPA Journal* 78: 12.

8

Comparison of Prediction Models Applied in Economic Recession and Expansion

Dagmar Camska *[ID] and **Jiri Klecka**

Department of Economics and Management, University of Chemistry and Technology Prague, Technická 5, 166 28 Prague 6, Czech Republic; jiri.klecka@vscht.cz
* Correspondence: dagmar.camska@email.cz

Abstract: As a rule, the economy regularly undergoes various phases, from a recession up to expansion. This paper is focused on models predicting corporate financial distress. Its aim is to analyze impact of individual phases of the economic cycle on final scores of the prediction models. The prediction models may be used for quick, inexpensive evaluation of a corporate financial situation leading to business risk mitigation. The research conducted is drawn from accounting data extracted from the prepaid corporate database, Albertina. The carried-out analysis also highlights and examines industry specifics; therefore, three industry branches are under examination. Enterprises falling under Manufacture of metal products, Machinery, and Construction are categorized into insolvent and healthy entities. In this study, 18 models are selected and then applied to the business data describing recession and expansion. The final scores achieved are summarized by the main descriptive statistics, such as mean, median, and trimmed mean, followed by the absolute difference comparing expansion and recession. The results confirm the expectations, assuming that final scores with higher values describe better corporate financial standing during the expansion phase. Similar results are achieved for both healthy and insolvent enterprises. The paper highlights exceptions and offers possible interpretations. As a conclusion, it is recommended that users need to respect the current phase of the economic cycle when interpreting particular results of the prediction models.

Keywords: models predicting financial distress; phases of economic cycle; Czech Republic

1. Introduction

Forecasting corporate bankruptcy is a crucial task for modern risk management. The current economic environment shaped by globalization, turbulent economic changes, and fierce competition impose challenging conditions for businesses and their prosperity. Contrariwise, many enterprises do not survive in the long run, and they have to withdraw from the market. The findings of the European Commission (2012) show that almost half of new companies went bankrupt within the first five years of their existence. Although corporate defaults seem natural in a market economy, corporate failures have enormous consequences for whole economic systems (Peng et al. 2010; Lee et al. 2011). The consequences can be recognized not only on the macroeconomic but also on the microeconomic level. The parties affected could be suppliers, customers, managers, employees, investors, governmental bodies, and financial creditors. All of these entities want to mitigate business risks and protect themselves from entering or continuing business activities with potentially default entities.

Prediction of corporate bankruptcy or corporate default has been a significant research issue since the 1960s. Pioneering works were associated with names such as Altman (1968) or Beaver (1966). These efforts have led to the construction of prediction models (also called bankruptcy models or models predicting financial distress). These models provide a controlled description of a particular economic reality. It should not be neglected that these models are never 100% accurate as they work on probability roots based on empirical observations (De Laurentis et al. 2010). The most popular statistical techniques applied are multivariate discriminant analysis and logistic regression (Balcaen and Ooghe 2006; Ohlson 1980). Since 2000, statistical methods have been replaced by artificial intelligence and machine learning methods. These current approaches include neural networks, genetic algorithms, fuzzy logic, vector support machines, or ensemble classifier methods (Alaka et al. 2018; Kumar and Ravi 2007; Lessmann et al. 2015; Acosta-González and Fernández-Rodríguez 2014; Ahn et al. 2000; Du Jardin 2018; Lensberg et al. 2006; Min and Lee 2005; Ravisankar and Ravi 2010; Wu et al. 2010).

De Laurentis et al. (2010) point out that prediction models are part of a broader framework: their limits have to be perfectly understood, and their general application should be avoided. The current modelling approaches make it difficult to fulfill the conditions mentioned above. They do not follow the recommendation by Zellner (1992) known as the KISS principle: Keep It Sophisticatedly Simple, which is often paraphrased as Keep It Simple Stupid. Large financial providers of different types can use the most up-to-date techniques, but credit risk management of small- and medium-sized enterprises (SMEs) differs (Belás et al. 2018).

This different approach used by SMEs causes the popularity of basic statistical techniques to remain unchanged in daily practice and a number of scientific papers can be found as well. Prusak (2018) or Klieštik et al. (2018) provide an overview of the research conducted in selected central and eastern European countries. Research carried out in the area of the Czech Republic involves the works by Karas and Režňáková (2013), Klečka and Scholleová (2010), Čámská (2015, 2016), Machek (2014), and Pitrová (2011). Despite the simplicity, the models predicting financial distress should not be used as dogmas. Two issues discussed in detail within the literature review need to be taken into account. The first is the influence attributed to the economic cycle phases. The second aspect that needs to be considered is the sensitivity of belonging to particular industry sectors. The paper's main aim is to analyze the impact of the economic cycle phases upon final values of the models predicting financial distress, as designed by statistical techniques. The principal conclusions lead to a recommendation that while applying models predicting financial distress, the present current phase of the economic cycle should be respected without regard to a particular industry branch and general corporate financial standing.

This paper has a standard structure and consists of five parts. Section 1 sets the research into a broader context. It describes the terms of the business environment, consequences of corporate defaults, reviews of the current research in this respective field, and explains the paper's main goal. Financial distress and the financially healthy position of a company is defined in Section 2; specific issues, such as the influence of the economic cycle and the role of particular industry sectors are also to be found in this section. Section 3 focuses on the materials and methods, explaining the extraction of the data sample and models predicting financial distress applied. Finally, Sections 4 and 5 present the results of the analysis along with their interpretation, summary, conclusions, and recommendations.

2. Literature Review

The review on the sensitivity of the economic cycles can be considered to be helpful for readers to gain an insight into this research. The theoretical background also refers to some other issues related to models predicting financial distress. The first defines financial standing, considering healthy and distressed. It is necessary to classify companies correctly before prediction models are applied. Secondly, the companies under investigation must be assigned into relevant industry sectors. The type of industry influences the risk of bankruptcy, sensitivity to the economic cycles, and, particularly, the values of financial ratios entering into prediction models. The models applied will be discussed separately in Section 3.

Deterioration of the overall economic situation results in an increased number of bankruptcies (Svobodová 2013; Achim et al. 2012; Smrčka et al. 2013). Bruneau et al. (2012) examined whether corporate bankruptcies are influenced by macroeconomic variables and whether defaults determine the business cycle in France. Altman (2004) emphasized the impact of a turbulent economic environment on an increasing unexpected number of bankruptcies in the United States in 2001 and 2002. Liou and Smith (2007) considered including macroeconomic variables into prediction models as a logical step but also admitted that it happens only very rarely. Several other studies confirm that the use of macroeconomic variables improves the predictive accuracy of models (Korol and Korodi 2010; Hol 2007; Zhou et al. 2010). The main drawback of these approaches applied is that only one economic period is scrutinized and comparison over time is missing. Surprisingly, Topaloglu (2012) is an exception because the paper covers American bankruptcies in the manufacturing industry during the period 1980–2007, which allows the conclusion that accounting variables lose predicting ability when market-driven variables are included.

Macroeconomic deterioration triggers the increase of corporate defaults and it probably also influences values of financial ratios, which would result in the changed final values of models predicting financial distress. During the recession phase, the values of economic indicators could be expected to deteriorate contrary to the phase of expansion when these values would get improved. The question arises whether the impact described is significant and observable in most economic indicators, entering into the models predicting financial distress. Li and Faff (2019) concluded that market-based information assumes importance during periods of financial crisis, in contrast to accounting-based information, the importance of which in the same phase is reduced. It seems that bankruptcy models based on macroeconomic variables are not stable over time since they are not used recurrently, and neither are they scrutinized in the longer time horizons. It seems that the life cycle of prediction models containing macroeconomic variables is not long enough and cannot be used for more economic cycles.

To achieve the required accuracy in model testing, it is essential to categorize the enterprises correctly; basically, into one of two main groups, either as healthy or distressed entities. Financial distress can be defined in many different ways, and similarly, the terminology referring to such companies also differs (bankrupt, insolvent, in default). Merton (1974) defines the default as a situation when the enterprise value is lower than the value of debts. Moyer (2005) compares corporate financial distress to the situation when the box of assets becomes smaller than the box of debts. Using this approach, the enterprises are distinguished through their over indebtedness, such as in Schönfeld et al. (2018). Insolvency is mostly connected with the inability to pay debts, which can be short or long-termed (Crone and Finlay 2012; Deakin 1972; Du Jardin 2017; Foster 1986). Another possibility to define a default is a definition provided by credit rating agencies. The approach used by Moody's can be found in Hamilton et al. (2001). For research purposes, data availability has to be respected. Some research works are based on non-public information provided by financial creditors. In this research, however, only publicly available information is used exclusively. As a result, financial default is defined as corporate insolvency under the Czech Insolvency Act (Act No. 182/2006 Coll.). Insolvency can be declared because of an inability to pay claims or because of over indebtedness. The second group of companies examined is presented as healthy companies. Less attention is given to the definition of healthy enterprises in literature. In this paper, healthy companies are considered to be those having positive economic value added (Jordan et al. 2011). This approach was applied in Čámská (2015, 2016).

The last issue covered in this literature review is the sensitivity of belonging to a particular industry branch. Ganguin and Bilardello (2004) point out that some industries are riskier than others. They conclude that the type of industry influences the risk of deterioration. One reason for industry sensitivity is its exposure to the risk of default. Another reason is that different industries achieve different performance. The literature provides numerous pieces of evidence for this statement. Structure of capital sources (proportion of equity and liabilities) is determined by belonging to industry sectors (Frank and Goyal 2009; Öztekin 2015). Structure of working capital and connected corporate liquidity are also influenced by industries (Vlachý 2018). The same can be said about corporate profitability (Jackson et al. 2018). Belonging to a particular industry sector has an impact on the quality of financial performance predicted (Fairfield et al. 2009; Lee and Alnahedh 2016). Chava and Jarrow (2004) even highlighted that the coefficients of the models predicting financial distress should be calibrated according to the particular industry branches. This leads to a conclusion that financial ratios influenced by industry specifics entering into bankruptcy models could influence the results achieved. Due to these reasons, this paper strictly separates individual industry branches.

3. Materials and Methods

This part describes the materials and methods employed herein. The materials include the observations extracted from the prepaid corporate database, Albertina. The selected observations all have to meet some predefined requirements. Each observation describes one company and is based on the annual financial statements. The methods specify the steps conducted during the analysis leading to the results achieved. The description provided below contains a sufficient number of details, therefore allowing any professionals to replicate this research work.

3.1. Materials

This paper's idea is verified by the data specified in this subchapter. Information about corporate financial performance is mainly included in financial statements, such as a balance sheet and income statement. This quantitative research includes hundreds of companies, which means that the data analysis is based on publicly available financial statements. The selected financial statements were extracted from the prepaid corporate database, Albertina. What proved to be the main obstacle was rather complicated access to data since many companies do not report on time or they tend not to report at all despite reporting being an obligatory legal requirement in the Czech Republic. Some further details concerning the Czech disclosure discipline can be found in Strouhal et al. (2014) focusing on TOP100 companies according their sales and in Bokšová and Randáková (2013) focusing on insolvent entities.

The data selected and obtained can be divided into several subcategories. The first category includes data strictly polarized; on one hand, there are enterprises which declared insolvency. On the other hand, there are companies considered financially healthy due to their positive economic value added creation (Jordan et al. 2011). Their return on equity exceeds the required level of return published by the Ministry of Industry and Trade (2013, 2018). Both groups can be divided into two subparts describing different time periods. There are the companies which announced insolvency as a consequence of the latest global economic crisis in 2012 and 2013, and businesses which announced their insolvency after the year 2014 until the first quarter of 2019 during economic expansion. The analyzed financial statements always describe the accounting year one or two periods before the companies had become insolvent. The same process was applied to the healthy entities. The preceding sample focuses on the accounting year 2012 and the current one describes the year 2017. The year 2017 was selected for this research for the following reasons. The financial data for the year 2019 have not been reported yet and neither those for the year 2018 have been published in full. Secondly, the data sample contains three industry branches, specifically, Manufacture of fabricated metal products, except machinery and equipment (CZ-NACE 25), Manufacture of machinery and equipment (CZ-NACE 28), and Construction (CZ-NACE F). Previous works mentioned in the literature review confirmed that industry specifics are relevant. The companies in this research, therefore, needed to be classified according to their industry sectors. These sectors provide one of the largest homogenous data samples, i.e., for the purposes of this research they were not selected randomly.

Table 1 shows the structure of the data sample following the aforementioned description. Healthy and insolvent enterprises are strictly polarized. The years 2012 and 2017 reflect different periods for comparison. According to the economic cycle, the year 2012 represents a recession phase and the year 2017 an economic expansion phase. Special emphasis should be placed on the analyzed industry sectors—CZ-NACE 25, CZ-NACE 28, and CZ-NACE F. It seems that a particular phase of the economic cycle influenced the number of the businesses extracted from the Albertina database, confirming the logical premises of economic cycles in general. Significantly, healthy companies can be observed more frequently in the expansion phase, however, insolvent enterprises can be found more frequently in the recession phase. This also explains why the second time period for extracting insolvent enterprises cannot be shorter. The sample size for the insolvent companies would be negligible if the period was shortened. The only exception observed is the number of insolvent entities within the construction industry during the expansion period. This number is three times larger than during the recession period. This can be explained by the ongoing construction sector crisis or better disclosure discipline.

Table 1. Size of the analyzed sample.

Industry Branch	Healthy 2012	Insolvent 2012	Healthy 2017	Insolvent 2017
CZ-NACE 25	383	36	786	25
CZ-NACE 28	33	10	321	11
CZ-NACE F	229	33	1997	105

Source: authors' own work.

3.2. Methods

The analysis carried out was based on models predicting financial distress, whose accuracy was confirmed and verified on Czech businesses in previous works (Čámská 2015, 2016). Methods such as linear discriminant analysis and logistic regression belong to classical statistical methods applied in prediction of corporate default risk. The models applied were designed using these statistical techniques. Their frequent reuse depends on their ease of use and clear interpretability. Users do not need to have deep insight into advanced statistical, as well as non-statistical, techniques.

The conducted analysis was based on the 18 following models predicting financial distress. The bankruptcy models in this paper are marked by the following numbers: 1—Altman, 2—IN01, 3—IN05, 4—Doucha, 5—Kralicek, 6—Bonita, 7—Prusak 1, 8—Prusak 2, 9—PAN-E, 10—PAN-F, 11—PAN_G, 12—D2, 13—D3, 14—Hajdu and Virág, 15—Šorins and Voronova, 16—Merkevicius, 17—R model, and 18—Taffler. The exact models' specifications are accessible in the relevant literature cited below. The models introduced were designed in different countries and in different periods. Some models were constructed in the most developed economies and at the beginning of 1990s, were assumed to be best practice in the Czech Republic. In the late 1990s, these foreign designs were replaced by domestically designed models. These efforts were visible not only in the Czech Republic, but also in other countries in the Central and Eastern European region. Countries like Poland, Hungary, Lithuania, and Latvia, due to historical circumstances, underwent similar political and economic development as the Czech Republic.

The approaches imported from the most developed economies are represented by the American Altman Z-Score formula (Altman 1993), German Bonita Index (from the German original Bonitätsanalyse) (Wöber and Siebenlist 2009), Austrian Kralicek Quick Test (Kralicek 2007), and British Taffler (Agarwal and Taffler 2007). National efforts from previously transitioned economies described in this research include Czech IN01 (Neumaierová and Neumaier 2002), IN05 (Neumaierová and Neumaier 2005), Balance Analysis System by Rudolf Doucha (Doucha 1996), Polish Prusak 1, Prusak 2, PAN-E, PAN-F, PAN-G, D2, D3 (all described in Kisielińska and Waszkowski 2010), Hungarian Hajdu and Virág (Hajdu and Virág 2001), and Baltic approaches, such as Šorins and Voronova (Jansone et al. 2010), Merkevicius (Merkevicius et al. 2006), and R model (Davidova 1999).

The conducted analysis was then divided into the following phases. At the beginning, final values of the aforementioned models predicting financial distress were calculated for individual companies included in the data sample. Then, the final values calculated were summarized. Their summary was performed by general descriptive statistics, such as mean, median, or trimmed mean. Finally, the comparison between the time period of expansion and recession was conducted. The time of expansion was represented by the data sample describing the year 2017 defined previously. In contrast, the time of recession was presented by the data sample of the year 2012. The comparison was based on absolute differences expressed by Equations (1) and (2).

$$\text{Absolute difference} = \text{Indicator value}_{2017} - \text{Indicator value}_{2012}, \tag{1}$$

$$\text{Absolute difference} = (\text{Indicator value2017} - \text{Indicator value2012}) \times (-1). \tag{2}$$

The first equation was applied to 17 tested models whose higher values mean better financial standing. The second equation was applied to one model only. This exception is the Kralicek Quick Test (marked by the number 5) which has an opposite metric. Better financial standing is connected with a lower, not higher, final value. This explains why other forms to express the absolute difference were used. As for the two differences displayed above, their positive value reflects a more favorable classification of companies in 2017 and a negative value indicates a more favorable classification of companies in 2012.

4. Results

This part is dedicated to the results achieved. The main aim of this study was to examine the difference in corporate financial standing during a recession and expansion phase of the economic cycle. It also emphasizes the sensitivity of industry sectors and general differences in financial standing (healthy contrary to insolvent companies). The results are most frequently demonstrated by their visualization, as proposed by Čámská (2019). This process was chosen as a number of models were employed and it highlights the differences between the industry branches.

Statistical characteristics, such as the mean, median, and trimmed mean, were calculated for each subsample. Table 2 shows an example of the results when applying the Altman model for the insolvent and healthy enterprises in 2017. It seems that from a statistical point of view, some enterprises could serve as outliers. Since these entities represent realistic financial standing, the question whether to exclude them from the sample can be considered rather controversial. The healthy group contains mainly positive outliers whose financial standing is significantly better. In contrast, the insolvent group mostly consists of negative outliers whose financial standing is considerably worse. This affects the mean value. The trimmed mean cannot rely on the same assumption due to the different sample sizes. For healthy enterprises, the mean limitation of 1/20 (5%), except CZ-NACE 28 in 2012 (which uses 1/10 (10%)), was applied. The situation is much more difficult in the case of insolvent companies. The mean limitation of 1/10 (10%), except CZ-NACE 28 in 2012 and also in 2017 (in these cases applied limitation of 1/5 (20%)), was used. This suggests that the median is an optimal indicator for visualization.

Table 2. Descriptive statistics for Altman's Z-score in 2017.

Statistics	Healthy Mean	Healthy Median	Healthy Trimmed Mean	Insolvent Mean	Insolvent Median	Insolvent Trimmed Mean
CZ-NACE 25	4.17	3.71	3.98	−1.23	0.74	−0.04
CZ-NACE 28	4.27	3.70	4.09	1.55	1.68	1.52
CZ-NACE F	4.22	3.73	4.04	0.72	0.83	0.76

Source: authors' own work.

Visualization can also express several criteria. The first takes into account a type of time period. In our case, the periods monitored (2012 and 2017) are different. The second criterion takes into consideration the type of industry branches. Again, the companies selected for the purpose of this study belong to three different industry branches. The third criterion applied here distinguishes companies according to their financial standing. The companies surveyed herein differ in their financial standing, presenting a strict polarization. Figures 1 and 2 display the results for the industry sector CZ-NACE F Construction. Figure 1 demonstrates healthy entities contrary to the insolvent companies presented in Figure 2. The different phases of the economic cycle are displayed by the separated curves in each figure. Models 5 and 18 (Kralicek and Taffler) are not included in the final visualization. It has been already highlighted that the Kralicek model is based on a different metric system, which leads to different results from the other applied models. The Taffler model has also been excluded due to its values range exceeding other prediction tools by 2–3 times. Higher total values are caused by the used individual indicators and especially assigned weights, which were chosen during the model's design.

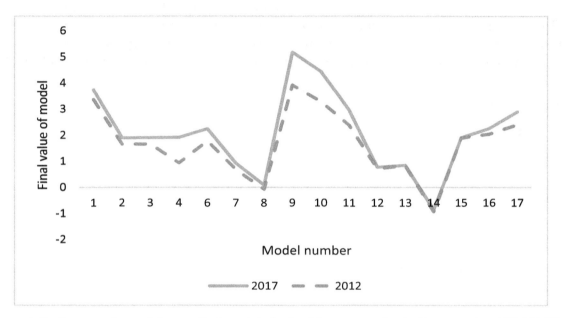

Figure 1. Indicator values of the studied models for healthy companies in Construction (CZ-NACE F). Source: authors' own work.

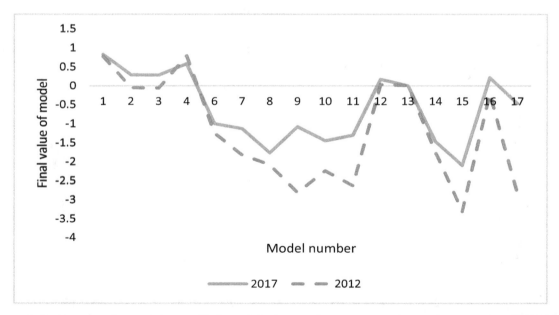

Figure 2. Indicator values of the studied models for insolvent companies in Construction (CZ-NACE F). Source: authors' own work.

Figure 1 confirms the research hypothesis that the recession phase leads to lower final values of models predicting financial distress. Figure 1 works with the companies defined as financially healthy. Figure 2 provides additional support for this claim and the differences for insolvent companies are even more significant. In the case of the models marked as 12 and 13, it should be noted that they were constructed by logistic regression and therefore their range of final values is from 0 to 1. Their visualized differences are insignificant in comparison with other models designed by linear discriminant analysis. The changed scale of graph would reveal that the differences are observable also for the models based on logistic regression.

Both Figures 1 and 2 concentrate on just one particular industry branch. They demonstrate the differences of the economic phases for the economic activity of CZ-NACE F Construction. The need to differentiate between sectors has already been emphasized in the theoretical part. The literature review highlighted the sensitivity of models predicting financial distress to particular industry branches. Figures 3 and 4 display results achieved in all branches included in the sample. The sample includes not only Construction (CZ-NACE F), but also Manufacture of fabricated metal products, except machinery and equipment (CZ-NACE 25), and Manufacture of machinery and equipment (CZ-NACE 28).

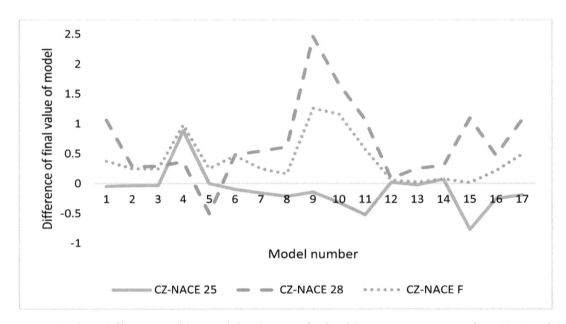

Figure 3. Absolute differences of the model indicators for healthy companies regarding 2012 and 2017 by branches. Source: authors' own work.

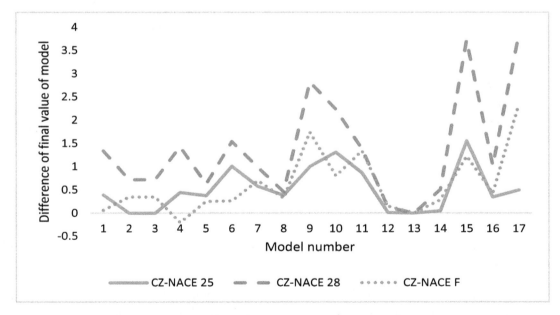

Figure 4. Absolute differences of the model indicators for insolvent companies regarding 2012 and 2017 by branches. Source: authors' own work.

Table 3 displays the results of the Wilcoxon test applied to all three industry branches studied. The null hypothesis is that there is no difference between the year 2012 and the year 2017. Small p-values lead to the rejection of the null hypothesis and to the acceptance of alternatives. The alternative can be presented as there are differences in the indicator values of the tested models between the recession phase (2012) and the expansion one (2017). The analysis was conducted for the healthy and also insolvent enterprises. p-values smaller than 10% are highlighted in the table. In these cases, the null hypothesis was rejected and the alternative was accepted. CZ-NACE 28 (Machinery) and CZ-NACE F (Construction) have reached convincing results for most models in the healthy, and also insolvent, sample. CZ-NACE 25 (Manufacture of metal products) does not support the alternative in many cases.

Table 3. p-values of the Wilcoxon test.

Company Type	Healthy	Healthy	Healthy	Insolvent	Insolvent	Insolvent
Model	CZ-NACE 25	CZ-NACE 28	CZ-NACE F	CZ-NACE 25	CZ-NACE 28	CZ-NACE F
Model 1	0.1246	0.0094	0.0177	0.3556	0.0167	0.4495
Model 2	0.9158	0.0219	0.0003	0.2126	0.1213	0.2582
Model 3	0.9118	0.0220	0.0003	0.2072	0.1213	0.2541
Model 4	0.0000	0.0039	0.0000	0.2467	0.2908	0.4406
Model 5	0.0219	0.2928	0.0001	0.0455	0.1329	0.0390
Model 6	0.8835	0.1783	0.0002	0.1236	0.0573	0.0666
Model 7	0.3279	0.0582	0.0921	0.1347	0.0573	0.0768
Model 8	0.1380	0.0418	0.2294	0.0889	0.1213	0.1336
Model 9	0.4733	0.0083	0.0037	0.1309	0.0039	0.0811
Model 10	0.4938	0.0361	0.0007	0.1549	0.0290	0.0864
Model 11	0.2264	0.1174	0.0231	0.1347	0.0573	0.0156
Model 12	0.1269	0.0070	0.0002	0.2180	0.2599	0.3074
Model 13	0.9997	0.0262	0.3491	0.5379	0.1392	0.6407
Model 14	0.9026	0.0926	0.5013	0.9415	0.9439	0.4031
Model 15	0.0000	0.0465	0.5648	0.2910	0.0112	0.0245
Model 16	0.0084	0.0440	0.2563	0.2292	0.0060	0.0673
Model 17	0.4545	0.0397	0.0635	0.2292	0.0137	0.0029
Model 18	0.5437	0.1081	0.1799	0.2778	0.0167	0.0158

Source: authors' own work.

Figures 3 and 4 do not reflect any distinction between the economic phases as their curves show the absolute differences defined by Equations (1) and (2). This enables the inclusion also of the Kralicek Quick Test into the graphs. Taffler, however, remains excluded and will be presented in a separate table. The curves above the horizontal axis mean that the models predicting financial distress reached higher values for the economic phase of expansion. On the contrary, curves below the horizontal axis mean that the bankruptcy models had higher values during the economic phase of recession.

Figure 3 represents healthy enterprises. The results obtained in the sectors of Construction and Machinery confirm the expectations. Final values of models predicting financial distress were all higher in the expansion phase except for the Kralicek Quick Test in the case of CZ-NACE 28. Surprisingly, CZ-NACE 25 (Manufacture of fabricated metal products) did not meet the expectations of the conducted research. The blue curve is situated below the horizontal axis for most models. It means that most models predicting financial distress provided better results for the recession than for the expansion phase in the case of CZ-NACE 25. The reasons will be explained below in the discussion.

The results of healthy companies are followed by the results for insolvent enterprises displayed in Figure 4. There are no significant differences between the individual industry branches subjected to analysis. The curves are situated above the horizontal axis, except for the Doucha approach, which was applied to the Construction sector. The results achieved can interpret the financial situation of the insolvent companies as significantly worse in the recession phase or significantly better in the expansion phase of the economic cycle, which met the preliminary expectations.

Friedman's test for comparing model performances for the different branches was applied. The results of the test provide the following interpretation. In the case of healthy companies, the industry branches CZ-NACE 28 (Machinery) and CZ-NACE F (Construction) do not differ significantly. In contrast, the industry sectors CZ-NACE 25 (Manufacture of metal products) and CZ-NACE F (Construction), as well as the pair CZ-NACE 25 (Manufacture of metal products) and CZ-NACE 28 (Machinery), differ significantly. The interpretation in the case of insolvent companies is following. The pairs CZ-NACE 28 (Machinery) + CZ-NACE F (Construction) and CZ-NACE 25 (Manufacture of metal products) + CZ-NACE 28 (Machinery) differ significantly. On the other hand, the industry sectors CZ-NACE 25 (Manufacture of metal products) and CZ-NACE F (Construction) do not differ significantly.

Again, the Taffler model has been excluded from the visualization. Its results are presented separately and can be seen in Table 4. Taffler's absolute difference in the median confirms previous outcomes. The prediction models for the healthy enterprises belonging to the sector of Manufacture of metal products showed better scores in the recession phase (leading to the negative value of absolute differences). Other industry sectors, with no respect for basic financial standing, show positive values, which can be interpreted as better financial conditions in the expansion phase in contrast to the recession phase.

Table 4. Absolute differences of the Taffler model regarding 2012 and 2017 by branches.

Company Type	Healthy	Insolvent
CZ-NACE 25	−1.03	2.47
CZ-NACE 28	3.78	9.57
CZ-NACE F	2.08	5.94

Source: authors' own work.

The visualization submitted in the figures represents results without using in-depth statistical methods. The apparent advantage of this approach is the opportunity for quick interpretation by the user, without requiring in-depth statistical knowledge. Figures 5 and 6 show the summarized results achieved on statistical bases. As demonstrated in a visualization, the expectations failed to be met in all models predicting financial distress applied. Figures 5 and 6 contain results for descriptive statistics, such as the mean, median, and trimmed mean. A number of models confirming expectations (absolute frequency) is followed by the share of models confirming expectations (relative frequency). Models confirming expectations had the curves above the horizontal axis in Figures 3 and 4. Their values were higher in the expansion rather than in the recession period.

Figures 5 and 6 confirm that the selected descriptive statistic for visualization (median versus mean and trimmed mean) does not influence results significantly. The Machinery (CZ-NACE 28) and Construction (CZ-NACE F) sectors provided comparable results for most models, regardless whether companies were healthy or insolvent. As already discussed, the Kralicek Quick Test failed in the field of Machinery in the case of healthy enterprises. The same can be applied to the Šorins–Voronova model in the field of Construction. On the contrary however, the majority of models failed in the case of healthy enterprises belonging to the Manufacture of metal products. Only median analysis based on Doucha, D2, and Hajdu and Virág models reached a satisfactory outcome.

The situation of insolvent entities is displayed in Figure 6. The level of error seems much lower as many models detected insolvency correctly. The lowest accuracy occurs again in the Manufacture of metal products. In the case of median models, such as IN01, IN05, and D3, were against the expectations in CZ-NACE 25. All models applied to CZ-NACE 28 reached expectations. Unconvincing results (mean) were provided by models such as Doucha, Bonita, and Prusak 1 in the field of Construction. The Doucha model collapsed for all three descriptive statistics in this case.

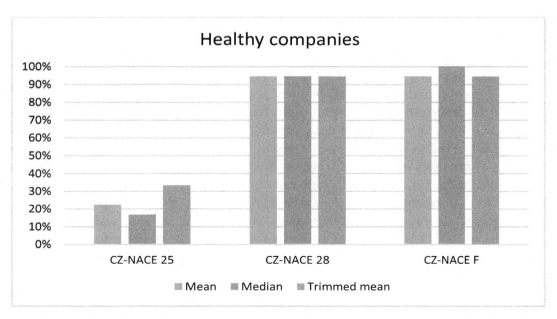

Figure 5. The number of models within each branch confirming better conditions for healthy companies. Source: authors' own work.

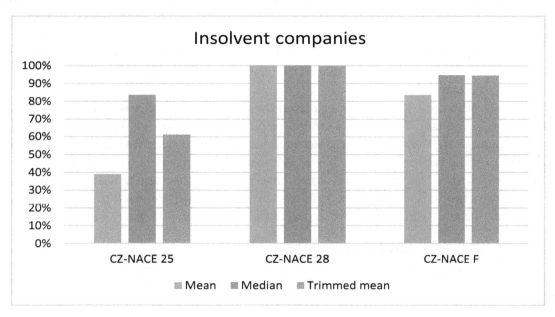

Figure 6. The number of models within each branch confirming better conditions for insolvent companies. Source: authors' own work.

5. Discussion and Conclusions

The results achieved, as described above, confirmed the working hypothesis that the phase of economic cycle influences corporate financial standing. Worse financial standing is expected in a recession phase and better financial conditions during an expansion phase. This finding has a significant consequence on models predicting financial distress related to forecasting corporate financial situation. If models predicting financial distress are applied, the users should respect overall economic conditions, including macroeconomic and industry development. The recession phase mostly leads to lower final scores of bankruptcy models; on the contrary, the expansion phase leads to higher final scores. The evaluation of a company, according to models predicting financial distress, should take into account the phases of the economic cycle. It seems it is not necessary to include macroeconomic variables into models, but the overall economic situation should be considered at least in an expert's decision when the final scores are interpreted.

The part describing the results emphasized the issue of healthy companies belonging to CZ-NACE 25. Figure 3 and Table 4 proved that most models predicting financial distress had better results in a recession period. This observation contradicts the expectations and results in other sectors (CZ-NACE 28 and CZ-NACE F). It should also be highlighted that the results of insolvent enterprises fulfilled the expectations. One explanation for this can be as follows. Firstly, the data sample of 2012 was previously extracted in the year 2014 for other research and the methodology applied was slightly different. Healthy companies should have created positive economic value added in three years in a row between the years 2010 and 2012, although only one year of positive economic value added was required for the data sample of 2017. This requirement excluded many companies as they were not deemed entirely financially healthy, but the same was applied to other analyzed sectors. Secondly, the industry situation and its development can influence the results. The development of the Manufacture of metal products (CZ-NACE 25) can be different from the development of Machinery (CZ-NACE 28) and Construction (CZ-NACE F).

Unconvincing results were obtained for different models predicting financial distress in three industry branches under examination. The unconvincing results are not a consequence of the models' design alone. If the users decide to predict financial distress promptly, they should use more than one prediction model. Multiple verifications can eliminate the randomness discussed previously. It is essential to realize that models predicting financial distress are designed for a quick evaluation of the corporate financial situation, they work on empirical bases, and they never function as natural law (De Laurentis et al. 2010). It should also be respected that economics belongs to the social sciences, although many processes can be quantified, and the behavior of economic entities can be described systematically.

Future research directions would benefit from the application of advanced statistical techniques. The methods enabling self-adaptation and learning are likely to have a unique position. Some approaches taking advantage of macroeconomic or industry variables are not published since they are part of the company's know-how. Although large financial providers of different kinds use these techniques, small- and medium-sized enterprises cannot apply them for mitigating their business risk. Unfortunately, as current research directions tend to move away from widespread application in practice, the primary intentions presented by Altman (1968) or Beaver (1966) are not met.

Author Contributions: Conceptualization, D.C. and J.K.; methodology, D.C.; validation, J.K.; formal analysis, J.K.; resources, D.C. and J.K.; data curation, J.K.; writing—original draft preparation, D.C.; writing—review and editing, D.C. and J.K.; visualization, J.K.; supervision, J.K.; project administration, D.C.; funding acquisition, D.C. All authors have read and agreed to the published version of the manuscript.

References

Achim, Monica Violeta, Codruta Mare, and Sorin Nicolae Borlea. 2012. A statistical model of financial risk bankruptcy applied for Romanian manufacturing industry. *Procedia Economics and Finance* 3: 132–37. [CrossRef]

Acosta-González, Eduardo, and Fernando Fernández-Rodríguez. 2014. Forecasting financial failure of firms via genetic algorithms. *Computational Economics* 43: 133–57. [CrossRef]

Agarwal, Vineet, and Richard Taffler. 2007. Twenty-five years of the Taffler z-score model: does it really have predictive ability? *Accounting and Business Research* 37: 285–300. [CrossRef]

Ahn, Byeong, Sung Cho, and Chang Kim. 2000. The integrated methodology of rough set theory and artificial neural network for business failure prediction. *Expert Systems with Applications* 18: 65–74. [CrossRef]

Alaka, Hafiz A., Lukumon O. Oyedele, Hakeem A. Owolabi, Vikas Kumar, Saheed O. Ajayi, Olungbenga O. Akinade, and Muhammad Bilal. 2018. Systematic review of bankruptcy prediction models: Towards a framework for tool selection. *Expert Systems with Applications* 94: 164–84. [CrossRef]

Altman, Edward I. 1968. Financial Ratios, Discriminant Analysis and the Prediction of Corporate Bankruptcy. *Journal of Finance* 23: 589–609. [CrossRef]

Altman, Edward I. 1993. *Corporate Financial Distress and Bankruptcy*, 2nd ed. New York: John Wiley & Sons, ISBN 978-0-471-55253-6.

Altman, Edward I. 2004. Predicting corporate distress in a turbulent economic and regulatory environment. *Rassegna Economica* 68: 483–524.

Balcaen, Sofie, and Hubert Ooghe. 2006. 35 years of studies on business failure: an overview of the classic statistical methodologies and their related problems. *The British Accounting Review* 38: 63–93. [CrossRef]

Beaver, William H. 1966. Financial Ratios as Predictors of Failure. *Journal of Accounting Research* 4: 71–111. [CrossRef]

Belás, Jaroslav, Luboš Smrčka, Beata Gavurova, and Jan Dvorský. 2018. The impact of social and economic factors in the credit risk management of SME. *Technological and Economic Development of Economy* 24: 1215–30. [CrossRef]

Bokšová, Jiřina, and Monika Randáková. 2013. Zveřejňují podniky, které procházejí insolvenčním řízením, své účetní závěrky (Do Firms in Insolvency Proceedings Publish Their Financial Statements?)? *Český finanční a účetní časopis* 8: 164–71. [CrossRef]

Bruneau, Catherine, Olivier de Bandt, and Widad El Amri. 2012. Macroeconomic fluctuations and corporate financial fragility. *Journal of Financial Stability* 8: 219–35. [CrossRef]

Čámská, Dagmar. 2015. Models Predicting Financial Distress and their Accuracy in the Case of Construction Industry in the Czech Republic. Paper presented at 7th International Scientific Conference Finance and Performance of Firms in Science, Education and Practice, Zlín, Czech Republic, April 23–24; Edited by Eliška Pastuszková, Zuzana Crhová, Jana Vychytilová, Blanka Vytrhlíková and Adriana Knápková. Zlín: Tomas Bata University in Zlin, pp. 178–90.

Čámská, Dagmar. 2016. Accuracy of Models Predicting Corporate Bankruptcy in a Selected Industry Branch. *Ekonomický časopis* 64: 353–66.

Čámská, Dagmar. 2019. Models predicting corporate financial distress and industry specifics. Paper presented at International Conference on Time Series and Forecasting (ITISE 2019), Universidad de Granada, Granada, Spain, September 25–27; Edited by Olga Valenzuela, Fernando Rojas, Hector Pomares and Ignacio Rojas. Granada: Godel Impresiones Digitales S.L., pp. 647–56.

Chava, Sudheer, and Robert Jarrow. 2004. Bankruptcy Prediction with Industry Effects. *Review of Finance* 8: 537–69. [CrossRef]

Crone, Sven, and Steven Finlay. 2012. Instance Sampling in Credit Scoring: An Empirical Study of Sample Size and Balancing. *International Journal of Forecasting* 28: 224–38. [CrossRef]

Davidova, G. 1999. Quantity method of bankruptcy risk evaluation. *Journal of Risk Management* 3: 13–20.

De Laurentis, Giacomo, Renato Maino, and Luca Molteni. 2010. *Developing, Validating and Using Internal Ratings: Methodologies and Case Studies*, 1st ed. Singapore: John Wiley & Sons, ISBN 978-0-470-71149-1.

Deakin, Edward B. 1972. A Discriminant Analysis of Prediction of Business Failure. *Journal of Accounting Research* 10: 167–69. [CrossRef]

Doucha, Rudolf. 1996. *Finanční Analýza Podniku: Praktické Aplikace (Corporate Financial Analysis: Practical Applications)*, 1st ed. Prague: Vox Consult, ISBN 80-902111-2-7.

Du Jardin, Philippe. 2017. Dynamics of Firm Financial Evolution and Bankruptcy Prediction. *Expert Systems with Application* 75: 25–43. [CrossRef]

Du Jardin, Philippe. 2018. Failure pattern-based ensembles applied to bankruptcy forecasting. *Decision Support Systems* 107: 64–77. [CrossRef]

European Commission. 2012. *Communication from the Commission to the European Parliament, The Council, The European Economic and Social Committee and The Committee of the Regions Entrepreneurship 2020 Action Plan, Reigniting the entrepreneurial spirit in Europe.* Brussels: European Communities, Available online: https://eur-lex.europa.eu/legal-content/EN/TXT/?uri=CELEX:52012DC0795 (accessed on 15 December 2019).

Fairfield, Patricia M, Sundaresh Rammath, and Teri Lombardi Yohn. 2009. Do Industry-Level Analyses Improve Forecasts of Financial Performance? *Journal of Accounting Research* 47: 147–78. [CrossRef]

Foster, George. 1986. *Financial Statement Analysis*, 2nd ed. New York: Prentice Hall, ISBN 978-0133163179.

Frank, Murray Z., and Vidhan K. Goyal. 2009. Capital Structure Decisions: Which Factors Are Reliably Important? *Financial Management* 38: 1–37. [CrossRef]

Ganguin, Blaise, and John Bilardello. 2004. *Standard & Poor's Fundamentals of Corporate Credit Analysis*. New York: McGrew-Hill Professional, ISBN 978-0071441636.

Hajdu, Ottó, and Miklós Virág. 2001. Hungarian Model for Predicting Financial Bankruptcy. *Society and Economy in Central and Eastern Europe* 23: 28–46.

Hamilton, David T., Greg M. Gupton, and A. Berthault. 2001. Default and Recovery Rates of Corporate Bond Issuers: 2000. Moody's Investor Service, New York, USA. Available online: http://papers.ssrn.com/sol3/ Delivery.cfm/SSRN_ID277999_code010803670.pdf?abstractid=277999&mirid=1 (accessed on 12 December 2019).

Hol, Suzan. 2007. The influence of the business cycle on bankruptcy probability. *International Transactions in Operational Research* 14: 75–90. [CrossRef]

Jackson, Andrew B, Marlene A. Plumlee, and Brian R. Rountree. 2018. Decomposing the market, industry, and firm components of profitability: implications for forecasts of profitability. *Review of Accounting Studies* 23: 1071–95. [CrossRef]

Jansone, Inga, Viktors Nespors, and Irina Voronova. 2010. Finanšu un ekonomisko risku ietekme uz Latvijas partikas mazumtirdzniecibas nozares attistibu (Impact of Financial and Economic Risks to Extension of Food Retail Industry of Latvia). *Scientific Journal of Riga Technical University Economics and Business Economy: Theory and Practice* 20: 59–64.

Jordan, Bradford, Randolph Westerfield, and Stephen Ross. 2011. *Corporate Finance Essentials*. New York: McGraw-Hill, ISBN 978-0-07-122115-3.

Karas, Michal, and Mária Režňáková. 2013. Bankruptcy Prediction Model of Industrial Enterprises in the Czech Republic. *International Journal of Mathematical Models and Methods in Applied Sciences* 7: 519–31.

Kisielińska, Joanna, and Adam Waszkowski. 2010. Polskie modele do prognozowania bankructwa przedsiębiorstw i ich weryfikacja (Polish Models to Predict Bankruptcy and Its Verification). *Ekonomika i Organizacja Gospodarki Żywnościowej* 82: 17–31.

Klečka, Jiří, and Hana Scholleová. 2010. Bankruptcy models enunciation for Czech glass making firms. *Economics and Management* 15: 954–59.

Klieštik, Tomáš, Jana Klieštiková, Mária Kováčová, Lucia Švábová, Katarína Valášková, Marek Vochozka, and Judit Oláh. 2018. *Prediction of Financial Health of Business Entities in Transition Economies*. New York: Addleton Academic Publishers, ISBN 978-1-942585-39-8.

Korol, Tomasz, and Adrian Korodi. 2010. Predicting Bankruptcy with the Use of Macroeconomic Variables. *Economic Computation and Economic Cybernetics Studies and Research* 44: 201–19.

Kralicek, Peter. 2007. Ertrags- und Vermögensanalyse (Quicktest) (Earnings and Wealth Analysis (Quicktest)). Available online: http://www.kralicek.at/pdf/qr_druck.pdf (accessed on 15 May 2019).

Kumar, P. Ravi, and Vadlamani Ravi. 2007. Bankruptcy prediction in banks and firms via statistical and intelligent techniques—A review. *European Journal of Operational Research* 180: 1–28. [CrossRef]

Lee, Gwendolyn K., and Mishari Alnahedh. 2016. Industries' Potential for Interdependency and Profitability: A Panel of 135 Industries, 1988–1996. *Strategy Science* 1: 285–308. [CrossRef]

Lee, Seung-Hyun, Yasuhiro Yamakawa, Mike W. Peng, and Jay B. Barney. 2011. How do bankruptcy laws affect entrepreneurship development around the world? *Journal of Business Venturing* 26: 505–20. [CrossRef]

Lensberg, Terje, Aasmund Eilifsen, and Thomas E. McKee. 2006. Bankruptcy theory development and classification via genetic programming. *European Journal of Operational Research* 169: 677–97. [CrossRef]

Lessmann, Stefan, Bart Baesens, Hsin-Vonn Seow, and Lyn C. Thomas. 2015. Benchmarking state-of-the-art classification algorithms for credit scoring: An update of research. *European Journal of Operational Research* 247: 124–36. [CrossRef]

Li, Leon, and Robert Faff. 2019. Predicting corporate bankruptcy: What matters? *International Review of Economics & Finance* 62: 1–19. [CrossRef]

Liou, Dah-Kwei, and MalcolmMalcolm Smith Malcolm Smith. 2007. Macroeconomic Variables and Financial Distress. *Journal of Accounting, Business & Management* 14: 17–31.

Machek, Ondřej. 2014. Long-term Predictive Ability of Bankruptcy Models in the Czech Republic: Evidence from 2007–2012. *Central European Business Review* 3: 14–17. [CrossRef]

Merkevicius, Egidijus, Gintautas Garšva, and Stasys Girdzijauskas. 2006. A Hybrid SOM-Altman Model for Bankruptcy Prediction. Paper presented at 6th International Conference Computational Science–ICCS 2006, Reading, UK, May 28–31; Berlin and Heidelberg: Springer, pp. 364–371, Part II. [CrossRef]

Merton, Robert C. 1974. On the pricing of corporate debt: The risk structure of interest rates. *The Journal of Finance* 29: 449–70. [CrossRef]

Min, Jae H., and Young-Chan Lee. 2005. Bankruptcy prediction using support vector machine with optimal choice of kernel function parameters. *Expert Systems with Applications* 28: 603–14. [CrossRef]

Ministry of Industry and Trade. 2013. Finanční analýza podnikové sféry se zaměřením na konkurenceschopnost sledovaných odvětví za rok 2012 (Financial Analysis of the Business Sphere with a Focus on the Competitiveness of the Monitred Sectors in 2012). Available online: https://www.mpo.cz/assets/dokumenty/ 48519/55958/605530/priloha001.xls (accessed on 10 April 2014).

Ministry of Industry and Trade. 2018. Finanční analýza podnikové sféry za rok 2017 (Financial Analysis of the Business Sphere in 2017). Available online: https://www.mpo.cz/assets/cz/rozcestnik/analyticke-materialy-a-statistiky/analyticke-materialy/2018/6/Tabulky2017.xlsx (accessed on 20 June 2019).

Moyer, Stephen G. 2005. *Distressed Debt Analysis: Strategies for Speculative Investors*. Boca Raton: J. Ross Publishing, ISBN 1-932159-18-5.

Neumaierová, Inka, and Ivan Neumaier. 2002. *Výkonnost a Tržní Hodnota Firmy (Performance and Company Market Value)*, 1st ed. Prague: Grada, ISBN 9788024701257.

Neumaierová, Inka, and Ivan Neumaier. 2005. Index IN05 (Index IN05). Paper presented at Evropské Finanční Systémy, Masarykova Univerzita, Brno, Czech Republic, June 21–23; Brno: Masarykova Univerzita, pp. 143–48.

Ohlson, James A. 1980. Financial ratios and the probabilistic prediction of bankruptcy. *Journal of Accounting Research* 18: 109–31. [CrossRef]

Öztekin, Özde. 2015. Capital structure decisions around the world: which factors are reliably important? *Journal of Financial and Quantitative Analysis* 50: 301–23. [CrossRef]

Peng, Mike W., Yasuhiro Yamakawa, and Seung-Hyun Lee. 2010. Bankruptcy Laws and Entrepreneur–Friendliness. *Entrepreneurship Theory and Practice* 34: 517–30. [CrossRef]

Pitrová, Kateřina. 2011. Possibilities of the Altman Zeta Model Application to Czech Firms. *EM Ekonomika a Management* 14: 66–76.

Prusak, Błażej. 2018. Review of research into enterprise bankruptcy prediction in selected central and eastern European countries. *International Journal of Financial Studies* 6: 60. [CrossRef]

Ravisankar, Pediredla, and Vadlamani Ravi. 2010. Financial distress prediction in banks using Group Method of Data Handling neural network, counter propagation neural network and fuzzy ARTMAP. *Knowledge-Based Systems* 23: 823–31. [CrossRef]

Schönfeld, Jaroslav, Michal Kuděj, and Luboš Smrčka. 2018. Financial Health of Enterprises Introducing Safeguard Procedure Based on Bankruptcy Models. *Journal of Business Economics and Management* 19: 692–705. [CrossRef]

Smrčka, Luboš, Markéta Arltová, and Jaroslav Schönfeld. 2013. Reasons for the failure to implement financial rehabilitation procedures in insolvent reality. *Politická Ekonomie* 61: 188–208. [CrossRef]

Strouhal, Jiří, Natalja Gurtviš, Monika Nikitina-Kalamäe, Tsz Wan Li, Anna-Lena Lochman, and Kathrin Born. 2014. Are Companies Willing to Publicly Present their Financial Statements on Time? Case of Czech and Estonian TOP100 Companies. Paper presented at 7th International Scientific Conference on Managing and Modelling of Financial Risks Modelling of Financial Risks, VSB Tech Univ Ostrava, Ostrava, Czech Republic, September 8–9; pp. 731–38.

Svobodová, Libuše. 2013. Trends in the number of bankruptcies in the Czech Republic. Paper presented at Hradecké ekonomické dny (Hradec Economic Days), Hradec Králové, Czech Republic, February 19–20; pp. 393–99.

Topaloglu, Zeynep. 2012. A multi-period logistic model of bankruptcies in the manufacturing industry. *International Journal of Finance and Accounting* 1: 28–37. [CrossRef]

Vlachý, Jan. 2018. *Corporate Finance*. Prague: Leges, ISBN 978-80-7502-291-2.

Wöber, André, and Oliver Siebenlist. 2009. *Sanierungsberatung für Mittel- und Kleinbetriebe, Erfolgreiches Consulting in der Unternehmenkrise (Restructuring Advice for Medium and Small Businesses, Successful Consulting in the Corporate Crisis)*. Berlin: Erich Schmidt Verlag GmbH, ISBN 978-3503112456.

Wu, Desheng Dash, Yidong Zhang, Dexiang Wu, and David L. Olson. 2010. Fuzzy multi-objective programming for supplier selection and risk modeling: A possibility approach. *European Journal of Operational Research* 200: 774–87. [CrossRef]

Zellner, Arnold. 1992. Statistics, Science and Public Policy. *Journal of the American Statistical Association* 87: 1–6.
    [CrossRef]
Zhou, Ligang, Kin Keung Lai, and Jerome Yen. 2010. Bankruptcy prediction incorporating macroeconomic variables
    using Neural Network. Paper presented at International Conference on Technologies and Applications of
    Artificial Intelligence, TAAI 2010, Hsinchu, Taiwan, November 18–20; pp. 80–85. [CrossRef]

9

An Ensemble Classifier-Based Scoring Model for Predicting Bankruptcy of Polish Companies in the Podkarpackie Voivodeship

Tomasz Pisula🆔

Department of Quantitative Methods, Faculty of Management, Rzeszow University of Technology, al. Powstancow W-wy 10, 35-959 Rzeszow, Poland; tpisula@prz.edu.pl

Abstract: This publication presents the methodological aspects of designing of a scoring model for an early prediction of bankruptcy by using ensemble classifiers. The main goal of the research was to develop a scoring model (with good classification properties) that can be applied in practice to assess the risk of bankruptcy of enterprises in various sectors. For the data sample, which included 1739 Polish businesses (of which 865 were bankrupt and 875 had no risk of bankruptcy), a genetic algorithm was applied to select the optimum set of 19 bankruptcy indicators, on the basis of which the classification accuracy of a number of ensemble classifier model variants (boosting, bagging and stacking) was estimated and verified. The classification effectiveness of ensemble models was compared with eight classical individual models which made use of single classifiers. A GBM-based ensemble classifier model offering superior classification capabilities was used in practice to design a scoring model, which was applied in comparative evaluation and bankruptcy risk analysis for businesses from various sectors and of different sizes from the Podkarpackie Voivodeship in 2018 (over a time horizon of up to two years). The approach applied can also be used to assess credit risk for corporate borrowers.

Keywords: bankruptcy prediction; ensemble classifiers; boosting; bagging; stacking; scoring models

---

1. Introduction

According to statistical data from 2018–2019, 30–60 businesses in Poland announce bankruptcy each month. Business bankruptcy is invariably an adverse phenomenon for the business itself and its employees, but it is also a problem for its creditors, banks and partners. The high number of bankruptcies reported may also lead to negative consequences locally—for the economic development and economic circumstances of the region—and on the national scale—for the economy of the whole country. For this reason, the issue of early prediction of business bankruptcy, and therefore the possibility of forecasting the risk of business bankruptcy over a long time horizon (even up to several years), is a very important financial and economic problem. In its financial and economic dimension, bankruptcy (i.e., business default) is defined as a situation in which a business is unable (for various reasons) to meet its liabilities towards creditors. For businesses operating in market economics conditions, a potential risk of bankruptcy always exists. The risk is the most commonly defined as the probability of defaulting on liabilities incurred (probability of default, PD). The subject of modeling risk of bankruptcy is also of enormous importance for institutions granting corporate loans, to whom the bankruptcy of a corporate debtor means a potential loss of the loan granted.

The main objective of this study was to design a scoring model based on ensemble classifiers which could be used to forecast the risk of bankruptcy for Polish businesses conducting activity in the Podkarpackie Voivodeship over a time horizon of up to two years. One of the reasons for using a developed scoring model based on ensemble classifiers to forecast bankruptcy risk for companies from the Podkarpackie region in this study is the fact that the Podkarpackie Voivodeship (along with several other Polish regions) just after a period of political transformation of Poland from socialism to market economy, was notably lagging behind in development. It belonged to the group of several eastern regions (voivodeships) from the so-called the eastern wall, which was overlooked and underestimated in the policies pursued by relevant governments. The selection of companies from the region was also influenced by the fact that the Podkarpackie Voivodeship is currently one of the "development tigers" in Poland and is catching up quickly. This is mainly due to the more effective policies of the current government aimed at equalizing the development opportunities of Polish regions. The Podkarpackie Voivodship is not a very large voivodeship in relation to other regions of Poland as it occupies 11th place in a ranking of all 16 voivodeships, with an area of 17,846 km^2 (source: Główny Urząd Statystyczny (2019) (Statistics Poland)—Local Data Bank, https://bdl.stat.gov.pl). The attractiveness of the voivodeship, however, is influenced by its geographical location, which is conducive to the development of ecological agriculture and tourism (also international—the Bieszczady Mountains). A big advantage of the region is also its border location (the region borders Ukraine and Slovakia—which also belongs to the EU). Due to its population size, the Podkarpackie region belongs to the group of medium-populated regions of Poland and takes 8th place in this ranking, with a population of approximately 2.1 million (source: Główny Urząd Statystyczny (2019) (Statistics Poland)—Local Data Bank, https://bdl.stat.gov.pl). The voivodeship also has no very developed industries, in comparison to other more industrialized regions of Poland. Nevertheless, the Podkarpackie Voivodeship belongs to the group of the fastest developing regions of Poland. In terms of income per capita, the Podkarpackie Voivodeship took 2nd place in 2018 in the ranking of 16 Polish regions-voivodships (revenues at the level of PLN 562.4 per inhabitant (source: Statistics Poland—Local Data Bank, https://bdl.stat.gov.pl). Also in 2018, the Podkarpackie region was the most dynamically developing region of Poland in terms of the growth of generated GDP (GDP). The Podkarpackie recorded an increase of 7.8% of GDP in 2018 compared to the previous year. In 2018, the GDP generated in the Podkarpackie already constituted 3.9% of Poland's GDP and was 9th place in the regions (ranking source: Statistics Poland—Local Data Bank, https://bdl.stat.gov.pl/BDL/start). This proves that the region's economy is already very dynamic but at present is still progressing. The economy of the Podkarpackie region stands out positively and has a very large impact on its potential cluster of aviation industry enterprises belonging to the so-called aviation valley and the dynamic development of road and transport infrastructure (e.g., the route of the international European North-South communication line Via Carpatia), as well as the development of innovation (innovative technologies) in the region. The companies that drive development in the region belong to Stowarzyszenie Dolina Lotnicza (2019) (Aviation Valley Association), that include many aviation industry companies that provide services to major aviation manufacturers around the world (e.g., Boeing, Airbus, source: http://www.dolinalotnicza.pl/en/business-card). These include companies such as 3M Poland, 3D Robot, Boeing Distribution Services, Pratt & Whitney Poland, Collins Aerospace, Goodrich Aerospace Poland, General Electric Company Poland, Hamilton Sundstrand Poland, Heli-One, Safran Transmission Systems Poland and MTU Aero Engines Poland. The very dynamic development of economic potential in the Podkarpackie region also affects the quality of life of its inhabitants. The Podkarpackie Voivodeship has been high in the quality of life rankings for several years. All these factors make it sensible to conduct a comprehensive analysis and an assessment of the risk of bankruptcy of enterprises operating in the Podkarpackie region using the most effective models of forecasting and assessing the risk of their bankruptcy. Therefore, first the work focused on developing an adequate scoring model for bankruptcy forecast using ensemble classifiers, and analyzing and verifying its prognostic capacity (classification efficiency), while only later on using it in practice to comprehensively assess the bankruptcy risk of enterprises from the Podkarpackie region belonging to various sectors of the economy (depending on the declared classification of their activities) that can also be distinguished by their size.

The article details the stages in which the scoring model was designed and implemented in practice. The scoring model design stage involved the comparison of the predictive capability of ensemble models used in this study with that of conventional single classifiers. The results of previous works of many authors (see e.g., Anwar et al. 2014; Barboza et al. 2017; Tsai et al. 2014) indicate that the models based on ensemble classifiers help achieve more accurate results and improve the discriminant capability of the model. On the basis of the scoring model designed, a bankruptcy risk assessment for businesses from the Podkarpackie Voivodeship was carried out based on the sector in which they operated and the size of the business.

The main innovation of the research presented in the article is that previous studies of other authors did not discuss the practical use of the scoring model for comprehensive analysis of the bankruptcy risk of companies (also from different sectors) operating in the Podkarpackie region, using the ensemble classifiers approach.

2. Literature Review

The various problems of bankruptcy of businesses are widely described in the literature. The significance and salience of the bankruptcy problem has motivated many authors to concentrate on this issue in their research. The first mentions of the subject of modeling business bankruptcy and forecasting its likelihood appeared in economic and financial literature in 1968. The first study on risk bankruptcy modeling was published by Altman (1968). The early bankruptcy prediction studies applied statistical methods and mainly concerned the use of different variants of discriminant analysis or logistic regression (Ohlson 1980; Begley et al. 1996). Since those models had significant limitations, artificial intelligence and machine learning methods that were successfully applied in image recognition tasks were gradually also implemented in bankruptcy forecasting. It was found that machine learning techniques such as neural networks (NNet), Support Vector Machines (SVM) and ensemble classifier methods have better forecasting capabilities and higher classification effectiveness than conventional approaches. An overview of the previous research on the application of statistical methods and machine learning techniques in business bankruptcy prediction can be found in studies such as the ones by Kumar and Ravi (2007) and Lessmann et al. (2015). Alaka et al. (2018) presented a comprehensive overview of literature and systematics of predictive models used in business bankruptcy forecasting, including: purpose of research, method of selecting variables for the model, sample size for analyzed businesses (also including bankrupt ones) and a comparison of the effectiveness of models' classification measures.

Some works deal with the issues of forecasting and assessing the risk of bankruptcy of enterprises, taking into account the specificities of the sector of their activity. Rajin et al. (2016) conducted a bankruptcy risk assessment for Serbian agricultural enterprises, which is one of the most significant sectors of the Serbian economy. The classification efficiency of several models was compared using the methods of linear discriminant analysis. Their research shows that models taking into account the specifics of economies and market characteristics (e.g., the European market—DF-Kralicek's model) give better results for the Serbian economy than models created for American markets (e.g., the classic Altman Z-Score model). Karas et al. (2017) dealt with similar problems, who showed that classic scoring models developed for the US economy (Z-Score Altman, Altman-Sabato's models) and IN05—designed and developed for the Czech enterprises—are less effective compared to the original validation results. This forces researchers to develop more adequate models, in particular taking into account the specificity and financial indicators of the agricultural sector and the economy of the country affecting the bankruptcy of enterprises. Receiver-Operating Characteristic (ROC) curves were used to measure the effectiveness of the models. Chen et al. (2013) dealt with the problems of forecasting the bankruptcy risk of industrial enterprises in the manufacturing sector in China. They used a modified variant of Multi-Criteria Linear Programming algorithm (so-called MC2LP algorithm) to forecast the risk of bankruptcy of 1499 Chinese enterprises from the studied sector and selected 36 financial indicators to assess their financial condition. The classification efficiency of the studied model was compared with the efficiency of the classic MCLP model and the SVM approach. Matrix correctness (compliance) matrices were used as measures of classification accuracy. The use of the model proposed by the authors enables setting up a variable value for the cut-off point (determining the expected belonging of objects to classes) and thus systematically correcting incorrect classification errors. Topaloglu (2012) dealt with the forecast of bankruptcy of American enterprises from the manufacturing sector using a multi-period logistic regression model, the so-called hazard models. The research period covered bankruptcies from 1980–2007 and the results show that macroeconomic diagnostic variables in a model such as GDP have the very large impact on the assessment of their bankruptcy. The study shows that accounting indicators for assessing the financial condition of enterprises used in the model lose their predictive power (become irrelevant) when global market and macroeconomic indicators are taken into account. Achim et al. (2012) studied the financial risk of bankruptcy for Romanian enterprises from the manufacturing sector using the Principal Component Analysis method in the period of 2000–2011, and thus taking into account the impact of the global crisis on financial markets. The research sample included 53 enterprises registered in Romania and operating in the production sector, including 16 selected and most frequently used financial indicators used in the study. The study shows good predictive quality of the model tested and presents its potential application possibilities. In the literature, you can also find works on the modeling of bankruptcy risk for enterprises operating in other sectors of the economy, e.g., Marcinkevicius and Kanapickiene (2014) for companies from the construction sector, as well as Kim and Gu (2010), Youn and Gu (2010) and Diakomihalis (2012) for companies in the hotel and restaurant sector.

It is also necessary to emphasize an important aspect in the research on the risk of bankruptcy of enterprises, which is taking into account the impact of economic cycles and selected macroeconomic variables of the market while considering the effect of cyclical economic conditions of countries. In Vlamis (2007) statistical logistic and probit regression models were used to forecast the risk of bankruptcy of American real estate companies in the period 1980–2001. It has been shown that financial indicators such as profitability, debt service and company liquidity are important determinants of the risk of bankruptcy of the surveyed enterprises. A number of key macroeconomic financial variables have also been used because the risk of borrowers' bankruptcy depends on the state of the economy and the current business cycle. Similar issues were dealt with in the publication by Hol (2007), which concerned the study of the impact of business cycles on the probability of bankruptcy of Norwegian companies. It has been shown that models that take into account the impact of economic cycles have better prognostic properties than models that only take into account the financial indicators of companies. In a similar study, Bruneau et al. (2012) analyzed the relationship between macroeconomic shocks and exposure to the risk of bankruptcy of companies in France belonging to different sectors of classification of activities. The study of the dependence of the risk of bankruptcy on economic cycles was carried out using the two-equation VAR model based on data from 1990–2010.

At this point one should also mention Polish authors' significant contribution to the development of bankruptcy forecast models which take into account the specific nature of the Polish economy. Their research is mostly based on classical techniques, using statistical methods or machine learning tools and the methods for predicting and evaluating the risk of business bankruptcy. The results obtained by Polish authors studying bankruptcy risk modeling can be found in publications by Korol (2010), Hadasik (1998), Hamrol and Chodakowski (2008), Mączyńska (1994), Prusak (2005) and Ptak-Chmielewska (2016). In the context of the research done by Polish authors, a very interesting and detailed comparative analysis of the subject of enterprise bankruptcy forecasting in East-Central Europe and an overview of models applied from the perspective of developing economies of the countries of the region in the transformation period was presented by Kliestik et al. (2018).

In recent years, ensemble classifiers have been successfully used for predicting bankruptcy of businesses. Some studies of this type include Barboza et al. (2017), Brown and Mues (2012) and Zięba et al. (2016). They are dedicated to the application of ensemble classifiers in forecasting bankruptcy of businesses and demonstrate that the ensemble classifiers offer better forecasting properties and accuracy than conventional statistical methods. Moreover, a study by Kim et al. (2015) proved that ensemble models are more resistant to the sample imbalance problem (for bankrupt businesses and those at no risk of bankruptcy) during the statistical data preparation phase.

Many studies on the application of ensemble classifiers in business bankruptcy forecasting refer to boosting and bagging methods (sequential correction and classification error minimization, as well as component classifier result sampling and combining) in order to increase classification performance of the entire forecasting system. In studies by Cortes et al. (2007) and Heo and Yang (2014), Adaboost (an adaptive boosting algorithm) was applied to decision trees as basic classification models. The use of ensemble classifiers with a classifier boosting technique based on neural network classifiers was discussed in studies by Alfaro et al. (2008), Fedorova et al. (2013), Kim and Kang (2010) and West et al. (2005). A different approach was adopted by Kim et al. (2015) and Sun et al. (2017) who used support vector machines (SVM) as base classifiers, which were boosted as a group of ensemble classifiers. Bagging is also a method frequently used in practical applications of ensemble classifiers. This subject dealt with studies which analyze the classification effectiveness of such ensemble classifiers by relying on several models of base classifiers developed by Hua et al. (2007), Zhang et al. (2010) and Twala (2010). The use of ensemble classifiers with combining (stacking) the results of several classifiers in a single meta-classifier was discussed in studies such as those by Iturriaga and Sanz (2015), Tsai and Wu (2008) and Tsai and Hsu (2013). Furthermore, many studies are dedicated to the use of various techniques of combining the results of base model classification: such as neural networks in the form of self-organizing maps (SOMs), rough sets techniques, case-based reasoning and classifier consensus methods. Examples of the use of this type of ensemble classifiers were examined by Ala'raj and Abbod (2016), Du Jardin (2018), Chuang (2013) and Li and Sun (2012).

3. Environmental Background of the Research Conducted

3.1. Statistical Description of Bankruptcies in Poland

According to data from Ogólnopolski Monitor Upadłościow (2019) (Coface Nationwide Bankruptcy Monitor—source: http://www.emis.com, http://www.coface.pl/en) a total of 798 businesses declared bankruptcy in 2018. Most bankruptcies were reported in October and September (76 and 74, respectively) and in the following months: March, April, May (67, 66 and 65, respectively), with 61 bankruptcies reported in January. The months with the relatively lowest number of bankruptcies were declared in August (42) and February and December (45 bankruptcies). Comparing the structure of business bankruptcies by voivodeships in 2018 (Figure 1), we may notice that the highest number of bankrupt businesses were reported in the Mazowieckie Voivodeship—156 (which constitutes 22% of all bankrupt enterprises). Further positions in the ranking, with a significantly lower number of bankruptcies, are held by: Ślaskie Voivodeship—84 (12%), Wielkopolskie Voivodeship—68 (10%), Dolnoślaskie Voivodeship—61 (9%), Podkarpackie Voivodeship—47 (7%) and Małopolskie Voivodeship—44 (6%). The lowest number of bankruptcies is reported in: Lubuskie Voivodeship—13 (2%), Opolskie Voivodeship—15 (2%), Podlaskie Voivodeship—19 (3%) and Świętokrzyskie Voivodeship—20 (3%). During the first three months of the year 2019, most bankruptcies were also reported in the Mazowieckie Voivodeship—27, Dolnoślaskie Voivodeship—15, Śląskie Voivodeship—14 and Wielkopolskie Voivodeship—11. Based on the latest available data from Q1 2019, the largest number of bankruptcies were recorded in the following voivodeships: Mazowieckie—27, Dolnoślaskie—15, Ślaskie—14, Wielkopolskie—11 and Łódzkie 10. The least in Świętokrzyskie—1, Opolskie—2, Podlaskie and Lubuskie—3, Warmińsko—Mazurskie—4. For the comparison in the Podkarpackie voivodeship, there were 6 bankruptcies.

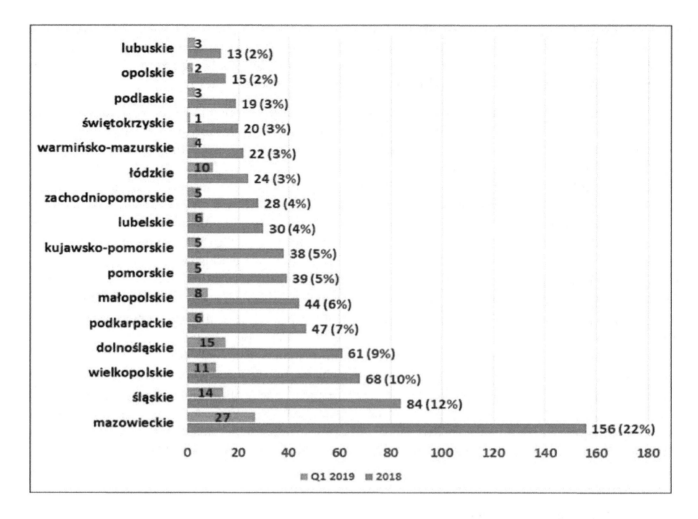

Figure 1. Number of bankruptcies in Polish voivodeships in Q1 2019 and in 2018. Source: own elaboration based on the data analyzed from Coface Nationwide Bankruptcy Monitor (http://www. emis.com).

When analyzing the number of bankrupt businesses in Poland in the year 2019 depending on their business activity, we may notice that the highest number of bankruptcies concerned businesses carrying out varied individual activities (one-person businesses, self-employment)—108 (27% bankrupt), followed by commercial law companies from the commerce (trade) sector—91 (22%), and from the industrial and service sector—70 (17%) and 63 (16%), respectively. In 2019, 51 (13%) businesses from the construction sector, 11 (3%) transport and logistics businesses and 9 (2%) businesses involved in other activities declared their bankruptcy. Figure 2 shows the distribution of the number of bankrupt businesses by their type and the sector of their activity.

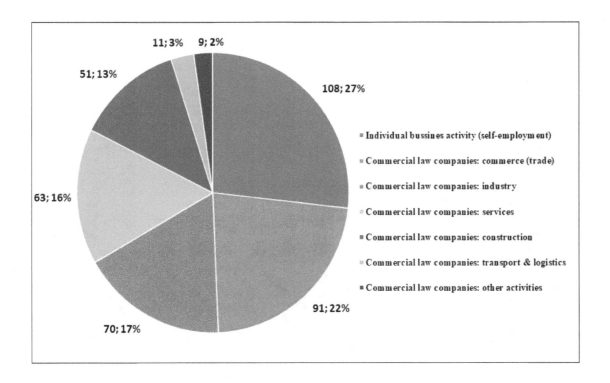

Figure 2. Number of business bankruptcies in Poland in 2019 by sector of activity. Source: own elaboration based on the data analyzed from Coface Nationwide Bankruptcy Monitor (http://www. emis.com).

3.2. Characteristics of Companies Operating in the Podkarpackie Voivodeship

According to Emerging Markets Information Service (2019)—EMIS (http://www.emis.com), in 2018 about 3679 companies and partnerships were registered and operating in the Podkarpackie Voivodeship (the number of available financial statements for 2018 in the database). Their reported sector of activity belonged to one of the following 18 areas: A—farming, forestry and fishing, B—mining and extraction, C—industrial processing, D—production of energy, supply of water, gas and other energy sources, E—waste, waste water and sewage management, F—construction, G—wholesale and retail, and servicing vehicles and motorcycles, H—transport and storage management, I—accommodation and food services, J—information and communications, K—finance and insurance, L—services for the property market, M—scientific, specialist and technological activity, N—administration and support, P—education, Q—health and social care, R—culture, entertainment and leisure, S—other services. Figure 3 presents the structure of the number of businesses operating in the Podkarpackie Voivodeship by sector.

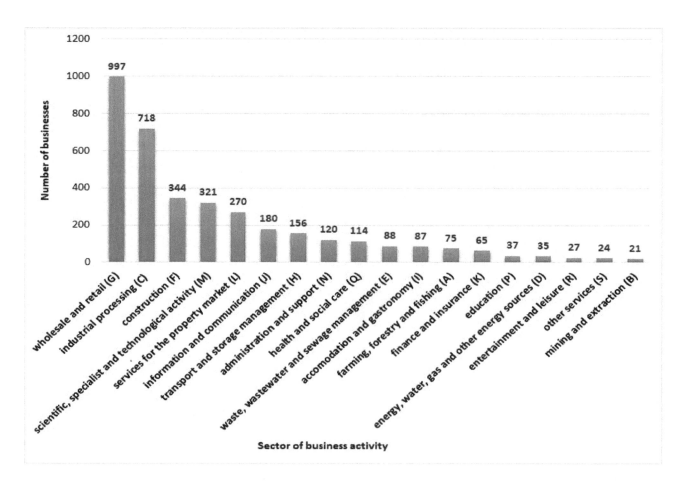

Figure 3. Businesses in the Podkarpackie Voivodeship by sector of activity. Source: own elaboration based on the data analyzed from 2018 (http://www.emis.com).

In 2018, 997 businesses in the Podkarpackie Voivodeship, a vast majority of this area's businesses, operated in the wholesale and retail sector. Economic activity in the field of industrial processing was declared by 718 enterprises, followed by sectors such as the construction, scientific, specialist and technological activity, and services for the property market sectors (344, 321, 270 businesses, respectively). The lowest number of businesses operated in sectors such as education—37, production of energy and supply of energy sources—35, culture—27, other services—24, as well as mining and extraction—21.

Figure 4 presents the structure of the number of businesses in the Podkarpackie Voivodeship by the duration for which they have functioned (in years). Most businesses, i.e., 1792 (which corresponds to 49% of all analyzed entities) have operated in the market for a very long time—10 years. Nearly as many businesses, i.e., 1720 (47% of the total number), have been active for a medium number of years, whereas 'young' enterprises (167), established in the period from 2017 to 2019 and active for up to two years, constituted only 4% of all businesses analyzed.

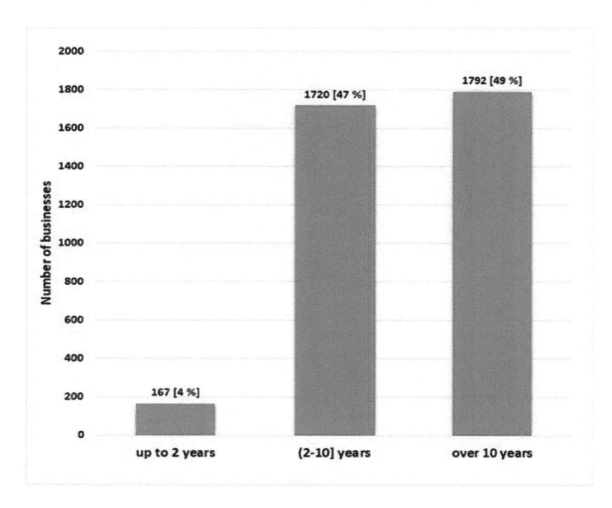

Figure 4. The structure of the number of businesses in the Podkarpackie Voivodeship by the duration of business activity (in years). Source: own elaboration based on the data analyzed from 2018 (http://www.emis.com).

An analysis of businesses operating in the Podkarpackie Voivodeship according to their size (Figure 5) shows that 40% (1461) of all enterprises are very small, they are the so-called micro-enterprises. Small businesses constituted a further 15%. Overall, over a half of businesses (55%) were either micro-enterprises or small enterprises. The number of medium and small enterprises was more or less equal, which corresponds respectively to 22% and 23% of all entities analyzed. The size of the enterprise was identified in accordance with the legal provisions of the classification of Polish enterprises adapted to EU law and directives. Micro enterprises were identified according to the rule: number of employees <10 and annual Turnover <= 2 m €. Small enterprises were identified as not being micro enterprises and fulfilling the conditions: number of employees <50 and annual Turnover <= 10 m €. Medium enterprises were identified as not being small and fulfilling the conditions: number of employees <250 and annual Turnover <= 50 m €. Therefore, large enterprises were identified according to the rule: number of employees >= 250 and annual Turnover >50 m € (source: https://ec.europa.eu/growth/smes/business-friendly-environment/sme-definition_pl).

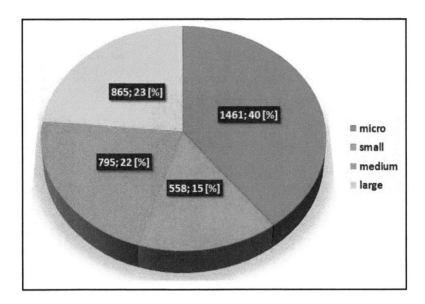

Figure 5. Structure of the number of businesses operating in the Podkarpackie Voivodeship by enterprise size. Source: own elaboration based on the data analyzed from 2018 (http://www.emis.com).

Among all businesses operating in the Podkarpackie Voivodeship, only 7 were listed in the stock market, while 3672 were non-listed companies. An analysis of legal forms of businesses in the Podkarpackie Voivodeship (Figure 6) shows that the vast majority (73.6%) are limited liability companies (private limited companies). There are 2.9% enterprises operating as public limited companies, and only 0.5% are limited partnerships. The remaining businesses, having other legal forms, constitute 23% of all enterprises analyzed in this study.

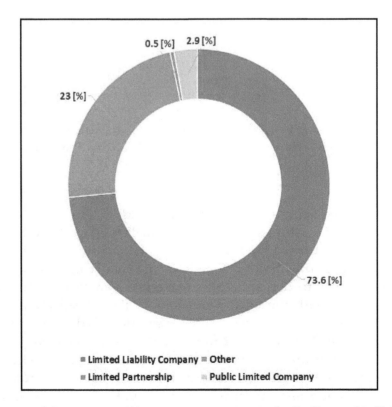

Figure 6. Distribution of the structure of businesses operating in the Podkarpackie Voivodeship by legal form of activity. Source: own elaboration based on the data analyzed from 2018 (http://www.emis.com).

4. Materials and Methods

As can be seen in the above analysis of literature, in practice business bankruptcy risk assessment makes use of various classifier models. Both classical statistical methods and more advanced non-statistical methods are used, with the latter based on various machine learning techniques. The use of so-called ensemble classifiers, i.e., classifiers designed to increase classification efficiency in relation to the conventional approach (which is based on single classifiers), are becoming increasingly popular—for obvious reasons. Table 1 contains an overview of business bankruptcy risk forecasting models that are most often used in practice.

Classical business bankruptcy forecasting models using single classifier models are very-well known and presented in many publications. Meanwhile, the presents study focuses mainly on a detailed presentation of the ensemble classifier methodology. A detailed discussion of classical models and models used in business bankruptcy forecasts can be found e.g., in monographs by Kuhn and Johnson (2013) and Hastie et al. (2013).

Table 1. List of methods applied in forecasting business bankruptcy risk.

Methods Used in Forecasting Business Bankruptcy Risk		
Conventional Approach Based on Single Classifiers		**Ensemble Classifiers**
Statistical Methods	**Non-Statistical Methods and Machine Learning**	
Logistic regression (LOGIT)	Mathematical programming	Stacking: - a level 2 meta-classifier aggregating classification results from base classifiers
Linear discriminant analysis (LDA)	Expert systems	Boosting (e.g.): - boosted trees, - GBM (Stochastic Gradient Boosting Machine), - boosted C5.0 trees, - boosted Logit, - other.
Classification and Regression Trees (C&RT)	Neural networks (NNet)	Bagging (e.g.): - Random Forest (RF), - bagged (LDA), - averaged Neural Networks (avNNet), - other.
Nearest Neighbor algorithm (k-NN) k-Nearest Neighbors	Support Vector Machine (SVM)	
Naive Bayes classifier (NB)	Generalized Additive Models (GAM)	
	Multivariate Adaptive Regression Splines (MARS)	

Source: own elaboration based on the literature analyzed.

4.1. Ensemble Classifier Methodology

The ensemble classifier methodology involves combining several single classifiers into an ensemble of classifiers performing the same task in order to improve the effectiveness of classification (the discriminant capability of the entire model) defined as correct assignment of objects into expected classes. This is done by suitably aggregating (often by weighing) results of classification obtained from component classifiers to arrive at a resultant classifier with the best possible forecasting capabilities (surpassing those of all base classifiers in use). Figure 7 shows a functional diagram of ensemble classifiers.

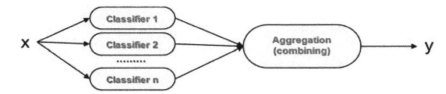

Figure 7. A diagram presenting the idea of using ensemble classifiers. Source: own elaboration.

A detailed description of ensemble classifier methodology, their types, characteristics and numerous practical applications can be found in monographs by Zhang and Ma (2012) as well as Zhou (2012). In practice, three well-known approaches: boosting, bagging and combining are applied in ensemble classifier methods. The terminology of boosting ensemble classifiers refers to a broad class of algorithms which enable boosting "weak classifiers", turning them into "strong qualifiers" (of excellent classification performance approaching that of perfect models). An example of such approach is AdaBoost—an adaptive boosting algorithm (Freund and Schapire 1997). In AdaBoost, classifiers of the same type, e.g., boosted classification trees, serve as base classifiers. Voting strategies are most commonly used in order to determine object classes, aggregating their output classifications, such as majority voting, plurality voting, weighted voting or soft voting. The AdaBoost.M1 adaptive boosting algorithm in the case of object classification for two classes contains the following steps (see: Algorithm 1, Zhang and Ma 2012, p. 14).

Algorithm 1 AdaBoost.M1 algorithm

---

1. *Inputs:* a set of input data for the training sample $\{x_i, y_i\}$, $i = 1, \ldots, N$, $y_i \in \{\omega_1, \omega_2\}$—learning with a pattern
2. Ensemble classifier: an ensemble classifier with the number of boosting cycles T—iterations
3. Initialization: initial distribution of weights for observation from training set $D_1(i) = 1/N$
4. Perform in loop FOR $t = 1, 2, \ldots, T$

    - Pick a random training subset S_t with distribution D_t
    - Train the base classifier on subset S_t, assume hypothesis $h_t : X \rightarrow Y$ concerning classification accuracy relative to the pattern
    - Calculate classification error for hypothesis h_t : $\varepsilon_t = \sum_i I[\![h_t(x_i \neq y_i)]\!]D_t(x_i)$
    - Interrupt if $\varepsilon_t > 1/2$.
    - Assume $\beta_t = \varepsilon_t / (1 - \varepsilon_t)$
    - Adjust weight distribution: $D_{t+1}(i) = \frac{D_t(i)}{Z_t} \cdot \begin{cases} \beta_t, & if \ h_t(x_i) = y_i \\ 1, & otherwise \end{cases}$, where $Z_t = \sum_i D_t(i)$—is the normalization constant enabling D_{t+1} to become the correct probability distribution

5. End FOR loop
6. Weighted majority voting. For a given unnamed instance of z obtain a voting result concerning case membership in each of the classes $V_c = \sum_{t:h_t(z)=\omega_c} log\left(\frac{1}{\beta_t}\right), c = 1, 2$.
7. *Output:* Membership in the class of the greatest value of V_c.

The name of the second group of ensemble classifier making use of the bagging method is derived from the English abbreviation: Bootstrap AGGregatING (Breiman 1996). This group of ensemble classifiers involves bootstrap sampling to obtain training subsets for base classifiers. Each the classifier is therefore trained on a different training sample, and the results are aggregated. Here, classifiers of the same type are used most often as base classifiers. An example of such a type of ensemble classifiers is Random Forest. The bootstrap aggregation algorithm for object classification into two classes has the following steps (see: Algorithm 2, Zhang and Ma 2012, p. 12).

Algorithm 2 Bagging algorithm

---

1. *Inputs:* a set of input data for the training sample S; training algorithm with a pattern, base classifier T—ensemble size; R—percentage of the sample for determining training subsets for sampling
2. Perform in loop FOR $t = 1, 2, \ldots, T$

   - Randomly select a replication subset—training sample S_t by selecting R % of S at random
   - Train the base classifier on subset S_t, obtain hypothesis for classifier h_t concerning classification accuracy relative to the pattern
   - Add h_t to ensemble, $\varepsilon \leftarrow \varepsilon \cup \{h_t\}$

3. End FOR loop
4. Combine classification results in an ensemble combination—simple majority voting: for a given unnamed instance of x, obtain a voting result concerning case membership in each of the classes
5. Evaluate class membership results on the basis of ensemble classifier $\varepsilon = \{h_1, \ldots, h_T\}$ for the analysed case x
6. Let $v_{t,c} = 1$, if h_t selects class ω_c, otherwise 0
7. Obtain overall final vote result for each class $V_c = \sum_{t=1}^{T} v_{t,c}$, $c = 1, 2$
8. *Output:* Membership in the class of the greatest value of V_c.

A group of methods called ensemble combining represents a wholly different approach. The group includes the so-called combined methods utilizing results of classification functions for single (base) classifiers and aggregating them into the result classification function using the averaging approach (simple or weighted averaging of base classifier results), voting approach (using various types of voting strategies, e.g., majority voting) or stacked generalization approach. The stacking ensemble methodology, pioneered by Wolpert (1992), is based on a combined approach whereby base classifiers (level 1 classifiers) are trained on the same random samples, and then relevant classification results (their classification functions) are used as training samples for the new meta-classifier (level 2 classifier) and aggregated in result classifications.

4.2. Feature Selection Process in Bankruptcy Prediction

A deeply significant classification-related issue is the problem of choosing the appropriate (optimum) set of diagnostic variables (i.e., the feature selection problem). Detailed characteristics of methods used for the selection of relevant variables for forecast models can be found in studies by John et al. (1994) and Jovic et al. (2015). Wrapper methods are frequently used techniques which analyze possible predictor subsets and determine the effectiveness of their impact on the model's dependent variable on the basis of a search algorithm, the best subset of variables and the classification method applied. In order to search all variable subsets, the search algorithm is 'wrapped' around the classification model, hence the name of this group of methods. Wrapper feature selection methods are based on various approaches of searching for the optimum subset of predictors. Such approaches can be divided into two basic groups: deterministic and randomized. This group of deterministic methods applies various types of sequential algorithms, e.g., progressive stepwise selection or backward stepwise elimination. Wrapper feature selection methods most frequently use random algorithms such as simulated annealing, genetic algorithms or ant colony optimization. A method employing a genetic algorithm in order to search for the optimum subset of predictors is often used to select variables for bankruptcy models. The genetic algorithm of Feature Selection (see: Algorithm 3) is executed according to the procedure designed by Kuhn and Johnson (2013).

Algorithm 3 Genetic Algorithm Feature Selection (GAFS)

---

1. *Define:* stopping criteria, number of children for each generation (*gensize*), and probability of mutation (*pm*)
2. *Generate:* an initial random set of m binary chromosomes, each of length p
3. REPEAT
4. FOR each chromosome DO

    Tune and train a model and compute each chromosome's fitness
5. END
6. FOR reproduction k = 1, ... , *gensize*/2 DO

    Select two chromosomes based on the fitness criterion
    Crossover: Randomly select a locus and exchange each chromosome's genes beyond the loci
    Mutation: Randomly change binary values of each gene in each new child chromosome with probability *pm*
7. END
8. UNTIL stopping criteria are met

4.3. Data Samples Description

The original research sample used in the study included data for 1739 Polish enterprises (bankrupt and not threatened with bankruptcy). This sample included calculated values for 19 financial indicators determining the financial condition of selected enterprises (characterized in detail in Section 5.1 and selected for the study using the wrapper search technique and genetic algorithm discussed in detail in Section 4.2). For bankrupt enterprises, the values of diagnostic variables were set at 1 or 2 years before the actual period of their bankruptcy. Statistical data came from the financial statements of enterprises from 2010–2018 available in the EMIS database (http://www.emis.com). Bankruptcy episodes were identified on the basis of statistics from the EMIS database source: Ogólnopolski Monitor Upadłościow (2019) (Coface Polish National Bankruptcy Monitor, source: http://www.emis.com, http://coface.pl/en). The balanced sample used included a total of 1739 research cases from all major sectors of the economy (865—cases for bankrupt enterprises and 874—randomly selected cases for enterprises not at risk of bankruptcy with strong financial conditions). The condition for the non-defaulted enterprises was evaluated on the basis of careful analysis and evaluation of values of many financial indicators, such as profitability ratios, debt ratios, management performance indicators etc., which determined their financial condition and low exposure to the bankruptcy risk. A 70% teaching sample was drawn from the research sample (1217 enterprises: 592—bankrupt and 625—not threatened with bankruptcy), which was used to train and calibrate the parameters of the bankruptcy models used. The remaining cases constituted a random 30% set for the test-validation sample (522—enterprises: 273—bankrupt and 249—not threatened with bankruptcy), which was used at the stage of validation of models to check their predictive properties for new, unknown cases. A separate research sample was designated for enterprises from the Podkarpackie Voivodeship, which included 2133 enterprises of various sizes from the Podkarpackie region registered in various sectors of economic activity. This sample included all enterprises operating in the Podkarpackie for which financial statements (in EMIS database) for 2018 were available. This sample was used as a research set to assess the risk of bankruptcy (in the 2-year horizon up to 2020) of enterprises in the Podkarpackie region under analysis based on an estimated scoring model using the approach of ensemble classifiers.

4.4. Procedure of Mapping PD into Scores

In this study, the score scaling approach discussed in detail in the literature was used (see e.g., Siddiqi 2017, pp. 240–41). The relationship between the score and logarithms for the so-called odds ratio: $Odds = \frac{1-PD}{PD}$—expressing the ratio of odds: (1-PD)—that the business in question will be classified as healthy versus the odds that the business will be bankrupt (PD) is:

$$Score = a_0 + a_1 \cdot \ln(Odds). \tag{1}$$

By introducing the concept of *pdo*—the number of points in the scoring system which doubles the value of the odds ratio, for a given value of the score we obtain the following relationship:

$$Score + pdo = a_0 + a_1 \cdot \ln(2 \cdot Odds). \tag{2}$$

By solving the system of Equations (1) and (2) we obtain formulas of the linear relationship ratios of score scaling depending on ln(*Odds*), and therefore on the probability of default (PD):

$$a_1 = \frac{pdo}{\ln(2)},$$
$$a_0 = Score_0 - a_1 \cdot \ln(Odds). \tag{3}$$

4.5. Validation Measures of Bankruptcy Prediction Models

Commonly used measures of classification accuracy were applied in the validation of estimated bankruptcy models. They are described by Siddiqi (2017) and Thomas (2009) clearly and in detail. The confusion matrix is probably the most frequent approach in the assessment of classification accuracy of models. Table 2 presents a general form of the confusion matrix.

Table 2. Confusion matrix for the validation of classification consistency of the bankruptcy model.

ReportedBankruptcy	Forecast Bankruptcy	
	B	**NB**
B (negative class: bankrupt)	TN (True Negative)	FN (False Negative)
NB (positive class: non-bankrupt)	FP (False Positive)	TP (True Positive)

Source: own elaboration.

Quantities shown in the table have the following meaning: TN—number of actually bankrupt businesses correctly classified by the model, TP—number of healthy businesses correctly classified by the model as healthy businesses, FN—number of actually bankrupt businesses incorrectly classified by the model as healthy businesses, FP—number of actually healthy businesses incorrectly classified by the model as bankrupt. $AC = \frac{TN+TP}{TN+FN+FP+TP} \cdot 100\%$ is the measure of the overall effectiveness of correct classification. The effectiveness of correct classifications for the 'bankrupt' class alone can be specified as: $AC_B = \frac{TN}{TN+FN} \cdot 100\% = 1 - Err_B$, where: Err_B—is the so-called type I error of incorrect classifications for the class of bankrupt businesses. Likewise, the effectiveness of correct classification for the businesses at no risk of bankruptcy alone can be determined as follows: $AC_{NB} = \frac{TP}{FP+TP} \cdot 100\% = 1 - Err_{NB}$, where: Err_{NB}—is the so-called type II error of incorrect classification for the class of healthy businesses. Obviously, the higher the values of classification accuracy measures, the better the effectiveness of the models assessed.

The GINI coefficient and the related area under curve ROC (Receiver Operating Characteristic) AUC_{ROC} are also often used as measures of bankruptcy model classification effectiveness (see e.g., Agarwal and Taffler 2008, Barboza et al. 2017). The ROC curve is a graphic representation in a coordinate system (Y = Sensitivity, X = (1 − Specificity)) of a relationship of the cumulative percentage (structural ratio) for bankrupt businesses from the contingency table for the predicted *i*th category of a point score (*score_i*): $\omega\_sk_{B,i} = \frac{\sum_{j=1}^{i} n_{B,j}}{n_B}$ and the corresponding cumulative structural ratio for businesses at no risk of default: $\omega\_sk_{NB,i} = \frac{\sum_{j=1}^{i} n_{NB,j}}{n_{NB}}$. In the case of classification results ordered relative to the score in the contingency table with k different scoring categories, the GINI coefficient, and thus AUC$_{ROC}$, is determined by the following formula (see e.g., Thomas 2009, pp. 117–18):

$$GINI = 1 - \sum_{i=1}^{k-1}(\omega_{skB,i+1} - \omega_{skB,i}) \cdot (\omega_{skNB,i+1} + \omega_{skNB,i}) = 2 \cdot AUC\ (ROC) - 1. \tag{4}$$

The GINI coefficient takes values from interval [0,1]. High values of the coefficient, approaching 1, mean that the model being assessed is highly effective (nearly perfect). Meanwhile, the measure of the area under curve AUC$_{ROC}$ ranges from 0.5 to 1. Value 0.5 means that the model classifies businesses in the analyzed classes in a completely random way (i.e., its use is pointless), while 1 is a value attained by the best model which perfectly identifies membership in a class.

Information Value (IV), Kolmogorov-Smirnov (KS) statistics and less frequently, the divergence coefficient (Div) are also used to evaluate the effectiveness of bankruptcy forecasting models at the validation stage. IV is calculated by the following formula (see e.g., Thomas 2009, p. 106):

$$IV = \sum_{i=1}^{k}\left(\frac{n_{NB,i}}{n_{NB}} - \frac{n_{B,i}}{n_B}\right) \cdot \ln\left(\frac{n_{NB,i}/n_{NB}}{n_{B,i}/n_B}\right) \tag{5}$$

where: n_B is the number of bankrupt businesses, n_{NB} is the number of businesses with no risk of bankruptcy, $n_{B,i}$ is the number of businesses for the ith scoring category and $n_{NB,i}$ is the corresponding number of businesses with no risk of bankruptcy. The higher IV values, the better discriminant properties of the model subjected to assessment.

The Kolmogorov-Smirnov (KS) statistic compares the empirical distributions of populations containing bankrupt businesses and healthy businesses (a goodness of fit measure). The greater the differences in cumulative distribution functions for the score (higher KS values), the better discriminant capabilities of the model (i.e., the better the scoring model is in separating bankrupt businesses from healthy ones). KS statistic values are calculated by the following formula (see e.g., Thomas 2009, p. 111):

$$KS = \max_{i=1,\ldots,k}\left|\omega\_sk_{B,i} - \omega\_sk_{NB,i}\right|. \tag{6}$$

The last validation measure applied to the bankruptcy forecasting models assessed is distribution divergence (Div) given by the formula (see e.g., Siddiqi 2017, p. 261):

$$Div = \frac{(\mu_{NB} - \mu_B)^2}{0.5 \cdot (var_{NB} + var_B)} \tag{7}$$

where: μ_{NB}—mean score distribution value for the healthy businesses population, μ_B—mean score distribution value for bankrupt businesses population and var_{NB}, var_B—respective variances of these distributions.

4.6. Optimal Cut-Off Point for Scoring Determination

There are several methods of determination the optimal cut-off point for the scoring models. These methods are described in depth in the literature (see e.g., Zweig and Campbell 1993). One of the methods of determining the optimum cut-off point for the score (used in the research) was to find a score value that maximizes the value of the following expression:

$$\max_{score_i}\left\{M_1(score_i) = \omega\_sk_{B,i}(score_i) - \frac{k_{NB}}{k_B} \cdot \frac{1-p_B}{p_B} \cdot \omega\_sk_{NB,i}(score_i)\right\} \tag{8}$$

where: k_B is the cost of type I error: the model incorrectly classifies a bankrupt business as a healthy one, k_{NB} corresponds to the cost of type II error where the model incorrectly classifies a healthy business as bankrupt, and p_B is the probability of membership in the bankrupt class estimated on the basis of the training sample (the percentage of bankrupt businesses in the sample).

5. Research Results

The ensemble classifier methodology will be applied to design a scoring model in order to predict bankruptcy events of Polish businesses operating in the Podkarpackie Voivodeship. Each stage of design will be presented in detail together with its potential for a practical application.

The process of designing a scoring model using ensemble classifiers for businesses operating in the Podkarpackie Voivodeship was divided into several stages:

1. The choice of a suitable subset of financial ratios (bankruptcy predictors) determining the financial circumstances of the businesses analyzed (feature selection stage).
2. Training and calibration of base models applied and ensemble models selected on the basis of the training sample. Determining the function of the probability of default and membership in forecast classes for both samples: training sample, and test and validation sample (which is not taken into account at the stage of calibration of the evaluated models).
3. Determining the score value for the training sample and the test sample with a suitable scaling of the value of the resulting probability of default function for the estimated models and their transformation into corresponding resulting point score values.
4. Validation of estimated models. Determining the values of validation statistics for the models applied and analysis of their discriminant capabilities for the training sample and the test sample. Selection of the best forecasting model.
5. For the best model, determining the optimum cut-off point for the score value, i.e., the point below which a business should be categorized as bankrupt.
6. Bankruptcy forecasts for analyzed businesses from the Podkarpackie Voivodeship in individual sectors of economic activity and business size. Final comparative analysis of results and final conclusions.

5.1. Feature Selection Stage—Selection of Ratios/Bankruptcy Risk Determinants

Twenty-two financial ratios commonly applied in financial analysis of businesses were initially proposed for the assessment of the financial standing of analyzed business entities:

- Financial liquidity ratios: X1—Current ratio = Current assets to Short-term liabilities total (all liabilities with maturity shorter than one year): CA/STL, X2—Quick ratio = (Current assets − Inventories) to Short-term liabilities total: (CA-I)/STL, X3—Cash ratio = Cash and Cash equivalents to Short-term liabilities total: Cash/STL
- Profitability ratios: X4—Operating profit margin = Operating earnings to Net sales: OE/NS [%], X5—Return on assets (ROA) = Net profit (Total Revenue − Cost of Goods Sold − Operating Expenses − Other Expenses − Interest and Taxes) to Assets total (Balance sheet total): NP/BST [%], X6—Return on equity (ROE) = Net profit to Equity: NP/E [%], X7—Return on invested capital = Net profit to (Assets total − Short-term liabilities total): NP/(BST-STL) [%], X8—Net profitability = Net profit to Revenues from sales: NP/RS [%], X9—gross profit margin on sales = (Revenues from sales − Cost of goods sold) to Revenues from sales: (RS-CoGS)/RS [%], X10—operating return on assets = EBIT (Earnings Before Interest and Taxes) to Assets total: EBIT/BST [%]
- Debt ratios: X11—Overall debt = Liabilities total to Assets total (Balance sheet total): TL/BST [%], X12—Debt to equity = Liabilities total to Equity: (TL/E) [%], X13—Debt to EBITDA = Liabilities total to EBITDA: TL/EBITDA, X14—Financial leverage = Assets total (Balance sheet total) to Equity: BST/E [%]
- Management effectiveness ratios: X15—Receivable turnover = Revenues from sales to Short-term receivables: RS/STR, X16—Asset turnover = Revenues from sales to Assets total (Balance sheet total): RS/BST, X17—Inventory turnover = Revenues from sales to Inventories: RS/I, X18—Liability

turnover = (Revenues from sales + Inventories) to Short-term liabilities total: (RS+I)/STL, X19—Working capital turnover = Revenues from sales to (Current assets − Short-term liabilities total): RS/(CA-STL)

• Capital structure ratios: X20—Structure of Equity to Assets total (Balance sheet total): E/BST [%], X21—Structure of Fixed assets to total assets (Balance sheet total): FA/BST [%], X22—Structure of Fixed assets to Current assets: FA/CA [%]

With the help of *wrapper* techniques (discussed in Section 4.2 above), an optimum subset of predictors was selected by means of the genetic algorithm and a potentially best set of financial ratios for bankruptcy forecasting models being trained was determined. Linear discriminant analysis (LDA) was used as a forecasting model in the search algorithm, while the general classification accuracy (AC) measure was applied as the measure of the effectiveness of predictor subsets. The calculations were performed by means of the R statistical analyses package and function *gafs()* from the *caret* library. Parameters for the genetic algorithm were as follows: *poSize = 50*—the number of subsets assessed in each iteration, *pcrossover = 0.8* (crossover probability) —a high probability that the new generation will not be an exact copy of the chromosomes of parents from the previous generation, *pmutation = 0.1* (mutation probability)—a low probability of chromosome alterations in the subsequent mutation, *elite = 0*—the number of best subsets capable of survival in each generation. By means of a suitable genetic algorithm randomly searching for the best subset of diagnostic variables, a set of 19 optimum financial ratios (accuracy for the set was AC = 0.89) using 5-fold cross-validation (cv) procedure. Table 3 contains values of selected measures of discriminant capabilities and significance for individual diagnostic variables.

Table 3. Discriminant capability measures—ranking of predictors.

Ratio	Discriminant Measures		
	IV	GINI	V-Cramer
X9 (Z8)—Return On Sales (profit margin) (gross) [%]	5.81	0.86	0.84
X11 (Z10)—Overall Debt [%]	4.82	0.88	0.87
X12 (Z11)—Debt to Equity [%]	4.04	0.81	0.79
X13 (Z12)—Debt/EBITDA	2.76	0.72	0.66
X5 (Z4)—Return on Assets (ROA) [%]	1.66	0.68	0.60
X8 (Z7)—Net Profit Margin [%]	1.62	0.67	0.58
X10 (Z9)—Operating Return on Assets [%]	1.59	0.66	0.57
X4 (Z3)—Operating Profit Margin [%]	1.57	0.66	0.57
X7 (Z6)—Return On Invested Capital [%]	1.40	0.65	0.55
X20 (Z18)—Equity To Total Assets Structure [%]	1.39	0.65	0.55
X6 (Z5)—Return On Equity ROE [%]	1.18	0.63	0.51
X18 (Z16)—Liability Turnover	0.93	0.61	0.46
X21 (Z19)—Fixed Assets to Total Assets Structure [%]	0.89	0.57	0.38
X17 (Z15)—Inventory turnover	0.75	0.59	0.42
X15 (Z13)—Receivable Turnover	0.72	0.58	0.40
X19 (Z17)—Working Capital Turnover	0.66	0.58	0.39
X3 (Z2)—Cash Ratio	0.66	0.58	0.39
X1 (Z1)—Current Ratio	0.59	0.57	0.37
X16 (Z14)—Asset Turnover	0.28	0.52	0.22

Source: own elaboration using Statistica software.

5.2. Calibration of the Parameters of Bankruptcy Risk Forecast Models (Calibration Stage)

Eight single classifier models were used in forecasting the probability of default (PD) (Table 3). Classification functions for those models, the so-called level 1 classifiers, served as inputs for a level 2 ensemble meta-classifier, which aggregated them into final classification results. k-NN (k-Nearest Neighbors) was the stacking ensemble classifier. Alternatively, boosting and bagging ensemble classifier approaches were also applied. For comparison purposes, boosting ensemble classifiers were also used: GBM—Stochastic Gradient Boosting Machine (Friedman 2002) and boosted logistic regression classifier (Logit Boost). The Random Forest (RF) model and averaged Neural Networks (avNNet) were used as bagging classifiers (Breiman 2001). A bankruptcy prediction model calibration procedure was based on samples described in detail in Section 4.3. Calculations were performed with the help of procedures written with the use of the R package libraries (https://cran.r-project.org/). In particular, the following libraries were used: *caret, caretEnsemble, caTools, pROC, MASS, nnet, kernlab, rpart, earth, mgCV, klaR, gbm, plyr, randomForest* and other auxiliary ones. A cross validation approach was employed in the calibration procedure of the optimum model (k = 5-fold CV cross-validation). The approach assumed an area under ROC curve values (AUC_{ROC}) as a measure of models' discriminant quality (effectiveness). Figure 8 illustrates the process of increasing classification effectiveness for the boosting ensemble model depending on the number of iterations of the boosting algorithm for various complexity of classification trees trained. It very clearly shows why ensemble classifiers surpass single (individual) classifiers in terms of quality.

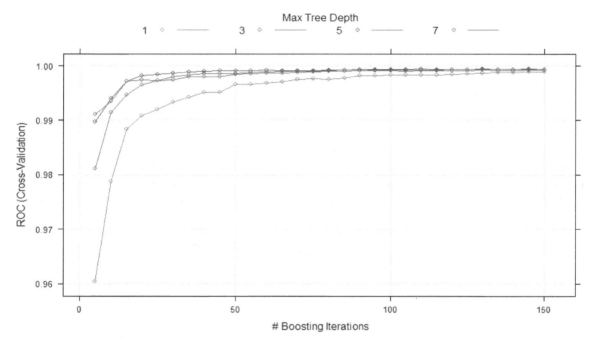

Figure 8. GBM model training process with the use of the stochastic gradient boosting algorithm. Source: own elaboration using R package.

A table in Appendix A (Table A1) presents the final best configurations of the considered bankruptcy prediction models and optimum values of their parameters.

5.3. Determining Score for the Optimum Model (Score Scaling Stage)

Forecast values of classification functions of the models analyzed (probability of default, PD) in the scoring model should be transformed into corresponding values of score through appropriate scaling. In the calculations, it was assumed that for $Score_0 = 600$ the number points which doubles the odds that the business is not at risk of default, evaluated as 50:1 (Odds = 50), is pdo = 20. With the above assumptions, scaling parameters were estimated and the score function was described by the following relationship: $Score = 487.12 + 28.85 \cdot \ln\left(\frac{1-PD}{PD}\right)$. Figure 9 illustrates the scaling obtained for the score when the GBM ensemble model is used for the training sample.

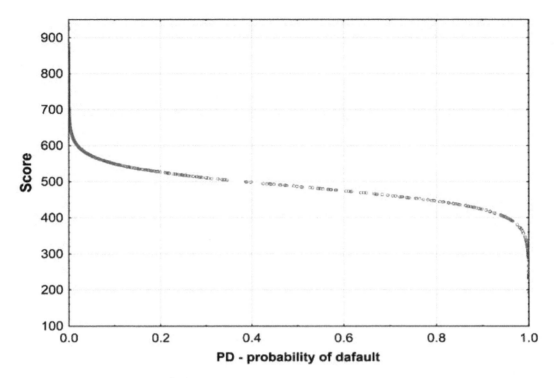

Figure 9. Score scaling in relation to the corresponding probability of default (PD) for the GBM model. Source: own Elaboration using Excel.

5.4. Model Validation (validation Stage)

Figure 10 presents ROC curves for five classification models assessed. It is clear that the GBM model perfectly (in 100% cases) predicted membership of businesses in either class (bankrupt and healthy) (AUC = 1). The worst of the models compared, NB—Naive Bayes, also had high prediction accuracy expressed by measure (AUC = 0.92), although it was still significantly inferior to other models.

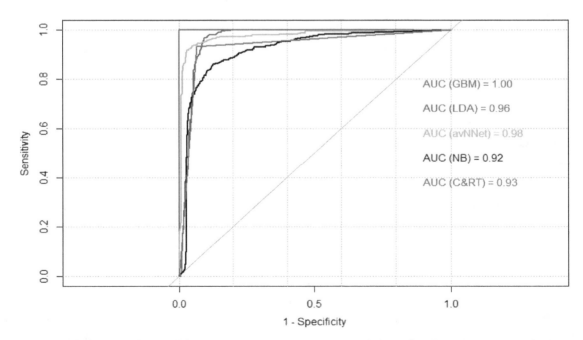

Figure 10. ROC curves for models LDA, NB, C&RT, avNNet and GBM for the training sample. Source: own elaboration using the R package.

Figure 11 presents a graphic interpretation of KS = 0.89 (for score = 468) for the LDA model when testing its effectiveness with regard to the test and validation sample. High values for this KS statistics mean that the model is rather effective.

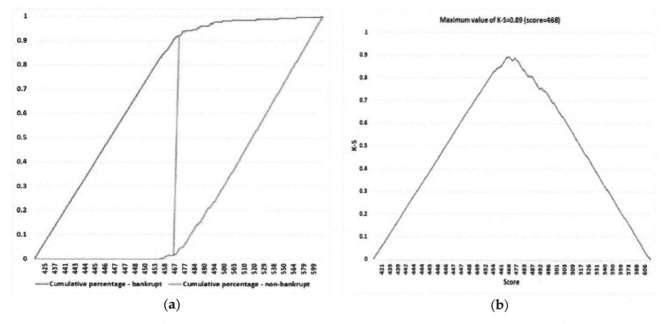

(a)   (b)

Figure 11. Interpretation of the Kolmogorov-Smirnov validation statistic for the LDA model and the test and validation sample: (**a**) Difference in cumulative distribution function for both classes relative to score; (**b**) Relationship of KS as the maximum difference between cumulative distribution functions for both classes relative to score. Source: own elaboration using Excel.

Figure 12 presents a comparison and interpretation of a very high discriminant capability of the ensemble GBM model (divergence Div = 92.1) and the LDA model with a relatively weaker discriminant capability (divergence Div = 2.6) rated on the basis of the training sample.

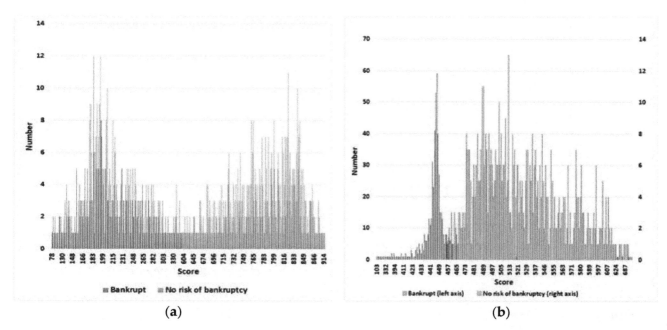

(a)   (b)

Figure 12. Score distribution for healthy and bankrupt businesses: (**a**) for the GBM model and very high divergence of distributions Div = 92.1; (**b**) for the LDA model and low divergence of distributions Div = 2.6. Source: own elaboration using Excel.

5.5. Optimal Cut_Off Point Determination Stage

The next step for the ensemble GBM classifier-based forecasting model with the best classification properties expressed by the value of validation measures involved determining values of the optimum cut_off point below which the businesses analyzed were regarded as being at risk of default (bankrupt). In the calculations, it was assumed that the ratio of the above costs is $\frac{k_{NB}}{k_B} = \frac{1}{2}$ (double cost for the incorrect classification of bankrupts, as the event appears to be more detrimental for the practical application of the model) and a probability of $p_B = 0.486$ in the training sample was determined. The optimum cut_off point was calculated for $score_{cut\_off} = 386$ by means of formula (8). Therefore, all businesses for which the point value of the score is score ≤ 386 must be forecast as members of the bankruptcy (B) class, while the remaining ones as members of the non-bankruptcy (NB) class. Still, for the estimated optimum ensemble GBM model in the score value interval [387–486], there is a very high potential risk of default (PD > 0.5), determined on the basis of the training sample (contained in the interval [0.96–0.51]). Consequently, if we rely on the classical procedure allowing us to consider a business (for which PD > 0.5) bankrupt (at risk of default), then the score interval (387 <= score <= 486) should be defined as a "gray zone", where it is difficult to clearly determine the membership of a given business in either the bankruptcy class or the non-bankruptcy class. Businesses of this type were assessed as uncertain, leaning towards potential bankruptcy (contingent on unfavorable circumstances affecting their financial health).

Figure 13 presents an interpretation of the optimum cut-off point for the score, determined in the above manner.

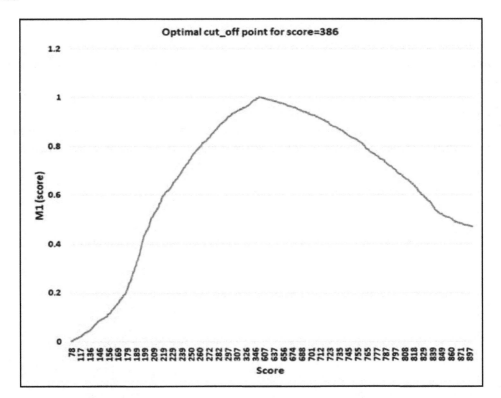

Figure 13. Optimal score cut-off point for the GBM model. Source: own elaboration using Excel.

5.6. Classification of Enterprises from the Podkarpacie Region (Prediction Stage) Depending on the Risk of Their Bankruptcy

Applying the classification rule:

$$\text{IF } (score \leq 386) \text{ THEN bankrupt within } h \leq 2 \text{ years};$$
$$\text{IF } (score > 486) \text{ THEN healthy};$$
$$\text{IF } (score > 386 \text{ AND } score \leq 486) \text{ THEN uncertain (grey zone)};$$

(9)

a forecast of bankruptcy (membership in either risk class) was determined over a time horizon of maximum 2 years (up to 2020) for businesses operating in the Podkarpackie Voivodeship in various sectors of economic activity and depending on the enterprise size. Table 4 is a contingency table presenting the forecast number of businesses classified as members of each of the 3 bankruptcy risk classes by different economic activity sectors.

Table 4. Predicted number of businesses at risk of bankruptcy in time horizon h = 2 (until 2020) and predicted number of businesses in an uncertain condition in the Podkarpackie Voivodeship for various sectors.

Sector	Number of Businesses Forecast by the Ensemble Scoring Model in a Given Bankruptcy Risk Class (h = 2 years, until 2020)		
	Bankrupt (B)	Uncertain ("Grey Zone")	Healthy (No Risk of Bankruptcy) (NB)
A—farming, forestry and fishing	2 (4%) (small = 1; medium = 1)	3 (6%) (micro = 1; small = 1; large = 1)	45 (90%) (micro = 10; small = 12; medium = 10; large = 13)
B—mining and extraction	0	0	12 (100%) (micro = 4; small = 1; medium = 4; large = 3)
C—industrial processing	11 (2%) (micro = 1; small = 4; medium = 5; large = 1)	27 (5%) (micro = 6; small = 9; medium = 3; large = 9)	543 (93%) (micro = 84; small = 83; medium = 175; large = 201)
D—energy, water, gas and other energy sources	0	0	25 (100%) (micro = 4; small = 3; medium = 6; large = 12)
E—waste, wastewater and sewage management	0	2 (3%) (small = 1; medium = 1)	65 (97%) (micro = 11; small = 5; medium = 18; large = 31)
F—construction	7 (3%) (micro = 2; small = 1; medium = 2; large = 2)	10 (5%) (micro = 9; large = 1)	203 (92%) (micro = 55; small = 44; medium = 52; large = 52)
G—wholesale and retail	17 (2%) (micro = 9; small = 3; large = 5)	19 (3%) (micro = 5; small = 4; medium = 5; large = 1)	698 (95%) (micro = 185; small = 121; medium = 226; large = 166)
H—transport and storage management	2 (3%) (micro = 1; small = 1)	3 (4%) (small = 1; large = 2)	70 (93%) (micro = 18; small = 10; medium = 20; large = 22)
I—accommodation and gastronomy	7 (13%) (micro = 4; medium = 2; large = 1)	4 (7%) (micro = 1; medium = 2; large = 1)	45 (80%) (micro = 17; small = 8; medium = 6; large = 14)
J—information and communication	0	3 (5%) (micro = 3)	52 (95%) (micro = 16; small = 7; medium = 11; large = 18)
K—finance and insurance	0	4 (33%) (micro = 1; small = 2; large = 1)	8 (67%) (small = 2; medium = 4; large = 2)
L—services for the property market	2 (3%) (micro = 1; small = 1)	10 (14%) (micro = 5; small = 2; medium = 2; large = 1)	61 (83%) (micro = 20; small = 8; medium = 12; large = 21)
M—scientific, specialist and technological activity	1 (2%) (micro = 1)	2 (3%) (micro = 1; large = 1)	58 (95%) (micro = 24; small = 8;medium = 14; large = 12)

Table 4. *Cont.*

Sector	Number of Businesses Forecast by the Ensemble Scoring Model in a Given Bankruptcy Risk Class (h = 2 years, until 2020)		
	Bankrupt (B)	Uncertain ("Grey Zone")	Healthy (No Risk of Bankruptcy) (NB)
N—administration and support	2 (5%) (micro = 2)	3 (7%) (micro = 1; large = 2)	38 (88%) (micro = 11; small = 3; medium = 8; large = 16)
P—education	0	0	9 (100%) (micro = 1; small = 2; medium = 2; large = 4)
Q—health and social care	1 (3%) (large = 1)	2 (5%) (small = 1; large = 1)	35 (92%) (micro = 10; small = 5; medium = 8; large = 12)
R—entertainment and leisure	0	2 (18%) (micro = 2)	9 (82%) (micro = 5; small = 2; medium = 2)
S—other services	0	1 (9%) (micro = 1)	10 (91%) (micro = 3; medium = 5; large = 2)
Total	52 (2%) micro = 4%; small = 3%; medium = 2%; large = 2%	95 (5%) micro = 7%; small = 6%; medium = 2%; large = 4%	1986 (93%) micro = 89%; small = 91%; medium = 96%; large = 94%

Source: own elaboration using Statistica software.

Figure 14 presents the forecast probability of potential bankruptcy risk (up to h = 2 years) for the enterprises surveyed from the Podkarpacie for various sectors of classification of their activities, which were estimated on the basis of the optimal ensemble model (GBM) for which the classification functions were used in the developed scoring model.

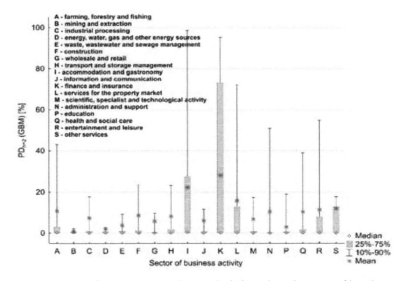

Figure 14. Descriptive statistics characterizing the probability distribution of bankruptcy (over a 2-year time horizon) for the surveyed enterprises from the Podkarpacie for various sectors of their business activities. Source: own elaboration using Statistica.

Figure 15, on the other hand, shows the predicted values of such probability of bankruptcy for the surveyed enterprises from the Podkarpackie, depending on their enterprise size.

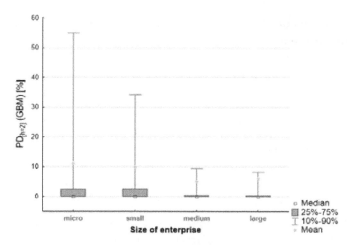

Figure 15. Descriptive statistics characterizing the probability distribution of bankruptcy (over a 2-year time horizon) for the surveyed enterprises from Podkarpackie depending on the size of the enterprise. Source: own elaboration using Statistica.

Table 5 presents a proper assessment of the classification effectiveness of the developed bankruptcy early warning model on observed and available at the time of conducting the confirmed court tests of 39 actual enterprises that declared bankruptcies in the Podkarpackie Voivodeship (in 2019). They were included in the test sample of 2133 enterprises. This confirms the fairly good quality of the model for which the effectiveness (ex-post) of correct recognition by the implemented scoring model for new (not taken into account at the calibration stage) of actually bankrupt enterprises is about 79% (which seems to be acceptable result), while for enterprises not threatened with bankruptcy, the efficiency of the model is much better and is equal to 95%.

Table 5. The actual effectiveness of the classification compatibility of the model verified on the basis of a sample of enterprises from the Podkarpackie Voivodeship.

Reported Bankruptcy	Forecast Bankruptcy (h = 2 years) to 2020		
	Bankrupt	**Uncertain (Potentially Bankrupt)**	**Healthy (No Risk of Bankruptcy)**
Bankrupt	31 (79%)	3 (8%)	5 (13%)
No risk of bankruptcy	21 (1%)	92 (4%)	1981 (95%)

Source: own elaboration.

6. Discussion

The comparative analysis of the classification effectiveness of ensemble models in juxtaposition with several classical bankruptcy forecasting methods indicates that ensemble classifiers are characterized by considerably better values of validation measures, both for the training sample and the test sample, surpassing all of the analyzed base classifiers in terms of accuracy. The best ensemble classifier, GBM (decision trees supported by a stochastic gradient boosting algorithm) offered full accuracy of correctly classified bankrupt and healthy businesses (AC = 100%, AC_B = 100%, AC_{NB} = 100%) for the training sample and over 99% for the test sample (Tables A2 and A3). In addition, other values of validation statistics demonstrate nearly perfect predictive capability of the GBM ensemble model for the training sample: AUC_{ROC} = 1, statistic KS = 1, divergence Div = 92.1 and information value IV = 5.3 and the test sample: AUC_{ROC} = 0.99, statistic KS = 0.99, divergence Div = 22.1 and information value IV = 7.1. The Generalized Additive Model (GAM) seems to be the best classical model, yet it displays inferior values of validation statistics, both for the training sample: AC = 97, AUC_{ROC} = 0.99, KS = 0.96, Div = 5.8, IV = 5.3, and for the test sample: AC = 97%, AUC_{ROC} = 0.99, KS = 0.96, divergence Div = 43.0, IV = 7.1. This confirms the earlier findings of other authors and allows us to say that in practical applications, bankruptcy models based on ensemble classifiers outperform other classical approaches and are an interesting alternative to the conventional method of using single classifiers.

Based on the analysis of the value of the probability of bankruptcy (Figure 14) of the enterprises surveyed in the Podkarpackie Voivodeship in individual sectors of their business activity (estimated on the basis of the best ensemble classifier model—GBM, which has the best forecasting and classification capabilities) and on the basis of an analysis of their predicted belonging to three Bankruptcy risk classes (Table 4), the following comparative analysis can be carried out assessing the exposure to bankruptcy risk of enterprises operating in the region in 2018 in view of their potential bankruptcy by 2020.

In sector A (farming, forestry and fishing) with a total of 50 enterprises surveyed, the developed scoring model predicted bankruptcy within a time horizon of up to two years (up to 2020) 4% of all enterprises in this sector, including uncertain enterprises from the second class of bankruptcy risk (from the so-called "gray zone"), i.e., with a significant probability of bankruptcy (PDt = 2 > 50%), the percentage of potentially bankrupt enterprises (over a 2-year horizon) increases to 10%. The average probability of bankruptcy for enterprises in this sector is 11% (min = 0%, max = 99.9%). Every 10 enterprise in this sector had a probability of bankruptcy over a 2-year horizon (up to 2020) in the range of 43%–99.9%. It is therefore quite heavily exposed to the risk of bankruptcy.

In sector B (mining and extraction) with a total of 12 enterprises, the scoring model qualified all enterprises as not being threatened with bankruptcy. The average probability of bankruptcy for enterprises in this sector is 1% (min = 0%, max = 6.8%). Every one of the 10 enterprises in this sector had a probability of bankruptcy in the 2-year horizon (up to 2020) in the range of 2.3%–6.8%. Therefore, it was the first of the three least risky sectors of the region's economy.

In sector C (industrial processing) with a total of 581 enterprises, the scoring model predicted bankruptcy for 2% of all enterprises in this sector within a time horizon of up to two years (up to 2020), including uncertain enterprises from the second class of bankruptcy risk (from "grey zone"), while the number of potentially bankrupt enterprises increased to 7%. The average probability of bankruptcy for enterprises in this sector is 7.4% (min = 0%, max = 100%). Every enterprise in this sector had a probability of bankruptcy over a 2-year horizon (up to 2020) greater than 17.7%.

Sector D (energy, water, gas and other energy sources) with a total of 25 enterprises was the second of the three least risky sectors in the region's economy. The scoring model qualified all enterprises as not being threatened with bankruptcy. The average probability of bankruptcy for enterprises in this sector is 2.2% (min = 0%, max = 43.3%). Every 10 enterprises in this sector had a probability of bankruptcy in the 2-year horizon (up to 2020) that was greater than 1.7%.

In sector E (waste, wastewater and sewage management) with a total of 67 enterprises, the scoring model qualified 97% of enterprises as not being threatened with bankruptcy, and 3% as uncertain. The average probability of bankruptcy for enterprises in this sector is 3.8% (min = 0%, max = 83.7%). Every 10 enterprises in this sector had a probability of bankruptcy in the 2-year horizon (up to 2020) that was greater than 9.2%.

In F sector (construction) with a total of 220 enterprises, the scoring model predicted bankruptcy within a time horizon of up to two years (up to 2020) for 3% of all enterprises in this sector, though after including uncertain enterprises with the second class of bankruptcy risk (from the "grey zone"), the percentage of potentially bankrupt enterprises increases to 8%. The average probability of bankruptcy for enterprises in this sector is 8.6% (min = 0%, max = 100%). Every 10 enterprises in this sector had a probability of bankruptcy over a 2-year horizon (up to 2020) that was greater than 23.5%.

In sector G (wholesale and retail) with a total of 734 enterprises, the scoring model predicted bankruptcy for 2% of all enterprises in this sector for up to two years (up to 2020). After including uncertain enterprises from the second class of bankruptcy risk (from the "gray zone"), the percentage of potentially bankrupt enterprises rose to 5%. The average probability of bankruptcy for enterprises in this sector is 5.7% (min = 0%, max = 100%). Every 10 enterprises in this sector had a probability of bankruptcy over a 2-year horizon (up to 2020) that was greater than 9.8%.

In the H (transport and storage management) sector with a total of 75 enterprises, the scoring model predicted bankruptcy for 3% of all enterprises in this sector for up to two years (up to 2020), including uncertain enterprises from the second class of bankruptcy risk (from the "gray zone"), while the percentage of potentially bankrupt enterprises increased to 7%. The average probability of bankruptcy for enterprises in this sector is 8.2% (min = 0%, max = 100%). Every 10 enterprises in this sector had a probability of bankruptcy over a 2-year horizon (up to 2020) that was greater than 23.2%.

The I sector (accommodation and gastronomy) with a total of 56 enterprises was the sector most exposed to the risk of bankruptcy. The scoring model predicts bankruptcy in the time horizon of up to two years (up to 2020) for as much as 13% of all enterprises in this sector, including uncertain enterprises in the second class of bankruptcy risk (from the "gray zone"), meaning the percentage of potentially bankrupt enterprises increased to 20%. The average probability of bankruptcy for enterprises in this sector is 22.2% (min = 0%, max = 100%). Every 10 enterprises in this sector had a probability of bankruptcy over a 2-year horizon (up to 2020) that was greater than 98.6%.

In the J (information and communication) sector with a total of 55 enterprises, the scoring model qualified 95% of enterprises as not being threatened with bankruptcy, and 5% as uncertain. The average probability of bankruptcy for enterprises in this sector is 6.1% (min = 0%, max = 89.4%). Every 10 enterprises in this sector had a probability of bankruptcy in the 2-year horizon (up to 2020) greater than 11.6%.

In the K (finance and insurance) sector with a total of 12 enterprises, the scoring model qualified 67% of enterprises as not being threatened with bankruptcy, and 33% as uncertain. The average probability of bankruptcy for enterprises in this sector is 28.2% (min = 0%, max = 96%). Every 10 enterprises in this sector had a probability of bankruptcy in a 2-year horizon (up to 2020) within 95.2–96%. This is a very specific sector (financial sector), hence the ambiguous interpretation of the results of the examined model belonging to risk classes.

In the L sector (services for the property market) with a total of 73 enterprises, the scoring model predicted bankruptcy for 3% of all enterprises in this sector within a 2-year horizon (up to 2020), including uncertain enterprises from the second class of bankruptcy risk (from the "gray zone"), where the percentage of potentially bankrupt enterprises increases to 17%. The average probability of bankruptcy for enterprises in this sector is 15.8% (min = 0%, max = 99.7%). Every 10 enterprises in this sector had a probability of bankruptcy over a 2-year horizon (up to 2020) in the range of 72.1%–99.7%. It is therefore also one of the sectors with high exposure to the risk of bankruptcy.

In the sector M (scientific, specialist and technological activity) with a total of 61 enterprises, the scoring model predicted bankruptcy for 2% of all enterprises in this sector within a time horizon of up to 2 years (up to 2020). After including uncertain enterprises from the second class of bankruptcy risk (from the "gray zone"), the percentage of potentially bankrupt enterprises increased to 5%. The average probability of bankruptcy for enterprises in this sector is 6.9% (min = 0%, max = 98.1%). Every 10 enterprises in this sector had a probability of bankruptcy over a 2-year horizon (up to 2020) greater than 17.4%.

The N sector (administration and support) with a total of 43 enterprises was also one of the sectors with a high exposure to the risk of bankruptcy. The scoring model predicted bankruptcy within a 2-year horizon (up to 2020) for 5% of all enterprises in this sector, including uncertain enterprises from the second class of bankruptcy risk (from the "gray zone"), when the percentage of potentially bankrupt enterprises increases to 12%. The average probability of bankruptcy for enterprises in this sector is 10.3% (min = 0%, max = 99.8%). Every 10 enterprises in this sector had a probability of bankruptcy over a 2-year horizon (up to 2020) greater than 51%.

Sector P (education) with a total of only nine enterprises was the third least risk affected sectors in the region's economy. The scoring model qualified all enterprises as not threatened with bankruptcy. The average probability of bankruptcy for enterprises in this sector is 3% (min = 0%, max = 19.1%). Every 10 enterprises in this sector had a probability of bankruptcy within a 2-year horizon (up to 2020) greater than 19%.

In the Q (health and social care) sector with a total of 38 enterprises, the scoring model predicted bankruptcy within a 2-year horizon (up to 2020) for 3% of all enterprises in this sector, including uncertain enterprises from the second class of bankruptcy risk (from "gray zone"), when the percentage of potentially bankrupt enterprises increases to 8%. The average probability of bankruptcy for enterprises in this sector is 10.3% (min = 0%, max = 98.8%). Every 10 enterprise in this sector had a probability of bankruptcy over a 2-year horizon (up to 2020) greater than 39%.

In the R (entertainment and leisure) sector with a total of 11 enterprises, the scoring model qualified 82% of enterprises as not being threatened with bankruptcy, and much because 18% as uncertain. The average probability of bankruptcy for enterprises in this sector is 11.3% (min = 0%, max = 61%). Every 10 enterprises in this sector had a probability of bankruptcy in the 2-year horizon (up to 2020) in the range of 54.9%–61%. Therefore, it is a sector in which ambiguity in the interpretation of the results of the examined model to risk classes can also be observed.

In the last sector S (other services) with a total of 11 enterprises, the scoring model qualified 91% of enterprises as not threatened with bankruptcy, and 9% as uncertain. The average probability of bankruptcy for enterprises in this sector is 12% (min = 0%, max = 91.7%). Every 10 enterprises in this sector had a probability of bankruptcy in the 2-year horizon (up to 2020) greater than 17.7%. It is also a sector in which ambiguity can be observed in interpreting the belonging of the results of the examined model to risk classes.

Based on the results from Table 4 and based on the analysis of the value of the probable bankruptcy probability (Figure 15) for the surveyed enterprises depending on their size, the following relationships illustrating the degree of their exposure to the risk of bankruptcy can be seen. In the sector for very small (micro) enterprises (535 of which were included in the study), the developed scoring model qualified 89% of these enterprises as not threatened with bankruptcy, 4% as bankrupt and a further 7% as uncertain (from the "gray zone"), but potentially with a significant risk of their bankruptcy above 50%. In the sector of small sized enterprises, of which 356 was developed in the study, the scoring model qualified 91% of such enterprises as not threatened with bankruptcy, 3% as bankrupt and another 6% as uncertain (from the "gray zone"). In the sector of medium enterprises (606 included in the study), the scoring model qualified 96% of enterprises as not threatened with bankruptcy, 2% as bankrupt and another 2% as uncertain (from the "gray zone"). Similarly for the large enterprise sector (636 enterprises) the scoring model in the study classified 94% of enterprises as not at risk of bankruptcy, 2% as bankrupt and another 4% as uncertain (from the "gray zone").

One also should pay attention to limitations of the analyses presented. The limitation of the model developed may be the fact that the developed and implemented scoring model has been estimated on the basis of statistical data for enterprises from various sectors of activity. It is very difficult to develop a model with good accuracy (a sufficiently high classification efficiency) that would be good in such a situation, since various sectors often very specific and incomparable. However, on the other hand, the results obtained (Table 5) for 39 actual bankruptcies of enterprises in the Podkarpackie Voivodeship observed and confirmed in 2018, the efficiency of correct recognition by the scoring model of really bankrupt enterprises is about 79%, while for non-bankrupt enterprises the equivalent figure is 95%. The effectiveness of the scoring model for the separate class: bankrupt at 79% is sufficient and acceptable, but of course can be discussed further. It can show that designed model includes three classes of bankruptcy risk (bankrupt, non-bankrupt and "gray zone"—difficult to say, but potentially also bankrupt). In the classic approach with only two classes (bankrupt, non-bankrupt), one should add another 8% to the model effectiveness (including the class of uncertain enterprises—"gray zone" for which the probability of bankruptcy is high and greater than 0.5). Then the efficiency of the correct classifications of estimated model increases to 87%, which seems to be a good result. Overall accuracy for the model (without division into classes) is 94%.

Also, the selection of such a large set of as many as 19 indicators as determinants of the financial condition of enterprises in the models raises the question of whether it should not be limited to the set of only a few most important indicators. Such a large collection may raise suspicions that many of the variables may be strongly correlated with each other, which may affect the quality, especially of classic models, such as LDA. In the study, such a large set of factors was conditioned by the choice using the wrapper method and genetic algorithm, and the final application of the type of ensemble classifiers that are not so sensitive to the interdependence of variables. However, for the sake of accuracy, it is worth emphasizing that the correlation between variables has never been greater than 0.87. However, in future research, it is worth considering reducing the number of predictors of bankruptcy.

7. Conclusions

The results of the analyses presented in the paper lead to several general conclusions that can be a summary of the research:

- The scoring model designed for the early prediction of bankruptcy risk for Polish businesses from the Podkarpackie Voivodeship using ensemble classifiers was highly effective in forecasting and accurately evaluating the risk of default of the analyzed businesses.

- An analysis of the forecast is obtained suggests that small enterprises are more exposed to risk of default than medium or large enterprises.

- The sector of business activity and unique characteristics of the economic activity influences a potentially higher risk of business bankruptcy. A higher number of potential bankruptcies is reported in some sectors of economic activity than in others.

- A higher risk of business bankruptcy for some particular industry branches may be caused the situation where bankruptcy models are sensitive to enterprises belonging to industry sectors. This can be considered as one of the limitations of the study presented in the paper. A potentially higher risk of business bankruptcy for some particular industry branches can be influenced by the model design. It would have to be examined in further research whether the estimated separate models for each sector would indicate lower values of PD and therefore lower exposure to the risk of bankruptcy of companies.

- Another limitation of the study is that bankruptcy models are sensitive to the phase of economic cycle (presented model does not cover it), but the influence of economic cycles on bankruptcy risk can be considered in further extensions of research.

- The approach presented in the paper can be used not only to assess the risk of bankruptcy of enterprises by market analysts and regional analysts, but also in banking activities to assess credit risk for corporate loans, where similar models are of course successfully implemented.

- The study may be extended in the future with an analysis and an assessment of the risk of bankruptcy for enterprises from other regions of Poland with the development of individual separate ensemble models for enterprises from key sectors of the country's economy. It can also be extended to a comparative analysis of the risk of bankruptcy in given sectors of the economy for a group of countries, e.g., EU, Visegrad Group countries or the Three Seas Initiative countries.

Appendix A

Table A1. Optimum configuration and set of parameters for bankruptcy models applied.

Classification Model Applied	Optimum Model Configuration (Training Sample) Parameter Selection Criterion: AUC (ROC) Sampling: (k = 5 fold) Cross-Validation
	Model Parameters:
Individual (single) classifier	
LDA (M1) linear discriminant analysis model $LDA = \alpha_1 Z_1 + \ldots + \alpha_m Z_m$	$\alpha_1 = -8.3 * 10^{-3}, \alpha_2 = 6.6 * 10^{-3}, \alpha_3 = -8.1 * 10^{-5}$ $\alpha_4 = 5.0 * 10^{-3}, \alpha_5 = -2.1 * 10^{-5}, \alpha_6 = 1.1 * 10^{-6}$ $\alpha_7 = 8.3 * 10^{-5}, \alpha_8 = 2.7 * 10^{-4}, \alpha_9 = -4.1 * 10^{-3}$ $\alpha_{10} = -3.7 * 10^{-2}, \alpha_{11} = -1.8 * 10^{-5}, \alpha_{12} = 3.2 * 10^{-5}$ $\alpha_{13} = 2.3 * 10^{-5}, \alpha_{14} = -2.7 * 10^{-2}, \alpha_{15} = -1.3 * 10^{-8}$ $\alpha_{16} = 9.8 * 10^{-3}, \alpha_{17} = -1.5 * 10^{-6},$ $\alpha_{18} = -3.7 * 10^{-2}, \alpha_{19} = -6.6 * 10^{-8}$
LOGIT (M2) logistic regression model $L = LOGIT = ln\left(\frac{p}{1-p}\right) = \alpha_0 + \alpha_1 Z_1 + \ldots + \alpha_m Z_m$	$\alpha_0 = 1.0 * 10^{15}, \alpha_1 = -6.9 * 10^{12}, \alpha_2 = 2.1 * 10^{12}$ $\alpha_3 = -5.1 * 10^{11}, \alpha_4 = 6.9 * 10^{12}, \alpha_5 = -1.3 * 10^{10}$ $\alpha_6 = 4.0 * 10^{8}, \alpha_7 = 4.9 * 10^{11}, \alpha_8 = 9.2 * 10^{11}$ $\alpha_9 = -3.7 * 10^{12}, \alpha_{10} = -1.4 * 10^{13}, \alpha_{11} = -3.7 * 10^{9}$ $\alpha_{12} = 9.0 * 10^{10}, \alpha_{13} = -6.5 * 10^{9}, \alpha_{14} = 2.2 * 10^{13}$ $\alpha_{15} = 1.8 * 10^{6}, \alpha_{16} = 4.4 * 10^{12}, \alpha_{17} = -4.1 * 10^{10}$ $\alpha_{18} = -1.1 * 10^{13}, \alpha_{19} = -2.2 * 10^{8}$
NNet (M3) neural network (single hidden layer network)	Network configuration: 19-5-1 Neuron activation function: logistic Error function = entropy fitting Calibrated parameter for weights: decay = 0.1
SVM Radial (M4) Support Vector Machine	Cost parameter: C = 1 Hyper parameter: sigma = 11.969
C&RT (M5) classification tree model	Tree complexity parameter (cp = 0.037) Tree split: $X_{11} \geq 40.79$ (class: bankrupt) $X_{11} < 40.79$ (class: no risk of bankruptcy)
MARS splines (M6)	product degree = 1 (degree of interaction); nprune = 12 (number of base functions);
Generalized Additive Model (GAM—M7)	Select = TRUE (feature selection); Link Function = Logit; Method = GCV.Cp (GCV method for an unknown parameter of model complexity)
Naive Bayes (M8)	Laplace Correction fL = 0 Distribution type usekernel = FALSE (Binomial) Bandwidth adjustment adjust = 1
Ensemble meta-classifier (stacking)	
k-NN k-nearest neighbours, inputs: classification functions for base models (M1-M8)	Nearest neighbour parameter k = 9
Ensemble classifier (boosting)	
Stochastic Gradient Boosting Machine (GBM)	Shrinkage = 0.2; n.minobsinnode = 15 (min. node size); n.trees = 130–boosting iterations interaction.depth = 5 (max. tree depth)
Boosted Logistic Regression (Logit Boost)	nIter = 13 (boosting iterations)

Table A1. *Cont.*

Classification Model Applied	Optimum Model Configuration (Training Sample) Parameter Selection Criterion: AUC (ROC) Sampling: (k = 5 fold) Cross-Validation
	Model Parameters:
Ensemble classifier (bagging)	
Random Forest (RF)	mtry = 5 randomly selected predictors ntree = 500 (number of trees)
Averaged NNet (avNNet)	*bag = TRUE; n = 5*—bootstraps; *size = 5*—number of neurons in the hidden layer for component networks; *decay = 0.9*—decay parameter for weights;

Source: own elaboration and calculations using R and Statistica software.

Table A2. Validation statistics for selected classical models of single bankruptcy classifiers in comparison to ensemble classifiers applied for the training sample.

Classification Model	Training Sample						
	AC	AC$_B$	AC$_{NB}$	AUC$_{ROC}$ (GINI)	KS Statistics	Divergence (Div)	Information Value (IV)
Base classifiers							
Linear discriminant analysis (LDA)—M1	88.4	94.6	82.5	0.96 (0.92)	0.87	2.6	5.2
Logistic regression (Logit)—M2	96.8	96.1	97.6	0.97 (0.94)	0.94	28.9	5.3
Neural network (NNet)—M3	93.0	94.1	92.0	0.95 (0.90)	0.86	7.5	5.2
Support Vector Machine (SVM Radial—M4)	96.4	95.4	97.4	0.99 (0.98)	0.93	17.2	5.2
Classification tree (C&RT)—M5	93.2	93.2	93.3	0.93 (0.86)	0.87	11.9	5.2
MARS splines—M6	96.0	95.8	96.3	0.99 (0.98)	0.94	8.0	5.2
Generalized Additive Model (GAM)—M7	97.7	98.0	97.4	0.99 (0.98)	0.96	5.8	5.3
Naive Bayes—M8	70.9	42.1	98.2	0.91 (0.82)	0.73	1.0	5.2
Ensemble classifier (stacking)							
Meta-classifier ensemble: kNN—model results M1-M8 as inputs	97.3	97.1	97.4	0.99 (0.98)	0.96	23.0	5.3
Ensemble classifiers (boosting)							
Stochastic Gradient Boosting Machine (GBM)	100	100	100	1.0 (1.0)	1.0	92.1	5.3
Logit Boost	97.9	97.3	98.5	0.99 (0.98)	0.96	20.5	5.3

Table A2. *Cont.*

Classification Model	Training Sample						
	AC	AC$_B$	AC$_{NB}$	AUC$_{ROC}$ (GINI)	KS Statistics	Divergence (Div)	Information Value (IV)
Ensemble classifiers (bagging)							
Random Forest (RF)	100	100	100	1.0 (1.0)	1.0	6.4	5.3
Averaged NNet (avNNet)	94.0	94.6	93.4	0.98 (0.96)	0.89	11.6	5.3

Source: own elaboration and calculations using R and Statistica software.

Table A3. Validation statistics for selected classical models of single bankruptcy classifiers in comparison to ensemble classifiers applied for the test/validation sample.

Classification Model	Test Sample						
	AC	AC$_B$	AC$_{NB}$	AUC$_{ROC}$ (GINI)	KS Statistics	Divergence (Div)	Information Value (IV)
Base classifiers							
Linear discriminant analysis (LDA)—M1	90.2	96.0	84.0	0.98 (0.96)	0.89	11.8	7.1
Logistic regression (Logit)—M2	96.5	94.5	98.8	0.97 (0.94)	0.93	46.2	7.1
Neural network (NNet)—M3	92.1	94.5	89.5	0.95 (0.90)	0.86	11.2	7.1
Support VectorMachine (SVM Radial)—M4	89.8	92.3	87.1	0.97 (0.94)	0.82	10.8	7.1
Classification tree (C&RT)—M5	94.2	95.2	93.1	0.94 (0.88)	0.88	14.8	7.1
MARS splines—M6	96.7	96.3	97.2	0.99 (0.98)	0.95	41.7	7.1
Generalized Additive Model (GAM)—M7	97.5	97.8	97.2	0.99 (0.98)	0.96	43.0	7.1
Naive Bayes—M8	68.4	41.7	97.6	0.93 (0.86)	0.78	7.8	7.1
Ensemble classifier (stacking)							
Meta-classifier ensemble: kNN model result M1-M8 as inputs	98.1	97.8	98.4	0.99 (0.98)	0.97	22.2	7.1
Ensemble classifiers (boosting)							
Stochastic Gradient Boosting Machine (GBM)	99.4	99.3	99.6	0.999 (0.998)	0.99	57.6	7.1
Logit Boost	98.5	98.2	99.6	0.99 (0.98)	0.98	20.6	7.1

Table A3. *Cont.*

Classification Model	Test Sample						
	AC	AC$_B$	AC$_{NB}$	AUC$_{ROC}$ (GINI)	KS Statistics	Divergence (Div)	Information Value (IV)
Ensemble classifiers (bagging)							
Random Forest (RF)	98.6	98.2	99.2	1.0 (1.0)	0.98	4.5	7.1
Averaged NNet (avNNet)	93.8	96.0	91.5	0.97 (0.94)	0.89	10.2	7.1

Source: own elaboration and calculations using R and Statistica software.

References

Achim, Monica V., Codruta Mare, and Sorin N. Borlea. 2012. A statistical model of financial risk bankruptcy applied for Romanian manufacturing industry. *Procedia Economics and Finance* 3: 132–37. [CrossRef]

Agarwal, Vineet, and Richard Taffler. 2008. Comparing the performance of market-based and accounting-based bankruptcy prediction models. *Journal of Banking & Finance* 32: 1541–51.

Ala'raj, Maher, and Maysam F. Abbod. 2016. Classifiers consensus system approach for credit scoring. *Knowledge-Based Systems* 104: 89–105. [CrossRef]

Alaka, Hafiz A., Lukumon O. Oyedele, Hakeem A. Owolabi, Vikas Kumar, Saheed O. Ajayi, Olungbenga O. Akinade, and Muhammad Bilal. 2018. Systematic review of bankruptcy prediction models: Towards a framework for tool selection. *Expert Systems with Applications* 94: 164–84. [CrossRef]

Alfaro, Esteban, Noelia Garcia, Matias Gamez, and David Elizondo. 2008. Bankruptcy forecasting: An empirical comparison of AdaBoost and neural networks. *Decision Support Systems* 45: 110–22. [CrossRef]

Altman, Edward I. 1968. Financial ratios, discriminant analysis and the prediction of corporate bankruptcy. *Journal of Finance* 23: 589–609. [CrossRef]

Anwar, Hina, Usman Qamar, and Abdul W. M. Qureshi. 2014. Global Optimization Ensemble Model for Classification Methods. *The Scientific World Journal* 2014: 1–9. [CrossRef]

Barboza, Flavio, Herbert Kimura, and Edward Altman. 2017. Machine learning models and bankruptcy prediction. *Expert Systems with Applications* 83: 405–17. [CrossRef]

Begley, Joy, Jin Ming, and Susan Watts. 1996. Bankruptcy classification errors in the 1980s: An empirical analysis of Altman's and Ohlson's models. *Review of Accounting Studies* 1: 267–84. [CrossRef]

Breiman, Leo. 1996. Bagging predictors. *Machine Learning* 24: 123–40. [CrossRef]

Breiman, Leo. 2001. Random Forests. *Machine Learning* 45: 5–32. [CrossRef]

Brown, Iain, and Christophe Mues. 2012. An experimental comparison of classification algorithms for imbalanced credit scoring data sets. *Expert Systems with Applications* 39: 3446–53. [CrossRef]

Bruneau, Catherine, Olivier de Brandt, and El A. Widad. 2012. Macroeconomic fluctuations and corporate financial fragility. *Journal of Financial Stability* 8: 219–35. [CrossRef]

Chen, Yibing, Lingling Zhang, and Liang Zhang. 2013. Financial Distress Prediction for Chinese Listed Manufacturing Companies. *Procedia Computer Science* 17: 678–86. [CrossRef]

Chuang, Chun-Ling. 2013. Application of hybrid case-based reasoning for enhanced performance in bankruptcy prediction. *Information Sciences* 236: 174–85. [CrossRef]

Cortes, Esteban A., Matias G. Martinez, and Noelia G. Rubio. 2007. A boosting approach for corporate failure prediction. *Applied Intelligence* 27: 29–37. [CrossRef]

Diakomihalis, Mihail. 2012. The accuracy of Altman's models in predicting hotel bankruptcy. *International Journal of Accounting and Financial Reporting* 2: 96–113. [CrossRef]

Du Jardin, Philippe. 2018. Failure pattern-based ensembles applied to bankruptcy forecasting. *Decision Support Systems* 107: 64–77. [CrossRef]

Emerging Markets Information Service (EMIS). 2019. EMIS Database. Available online: http://www.emis.com (accessed on 10 September 2019).

Fedorova, Elena, Evgenii Gilenko, and Sergey Dovzhenko. 2013. Bankruptcy prediction for Russian companies: Application of combined classifiers. *Expert Systems with Applications* 40: 7285–93. [CrossRef]

Freund, Yoav, and Robert E. Schapire. 1997. A decision theoretic generalization of online learning and an application to boosting. *Journal of Computer and System Sciences* 55: 119–39. [CrossRef]

Friedman, Jerome H. 2002. Stochastic gradient boosting. *Computational Statistics and Data Analysis* 38: 367–78. [CrossRef]

Główny Urząd Statystyczny (Statistics Poland). 2019. Bank Danych Lokalnych (Local Data Bank). Available online: https://bdl.stat.gov.pl (accessed on 10 September 2019).

Hadasik, Dorota. 1998. *The Bankruptcy of Enterprises in Poland and Methods of Its Forecasting.* Poznań: Wydawnictwo Akademii Ekonomicznej w Poznaniu.

Hamrol, Mirosław, and Jarosław Chodakowski. 2008. Prognozowanie zagrożenia finansowego przedsiębiorstwa. Wartość predykcyjna polskich modeli analizy dyskryminacyjnej. *Badania Operacyjne i Decyzje* 3: 17–32.

Hastie, Trevor, Robert Tibshirani, and Jerome Friedman. 2013. *The Elements of Statistical Learning: Data Mining, Inference, and Prediction.* New York: Springer.

Heo, Junyoung, and Jin Y. Yang. 2014. AdaBoost based bankruptcy forecasting of Korean construction companies. *Applied Soft Computing* 24: 494–99. [CrossRef]

Hol, Suzan. 2007. The influence of the business cycle on bankruptcy probability. *International Transactions in Operational Research* 14: 75–90. [CrossRef]

Hua, Zhongsheng, Yu Wang, Xiaoyan Xu, Bin Zhang, and Liang Liang. 2007. Predicting corporate financial distress based on integration of support vector machine and logistic regression. *Expert Systems with Applications* 33: 434–40. [CrossRef]

Iturriaga, Felix J. L., and Ivan P. Sanz. 2015. Bankruptcy visualization and prediction using neural networks: A study of U.S. commercial banks. *Expert Systems with Applications* 42: 2857–69. [CrossRef]

John, George H., Ron Kohavi, and Karl Pfleger. 1994. Irrelevant features and the subset selection problem. In *Machine Learning Proceedings 1994. Proceedings of the Eleventh International Conference.* Edited by William Cohen and Haym Hirsh. San Francisco: Morgan Kaufmann Publishers, pp. 121–29. [CrossRef]

Jovic, Alan, Karla Brkic, and Nikola Bogunovic. 2015. A review of feature selection methods with applications. In *2015 38th International Convention on Information and Communication Technology, Electronics and Microelectronics.* Edited by Peter Biljanovic, Z. Butkovic, K. Skala, B. Mikac, M. Cicin-Sain, V. Sruk, S. Ribaric, S. Gros, B. Vrdoljak, M. Mauher and et al. New York: IEEE, pp. 1200–5. [CrossRef]

Karas, Michal, Maria Reznakova, and Petr Pokorny. 2017. Predicting bankruptcy of agriculture companies: Validating selected models. *Polish Journal of Management Studies* 15: 110–20. [CrossRef]

Kim, Hyunjoon, and Zheng Gu. 2010. A Logistic Regression Analysis for Predicting Bankruptcy in the Hospitality Industry. *Journal of Hospitality Financial Management* 14: 17–34. [CrossRef]

Kim, Myoung-Jong, and Dae-Ki Kang. 2010. Ensemble with neural networks for bankruptcy prediction. *Expert Systems with Applications* 37: 3373–79. [CrossRef]

Kim, Myoung-Jong, Dae-Ki Kang, and Hong B. Kim. 2015. Geometric mean based boosting algorithm with over-sampling to resolve data imbalance problem for bankruptcy prediction. *Expert Systems with Applications* 42: 1074–82. [CrossRef]

Kliestik, Tomas, Jana Kliestikova, Maria Kovacova, Lucia Svabova, Katarina Valaskova, Marek Vochozka, and Judit Olah. 2018. *Prediction of Financial Health of Business Entities in Transition Economies.* New York: Addleton Academic Publishers.

Korol, Tomasz. 2010. *Early Warning Systems of Enterprises to the Risk of Bankruptcy.* Warsaw: Wolters Kluwer.

Kuhn, Max, and Kjell Johnson. 2013. *Applied Predictive Modeling.* New York: Springer.

Kumar, Ravi P., and Vadlamani Ravi. 2007. Bankruptcy prediction in banks and firms via statistical and intelligent techniques—A review. *European Journal of Operational Research* 180: 1–28. [CrossRef]

Lessmann, Stefan, Bart Baesens, Hsin-Vonn Seow, and Lyn C. Thomas. 2015. Benchmarking state-of-the-art classification algorithms for credit scoring: An update of research. *European Journal of Operational Research* 247: 124–36. [CrossRef]

Li, Hui, and Jie Sun. 2012. Case-based reasoning ensemble and business application: A computational approach from multiple case representations driven by randomness. *Expert Systems with Applications* 39: 3298–310. [CrossRef]

Mączyńska, Elżbieta. 1994. Assessment of the condition of the enterprise. Simplified methods. *Życie Gospodarcze* 38: 42–45.

Marcinkevicius, Rosvydas, and Rasa Kanapickiene. 2014. Bankruptcy prediction in the sector of construction in Lithuania. *Procedia—Social and Behavioral Sciences* 156: 553–57. [CrossRef]

Ogólnopolski Monitor Upadłościowy (Coface Polish National Bankruptcy Monitor). 2019. Available online: http://www.coface.pl/en (accessed on 10 September 2019).

Ohlson, James A. 1980. Financial ratios and the probabilistic prediction of bankruptcy. *Journal of Accounting Research* 18: 109–31. [CrossRef]

Prusak, Błażej. 2005. *Nowoczesne Metody Prognozowania Zagrożenia Finansowego Przedsiębiorstw.* Warsaw: Wydawnictwo Difin.

Ptak-Chmielewska, Aneta. 2016. Statistical models for corporate credit risk assessment—Rating models. *Acta Universitatis Lodziensis Folia Oeconomica* 3: 98–111. [CrossRef]

Rajin, Danica, Danijela Milenkovic, and Tijana Radojevic. 2016. Bankruptcy prediction models in the Serbian agricultural sector. *Economics of Agriculture* 1: 89–105. [CrossRef]

Siddiqi, Naeem. 2017. *Intelligent Credit Scoring*, 2nd ed. Hoboken: John Wiley & Sons.

Stowarzyszenie Dolina Lotnicza (Aviation Valley Association). 2019. Available online: http://www.dolinalotnicza.pl/en/business-card (accessed on 10 September 2019).

Sun, Jie, Hamido Fujita, Peng Chen, and Hui Li. 2017. Dynamic financial distress prediction with concept drift based on time weighting combined with AdaBoost support vector machine ensemble. *Knowledge-Based Systems* 120: 4–14. [CrossRef]

Thomas, Lyn C. 2009. *Consumer Credit Models.* New York: Oxford University Press.

Topaloglu, Zeynep. 2012. A Multi-period Logistic Model of Bankruptcies in the Manufacturing Industry. *International Journal of Finance and Accounting* 1: 28–37. [CrossRef]

Tsai, Chih-Fong, and Yu-Feng Hsu. 2013. A meta-learning framework for bankruptcy prediction. *Journal of Forecasting* 32: 167–79. [CrossRef]

Tsai, Chih-Fong, and Jhen-Wei Wu. 2008. Using neural network ensembles for bankruptcy prediction and credit scoring. *Expert Systems with Applications* 34: 2639–49. [CrossRef]

Tsai, Chih-Fong, Yu-Feng Hsu, and David C. Yen. 2014. A comparative study of classifier ensembles for bankruptcy prediction. *Applied Soft Computing* 24: 977–84. [CrossRef]

Twala, Bhekisipho. 2010. Multiple classifier application to credit risk assessment. *Expert Systems with Applications* 37: 3326–36. [CrossRef]

Vlamis, Prodromos. 2007. Default Risk of the UK Real Estate Companies: Is There a Macro-economy Effect? *The Journal of Economic Asymmetries* 4: 99–117. [CrossRef]

West, David, Scott Dellana, and Jingxia Qian. 2005. Neural network ensemble strategies for financial decision applications. *Computers & Operations Research* 32: 2543–59.

Wolpert, David H. 1992. Stacked generalization. *Neural Networks* 5: 241–59. [CrossRef]

Youn, Hyewon, and Zheng Gu. 2010. Predict US restaurant firm failures: The artificial neural network model versus logistic regression model. *Tourism and Hospitality Research* 10: 171–87. [CrossRef]

Zhang, Cha, and Yunqian Ma. 2012. *Ensemble Machine Learning. Methods and Applications.* New York: Springer.

Zhang, Defu, Xiyue Zhou, Stephen C. H. Leung, and Jiemin Zheng. 2010. Vertical bagging decision trees model for credit scoring. *Expert Systems with Applications* 37: 7838–43. [CrossRef]

Zhou, Zhi-Hua. 2012. *Ensemble Methods. Foundations and Algorithms.* Boca Raton: CRC Press.

Zięba, Maciej, Sebastian K. Tomczak, and Jakub M. Tomczak. 2016. Ensemble boosted trees with synthetic features generation in application to bankruptcy prediction. *Expert Systems with Applications* 58: 93–101. [CrossRef]

Zweig, Mark H., and Gregory Campbell. 1993. Receiver-Operating Characteristic (ROC) plots: A fundamental evaluation tool in clinical medicine. *Clinical Chemistry* 39: 561–77. [CrossRef] [PubMed]

10

Tax Arrears Versus Financial Ratios in Bankruptcy Prediction

Oliver Lukason * and Art Andresson

Faculty of Economics and Business Administration, University of Tartu, Liivi 4, 50409 Tartu, Estonia; art@taust.ee
* Correspondence: oliver.lukason@ut.ee

Abstract: This paper aims to compare the usefulness of tax arrears and financial ratios in bankruptcy prediction. The analysis is based on the whole population of Estonian bankrupted and survived SMEs from 2013 to 2017. Logistic regression and multilayer perceptron are used as the prediction methods. The results indicate that closer to bankruptcy, tax arrears' information yields a higher prediction accuracy than financial ratios. A combined model of tax arrears and financial ratios is more useful than the individual models. The results enable us to outline several theoretical and practical implications.

Keywords: bankruptcy prediction; tax arrears; payment defaults; financial ratios

1. Introduction

In the year 2018, half a century had passed from the foundational multivariate bankruptcy prediction study conducted by Altman (1968). During this time, hundreds of financial ratio-based prediction models have been published (see e.g., reviews by Ravi Kumar and Ravi 2007; Sun et al. 2014; Alaka et al. 2018). The area has especially flourished with the advances in artificial intelligence, and substantial amount of new tools are being introduced annually. Although high prediction accuracies have been achieved with financial ratios, due to several reasons, they can never be fully relied on in bankruptcy prediction.

The first set of reasons includes the availability and accuracy of financial reports. Financial reporting delays or non-submission of reports are fairly common in case of SMEs, especially for financially distressed firms (Clatworthy and Peel 2016; Luypaert et al. 2016). The latter is characteristic to Estonia as well (Lukason 2013; Lukason and Camacho-Miñano 2019). In addition, as annual reports of SMEs are usually non-audited, they are at a higher risk of including faulty information (Altman et al. 2010). Thus, the financial ratios needed for prediction might be incorrect or not available.

The other substantial reason concerns how capable financial ratios are in signaling future bankruptcy of firms. It is an established fact that a fair share of firms regardless of their age can follow a failure process, where (serious) financial problems or performance declines are not observable in the last financial report before bankruptcy (Lukason et al. 2016; Lukason and Laitinen 2019). In addition, a remarkable number of firms perform poorly, but will never fail, and therefore, cannot be distinguished from their bankrupting counterparts, leading to a Type II error in classification models (du Jardin 2017).

Because of these reasons, an ongoingly important research question is whether there is a substitute for financial ratios in bankruptcy prediction. Various attempts have been utilized in this area, for instance using information about corporate governance, business environment, past payment defaults, and audit resolution (Lussier 1995; Back 2005; Ciampi 2015; Liang et al. 2016; Iwanicz-Drozdowska et al. 2016; Munoz-Izquierdo et al. 2019; Ciampi et al. 2019). Such studies have concluded that variables other than financial ratios can be individually better predictors or can at least provide some incremental value, when applied with financial ratios.

Relying on the aforementioned general motivation, this study aims to find out how accurately future bankruptcy can be predicted by using tax arrears information and whether the accuracy exceeds the level of a financial ratio-based model. In the following literature review section, we synthesize the past findings of failure (prediction) studies in order to lay a foundation for the follow-up empirical part of the paper. The literature review section is followed by a thorough explanation of our dataset, variables calculated, and methods used. Then, empirical results with relevant discussion are presented, succeeded by both theoretical and empirical implications. This is followed by a separate section about the study's limitations and the paper ends with conclusive remarks, while also including multiple novel research directions.

2. Literature Review

2.1. Firm Failure Process Leading to Bankruptcy

The general theoretical foundation for the choice of variables for bankruptcy prediction is firm failure process, i.e., a pathway to bankruptcy. A firm failure process depicts in a certain timeframe how managerial actions in certain environmental conditions lead to an outcome such as poor profitability or illiquidity of a firm (Crutzen and Caillie 2008; Ooghe and Prijcker 2008). The theoretical models of firm failure processes (e.g., Weitzel and Jonsson 1989; Crutzen and Caillie 2008; Amankwah-Amoah 2016) have broken the pathway to bankruptcy into multiple consecutive stages, and concluded that in the earlier stages, problems might not be signaled through financial reports, and thus, finally bankrupting firms might not be (well) distinguishable from poorly performing, but finally surviving firms. Therefore, empirical studies have concluded that in the longer time horizon, financial ratios are not accurate in bankruptcy prediction (du Jardin 2017) and variables other than financial ratios would be beneficial (Iwanicz-Drozdowska et al. 2016).

Recent studies have indicated that the pre-bankruptcy problems indicated through the values of financial ratios or failure risk might not be observable enough through the pre-bankruptcy annual reports of SMEs more than one year before bankruptcy is declared. For instance, Lukason and Laitinen (2019) showed that for 73% of analyzed European SMEs, bankruptcy risk became over 50% and known financial ratios obtained negative values only in the last annual report before bankruptcy. Still, the latter result was obtained when looking at the median values of respective variables, and thus, a fair share of firms might not witness any observable problems in the last financial report (see e.g., Lukason et al. 2016).

A practical issue when using information from annual reports is the delay in information disclosure. Multiple studies (e.g., Altman et al. 2010; Luypaert et al. 2016) have vividly pointed to the issue that firms in (high) failure risk tend to delay the presentation of negative information. In the worst scenario, this can mean not submitting the pre-bankruptcy annual report at all, while the delay of the annual report beyond a deadline set in law (e.g., in Estonia 6 months after the fiscal year) becomes more like a "rule" rather than an exception (Lukason 2013).

2.2. Financial Ratios as Predictors of Bankruptcy

A vast amount of studies exploiting financial ratios for bankruptcy prediction have been composed so far with largely varying results (see e.g., literature reviews by Dimitras et al. 1996; Ravi Kumar and Ravi 2007; Sun et al. 2014; Alaka et al. 2018). As the situation of bankruptcy points to either a shortage of cash (liquidity crisis) and/or liabilities exceeding assets (solidity crisis) (Uhrig-Homburg 2005), the theoretical explanations of which ratios could be useful rely on both of them. The cash flow-based explanation to predictors' choice originates from Beaver (1966) idea of firm as a reservoir of liquid assets, while a (negative) equity-based explanation is most vividly explained in the probabilistic theory of bankruptcy developed by Scott (1981). Still, since the earlier multivariate contributions (e.g., Altman 1968; Ohlson 1980), the financial ratios for bankruptcy prediction have mostly been chosen on empirical grounds, without focusing on the mechanism leading to corporate collapse. The usual ratio domains applied in bankruptcy prediction, although occasionally phrased differently, concern liquidity, solidity, capital/financial structure, profitability, and turnover (Lukason et al. 2016; du Jardin 2017).

The recent cross-sectional studies using very large populations of European firms and t-1 period for bankruptcy prediction have indicated that areas under the curve (AUCs) remain on an average level, namely in the range of 0.7–0.9 and only on rare occasions exceed 0.9 (Laitinen and Suvas 2013; Altman et al. 2017). In a meta-analysis of bankruptcy prediction studies, du Jardin (2017) found the average t-1 classification accuracy to be 85%. Recently, studies have shown that prediction accuracies can be enhanced by accounting for the financial dynamics and patterns occurring before bankruptcy (e.g., du Jardin 2015, 2017, 2018), but still the misclassification rates have remained at 10–20%. This provides a clear indication that financial ratios have inherent problems (see also Section 2.1), which cannot be overcome by using more sophisticated classification methods.

2.3. Payment Defaults as Predictors of Bankruptcy

A domain in the literature scantly developed is the usage of past payment defaults to predict bankruptcy. The few available studies (e.g., Laitinen 1999; Back 2005; Altman et al. 2010; Wilson and Altanlar 2014; Iwanicz-Drozdowska et al. 2016; Ciampi et al. 2019) have all indicated that past payment behavior can be valuable in bankruptcy prediction and lead to either higher classification accuracies individually or at least provide an increment to classification accuracies, when applied with financial ratios.

Despite substantial contribution to the area, the available studies have treated payment defaults in a rather simple way: by accounting their presence, number and size. Still, the extant studies do not pay attention to defaults in the longer time horizon, i.e., their exact dynamic behavior in respect to what pattern they follow. Another substantial issue in the portion of extant literature is that the applied payment defaults are permanent, namely they are a logical precedent to the future bankruptcy. Such application can lead to using de facto insolvency to predict de jure insolvency, reducing the practical applicability of such models, i.e., they do not lead to remarkable benefits for creditors aiming to reduce their misclassifications. Therefore, the practical usage of relevant prediction models can be enhanced by taking into account temporary payment defaults as well. In addition, to our knowledge tax arrears as a type of payment default has so far not been applied in bankruptcy prediction, although their existence has successfully been used as a dependent variable with financial ratios being independent (see Höglund 2017).

2.4. Research Propositions

We would argue that as many SMEs do not witness financial problems one year before bankruptcy portrayed through the annual report, but in turn start witnessing temporary liquidity problems, models based on tax arrears are more accurate than models based on financial ratios in the short-run. Further away from bankruptcy, liquidity problems are equally frequent for future bankrupt and non-bankrupt firms, and thus, financial ratio-based models are more beneficial in the long-run. As different types of variables are beneficial in the short- and long-run, their conjoint usage should logically lead to the highest classification accuracy. Relying on the latter theoretical explanations and past achievements in the literature, we phrase three research propositions for the empirical part of the paper, while we consider one specific type of payment defaults, i.e., tax arrears, in this study:

P1:   *A model based on payment defaults leads to a higher accuracy in bankruptcy prediction than a model based on financial ratios only in the short-run.*

P2:   *The accuracy of a model based on payment defaults decreases further away from bankruptcy.*

P3:   *A model incorporating both payment defaults and financial ratios leads to a higher accuracy than the individual models incorporating these variables.*

3. Data and Methods

3.1. Dataset and General Setting of the Study

The dataset of this paper includes all Estonian bankrupted firms from 2013–2017, in case of which the following restrictions have been applied. First, all firms must have information available to calculate variables outlined in Sections 3.2 and 3.3. Second, we demand the financial report of a bankrupted firm to be not older than two years from the moment of bankruptcy declaration. With this restriction, we guarantee that the annual report portrays pre-bankruptcy financial situation homogenously for firms included in the analysis and is available for comparative purposes with payment defaults. On average, the financial report in the dataset portrays financial situation one year before bankruptcy declaration. In total, 512 bankrupted firms are included in the analysis, which are all SMEs.

Concerning survived firms, 4003 firms are used which are functional at the time of the analysis. All firms which have financial information available from 2011 to 2015 are chosen, irrespective of how well they perform. The latter is important to avoid a bias of discriminating only in between bankrupt and "successful" survived firms. The time 2011–2015 is determined by the fact that the reports of bankrupted firms originate from the same time interval. In the viewed period, Estonia had recovered from the consequences of the global financial crisis and these years were characterized by stable economic growth. Thus, the viewed period is not subject to any abnormal performance of firms due to economic recession.

For calculating financial ratios of bankrupt firms, we use the last available annual financial report before bankruptcy. In case of survived firms, we calculate the financial ratios for all firms for all five years incorporated to the analysis. In Estonia, firms are responsible for submitting an annual report in maximum six months after the end of the fiscal year, which for the vast majority of firms overlaps with the calendar year.

Concerning taxes, firms need to submit tax reports and pay taxes twice in the month following the month that the taxes were incurred. Specifically, on the 10th day of the month for taxes concerned with salaries and on the 20th day of the month for value added tax. Estonia is among a few countries in the world where profit is not taxed on an accrual basis, but only when dividends are paid. When dividends are paid, the respective income tax is subject to the same principles as salaries. When tax arrears (i.e., unpaid tax debt due) occur, this is observable live on the Estonian Tax and Customs Board database. From the latter database, we have obtained the values of tax arrears for the whole population for each month end in the viewed period of 2011–2017. The usage of the month end is a more suitable option when compared with for instance one day delay of paying taxes. This is because a few days' delays of paying taxes is common in Estonia and are more subject to administrative or diligence reasons, rather than pointing to a temporary liquidity crisis. Thus, tax arrears' information can be used dynamically to view the emergence of problems up to the exact month when bankruptcy occurred. As the annual reports are up to 2 years old, in case of tax arrears data, we consider a 24 month long period before bankruptcy is declared. For survived firms, we use multiple 24 month long periods within the years from 2011 to 2016.

We do not apply other payment defaults (i.e., to private creditors, such as banks and suppliers) in this study for multiple reasons. First, in Estonia no single database incorporates all payment defaults to private creditors. Second, some of such defaults might not be documented, for instance because of their small size or creditors executing their claims in a different way (e.g., suing managers who have guaranteed the credit). Third, such defaults might not be documented precisely in respect to their start or end period, e.g., due to the fact that creditors could be delaying the execution of a claim because of groundless promises by debtors to pay the debt.

To provide an answer in which period tax arrears' information is more useful than financial ratios, we consider different pre-bankruptcy periods concerning tax arrears. The usage of financial information in this study has been consolidated into Table 1.

Table 1. The logic of calculating financial ratios and variables portraying tax arrears in this study.

Information Sources for Calculating Financial Ratios in This Study	
Bankrupted firms	Last annual report (not older than two years from bankruptcy moment)
Survived firms	All annual reports from 2011 to 2015
Information sources for calculating tax arrears variables in this study	
Bankrupted firms	12 month long periods before bankruptcy, where the respective numbers indicate month x to month y before the bankruptcy declaration month: 1–12, 4–15, 7–18, 10–21, 13–24. A single 24 month long period before bankruptcy, where the respective numbers indicate month x to month y before the bankruptcy declaration month: 1–24.
Survived firms	12 month long periods are used as six full years from 2011 to 2016. A single 24 month period is used as five two-year periods: 2011–2012, 2012–2013, 2013–2014, 2014–2015, 2015–2016. As there are proportionally much less bankruptcies from 2017, then in case of survived firms that year is neglected from the analysis.

Source: own elaboration.

3.2. Financial Ratios Portraying Different Domains

The financial ratios for this study have been chosen based on their previous usage for bankruptcy prediction and taking into account that all important financial ratio domains would be covered (see the formulas and ratio domains in Table 2). Firm leverage is reflected by the total debt to total assets ratio (DA). This ratio in its different forms (e.g., total equity to total assets or total equity to total debt) might be the most common and useful failure predictor. The ratio has a strong intersection with legislation, as business and insolvency codes in different countries often set minimum requirements for firms' equity. Profitability is captured with two ratios, i.e., net income to total assets and net income to operating revenue. The former is a more common profitability ratio in bankruptcy prediction and was used already in the Altman (1968) model, although having EBIT instead of net income in the numerator. Static liquidity is portrayed with two ratios, namely either the quotient of cash minus current liabilities to total assets or the quotient of current assets minus current liabilities to total assets. These ratios have been frequently used in the form of cash to current liabilities (quick ratio) and current assets to current liabilities (current ratio), but the usage of such ratios is problematic. Namely, as among survived firms there might be a fair amount of companies with no or very low level of current liabilities, such ratios would obtain extreme values or the value cannot be calculated at all. Moreover, the division with total assets helps us to have a better overview how large the surplus or deficit of cash or current assets is in comparison to all assets a firm possesses. A firm's cash flow creation is portrayed with two ratios reflecting the quotient of operating cash flow to either operating revenue or total assets. The productivity (efficiency) of a firm's assets is reflected by the quotient of operating revenue to total assets. Finally, the burden of interest paid on debt is proxied with two ratios, specifically the quotient of total financial revenues minus total financial expenses to either total assets or operating revenue. The latter two variables (with similar, but not necessarily identical formulas) have been often classified as solvency (solidity) ratios.

The ten applied financial ratios reflect the most usual domains used in previous bankruptcy prediction studies, i.e., profitability, cash flow creation, leverage, liquidity, solidity, and profitability. We acknowledge that many more financial ratios have been applied in previous studies, but they are mostly very similar (or mere modifications) to the ones used, and thus, would evidently provide only a marginal surplus (if at all) to classification accuracies. In addition, the calculation of very specific financial ratios is altered by the availability of financial information, as the financial reports of SMEs are often quite brief. Because of the latter, we can for instance use the difference of financial revenues and financial expenses, rather than specific types of those revenues/expenses. In case of all applied financial ratios, the general rule is that higher values should reduce the bankruptcy probability on a univariate principle. The exception is DA, where the situation is the reverse.

Table 2. Financial ratio abbreviations, domains, and formulas used in this study.

Ratio Abbreviation	Domain	Formula
CCLA	liquidity	(cash—current liabilities)/total assets
CACLA	liquidity	(current assets—current liabilities)/total assets
NIA	profitability	net income/total assets
NIOR	profitability	net income/operating revenue
DA	leverage/solidity	total debt/total assets
ORA	productivity	operating revenue/total assets
FREOR	interest burden	(financial revenues—financial expenses)/operating revenue
FREA	interest burden	(financial revenue—financial expenses)/total assets
OCFA	cash flow creation	operating cash flow/total assets
OCFOR	cash flow creation	operating cash flow/operating revenue

Source: own elaboration.

3.3. Variables Portraying Tax Arrears

Unlike with financial ratios, there are no uniform guidelines on how to calculate variables portraying the dynamics and content of tax arrears. Still, past theoretical and empirical research provides hints that larger and/or more frequent payment defaults increase the likelihood of failure. Derived from that logic, both of those dimensions should be incorporated into the analysis. To capture the scale of tax arrears, we calculate the maximum of tax arrears occurring in the viewed period. As large tax arrears can occur only episodically (e.g., only during one month in the sequence of 12 months), we extend the scale variable to incorporate frequency context as well by calculating the median of tax arrears in the viewed period. The frequency of tax arrears is captured by a variable counting the month ends when tax arrears were present. Still, the latter variable might be limited, because tax arrears can occur for instance every second month, i.e., they occur frequently, but still episodically. In order to enhance the frequency analysis by also incorporating the severity of ongoingness of payment defaults, we also introduce a variable measuring the longest sequence of month ends when tax arrears occurred. Thus, the four applied tax arrears' variables (see Table 3) also incorporate both the scale and frequency of payment defaults in a combined manner.

Table 3. Abbreviations and calculation explanations of variables portraying tax arrears in this study.

Variable Abbreviation	Calculation Explanation
TMAX	Maximum tax arrears in the viewed sequence on month ends
TMEDIAN	Median tax arrears in the viewed sequence of month ends
TCOUNT	Number of month ends with tax arrears in the viewed sequence
TCONSMON	Length of the longest sequence of month ends with tax arrears

Source: Own elaboration; Note: we consider the presence of tax arrears as over 100 euros unpaid tax debt, as tax authority does not add a disclaimer of owing taxes in case of very small arrears, and also, managers can occasionally forget paying very small tax arrears.

3.4. Methods

We apply one classical statistical (i.e., logistic regression, noted as LR) and one machine learning (i.e., multilayer perceptron with two hidden layers, noted as MP) tool for composing the prediction models. In case of using only one method, the results could be biased towards that specific method, and therefore, not generalizable. These two methods are probably the most exploited classical and novel methods in bankruptcy prediction, thus their choice is fairly justified based on the developments in previous research. We acknowledge that there is nowadays a myriad of different methods (especially in the area of machine learning) available for failure prediction. Still, as the first and foremost aim of the paper is to show whether and in what context the information about tax arrears can be exploited in bankruptcy prediction, we find the usage of two methods a sufficient choice. In addition, based on the results in the empirical section, we thoroughly explain why the usage of additional methods would probably not have provided a surplus to the obtained results.

In bankruptcy prediction, there are different streams concerning how to use observations in the analysis. The classical studies have used (rather) equal samples for bankrupted and survived firms. This definitely guarantees that the analysis reaches a clear conclusion how accurately bankrupted and survived firms can be discriminated from each other. Still, such selection of survived firms should be avoided, as there is a serious risk of creating a bias, i.e., the sample of survived firms does not represent the population it originates from. Moreover, when for instance a credit analyst is solving a practical classification problem, a firm under consideration originates from the whole population without any preselection. Thus, if available, the population of survived firms should be used irrespective of their characteristics. Therefore, our dataset (see Section 3.1) incorporates all bankrupted firms and all their survived counterparts, for which the respective annual reports were available.

There are different options on how to use LR and MP. When the frequencies in two groups (i.e., bankrupted and non-bankrupted firms) are very imbalanced (which is the usual case and also applies for this study), algorithms can result in classifying a majority group (i.e., non-bankrupt firms) as correctly as possible, at the same time creating (huge) misclassification errors in case of the minority group (i.e., bankrupt firms). Therefore, we administer a procedure frequently used in bankruptcy prediction research (see e.g., Altman et al. 2017) by weighting the two groups of firms to be equal in the analysis. In case of LR, the weights for observations are calculated as 0.5 divided by the share of respective group in the population used. In case of MP, we achieve the same by making synthetic observations. Such a method, i.e., a synthetic minority oversampling technique (SMOTE), has been frequently used in case of machine learning classification applications for bankruptcy prediction (Kim et al. 2015). SMOTE is achieved by repeating the observations of bankrupt firms as long as their population size equals that of non-bankrupt firms. We acknowledge that different weights could be applied in this study, but this is specifically dependent on how large the misclassification costs of (non-)bankrupt firms are (in practice). Likewise with majority of previous studies in the area, we do not incorporate misclassification costs in the analysis.

In order to understand what are the prediction abilities of individual variables, we first provide the results in case of LR by using only single variables from Tables 2 and 3. After that, we conduct three types of analyses: (a) using all financial ratios together for LR and MP, (b) using all tax arrears' variables together for LR and MP, (c) using financial ratios and tax arrears' variables together for LR and MP. When the comparison of (a) and (b) enables us to outline the individual prediction abilities of the specific variables through the two applied methods, then (c) introduces a joint analysis. Results are provided for both test and hold-out samples.

4. Results and Discussion

4.1. Univariate Prediction Abilities of Variables

We first outline the univariate prediction abilities of the applied variables (see Table 4), while the descriptive statistics of the variables have been provided in Appendix A Tables A1–A3. The results in Table 4 have been presented for descriptive purposes and obtained from LR by applying each variable individually. The most useful financial ratio on a univariate principle is DA, which is a fairly common and useful predictor in previous studies (usually also in the form of total equity to total assets ratio). Still, the accuracy (77.1%) of this solidity ratio remains modest, closely followed by a liquidity ratio CCLA with 75.7% accuracy.

The tax arrears' variables indicate better predictive performance. For instance, when calculated for the period 1–12 months before bankruptcy declaration, all of them outperform DA. When further away from bankruptcy, the individual predictive power of tax arrears' variables deteriorates. For instance, when the period 13–24 months before bankruptcy prediction is applied, the most accurate tax arrears variable is TMAX, indicating that the largest tax arrears in that period obtains the same predictive power as DA, i.e., 77.1%. Thus, the univariate results provide an initial indication that tax arrears have remarkable predictive power and this result is further elaborated with multivariate analysis in the next section.

Table 4. Univariate prediction accuracies (%) of variables.

Financial Ratios			
CCLA	75.7	ORA	60.5
CACLA	70.1	FREOR	59.5
NIA	61.4	FREA	63.6
NIOR	59.5	OCFA	49.3
DA	77.1	OCFOR	42.2
Tax Arrears Variables			
TMAX1–12	85.3	TMAX10–21	77.6
TMEDIAN1–12	78.5	TMEDIAN10–21	71.5
TCOUNT1–12	84.9	TCOUNT10–21	76.3
TCONSMON1–12	85.1	TCONSMON10–21	76.9
TMAX4–15	82.1	TMAX13–24	77.1
TMEDIAN4–15	74.8	TMEDIAN13–24	70.3
TCOUNT4–15	81.6	TCOUNT13–24	74.7
TCONSMON4–15	81.0	TCONSMON13–24	75.4
TMAX7–18	79.3	TMAX1–24	85.9
TMEDIAN7–18	73.5	TMEDIAN1–24	74.0
TCOUNT7–18	77.9	TCOUNT1–24	83.0
TCONSMON7–18	79.0	TCONSMON1–24	83.8

Source: own elaboration; Note: Tx-y indicates tax arrears variable from period month x to month y before bankruptcy is declared.

4.2. Multivariate Approach with Logistic Regression and Multilayer Perceptron

The classification accuracies of the logistic regression and multilayer perceptron models are quite similar, although the logistic regression models are somewhat more precise on holdout sample when tax arrears' variables are applied. The higher accuracy in case of non-bankrupt firms observable in Table 5 for tax arrears' models can be explained by a simple financial logic. Type I error (i.e., bankrupt firms classified as non-bankrupt) is caused by a certain proportion of bankrupt firms having no tax arrears during the viewed period. The survived firms normally do not witness tax arrears, or at least not in such scale and frequency as the bankrupt firms. Thus, when using tax arrears in bankruptcy prediction, no sophisticated logic about the occurring patterns is necessary, and rather, their existence with a certain frequency and magnitude is a sufficient proof of potential serious financial problems.

The few percentage points superiority of the LR models over the MP models in case of tax arrears' variables could mostly be explained by the MP models overtraining the relationship in between independent and dependent variables, i.e., it is considered to be more sophisticated than it actually is.

The prediction abilities of tax arrears' models gradually decrease when looking at periods further away from bankruptcy declaration. The logistic regression model TA10–21 and the multilayer perceptron model TA7–18 are the first ones being not able to outperform financial ratios in bankruptcy prediction. In case of the LR model, the latter means that when looking at the time before bankruptcy, then at a certain point in between the 7th and 10th month before the bankruptcy declaration, the usage of financial ratios becomes more beneficial than tax arrears' information. Thus, tax arrears' information is especially useful for predictive purposes in the short-run before a firm becomes bankrupt.

We find support for all three research propositions set for this study. Payment defaults' dynamics portrayed by tax arrears can lead to a higher bankruptcy prediction accuracy than financial ratios in the short-run (P1), but that accuracy reduces further away from bankruptcy (P2) and at a certain point is overrun by the accuracy of a model based on financial ratios. In addition, the model incorporating both variable domains leads to the highest accuracy (P3). The prediction accuracy of the financial ratios' model is similar to the findings in previous studies (e.g., Altman et al. 2017; du Jardin 2017), while the tax arrears' models obtain higher accuracies than previous models based on payment defaults (e.g., Back 2005; Ciampi et al. 2019). In addition, as suggested by previous studies (e.g., Iwanicz-Drozdowska et al. 2016; Ciampi et al. 2019), a combined model of financial ratios and payment defaults leads to the highest possible accuracy.

Table 5. Prediction accuracies (%) of composed multivariate models.

Variables	Logistic Regression				Multilayer Perceptron				
	Test Sample	Holdout Sample	AB	ANB	Training Sample	Test Sample	Holdout Sample	AB	ANB
Financial ratios	79.9	79.5	80.4	78.7	81.8	80.6	81.9	85.4	78.4
TA1–12	86.9	89.5	83.3	95.7	86.8	86.9	86.7	84.6	88.9
TA4–15	83.6	85.2	75.5	94.9	83.5	83.9	84.7	79.7	89.8
TA7–18	80.4	82.1	69.6	94.5	80.2	79.8	80.6	71.9	88.9
TA10–21	78.9	78.6	62.8	94.5	78.2	78.8	78.5	68.0	89.0
TA13–24	77.4	78.0	61.8	94.2	78.1	78.0	77.8	67.1	88.4
TA1–24	86.7	89.9	84.3	95.4	86.8	86.5	86.7	88.6	84.9
Financial ratios and TA1–24 combined	90.2	91.3	89.2	93.4	87.7	87.6	87.5	90.8	84.3

Source: Own elaboration; Note: TAx–y means tax arrears variables' model from period month x to month y before bankruptcy is declared. AB and ANB refer respectively to accuracies among bankrupt and non-bankrupt firms in the hold-out sample.

4.3. Theoretical Implications

The main theoretical implication from the study is that the dynamics of payment defaults can be very useful as a bankruptcy predictor shortly before bankruptcy. In addition, the finding complements previous studies (see Section 2.3) applying different types of payment defaults in a more simple manner. While tax arrears as a type of payment default have not been applied in previous studies, this study showed that they have remarkable value in bankruptcy prediction. Finally, we agree with the previous studies suggesting that variables other than financial ratios should be applied in SME failure prediction, but with a substantial extension. Namely, the individual usage of such variables could lead to a better predictive performance of models in the short-run or these variables could be used conjointly with other variables, such as financial ratios, in the long-run.

4.4. Practical Implications

This study provides multiple guidelines for various stakeholders, such as builders of insolvency prediction models, lenders (e.g., banks or trade credit providers), or credit information bureaus.

First, when used dynamically, past temporary payment defaults can include valuable individual and incremental information when aiming to build more accurate bankruptcy prediction models. In this respect, both the size and duration of payment defaults can matter.

Second, financial ratios are not very useful in predicting future bankruptcy, as when implementing models based on them for SMEs in practice, it is difficult to achieve accuracy levels that would avoid substantial losses for creditors.

Third, and maybe the most substantial practical implication, the usage of payment defaults is a vital substitution when annual reports of firms are not available in time or at all. Payment defaults are usually available on a live principle, as they are submitted by creditors, not by the firm itself.

4.5. Limitations

There are several limitations of this study that should be acknowledged. First, this study focused on a specific type of payment defaults, i.e., tax debt not paid when due, in one country. The tax laws and their practical application, i.e., enforcing tax claims by the relevant authority, can vary through different countries. Thus, when replicating the ideas proposed in this article in other environments, the country-specific tax laws and practice of dealing with tax arrears is of high essence.

Second, using payment defaults to other stakeholders, such as banks, trade credit providers, or employees could even enhance the prediction abilities. The incorporation of this information has proven to be valuable in previous relevant studies (e.g., Wilson and Altanlar 2014; Ciampi et al. 2019). Due to the variation in firms' business models, tax arrears might emerge not at all before bankruptcy, but other payment defaults might in turn be present.

Third, although tax arrears are not remarkably subject to the information disclosure issue compared to financial ratios, they are not fully free from it. Namely, some firms might engage in illegal practices, e.g., not submit tax declarations at all or provide false information in them.

5. Conclusions

This study aimed to compare the usefulness of tax arrears and financial ratios in bankruptcy prediction. The models created indicate that shortly before bankruptcy, tax arrears' models outrun the financial ratio-based models in terms of accuracy. Still, this accuracy reduces when further periods before bankruptcy declaration are considered. The highest accuracy is obtained by using tax arrears and financial ratios simultaneously.

The study provides important implications for the relevant research area. It indicates that the dynamic usage of only a certain type of payment defaults, i.e., tax arrears, can substantially outrun the accuracies of financial ratio-based models. Thus, despite the availability of hundreds of financial ratio-based prediction models, future researchers should pay more attention to payment default variables, which incorporate substantial possibilities to increase prediction accuracies.

This study can be extended in different ways. The main extension includes relaxing the previously outlined limitations, for instance by including different types of payment defaults. In addition, tax arrears' information could be supplemented by information about the tax payment behavior of firms, as during the retrenchment of activities in the decline process, small tax arrears could have a more important role than in usual circumstances. It is important to test the usefulness of tax arrears in bankruptcy prediction in other countries as well when such information is available. Last but not least, there might be potential to enhance the prediction accuracies by including variables about the background of managers, for instance concerning their past risk behavior in other firms.

Author Contributions: Both authors contributed to all parts.

Appendix A

Table A1. Descriptive statistics of financial ratios.

Status	Descriptive Statistic	CCLA	CACLA	NIA	NIOR	DA	ORA	FREOR	FREA	OCFA	OCFOR
NB	N						20,015				
	Mean	0.07	0.43	0.07	0.04	0.35	2.00	0.00	0.00	0.10	0.09
	Std. Deviation	0.49	0.42	0.26	0.36	0.31	2.06	0.03	0.01	0.27	0.33
	Median	0.03	0.47	0.05	0.03	0.26	1.33	0.00	0.00	0.07	0.06
	Minimum	−0.95	−0.65	−0.74	−1.30	0.00	0.03	-0.10	−0.04	−0.62	−0.92
	Maximum	0.96	1.00	0.65	0.79	1.12	8.92	0.09	0.04	0.74	0.88

Table A1. *Cont.*

Status	Descriptive Statistic	CCLA	CACLA	NIA	NIOR	DA	ORA	FREOR	FREA	OCFA	OCFOR
B	N						512				
	Mean	−0.79	−0.24	−0.31	-0.09	1.09	4.00	0.01	0.01	0.24	0.16
	Std. Deviation	0.99	1.00	1.03	0.32	1.10	5.18	0.03	0.03	1.25	0.78
	Median	−0.62	0.01	−0.01	0.00	0.87	2.39	0.00	0.00	0.04	0.01
	Minimum	−5.42	−5.08	−5.26	−1.48	0.12	0.19	−0.04	−0.07	−2.33	−0.83
	Maximum	0.27	0.80	0.57	0.31	6.29	27.57	0.11	0.10	5.58	3.60
	p-value of ANOVA Welch test	0.000	0.000	0.000	0.000	0.000	0.000	0.000	0.000	0.016	0.044

Source: own elaboration. Note: B—bankrupt, NB—non-bankrupt. For non-bankrupt firms, the population size 20,015 originates from using data from 5 years (2011–2015) for 4003 firms (see Section 3.1 for more information).

Table A2. Descriptive statistics of tax arrears variables (part 1).

Status	Descriptive Statistic	TMAX1-12	TMEDIAN1-12	TCOUNT1-12	TCONSMON1-12	TMAX4-15	TMEDIAN4-15	TCOUNT4-15	TCONSMON4-15	TMAX7-18	TMEDIAN7-18	TCOUNT7-18	TCONSMON7-18
NB	N							24,018					
	Mean	0.4	0.1	0.5	0.4	0.4	0.1	0.5	0.4	0.4	0.1	0.5	0.4
	Std. Dev.	3.8	1.7	1.8	1.6	3.8	1.7	1.8	1.6	3.8	1.7	1.8	1.6
	Median	0	0	0	0	0	0	0	0	0	0	0	0
	Min.	0	0	0	0	0	0	0	0	0	0	0	0
	Max.	187	125	12	12	187	125	12	12	187	125	12	12
B	N							512					
	Mean	59.1	36.9	7.4	7.1	48.9	29.8	6.8	6.3	41.5	23.9	6.2	5.7
	Std. Dev.	171.5	145.0	4.7	4.8	163.3	128.7	5.0	5.0	150.8	91.4	5.1	5.1
	Median	13.7	3.5	9.0	8.0	9.7	1.2	8.0	6.0	6.4	0.7	7.0	5.0
	Min.	0	0	0	0	0	0	0	0	0	0	0	0
	Max.	2427	2396	12	12	2427	2396	12	12	2427	1462	12	12
	p-value of ANOVA Welch test	0.000	0.000	0.000	0.000	0.000	0.000	0.000	0.000	0.000	0.000	0.000	0.000

Source: own elaboration. Note: B—bankrupt, NB—non-bankrupt. Mean, median and std. deviation presented in thousands euros for TMAX and TMEDIAN. For non-bankrupt firms, the population size 24,018 originates from using 6 years (2011–2016) for 4003 firms (see Section 3.1 for more information).

Table A3. Descriptive statistics of tax arrears variables (part 2).

Status	Descriptive statistic	TMAX10-21	TMEDIAN10-21	TCOUNT10-21	TCONSMON10-21	TMAX13-24	TMEDIAN13-24	TCOUNT13-24	TCONSMON13-24	TMAX1-24	TMEDIAN1-24	TCOUNT1-24	TCONSMON1-24
NB	N							24,018					
	Mean	0.4	0.1	0.5	0.4	0.4	0.1	0.5	0.4	0.6	0.1	0.9	0.6
	Std. Dev.	3.8	1.7	1.8	1.6	3.8	1.7	1.8	1.6	4.6	1.3	3.4	2.6
	Median	0	0	0	0	0	0	0	0	0	0	0	0
	Min.	0	0	0	0	0	0	0	0	0	0	0	0
	Max.	187	125	12	12	187	125	12	12	187	109	24	24

Table A3. *Cont.*

Status	Descriptive statistic	TMAX10–21	TMEDIAN10–21	TCOUNT10–21	TCONSMON10–21	TMAX13–24	TMEDIAN13–24	TCOUNT13–24	TCONSMON13–24	TMAX1–24	TMEDIAN1–24	TCOUNT1–24	TCONSMON1–24
	N					512							
	Mean	38.5	18.6	5.7	5.3	32.3	17.7	5.3	4.8	64.1	23.2	12.7	11.2
B	Std. Dev.	157.6	61.9	5.1	5.0	127.7	64.6	5.1	4.9	190.4	90.0	9.0	8.8
	Median	4.9	0	5.0	4.0	3.6	0	3.5	3.0	15.6	0.7	13.0	9.0
	Min.	0	0	0	0	0	0	0	0	0	0	0	0
	Max.	2427	872	12	12	1932	872	12	12	2427	1462	24	24
p-value of ANOVA Welch test		0.000	0.000	0.000	0.000	0.000	0.000	0.000	0.000	0.000	0.000	0.000	0.000

Source: own elaboration. Note: B—bankrupt, NB—non-bankrupt. Mean, median and std. deviation presented in thousands euros for TMAX and TMEDIAN. For non-bankrupt firms, the population size 24,018 originates from using 6 years (2011–2016) for 4003 firms, while for variables depicting 24 months (ending with "1–24") there are 5 periods used, resulting in 20,015 observations (see Section 3.1 for more information).

References

Alaka, Hafiz A., Lukumon O. Oyedele, Hakeem A. Owolabi, Vikas Kumar, Saheed O. Ajayi, Olugbenga O. Akinade, and Muhammad Bilal. 2018. Systematic review of bankruptcy prediction models: Towards a framework for tool selection. *Expert Systems with Applications* 94: 164–84. [CrossRef]

Altman, Edward I. 1968. Financial ratios, discriminant analysis and the prediction of corporate bankruptcy. *Journal of Finance* 23: 589–609. [CrossRef]

Altman, Edward I., Małgorzata Iwanicz-Drozdowska, Erkki K. Laitinen, and Arto Suvas. 2017. Financial distress prediction in an international context: A review and empirical analysis of Altman's Z-Score model. *Journal of International Financial Management & Accounting* 28: 131–71. [CrossRef]

Altman, Edward I., Gabriele Sabato, and Nick Wilson. 2010. The value of non-financial information in SME risk management. *The Journal of Credit Risk* 6: 95–127. [CrossRef]

Amankwah-Amoah, Joseph. 2016. An integrative process model of organisational failure. *Journal of Business Research* 69: 3388–97. [CrossRef]

Back, Peter. 2005. Explaining financial difficulties based on previous payment behavior, management background variables and financial ratios. *European Accounting Review* 14: 839–68. [CrossRef]

Beaver, William H. 1966. Financial ratios as predictors of failure. *Journal of Accounting Research* 4: 71–111. [CrossRef]

Ciampi, Francesco. 2015. Corporate governance characteristics and default prediction modeling for small enterprises. An empirical analysis of Italian firms. *Journal of Business Research* 68: 1012–25. [CrossRef]

Ciampi, Francesco, Valentina Cillo, and Fabio Fiano. 2019. Combining Kohonen maps and prior payment behavior for small enterprise default prediction. *Small Business Economics*. in press. [CrossRef]

Clatworthy, Mark A., and Michael J. Peel. 2016. The timeliness of UK private company financial reporting: Regulatory and economic influences. *The British Accounting Review* 48: 297–315. [CrossRef]

Crutzen, Nathalie, and Didier van Caillie. 2008. The business failure process. An integrative model of the literature. *Review of Business and Economics* 53: 287–316.

Dimitras, Augustinos I., Stelios H. Zanakis, and Constantin Zopounidis. 1996. A survey of business failures with an emphasis on prediction methods and industrial applications. *European Journal of Operational Research* 90: 487–513. [CrossRef]

du Jardin, Philippe. 2015. Bankruptcy prediction using terminal failure processes. *European Journal of Operational Research* 242: 286–303. [CrossRef]

du Jardin, Philippe. 2017. Dynamics of firm financial evolution and bankruptcy prediction. *Expert Systems with Applications* 75: 25–43. [CrossRef]

du Jardin, Philippe. 2018. Failure pattern-based ensembles applied to bankruptcy forecasting. *Decision Support Systems* 107: 64–77. [CrossRef]

Höglund, Henrik. 2017. Tax payment default prediction using genetic algorithm-based variable selection. *Expert Systems with Applications* 88: 368–75. [CrossRef]

Iwanicz-Drozdowska, Małgorzata, Erkki K. Laitinen, Arto Suvas, and Edward I. Altman. 2016. Financial and nonfinancial variables as long-horizon predictors of bankruptcy. *Journal of Credit Risk* 12: 49–78. [CrossRef]

Kim, Myoung-Jong, Dae-Ki Kang, and Hong Bae Kim. 2015. Geometric mean based boosting algorithm with over-sampling to resolve data imbalance problem for bankruptcy prediction. *Expert Systems with Applications* 42: 1074–82. [CrossRef]

Laitinen, Erkki K. 1999. Predicting a corporate credit analyst's risk estimate by logistic and linear models. *International Review of Financial Analysis* 8: 97–121. [CrossRef]

Laitinen, Erkki K., and Arto Suvas. 2013. International applicability of corporate failure risk models based on financial statement information: Comparisons across European countries. *Journal of Finance & Economics* 1: 1–26. [CrossRef]

Liang, Deron, Chia-Chi Lu, Chih-Fong Tsai, and Guan-An Shih. 2016. Financial ratios and corporate governance indicators in bankruptcy prediction: A comprehensive study. *European Journal of Operational Research* 252: 561–72. [CrossRef]

Lukason, Oliver. 2013. Firm bankruptcies and violations of law: An analysis of different offences. In *Dishonesty in Management: Manifestations and Consequences*. Edited by Tiia Vissak and Maaja Vadi. Bingley: Emerald, pp. 127–46.

Lukason, Oliver, and Maria-del-Mar Camacho-Miñano. 2019. Bankruptcy risk, its financial determinants and reporting delays: Do managers have anything to hide? *Risks* 7: 77. [CrossRef]

Lukason, Oliver, and Erkki K. Laitinen. 2019. Firm failure processes and components of failure risk: An analysis of European bankrupt firms. *Journal of Business Research* 98: 380–90. [CrossRef]

Lukason, Oliver, Erkki K. Laitinen, and Arto Suvas. 2016. Failure processes of young manufacturing micro firms in Europe. *Management Decision* 54: 1966–85. [CrossRef]

Lussier, Robert N. 1995. A Nonfinancial business success versus failure prediction model for young firms. *Journal of Small Business Management* 33: 8–20.

Luypaert, Mathieu, Tom Van Caneghem, and Steve Van Uytbergen. 2016. Financial statement filing lags: An empirical analysis among small firms. *International Small Business Journal* 34: 506–31. [CrossRef]

Munoz-Izquierdo, Nora, Maria Jesus Segovia-Vargas, Maria-del-Mar Camacho-Minano, and David Pasqual-Ezama. 2019. Explaining the causes of business failures using audit report disclosures. *Journal of Business Research* 98: 403–14. [CrossRef]

Ohlson, James A. 1980. Financial ratios and the probabilistic prediction of bankruptcy. *Journal of Accounting Research* 18: 109–31. [CrossRef]

Ooghe, Hubert, and Sofie de Prijcker. 2008. Failure processes and causes of company bankruptcy: A typology. *Management Decision* 46: 223–42. [CrossRef]

Ravi Kumar, Puvvala, and Vadlamani Ravi. 2007. Bankruptcy prediction in banks and firms via statistical and intelligent techniques—A review. *European Journal of Operational Research* 180: 1–28. [CrossRef]

Scott, James. 1981. The probability of bankruptcy: A comparison of empirical predictions and theoretical models. *Journal of Banking and Finance* 5: 317–44.

Sun, Jie, Hui Li, Qing-Hua Huang, and Kai-Yu He. 2014. Predicting financial distress and corporate failure: A review from the state-of-the-art definitions, modeling, sampling, and featuring approaches. *Knowledge-Based Systems* 57: 41–56. [CrossRef]

Uhrig-Homburg, Marliese. 2005. Cash-flow shortage as an endogenous bankruptcy reason. *Journal of Banking & Finance* 29: 1509–34. [CrossRef]

Weitzel, William, and Ellen Jonsson. 1989. Decline in organizations: A literature integration and extension. *Administrative Science Quarterly* 34: 91–109. [CrossRef]

Wilson, Nick, and Ali Altanlar. 2014. Company failure prediction with limited information: Newly incorporated companies. *Journal of the Operational Research Society* 65: 252–64. [CrossRef]

11

Assessment of Bankruptcy Risk of Large Companies: European Countries Evolution Analysis

Nicoleta Bărbuță-Mișu [1,*][iD] **and Mara Madaleno** [2][iD]

[1] Department of Business Administration, "Dunarea de Jos" University of Galati, 800008 Galati, Romania
[2] GOVCOPP—Research Unit in Governance, Competitiveness and Public Policy, Department of Economics, Management, Industrial Engineering and Tourism (DEGEIT), University of Aveiro, 3810-193 Aveiro, Portugal; maramadaleno@ua.pt
*   Correspondence: Nicoleta.Barbuta@ugal.ro

Abstract: Assessment and estimation of bankruptcy risk is important for managers in decision making for improving a firm's financial performance, but also important for investors that consider it prior to making investment decision in equity or bonds, creditors and company itself. The aim of this paper is to improve the knowledge of bankruptcy prediction of companies and to analyse the predictive capacity of factor analysis using as basis the discriminant analysis and the following five models for assessing bankruptcy risk: Altman, Conan and Holder, Tafler, Springate and Zmijewski. Stata software was used for studying the effect of performance over risk and bankruptcy scores were obtained by year of analysis and country. Data used for non-financial large companies from European Union were provided by Amadeus database for the period 2006–2015. In order to analyse the effects of risk score over firm performance, we have applied a dynamic panel-data estimation model, with Generalized Method of Moments (GMM) estimators to regress firm performance indicator over risk by year and we have used Tobit models to infer about the influence of company performance measures over general bankruptcy risk scores. The results show that the Principal Component Analysis (PCA) used to build a bankruptcy risk scored based on discriminant analysis indices is effective for determining the influence of corporate performance over risk.

Keywords: European large companies; bankruptcy risk; company performance; bankruptcy prediction; Principal Component Analysis

1. Introduction

Bankruptcy and bankruptcy prediction is a very real issue worldwide both in academic research and in practice considering the evolution at a global level: the upward trend in business insolvencies continued in 2018 (increase by 10% in 2018 compared to 2017), mainly due to the surge in China by 60% and, to a lesser extent, an increase in Western Europe by 2% (Euler Hermes Economic Research 2019).

In Western Europe, although a downside trend in insolvencies was recorded from 2014 to 2017, the increase mentioned by 2% in 2018 compared to 2017 was determined by different evolution by other countries: a noticeable upturn of 12% in the UK due to the Brexit-related uncertainties that added headwinds on businesses; a stabilization of insolvencies can be seen in France, Spain and Belgium, although in France in 2018, 54,751 companies went bankrupt, corresponding to a fairly high 1.3% of the active business universe (Dun & Bradstreet 2019); an increase in the Nordic countries of 10% in Sweden, 3% in Norway, 19% in Finland and 25% in Denmark. This trend comes from economic and fiscal reasons or exceptional factors, especially for Denmark and Finland. At the same time, other countries of the region registered slower declines in 2018 compared to 2017, notably the Netherlands (from −23% to −6%), Portugal (−12%), Ireland (−10%) and Germany (−4%). In Italy, 11,207 companies filed for bankruptcy in 2018, down by a significant 5.8%, but the newly-elected populist government is likely to embark on a series of populist policies that are at odds with improving the country's operating environment (Dun & Bradstreet 2019).

According to Euler Hermes Economic Research (2019), in Central and Eastern Europe, we can see economies that forecast to moderate in line with the slowdown in the Eurozone, but remain robust enough to see another decrease in insolvencies, albeit at more limited time, i.e., Hungary from −18% in 2018 to −11% in 2019 and the Czech Republic, respectively −17% and −10%. Romania registered a rebound in insolvencies, −3% in 2018 and +3% in 2019. Other countries continued to rise in insolvencies: 3% for Bulgaria in 2019 where the changes in the Insolvency law done in 2017 kept on boosting the bankruptcies of sole proprietorships, Slovakia of 16%, Poland of 5% where businesses have a structural problem of profitability and will face a noticeable deceleration of the economy.

Over time, researchers have tried to find diverse methods to estimate business failure: patrimonial method based on net working capital and treasury; financial ratios method especially based on individual analysis of profitability, liquidity, solvency and financial autonomy; and score method highlighted in numerous models for which Altman (1968), Ohlson (1980), and Zmijewski (1984) models are the most cited ones and that are based on accounting variables (Avenhuis 2013). These bankruptcy prediction models use different explanatory variables and statistical techniques and may provide valuable information about the financial performance of the companies and their risks. More than that, we must mention that the predictive power of these bankruptcy prediction models differ between countries, sectors of activity, time periods, firms' ages, or firms' sizes.

There is a constant effort to use the models developed for firms in different economies, even if decision makers know or at least should know that assumptions used for fitting the original models are probably not valid anymore. There is a continuous concern and preoccupation for designing models for prediction risk of bankruptcy. Assessing of the level of advancement of bankruptcy prediction research in countries of the former Eastern Bloc, in comparison to the latest global research trends in this area, Prusak (2018) found that the most advanced research in this area is conducted in the Czech Republic, Poland, Slovakia, Estonia, Russia, and Hungary. In addition, the best world practices are reflected in the research provided in Poland, the Czech Republic, and Slovakia.

The main problem of the bankruptcy prediction models developed in the literature is that these models cannot be generalized because these were developed using a specific sample from a specific sector, specific time period and from a specific region or country. As the above-mentioned statistics show, there are many other specific factors that increase the bankruptcies in a country: changes in economic environments, law frameworks, incomparability of populations of interest, etc. (Král' et al. 2016). That is why it is necessary to adapt these models to the specificity of the sector, country or time period analyzed and to use combined techniques of estimation in designing these specific models.

In this paper, considering the context presented, the large companies from the European Union are analysed. The aim of this research is twofold: to improve the knowledge of bankruptcy prediction for European large companies and to analyse the predictive capacity of factor analysis, such as Principal Component Analysis (PCA) using as a basis the discriminant analysis (models for assessing bankruptcy risk, commonly used in the literature). Our paper is distinguishing from other studies by using a sample of large companies active in the EU-28 countries in the period 2006–2015 and by own original selection of bankruptcy prediction models (Altman, Conan and Holder, Tafler, Springate and Zmijewski) used in the PCA analysis.

The rest of the paper is organised as follows: in Section 2, the literature review on risk, bankruptcy prediction, models and techniques used to assess and forecast the risk of bankruptcy is presented. The data and methodology are presented in the Section 3. The paper then follows with analysis of results and discussions in Section 4. Concluding remarks pointing out some policy implications, future research suggestions and limitations of the study are discussed in the Section 5.

2. Literature Review

Financial risks show the possibility of losses arising from the failure to achieve financial objectives. The financial risks related to the financial operation of a business may take many different forms: market risks determined by the changes in commodities, stocks and other financial instruments prices, foreign exchange risks, interest rate risks, credit risks, financing risks, liquidity risks, cash flow risk, and bankruptcy risk. These financial risks are not necessarily independent of each other, the interdependence being recognized when managers are designing risk management systems (Woods and Dowd 2008). The importance of these risks will vary from one firm to another, in function of the sector of activity of the firms, the firm size, development of international transactions, etc.

Bankruptcy refers to the situation in which the debtor company becomes unable to repay its debts and can be considered to be the consequence of a company's inability to survive market competition, reflected in terms of job losses, the destruction of assets, and in a low productivity (Aleksanyan and Huiban 2016). The risk of bankruptcy or insolvency risk shows the possibility that a company will be unable to meet its debt obligations, respectively the probability of a company to go bankrupt in the next few years. Assessing of bankruptcy risk is important especially for investors in making equity or bond investment decisions, but also for managers in financial decision making of funding, investments and distribution policy. Failure prediction models are important tools also for bankers, rating agencies, and even distressed firms themselves (Altman et al. 2017).

The essential information for executive financial decisions, but also for investors decisions are provided by financial statements. Thus, companies' financial managers should develop the financial performance analysis and problem-solving skills (Burns and Balvinsdottir 2005; Scapens 2006), without limiting their duties in verifying accounting data (Diakomihalis 2012) in order to maintain the firm attractive for investors. The image of financial performance of companies is affected by the estimation of its position in front of investors, creditors, and stakeholders (Ryu and Jang 2004). For this estimation there are used many indicators that reflect the company's position such as: net working capital, net treasury, liquidity, solvency, profitability, funding capacity, cash-flow, etc., or a mix between them, such as Z-scores.

The design of reliable models to predict bankruptcy is crucial for many decision-making processes (Ouenniche and Tone 2017). The approach used for bankruptcy prediction has evolved over time starting to Beaver (1966, 1968) model based on univariate analysis for selected ratios and which had very good predictive power. Then, Altman (1968) made strides by developing a multiple discriminant analysis model called the Z-Score model. Bankruptcy prediction models could be divided into two general categories depending on the type of variable used: static models (Altman 1968, 2000, 2002; Taffler 1982, 1983, 1984; Ohlson 1980; Zmijewski 1984; Theodossiou 1991) or dynamic models (Shumway 2001; Hillegeist et al. 2004).

In the literature of bankruptcy prediction, the models of Altman (1968), Ohlson (1980), and Zmijewski (1984) are the most cited ones that are based on accounting variables. These bankruptcy prediction models use different explanatory variables and statistical techniques. Therefore, the predictive power of these bankruptcy prediction models differs. However, when the original statistical techniques are used, the accuracy rates for the models of Altman (1968), Ohlson (1980), and Zmijewski (1984) are respectively 80.6%, 93.8%, and 95.3% (Avenhuis 2013). Studying the efficacy of Altman's z-score model in predicting bankruptcy of specialty retail firms doing business in contemporary times, Chaitanya (2005) found that all but two of the bankruptcies (94%) would have been accurately predicted.

Ashraf et al. (2019) found that both models by Altman (1968) and Zmijewski (1984) are still valuable for predicting the financial distress of emerging markets and can be used by businessmen, financial specialists, administrators, and other concerned parties who are thinking about investing in an organization and/or want to enhance their organization performance. Elviani et al. (2020) studied the accuracy of the Altman (1968), Ohlson (1980), Springate (1978) and Zmijewski (1984) models in bankruptcy predicting trade sector companies in Indonesia using binary logistic regression.

Their results proved that the most appropriate and accurate models in predicting bankruptcy of trade sector companies in Indonesia are the Springate and Altman models.

Related to methodologies used in creating bankruptcy risk models we can mention bankruptcy prediction models based on: statistical methodologies (Models of Altman 1968, 2000, 2002; Altman et al. 2017; Model of Springate 1978; Model of Conan and Holder 1979; Models of Taffler 1982, 1983, 1984; Model of Fulmer et al. 1984), stochastic methodologies (Model of Ohlson 1980; Model of Zmijewski 1984; Model of Zavgren 1985; Theodossiou 1991), and artificial intelligence methodologies (Zhang et al. 1999; Kim and Han 2003; Shin et al. 2005; Li and Sun 2011) and data envelopment analysis (DEA) methodologies (Koh and Tan 1999; Cielen et al. 2004; Paradi et al. 2004; Shetty et al. 2012; Ouenniche and Tone 2017). Aziz and Dar (2006) reviewed 89 studies on the prediction of bankruptcy risk in the period 1968–2003 in order to carry out a critical analysis of the methodologies and empirical findings of the application of these models across 10 different countries (Finland, Norway, Sweden, Belgium, UK, Italy, Greece, USA, Korea and Australia). They found that the multi-variable models (Z-Score) and logit were most popular in the 89 papers studied.

The multitude of models created demonstrate an intense concern for bankruptcy prediction, considering also the evolution of number of bankruptcies in the world. However, the first bankruptcy models are still applied and provide important information. For example, Altman's model was applied to Jordanian companies, non-financial service and industrial companies, for the years 1990–2006. The study shows that Altman's model has an advantage in company bankruptcy prediction, with a 93.8% average predictive ability of the five years prior to the liquidation incident (Alkhatib and Bzour 2011). Chung et al. (2008) also examined the insolvency predictive ability of different financial ratios for ten failed financial companies during 2006–2007 in New Zealand and found that, one year prior to failure, four of the five Altman (1968) ratios were superior to other financial ratios for predicting corporate bankruptcy. In other countries, such as Romania aggregate indexes of financial performance assessment for the building sector companies were created (Bărbuţă-Mişu 2009; Bărbuţă-Mişu and Codreanu 2014) or well-known modes, such as the Conan and Holder model were adjusted to the specificity of Romanian companies (Bărbuţă-Mişu and Stroe 2010). In studies about bankruptcy prediction, in Romania was preferred Conan and Holder (1979) model to evaluate the financial performance of the companies.

The majority of authors proposed models adapted to the specificity of the economies. Brédart (2014) developed an econometric forecasting model on United States companies using three simple and a few correlated and easily available financial ratios as explanatory variables and their results show a prediction accuracy of more than 80%. Dakovic et al. (2010) developed statistical models for bankruptcy prediction of Norwegian firms acting in the industry sector. They modelled the unobserved heterogeneity among different sectors through an industry-specific random factor in the generalized linear mixed model. The models developed are shown to outperform the model with Altman's variables.

To solve the problem of bankruptcy prediction some statistical techniques such as regression analysis and logistic regression are used (De 2014). These techniques usually are used for the company's financial data to predict the financial state of company as healthy, distressed, high probability of bankruptcy. As we know, Altman (1968) used financial ratios and multiple discriminant analysis (MDA) to predict financially distressed companies. However, further, it was found that the usage of statistical techniques or MDA depends on the constraint as linear separability, multivariate normality and independence of predictive variables (Ohlson 1980; Karels and Prakash 1987). Thus, bankruptcy prediction problem can be solved using various other types of classifiers, such as neural network that compared to MDA, logistic regression and k-nearest neighbour method proved a higher performance. For instance, Tam (1991) found that the neural network performs better than other prediction techniques.

Otherwise, Xu and Zhang (2009) have investigated whether the bankruptcy of certain companies can be predicted using traditional measures, such as Altman's Z-score, Ohlson's (1980) O-score, and the option pricing theory-based distance-to-default, previously developed for the U.S. market, in order to find if these models are useful for the Japanese market. They have found that the predictive power is substantially enhanced when these measures are combined.

In addition, Jouzbarkand et al. (2013) compiled two models for the prediction of bankruptcy, related to the Iranian economic situation. Using the logistic regression method, they studied the Ohlson (1980) and Shirata (1995) models, examining and comparing the performance of these models. Their results show that models created are able to predict the bankruptcy. For classifying and ranking the companies, they used their business law to determine the bankrupt companies and a simple Q-Tobin to specify the solvent companies.

Discriminant analysis was the prevailing method, and the most important financial ratios came from the solvency category, with profitability ratios also being important (Altman et al. 2017). The performance of five bankruptcy prediction models, such as Altman (1968), Ohlson (1980), Zmijewski (1984), Shumway (2001) and Hillegeist et al. (2004) was studied by Wu et al. (2010) building their own integrated model using a dataset for U.S.A. listed firms. Wu et al. (2010) found that Shumway's (2001) model performed best, Hillegeist et al.'s (2004) model performed adequately, Ohlson's (1980) and Zmijewski's (1984) models performed adequately, but their performance deteriorated over time, while Altman's Zscore performed poorly compared with all other four models analysed. However, the integrated model outperformed the other models by combining both accounting and market data, and firms' characteristics.

The factor analysis is often used together with other methodologies, in order to improve bankruptcy prediction models (Cultrera et al. 2017). Principal Component Analysis (PCA), the statistical procedure that uses an orthogonal transformation to convert a set of observations of possibly correlated variables into a set of values of linearly uncorrelated variables called principal components started to be used in analysis and prediction of bankruptcy risk. Adalessossi (2015) used discriminant function named Z-scores model of Altman, financial ratio analysis, and the principal component analysis on a sample of 34 listed companies from different sectors and sizes in order to find out if the three methods used in this study converge toward similarity results. The comparison of the three methods indicates unanimously that, out of the 34 companies, only eight companies have had the best financial performances and are not likely to go on to bankruptcy.

Onofrei and Lupu (2014) have built a quick warning model for the Romanian companies in difficulty, using the following methodologies: the Principal Components Analysis, the multivariate discriminant analysis and the logit analysis in order to determine which are the best predictors of bankruptcy for the Romanian companies. They found that the best predictor for the Romanian market is the multiple discriminant analysis method with a predictive power between 68–95%, while the logit method registering slightly weaker results with a predictive power between 53–82%.

De (2014) developed the principal component analysis (PCA) and general regression auto associative neural network (GRAANN) based hybrid as a one-class classifier in order to test the effectiveness of PCA-GRAANN on bankruptcy prediction datasets of banks from Spain, Turkey, US and UK. They concluded that PCA-GRAANN can be used as a viable alternative for any one-class classifier. Checking related literature, we found that PCA is more used with artificial neural network methods for prediction bankruptcy risk where the effectiveness was proved. However, in this paper we proposed to use PCA based on the five discriminant analysis measures, i.e., Z-score determined by the following models: revised Z-score Altman, Conan and Holder, Tafler, Springate and Zmijewski in order to test the efficiency in predicting the risk of bankruptcy. Afterwards, we made use of econometric techniques and the PCA score created by country and year to test its influence over performance. The principal component analysis to build the bankruptcy risk score of the five models selected is used, since there is no consensus in the literature so as to which is the best bankruptcy prediction model. In this way we may capture the components that will exert more impact in bankruptcy prediction.

3. Data and Methodology

In this section we describe the data and all methodologies used to assess bankruptcy risk, as well as to create the bankruptcy risk indexes by year and country that are presented in the results section. It starts by describing the models used to assess bankruptcy risk measures, which are commonly used in the literature and afterwards describes the Principal Component Analysis (PCA) used to create the bankruptcy risk index measures by year and country (by country, Greece had to be taken out from the sample due to missing data able to allow us to create the index for this country).

3.1. Data Description

The source of the data is Amadeus database, provided by Bureau van Dijk Electronics. In the sample we have included only large non-financial companies from the former EU-28 countries, for the period 2006–2015, that act in all sectors of activity (with the conclusion of the Brexit, the EU is now with 27 countries, instead of 28. However, UK was used because at the beginning of the analysis it belonged to the EU-28 and we will keep this representation through the article). The selection criteria for large companies included in the sample are in accordance with the classification of the small and medium enterprises (SMEs) published in Commission Recommendation of 6 May 2003 (European Commission 2003) concerning the definition of micro, small and medium-sized enterprises. Thus, in order to select the large companies for EU-28 countries, as selection criteria of these companies we used: number of employees greater than 250, total assets greater than €43 million and turnover greater than €50 million. These criteria were applied simultaneously for the data available for the last year included in the sample, i.e., year 2015. We found 22,581 active large companies. We did not consider small and medium enterprises (SMEs) due to the high fluctuations over time in foundation and closing of these firms compared to large companies. Our intention was to study the risk of bankruptcy to large companies that had a more stable activity over time. Our data period was from 2006 until 2015.

Where it was applicable, because of some data missing, we deleted data for years and companies with no available information for calculation of variables of risk of bankruptcy models. In addition, we eliminated from database the inconclusive values and outliers. Thus, remained in the study 154,459 valid year-observations. However, we still worked with an unbalanced panel, due to missing years of data in the sample. Additionally, we have taken out from our sample all countries which did not present a number of companies higher than 1000. From the 28 available countries we ended up working with 20 of these countries.

3.2. Models for Assessing Bankruptcy Risk

As we mentioned in the literature review, there are numerous models for bankruptcy risk prediction based on Z score method, but in this paper we selected the following five models: Altman's Models (1968, 2000), Conan and Holder Model (1979), Springate's Model (1978), Taffler's Model (1982, 1983), Zmijewski's Model (1984). We used these five models since these are the most referenced one's to predict bankruptcy and have a high level of accuracy as we presented in the Section 2. There are a number of key models that have been developed by various authors and presented in the bankruptcy prediction literature over the last three decades, but these five appear in most of the recent studies where bankruptcy models are tested. For these models we determined all variables necessary and the Z scores for all companies included in the sample for the period 2006–2015.

3.2.1. Altman's Models

Altman (1968) is the dean of insolvency prediction models and the first researcher that successfully used the step-wise multiple discriminate analysis to develop a prediction model with a high degree of accuracy of 95%. The original study included a sample comprising 66 industrial companies, 33 bankrupts and other 33 non-bankrupts for a period of analysis of 20 years (1946–1965).

The author found a total of 22 potential variables, based on data provided by annual reports of the companies, and by them, he retains five variables with the highest significance, as a result of using statistical techniques and discrimination analysis. Generally, these variables include profitability ratios, coverage ratios, liquidity ratios, capitalization ratios, and earnings variability (Altman 2000).

The final discriminant function of first Altman model (1968) takes the following form:

$$Z1\ Altman = 0.012\ X1 + 0.014\ X2 + 0.033\ X3 + 0.006\ X4 + 0.999\ X5 \qquad (1)$$

where:

Z1 Altman = Overall Index Altman

X1 = Working Capital/Total Assets

X2 = Retained Earnings/Total Assets

X3 = Earnings Before Interest and Taxes/Total Assets

X4 = Market Value Equity/Book Value of Total Debt

X5 = Sales/Total Assets

Because this original model cannot be applied to unlisted companies in the Stock Exchange, the model was completely re-estimated, substituting the Market Value of Equity with Book Values of Equity in X4 (Altman 2000), resulting the Revised Z-Score Model that is used for our sample.

A Revised Z-Score Model (rza)

This change of the Market Value of Equity determined not only the change of new variable's parameter, but determined the change of all coefficients, as well as the classification criterion and related cut-off scores.

The results of the revised Z-Score model with a new X4 variable is:

$$Z2\ Altman = 0.717\ X1 + 0.847\ X2 + 3.107\ X3 + 0.420\ X4 + 0.998\ X5 \qquad (2)$$

The description of the variable used is the following:

X1—Working Capital/Total Assets

This ratio is the measure of the net liquid assets of the firm relative to the total capitalization. Working capital is defined as the difference between current assets and current liabilities. Liquidity and size characteristics are explicitly considered in this ratio. Ordinarily, a company experiencing consistent operating losses will have shrinking current assets in relation to total assets.

X2—Retained Earnings/Total Assets

Retained earnings is the account which reports the total amount of reinvested earnings and/or losses of a firm over its entire life. The account is also referred to as earned surplus. Retained earnings may be affected by a substantial reorganization or stock dividend and for this reason, in research studies, some appropriate readjustments should be made to the accounts. In this ratio, the age of the company is considered implicitly. For example, a relatively young company will probably show a low ratio because it had not enough time to build up its cumulative profits. Therefore, it may be argued that a young company is somehow discriminated against in this analysis, and its chance of being classified as bankrupt is relatively higher than another older company. That's why we have included in our sample only large companies that have a higher chance of remaining on the market. This is precisely the situation manifested in the real world because the incidence of failure is much higher in a company's earlier years. Those companies with high retained earnings, relative to total assets, have financed their assets through retention of profits and have not utilized as much debt.

X3—Earnings before Interest and Taxes/Total Assets

This ratio is a measure of the true productivity of the company's assets, independent of any tax or leverage factors. Since a company's ultimate existence is based on the earning power of its assets, this ratio appears to be particularly appropriate for studies dealing with corporate failure.

Furthermore, insolvency in a bankruptcy sense occurs when the total liabilities exceed a fair valuation of the company's assets with value determined by the earning power of the assets.

X4—Book Value of Equity/Book Value of Total Debt

Equity is measured by the Book Value of Equity divided by Total Debt, debt including both current and long-term. The measure shows how much the firm's assets can decline in value (measured by book value of equity plus debt) before the liabilities exceed the assets and the company becomes insolvent.

X5—Sales/Total Assets

The capital-turnover ratio is a standard financial ratio illustrating the sales generating ability of the firm's assets. This ratio is quite important because it is the least significant ratio on an individual basis. Because of its unique relationship to other variables in the model, the Sales/Total Assets ratio ranks second in its contribution to the overall discriminating ability of the model.

The interpretation of the Z2 Altman is:

Z2 Altman > 2.9 – Safe zone
1.23 < Z2 Altman < 2.9 – Grey zone
Z2 Altman < 1.23 – Distress zone

In order to eliminate industry effects, the next change of the Z-Score model analysed the characteristics and accuracy of the model without variable X5—Sales/Total Assets (Altman 2002). He does this in order to minimize the potential industry effect which is more likely to take place when such an industry-sensitive variable as asset turnover is included. This particular model is also useful within an industry where the type of financing of assets differs greatly among firms and important adjustments, like lease capitalization, are not made (Bărbuţă-Mişu 2017).

In particular, Altman et al. (1998) have applied this enhanced Z Score model to emerging markets corporates, specifically Mexican firms that had issued Eurobonds denominated in US dollars. In the emerging market model, they added a constant term of +3.25 so as to standardize the scores with a score of zero equated to a default rated bond.

3.2.2. Conan and Holder's Model (zcc)

The Conan and Holder (1979) model was developed to analyse the degradation of the financial situation of small and medium enterprises (SMEs). The appraisals for the proposed score function were based on an initial set of 50 indicators studied by the category: the asset structure, the financial dependence, the treasury, the working fund, the exploitation, the profitability, etc. Then, the formulation and model results are based on the analysis of 31 rates (financial variables), applied on 190 small and medium enterprises acting in various fields: industry, trade, services and transport during 1970–1975. Of the 190 selected companies, 95 companies were bankrupt, and another 95 were healthy businesses whose activities were appropriate waist and bankrupt companies.

The model developed by Conan and Holder is included in the statistical tested methods, and has the advantage of simplifying the calculation, so that it continues to be used today.

The Conan and Holder model is:

$$Z \text{ Conan and Holder} = 0.24 X1 + 0.22 X2 + 0.16 X3 - 0.87 X4 - 0.10 X5 \tag{3}$$

where:

Z Conan and Holder = Overall Index Conan and Holder

X1 = Gross Operating Surplus/Total Debts, expresses the profitability by creditors, the profit achieved by using borrowed capital.

X2 = Permanent Capital/Total Liabilities, expresses the solvency of the company on long term, a measure of debt guarantees through permanent capital.

X3 = (Current assets – Stocks)/Total Liabilities, expresses the liquidity of the company, the capacity of paying debts by transforming into cash of receivables, financial short-term investments, cash, and cash equivalents.

X4 = Financial Expenditures/Net Sales, expresses the rate of financial expenses, the share of financial expenses in net sales.

X5 = Personnel Expenditures/Added Value, expresses the rate of personnel costs, i.e., the share of remuneration of the personnel by the added value of the company.

The interpretation of the Z Conan and Holder score function is as follows:

Z Conan and Holder < 0.04 – a probability of a bankruptcy risk of >65%;
0.04 < Z Conan and Holder < 0.16 – a probability of bankruptcy between 30–65%;
Z Conan and Holder > 0.16 – a probability of bankruptcy of <30%.

3.2.3. Springate's Model (zs)

This Canadian business insolvency prediction model was developed in 1978 at Simon Fraser University by Gordon L.V. Springate, following procedures developed by Altman in the US data. Springate (1978) used step-wise multiple discriminate analysis to select four out of 19 popular financial ratios that best distinguished between sound business and those that actually failed. This insolvency prediction model achieved an accuracy rate of 92.5% using the 40 companies tested by Springate.

The Springate model takes the following form:

$$Z\ Springate = 1.03\ X1 + 3.07\ X2 + 0.66\ X3 + 0.4\ X4 \tag{4}$$

Z Springate = Overall Index Springate
X1 = Working Capital/Total Assets measure of the net liquid assets of the firm relative to the total capitalization.

X2 = Earnings Before Interest and Taxes/Total Assets is a measure of the true productivity of the firm's assets, independent of any tax or leverage factors.

X3 = Earnings before Taxes/Current Liabilities is a measure of the true productivity of the firm's assets, independent of any leverage factors.

X4 = Sales/Total Assets illustrate the sales generating ability of the firm's assets. It is one measure of management's capability in dealing with competitive condition.

The interpretation of Z Springate model is:

Z Springate > 0.826, the company is performant;
Z Springate <= 0.826, the company is bankrupted.

3.2.4. Taffler's Model (ztta)

Taffler (1983) proposed a model based on an extensive survey of the vast array of data. The original model was developed to analyse industrial (manufacturing and construction) companies only with separate models developed for retail and service companies. Using computer technology, 80 carefully selected financial ratios were calculated using accounts of all listed industrial companies failing between 1968 and 1976 and 46 randomly selected solvent industrial firms (Agarwal and Taffler 2007).

This information was processed through a series of statistical methods, and the model was built using multivariate discriminant method. The Z-score model was derived by determining the best set of ratios which, when taken together and appropriately weighted, distinguished optimally between the two samples. Leverage, profitability, liquidity, capital adequacy and other parameters were evaluated for model creation. The model is applicable to companies in the form of joint stock companies, whose shares were subject to public offering and traded on various stock exchanges (Belyaeva 2014).

The Z Taffler model is:

$$Z \text{ Taffler} = 3.2 + 12.18\ X1 + 2.5\ X2 - 10.68\ X3 + 0.029\ X4 \tag{5}$$

where:

Z Taffler = Overall Index Taffler

X1 = Profit before Tax/Current Liabilities is a measure of the true productivity of the firm's assets, independent of any leverage factors.

X2 = Current Assets/Total Liabilities expresses the payment capacity on short-term of the company, i.e., the ability of current assets to be converted into cash to meet the payment obligations. This ratio estimates the liquidity of the company by showing the company can pay its creditors with its current assets if the company's assets ever had to be liquidated.

X3 = Current Liabilities/Total Assets shows the share of a company's assets which are financed through short-term debt. If the ratio is low, most of the company's assets are financed through equity and long-term debts. If the ratio is high, most of the company's assets are financed through short-term debt.

X4 = (Quick Assets − Current Liabilities)/Daily Operating Expenses with the denominator proxied by: (Sales − Profit Before Tax − Depreciation)/365

The interpretations of Z Taffler model is as follows:

Z Taffler > 0.3 shows that the company has good chances for performance

0.2 < Z Taffler < 0.3 shows the grey zone (undefined area)

Z Taffler < 0.2 shows that the company is almost bankrupt.

Thus, in the case of this model, if the computed Z Taffler score is positive, the firm is solvent and is very unlikely indeed to fail within the next year. However, if its Z Taffler score is negative, it lies in the "at risk" region and the firm has a financial profile similar to previously failed businesses. The high probability of financial distress is depending on how much negative is the Z Taffler score (Agarwal and Taffler 2007).

3.2.5. Zmijewski's Score (zzzmij)

The Zmijewski Score (Zmijewski 1984) is a bankruptcy model used to predict a firm's bankruptcy in two years. Zmijewski (1984) criticised previous models, considering that other bankruptcy scoring models oversampled distressed firms and favoured situations with more complete data.

Thus, in Zmijewski (1984) study, two methodological issues are examined that are related to the estimation of bankruptcy prediction models. The two biases are choice-based sample biases and sample selection biases. The choice based bias is the result of over-sampling distressed firms. When a matched-pair (one-to-one match) design is for a study to predict bankruptcy, the potential of bankruptcy is overstated. This lead to biased probabilities in the models. The sample selection biases occur when the probability of distress given complete data are significantly different from the probability of distress given incomplete data (Avenhuis 2013).

The ratio used in the Zmijewski (1984) score was determined by probit analysis (probit should be regarded as probability unit) in order to construct the bankruptcy prediction model. Like the logit function, the probit function maps the value between 0 and 1, and, in this case, scores greater than 0.5 represent a higher probability of default. The accuracy rate of the Zmijewski (1984) model for the estimation sample was 99%.

The constructed probit function with the variables and estimated coefficients from the study of Zmijewski (1984) is as follows:

$$Z \text{ Zmijewski} = -4.336 - 4.513\ X1 + 5.679\ X2 + 0.004\ X3 \tag{6}$$

where:

Z Zmijewski = Overall Zmijewski Index

X1 = Net Income/Total Assets is a profitability ratio that measures the net income produced by total assets during a period by comparing net income to the average total assets.

X2 = Total Liabilities/Total Assets shows the share of a company's assets which are financed through debt. If the ratio is less than 0.5, most of the company's assets are financed through equity. If the ratio is greater than 0.5, most of the company's assets are financed through debt.

X3 = Current Assets/Current Liabilities expresses the payment capacity on short-term of the company.

While Altman used the ratio Earnings before Interest and Taxes (EBIT)/Total Assets for profitability, where EBIT eliminates the effect of different capital structures and of taxation and make easier the comparing of the firm profitability, Zmijewski (1984) used the ratio: Net Income/Total Assets, thus considering the effects of funding sources used and of the firm taxation.

Zmijewski (1984) classified the companies thus:

(i)   Firms with probabilities greater than or equal to 0.5 were classified as bankrupt or having complete data.

(ii)   Firms with probabilities less than 0.5 were classified as non-bankrupt or having incomplete data.

3.3. Principal Component Analysis

There exist many indicators in financial analysis which allow to assess the risk of bankruptcy of a company (Armeanu et al. 2012; Armeanu and Cioaca 2015; Cultrera et al. 2017; Arroyave 2018; Prusak 2018).

In order to make an appropriate assessment, we need to reduce the number of indicators. A solution is indicated by Armeanu et al. (2012): using Principal Component Analysis (PCA), cluster and discriminant analysis techniques. The authors used these three methods to build a scoring function and afterwards to identify bankrupt companies. Their sample consisted on listed companies on Bucharest Stock Exchange. Heffernan (2005) points that bankruptcy risk predicting models, developed based on discriminant analysis (like Altman and Conan-Holder) can easily mislead. This is due to the fact that they rely on historical data, but also on the fact that the result is binary (either the debtor is solvent or not). However, in the present article we consider the following possible scenarios (Armeanu et al. 2012; Armeanu and Cioaca 2015): delays in monthly repayments, failure to pay them, failure to pay fees or penalty interest, and so on, and that is why we rely on large companies' data. Discriminant analysis models may not include the state of solvency, insolvency and restructuring at once, and we would like to infer about it using principal component analysis jointly with discriminant analysis. PCA methods are less recognized in the literature to predict bankruptcy risk (Cultrera et al. 2017).

We use PCA based on the five discriminant analysis measures identified previously in Section 3.2. Software Stata is used for studying the effect of performance over risk and bankruptcy scores were obtained by year of analysis and country. Descriptive statistics of this data and Pearson correlation values considering country scores and year scores are presented in tables presented in Section 4.

3.4. Econometric Methodologies

In order to analyse the effects of risk scores over firm performance, we applied a dynamic panel-data estimation model, with GMM estimators to regress earnings before interest and taxes to total assets over risk by year. By doing so in a Generalized Method of Moments (GMM) context, we may construct more efficient estimates of the dynamic panel data model (these models contain one or more lagged dependent variables, allowing for the modelling of a partial adjustment mechanism). In the context of panel data, we usually must deal with unobserved heterogeneity. Static models are (almost) always misspecified, because the within-group error terms are serially correlated, thereby invalidating both point estimates and statistical inference. Conversely, dynamic models tend to be correctly specified, because the dynamics are in the estimated part of the model rather than displaced into the error terms, which invalidates static FE/RE estimation. Dynamic models are much richer in economic content by virtue of being able to distinguish short-run and long-run effects of independent variables on dependent variables.

Additionally, we used Tobit models to infer about the influence of company performance measures over general bankruptcy risk scores. The Tobit model, also called a censored regression model, is designed to estimate linear relationships between variables when there is either left- or right-censoring in the dependent variable. Our dependent variable is censored from both below and above provided we have limited the risk variable to be between −3 and 3, inclusively. Tobit models to predict bankruptcy have also been used by Sigrist and Hirnschall (2019) recently. The assumption of the Tobit model is that there exists a latent variable Y* which follows, conditional on some covariates X a Gaussian distribution: $Y^*|X \sim N\big(F(X), \sigma^2\big)$. The mean F(X) is assumed to depend linearly on the covariates X through $F(X) = X^T\beta$ where β is a set of coefficients. This latent variable Y* is observed only if it lies in an interval. Mousavi et al. (2019) used instead of PCA, a DEA model to measure the operational efficiency scores of Japanese companies, in the first step. In the second step, the efficiency score is used as the dependent variable in a Tobit regression to investigate whether corporate governance variables influence the operational efficiency of firms.

4. Results and Discussion

As we presented in the Section 3.1, in this study we used data from European large companies where insolvencies are more present. Figure 1 plots the frequency of corporate insolvencies in Europe by country for 2018 (Euler Hermes Economic Research 2019). We can see that the first place in the frequency of bankrupties was occupied by France (with 26.02%) corresponding to 54,965 companies bankrupted, followed by United Kingdom with 10.26% frequency corresponding to 21,669 companies bankrupted and 9.16% to Germany with 19,350 companies bankrupted. In our sample we used a great part of these countries. As we are able to observe, among countries with a high number of corporate insolvencies were also Italy, Belgium, Romania, Denmark, Sweden, Hungary, Norway, and Austria. From the countries used in our sample, France, United Kingdom, Germany, Turkey, Italy, Belgium, Romania, Denmark and Sweden were in the top ten of the Frequency of corporate insolvencies in Europe in 2018 (Figure 1).

Table 1 presents the number of companies from EU-28 countries included in the sample. We can observe that a high number of firm-year observations from large companies came from United Kingdom i.e., 28.60% of all observations analysed (also the country with the second number of bankruptcies), followed by Germany with 16.17%, Italy with 11.49%, France with 9.97% and Spain with 7.28%. Related to the number of firm-year observations of large companies by years, we can observe that the highest number of observations was in 2014 (18,513 companies) and 2013 (18,395 companies), respectively 12.02% and 11.94% of the sample analysed.

Table 2 presents the data descriptive statistics for the variables used for calculation of Z score for all five models used. In average, the companies from the sample show a need of exploitation capital of 14% by the total assets, an operational profitability of 6%, a rotation speed of assets 1.48 times per year, a current liquidity by 2.31 showing the capacity to pay debts by converting of assets in cash, the share of financial expenditure of 0.11% by sales, the share of personnel expenses of 69% in value added and a degree of debts of 64% by total assets. In addition, from Table 2 it is visible the disparity of values of mean and standard deviation of the bankruptcy measures. Moreover, the different number of observations considered for both the creation of financial ratios as well as bankruptcy indicators of interest are clearly visible.

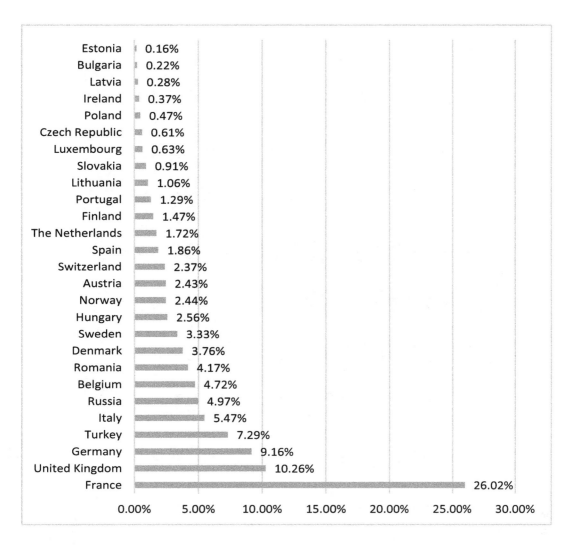

Figure 1. Frequency of corporate insolvencies in Europe, by country in 2018. Source: Euler Hermes Economic Research. 2019. Insolvency Outlook. Euler Hermes, Allianz, Economic Research, 1–14 January 2019. Own elaboration.

Table 1. Total number of companies within the sample by country and year.

Acronym	Country	Number Companies	Frequency	2006	2007	2008	2009	2010	2011	2012	2013	2014	2015
AT	Austria	2175	1.41%	1	56	5	96	340	372	380	401	428	96
BE	Belgium	5956	3.87%	579	535	604	610	618	626	633	636	639	476
BG	Bulgaria	1119	0.73%	101	92	110	110	106	119	120	120	121	120
CZ	Czech Republic	4270	2.77%	407	370	393	448	460	482	490	493	461	266
DE	Germany	24,917	16.17%	2105	2276	2603	2758	2908	3039	3106	3172	2667	283
ES	Spain	11,213	7.28%	1096	993	1179	1194	1228	1261	1285	1304	1298	375
FI	Finland	2304	1.50%	193	208	213	231	229	244	250	254	264	218
FR	France	15,356	9.97%	1775	1595	1560	1413	1593	1395	1114	1654	2099	1158
GB	Great Britain (UK)	44,060	28.60%	3558	3811	4078	4324	4612	4913	5155	5392	5550	2667
GR	Greece	1741	1.13%	167	131	177	188	191	192	194	194	193	114
HR	Croatia	1190	0.77%	101	96	116	117	125	126	127	128	128	126
HU	Hungary	1849	1.20%	42	137	212	223	236	230	235	237	173	124
IE	Ireland	1482	0.96%	97	136	140	145	171	175	189	198	194	37
IT	Italy	17,697	11.49%	1750	1519	1802	1828	1855	1930	1947	1979	1974	1113
NL	The Netherlands	5868	3.81%	345	471	258	597	500	705	785	817	879	511
PL	Poland	1668	1.08%	163	165	182	198	187	154	157	171	196	95
PT	Portugal	2555	1.66%	222	215	248	255	267	281	288	287	271	221
RO	Romania	2144	1.39%	234	64	0	0	297	303	310	311	322	303
SE	Sweden	5115	3.32%	475	476	548	570	517	506	512	524	537	450
SK	Slovakia	1382	0.90%	136	130	154	162	159	141	141	123	119	117
	Total	154,061		13,547	13,476	14,582	15,467	16,599	17,194	17,418	18,395	18,513	8870

Source. Performed by the authors based on data provided by Amadeus database.

Table 2. Variables, formulas, and descriptive statistics.

Formula	Variable	Obs	Mean	Std. Dev.	Min	Max
Working capital/Total assets	wcta	153,459	0.14	0.76	-198.44	113.86
Retained Earnings/Total Assets	reta	148,986	0.24	1.29	-364.35	274.07
EBIT/Total assets	ebitta	153,459	0.06	0.24	-42.14	61.11
Book Value of Equity/Book Value of Total Debt	bvebvtd	153,278	2.44	176.82	-657.29	50,409.00
Sales/Total assets	sta	153,459	1.48	3.99	0.00	1322.52
Revised Z Altman	rza	148,821	3.02	75.50	-306.70	21,172.06
EBIT/Current liabilities	ebitcliabil	151,123	240.93	101,682.60	-4,900,820.00	38,700,000.00
Permanent capital/Total debts	ppi	153,278	2.77	176.83	-656.29	50,410.00
(Current assets – Stocks)/Total Liabilities	curnt	153,278	2.31	172.72	-38.15	45,178.00
Financial expenditures/Sales	fs	145,515	0.11	8.93	-1.11	2169.55
Personnel Expenditures/Added Value	pexpenditura	140,104	0.69	3.81	-609.22	440.32
Z Connan	zcc	135,073	64.97	25,813.04	-1,176,196.00	9,298,852.00
Working capital/Total assets	wcta_1	153,459	0.14	0.76	-198.44	113.86
Earnings Before Interest and Taxes/Total Assets	ebitta_1	153,459	0.06	0.24	-42.14	61.11
Earnings Before Taxes/Current Liabilities	ebtcl	151,096	229.24	103,167.50	-5,151,934.00	39,400,000.00
Sales/Total Assets	sta_1	153,459	1.48	3.99	0.00	1322.52
Z Springate Model	zs	151,096	152.23	68,090.55	-3,400,276.00	26,000,000.00
Profit Before Tax/Current Liabilities	pbtcl	151,096	229.24	103,167.50	-5,151,934.00	39,400,000.00
Current Assets/Total Liabilities	cat	153,278	2.89	219.41	-39.30	55,223.00
Current Liabilities/Total Assets	clt	153,459	0.43	0.75	-113.76	199.44
(Quick Assets – Current Liabilities)/(Sales – Profit Before Tax – Depreciation)/365	qaclspbtd	144,735	-792,000,000,000	301,000,000,000,000	-115,000,000,000,000,000	10,200,000
Z Taffler	ztta	144,730	-23,000,000,000	8740,000,000,000	-3,320,000,000,000,000	47,900,0000
Net Income/Total Assets	nincomt	153,459	0.04	0.26	-62.33	26.68
Total Liabilities/Total Assets	tliat	153,432	0.64	1.12	-71.28	390.32
Current Assets/Current Liabilities	cac	151,123	-653.97	403,912.70	-90,700,000.00	84,800,000.00
Z Zmijewski	zzzmij	151,118	-3.44	1615.68	-362,744.00	339,315.60

Source. Performed by the authors based on data provided by Amadeus database.

Tables A1 and A2 (at the Appendix A) presents the correlation matrix among the variables used both to produce the bankruptcy risk indicators and the five bankruptcy risk scores. In addition, Tables A1 and A2 presents the Pearson correlation values and statistical significance. From here it is seen that there are ratios used to produce the bankruptcy indicators which are highly correlated among them, significantly, with negative or positive correlation (i.e., strong positive significant correlation (0.821) between Book Value of Equity/Book Value of Total Debt and Current Assets/Total Liabilities; strong positive significant correlation (0.778) between Book Value of Equity/Book Value of Total Debt and (Current assets − Stocks)/Total Liabilities, almost perfect positive correlation (0.998) between EBIT/Current liabilities and Profit Before Tax/Current Liabilities etc.), but mostly have low to moderate correlation. However, between bankruptcy indicators constructed through discriminant analysis, correlation values are very low, and very close to zero with statistical significance.

Table 3 indicates that after applying PCA, the number of observations decreased as compared to Table 2. In fact, by restricting the sample to all those values obtained for the general risk score greater than 3 or smaller than 3, our sample was reduced to 133,751 firm-year observations. Risk is the score computed through PCA considering all companies, years and countries.

Table 3. Descriptive Statistics of scores computed based over Principal Component Analysis (PCA).

Variable	Obs	Mean	Std. Dev.	Variable	Obs	Mean	Std. Dev.
risk	133,751	−0.00331	0.004657	riskAT	133,751	−0.23914	3.094626
risk2015	133,751	0.004167	0.006804	riskBE	133,751	0.433947	50.73316
risk2014	133,751	−0.01011	0.001642	riskBG	133,751	0.485776	14.48578
risk2013	133,751	0.264434	26.89755	riskCZ	133,751	0.555987	60.98777
risk2012	133,751	0.006104	1.469264	riskDE	133,751	−0.01741	0.468755
risk2011	133,751	0.085679	9.797604	riskES	133,751	0.188694	3.364935
risk2010	133,751	0.001579	1.400829	riskFI	133,751	1.197073	115.5954
risk2009	133,751	0.012124	2.556249	riskFR	133,751	−0.00996	0.00155
risk2008	133,751	0.029394	3.814389	riskGB	133,751	0.731819	71.07321
risk2007	133,751	−0.00539	0.608735	riskHR	133,751	0.226101	3.129303
risk2006	133,751	−0.01938	0.606729	riskHU	133,751	0.158191	19.79164
				riskIE	133,751	0.061467	10.7725
				riskIT	133,751	0.297428	2.719817
				riskNL	133,751	−0.29214	3.178018
				riskPL	133,751	−0.07491	3.281825
				riskPT	133,751	3.345667	299.3375
				riskRO	133,751	1.151802	109.7751
				riskSE	133,751	−0.30931	3.435378
				riskSK	133,751	0.317604	36.03616

Source. Performed by the authors based on data provided by Amadeus database.

Overall, countries presented higher mean scores as well as negative mean for some countries, and also standard deviation is higher for countries scores. A plot of year bankruptcy risk scores will allow us to see their behaviour along years. Figure 2 presents these data evolution for countries. After the final data treatment, the total number of companies available to analyse by country and year are presented in Table 4.

Correlation values (Table 5) seem to be very strong among Austria and Spain, Croatia, Italy, the Netherlands, Poland and Sweden; strong (higher than 90% and positive; some near perfect linear positive correlation) between Belgium, Czech Republic, Germany, Finland, France, Great Britain, Hungary, Portugal, Romania, and Slovakia; Bulgaria and Ireland; Germany, Finland, France, Great Britain, Hungary, Portugal, Romania, and Slovakia; Spain, Croatia, Italy, the Netherlands, Poland, and Sweden; Finland, France, Great Britain, Hungary, Portugal, Romania, and Slovakia; between France, Great Britain, Hungary, Portugal, Romania and Slovakia; among Great Britain and Hungary, Portugal, Romania, and Slovakia; Croatia, Italy, the Netherlands, Poland, and Sweden; between Hungary, Portugal, Romania, and Slovakia; Italy, Poland, and Sweden; the Netherlands, Poland and Sweden; Between Poland and Sweden; Portugal, Romania, and Slovakia; and finally between Romania and Slovakia. As such, no clear pattern is identified regarding for instant the geographic distance among the countries, but high correlation values maybe due to commercial transactions performed among these countries.

Regarding year, whose correlation values are presented in Table 6, the score Pearson correlation values were very high, near to one and positive. In the next we will be analysing the evolution plots of scores of bankruptcy risk by country and by year. Figures 2 and 3 present these evolutions respectively.

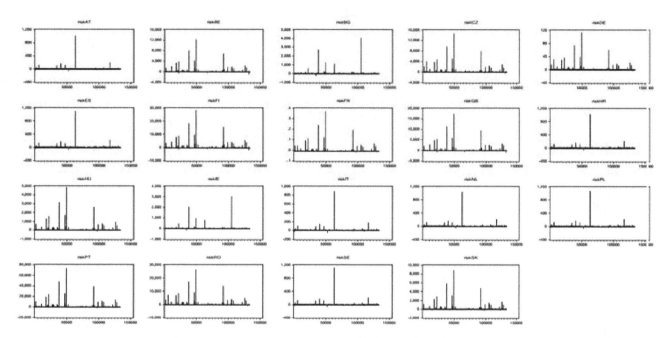

Figure 2. Plot of scoring bankruptcy risk by country. Source. Performed by the authors based on data provided by Amadeus database.

Table 4. Number of firms after limiting the risk values by country and year.

Country	2006	2007	2008	2009	2010	2011	2012	2013	2014	2015	Total
AT	1	0	4	90	315	347	352	363	396	80	1948
BE	576	463	600	606	613	620	628	634	635	471	5846
BG	95	65	107	104	102	119	120	120	121	120	1073
CZ	403	273	388	445	455	480	488	490	459	265	4146
DE	2018	1693	2501	2664	2840	2973	3042	3113	2613	273	23,730
ES	1086	760	1167	1172	1213	1241	1269	1286	1280	367	10,841
FI	155	138	174	186	194	204	207	211	223	170	1862
FR	1738	1265	1542	1389	1572	1381	1095	1633	2064	1132	14,811
GB	3217	2772	3702	3884	4078	4363	4553	4773	4890	2347	38,579
HR	100	64	116	117	124	124	126	127	128	126	1152
HU	36	99	202	212	220	217	222	224	162	115	1709
IE	89	93	125	127	149	153	170	166	160	30	1262
IT	1746	1221	1798	1825	1855	1930	1946	1976	1973	1113	17,383
NL	239	199	55	16	13	17	25	29	26	0	619
PL	72	52	76	85	75	51	59	61	83	17	631
PT	221	141	245	253	259	270	274	264	257	205	2389
RO	152	0	0	0	297	303	310	311	322	303	1998
SE	218	205	269	282	244	245	249	261	273	240	2486
SK	130	94	149	153	128	139	139	121	117	116	1286
Total	12,292	9597	13,220	13,610	14,746	15,177	15,274	16,163	16,182	7490	133,751

Source. Performed by the authors based on data provided by Amadeus database.

Table 5. Pearson correlation values among scoring PCA bankruptcy risk variables obtained by country.

Score	riskAT	riskBE	riskBG	riskCZ	riskDE	riskES	riskFI	riskFR	riskGB	riskHR	riskHU	riskIE	riskIT	riskNL	riskPL	riskPT	riskRO	riskSE	riskSK
riskAT	1																		
riskBE	0.093 ***	1																	
riskBG	0.037 ***	0.337 ***	1																
riskCZ	0.093 ***	0.998 ***	0.363 ***	1															
riskDE	0.093 ***	0.998 ***	0.363 ***	1.000 ***	1														
riskES	0.997 ***	0.016 ***	0.008 ***	0.016 ***	0.016 ***	1													
riskFI	0.093 ***	1.000 ***	0.337 ***	0.998 ***	0.998 ***	0.016 ***	1												
riskFR	0.093 ***	0.998 ***	0.363 ***	1.000 ***	1.000 ***	0.016 ***	0.998 ***	1											
riskGB	0.093 ***	1.000 ***	0.337 ***	0.998 ***	0.998 ***	0.016 ***	1.000 ***	0.998 ***	1										
riskHR	0.093 ***	0.098 ***	0.039 ***	0.098 ***	0.098 ***	0.997 ***	0.098 ***	0.098 ***	0.098 ***	1									
riskHU	0.093 ***	0.998 ***	0.363 ***	1.000 ***	1.000 ***	0.016 ***	0.998 ***	1.000 ***	0.998 ***	0.098 ***	1								
riskIE	0.037 ***	0.337 ***	1.000 ***	0.363 ***	0.363 ***	0.008 ***	0.337 ***	0.363 ***	0.337 ***	0.039 ***	0.363 ***	1							
riskIT	0.982 ***	-0.098 ***	-0.032 ***	-0.098 ***	-0.098 ***	0.994 ***	-0.098 ***	-0.098 ***	-0.098 ***	0.981 ***	-0.098 ***	-0.032 ***	1						
riskNL	0.997 ***	0.174 ***	0.065 ***	0.174 ***	0.174 ***	0.987 ***	0.174 ***	0.174 ***	0.174 ***	0.997 ***	0.174 ***	0.065 ***	0.963 ***	1					
riskPL	1.000 ***	0.085 ***	0.033 ***	0.085 ***	0.085 ***	0.998 ***	0.085 ***	0.085 ***	0.085 ***	0.999 ***	0.085 ***	0.033 ***	0.983 ***	0.996 ***	1				
riskPT	0.093 ***	0.998 ***	0.363 ***	1.000 ***	1.000 ***	0.016 ***	0.998 ***	1.000 ***	0.998 ***	0.098 ***	1.000 ***	0.363 ***	-0.098 ***	0.174 ***	0.085 ***	1			
riskRO	0.093 ***	0.998 ***	0.363 ***	1.000 ***	1.000 ***	0.016 ***	0.998 ***	1.000 ***	0.998 ***	0.098 ***	1.000 ***	0.363 ***	-0.098 ***	0.174 ***	0.085 ***	1.000 ***	1		
riskSE	0.999 ***	0.071 ***	0.029 ***	0.071 ***	0.071 ***	0.999 ***	0.071 ***	0.071 ***	0.071 ***	0.999 ***	0.071 ***	0.029 ***	0.986 ***	0.995 ***	0.999 ***	0.071 ***	0.071 ***	1	
riskSK	0.093 ***	0.998 ***	0.363 ***	1.000 ***	1.000 ***	0.016 ***	0.998 ***	1.000 ***	0.998 ***	0.098 ***	1.000 ***	0.363 ***	-0.098 ***	0.174 ***	0.085 ***	1.000 ***	1.000 ***	0.071 ***	1

Source. Performed by the authors based on data provided by Amadeus database. Note: *, **, ***, represent statistically significant at 10%, 5% and 1%, respectively.

Table 6. Pearson correlation variables among scoring PCA bankruptcy risk variables obtained by year.

Scores	risk	risk2015	risk2014	risk2013	risk2012	risk2011	risk2010	risk2009	risk2008	risk2007	risk2006
risk	1										
risk2015	1.000 ***	1									
risk2014	1.000 ***	1.000 ***	1								
risk2013	1.000 ***	1.000 ***	1.000 ***	1							
risk2012	1.000 ***	1.000 ***	1.000 ***	1.000 ***	1						
risk2011	0.998 ***	0.998 ***	0.998 ***	0.998 ***	0.998 ***	1					
risk2010	1.000 ***	1.000 ***	1.000 ***	1.000 ***	1.000 ***	0.998 ***	1				
risk2009	1.000 ***	1.000 ***	1.000 ***	1.000 ***	1.000 ***	0.998 ***	1.000 ***	1			
risk2008	0.998 ***	0.998 ***	0.998 ***	0.998 ***	0.998 ***	1.000 ***	0.998 ***	0.998 ***	1		
risk2007	1.000 ***	1.000 ***	1.000 ***	1.000 ***	1.000 ***	0.998 ***	1.000 ***	1.000 ***	0.998 ***	1	
risk2006	1.000 ***	1.000 ***	1.000 ***	1.000 ***	1.000 ***	0.998 ***	1.000 ***	1.000 ***	0.998 ***	1.000 ***	1

Source. Performed by the authors based on data provided by Amadeus database. Note: *, **, ***, represent statistically significant at 10%, 5% and 1%, respectively.

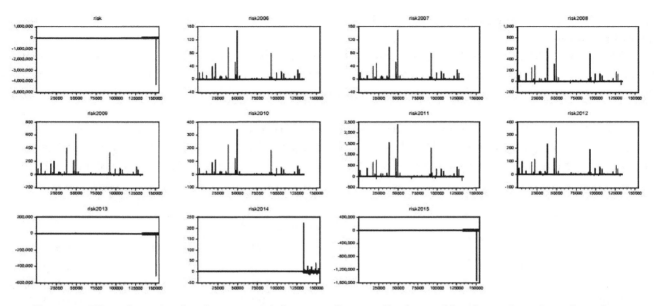

Figure 3. Plot of scoring bankruptcy risk by year. Source. Performed by the authors based on data provided by Amadeus database.

Figure 2 plots the evolution of the score values obtained through PCA from the discriminant indices calculous by country. There are some countries which evidence a very similar behaviour like Belgium, Czech Republic, Finland, France, Great Britain, Hungary, Portugal, Romania, Slovakia and Germany. Another group of similar behaviour in terms of scores is that of Austria, Spain, Italy, Croatia, the Netherlands, Poland and Sweden. The two other similar countries in terms of scores are Ireland and Bulgaria.

Regarding years, the years 2006 until 2012 were very similar years in terms of score behaviour. As such, unstable values are more observed in these years with peaks and downs, which included all countries. In the following we decided to apply first a dynamic panel-data model by regressing the ratio EBIT over Total Assets in the bankruptcy scoring variables by year and a probit estimation considering as dependent variable risk and as independent variables firm performance measures.

Table 7 presents the estimation results of the panel-data model.

Table 7. Dynamic panel data results.

Dynamic Panel-Data Estimation			
Wald chi2(4)		8.04	
Prob > chi2		0.0901	
ebitta	Coef.	z	P > |z|
risk2014	310280	2.04	0.041
risk2013	−9.35136	−2	0.045
risk2011	−0.03367	−0.33	0.743
risk2009	−101.797	−2.08	0.038
GMM-type:	L(2/.).wcta		

Source. Performed by the authors based on data provided by Amadeus database.

The dynamic panel data results indicate that the only score risk variables which have not been omitted due to collinearity issues were the risk measures for years 2014, 2013, 2011 and 2009. The years 2009 until 2011 are characterized by the financial crisis which has spread out through Europe, having a negative influence over firm performance as measured by the ratio of Earnings Before Interest and Taxes and Total Assets, but with significance only for the year 2009 at 5%.

Aleksanyan and Huiban (2016) study confirm also the dramatic increase in bankruptcy risk in the French food industry observed over the period 2010–2012, highlighting that among food industry sub-sectors, the meat industry was primarily responsible for the evolution of bankruptcy risk in the period mentioned.

The years of 2013 and 2014 were years of starting recovery, and we might infer from the results that despite the negative influence of 2013 risk score over performance, in 2014 we already have a positive contribution of bankruptcy risk score over performance, both years with statistical significance at 5%.

Table 8 reports the Tobit estimation results for general risk among countries, while Table 9 presents the same Tobit estimation results but this turn by country. This turn we are testing the influence of performance measures over risk scores since we are analysing the dependent censored variable risk.

Table 8. Tobit estimation results.

	Tobit Regression: Dependent = Risk					
	Coef	t	p > t	Coef	t	p > t
ebitta	0.00012 **	2.05	0.041	0.00019 *	1.90	0.057
sta				0.000006	0.96	0.339
wcta				0.0001 ***	3.68	0.000
const	−0.00332	−250.91	0.000	−0.00334 ***	−213.66	0.000
	LR chi2	4.19		LR chi2	18.9	
	prob chi2	0.0406		prob chi2	0.0003	

Source. Performed by the authors based on data provided by Amadeus database. Note: *, **, *** statistically significant at 10%, 5% and 1%, respectively. Ebitta = earnings before interest and taxes (ebit)/total assets; sta = sales/total assets; wcta = working capital/total assets.

Model significance was confirmed at 5% and results seem to indicate that performance measures positively influence risk scores. Thus the higher the performance is the higher will be the risk score and as such bankruptcy risk decreases with performance, a result which was expected. Bankruptcy is one of the most discussed topics in the literature, owing to its importance to the economy of any country. Bankruptcy costs are high and authors have tried to develop bankruptcy prediction models through years. Our scoring methodology through PCA applied to discriminant analysis of bankruptcy risk therefore indicates that performance is the solution to decrease this risk.

Discriminant analysis of bankruptcy risk argues that positive high values of bankruptcy risk positions companies in the safe zone, meaning a low risk of bankruptcy or a probability of bankruptcy lower than 30% (zcc index). Lower values positions firms between the grey zones or in the distress zone (see Section 3.2). Therefore, we may argue that for our sample of firms, these large companies had good chances for performance provided their higher results, thus being non-bankrupt or with lower chances to become so. However, these results depended on the year of analysis provided that Table 7 demonstrates that 2009, 2011 and 2013 were years of negative influence of bankruptcy risk scores over companies' results.

Company performance variables were all statistically significant and with a positive impact over the bankruptcy risk score in Austria, Bulgaria, Spain, Finland, Great Britain, Croatia, Ireland, Italy, The Netherlands, Portugal, Romania, and Sweden. The ratio sales to total assets had a negative and non-significant impact over the risk score in Belgium, Czech Republic, Hungary and Slovakia. It is positive and non-significant in Poland and France. The only countries where performance (independently of its measure) did not seem to exert an influence over the bankruptcy risk score were Germany and Poland.

Since Germany is on the top ten of the number of corporate insolvencies, this might mean that other corporate variables despite the ones considered here to represent performance in our analysis, might be influencing bankruptcy risk scores under the years in analysis. The Principal Component Analysis here employed to build a bankruptcy risk scored based on discriminant analysis indices was found to be effective for determining the influence of corporate performance over risk. It was useful to understand that different countries evidence different results regarding this influence, as well as different risk scores with respect to years reveal to be different. It could be useful to understand this impact in the future by using other scoring techniques, like data envelopment analysis, or even by detailing years and countries analysis.

Table 9. Tobit estimation results by country.

Tobit Regression: Dependent = Risk								
	AT = Austria			**BE = Belgium**			**BG = Bulgaria**		
Indep.	Coef	t	p > t	Coef	t	p > t	Coef	t	p > t
ebitta	0.00060 ***	39.82	0.0000	−0.00017	−0.53	0.598	0.00007 ***	19.19	0.0000
sta	0.000002 ***	8.01	0.0000	−0.00002	−0.89	0.375	0.000002 ***	4.30	0.0000
wcta	0.000032 ***	36.01	0.0000	0.00018 *	1.83	0.067	0.00004 ***	15.75	0.0000
const	−0.00337 ***	−6822.46	0.0000	−0.00332 ***	−74.97	0	−0.00337 ***	−3544.58	0.0000
LR chi2		2114.45			4.50			646.96	
prob chi2		0.0000			0.2126			0.0000	
	CZ = Czech Republic			**DE = Germany**			**ES = Spain**		
Indep.	Coef	t	p > t	Coef	t	p > t	Coef	t	p > t
ebitta	0.00020 ***	26.54	0.0000	0.00056	0.90	0.3710	0.00007 ***	5.04	0.0000
sta	−0.00000	−0.77	0.4440	−0.00006	−1.09	0.2760	0.000003 *	1.93	0.0530
wcta	0.00004 ***	12.80	0.0000	0.00011	1.38	0.1660	0.00002 ***	3.12	0.0020
const	−0.00337 ***	−2204.68	0.0000	−0.00310 ***	−27.57	0.0000	−0.00337 ***	−1570.65	0.0000
LR chi2		3370.88			3.62			53.54	
prob chi2		0.0000			0.3060			0.0000	
	FI = Finland			**FR = France**			**GB = Great Britain (UK)**		
Indep.	Coef	t	p > t	Coef	t	p > t	Coef	t	p > t
ebitta	0.00011 ***	19.32	0.0000	0.00102 **	2.37	0.0180	0.00005 ***	15.28	0.0000
sta	0.000004 ***	8.10	0.0000	0.00006	1.37	0.1720	0.000003 ***	6.45	0.0000
wcta	0.00003 ***	8.97	0.0000	0.00005	1.09	0.2770	0.00003 ***	15.21	0.0000
const	−0.00338 ***	−2800.20	0.0000	−0.00345 ***	−39.57	0.0000	−0.00337 ***	−4094.65	0.0000
LR chi2		527.87			9.77			787.56	
prob chi2		0.0000			0.0206			0.0000	
	HR = Croatia			**HU = Hungary**			**IE = Ireland**		
Indep.	Coef	t	p > t	Coef	t	p > t	Coef	t	p > t
ebitta	0.00006 ***	10.42	0.0000	0.00014 **	2.21	0.0270	0.00008 ***	26.52	0.0000
sta	0.000004 ***	5.64	0.0000	−0.00000	−0.07	0.9450	0.000003 ***	7.28	0.0000
wcta	0.00003 ***	13.65	0.0000	0.00011 ***	4.97	0.0000	0.00003 ***	27.08	0.0000
const	−0.00337 ***	−3219.78	0.0000	−0.00337 ***	−293.47	0.0000	−0.00337 ***	−5373.66	0.0000
LR chi2		476.75			34.35			1265.69	
	IT = Italy			**NL = The Netherlands**			**PL = Poland**		
Indep.	Coef	t	p > t	Coef	t	p > t	Coef	t	p > t
ebitta	0.00004 ***	5.25	0.0000	0.00006 ***	14.94	0.0000	0.00009	0.90	0.3710
sta	0.000004 ***	4.41	0.0000	0.000003 ***	9.42	0.0000	0.000012	1.28	0.2010
wcta	0.00004 ***	11.45	0.0000	0.00003 ***	12.46	0.0000	0.00005	1.26	0.2100
const	−0.00338 ***	−2531.81	0.0000	−0.00337 ***	−4554.27	0.0000	−0.00339 ***	−214.04	0.0000
LR chi2		247.05			428.15			6.47	
prob chi2		0.0000			0.0000			0.0909	
	PT = Portugal			**RO = Romania**			**SE = Sweden**		
Indep.	Coef	t	p > t	Coef	t	p > t	Coef	t	p > t
ebitta	0.00006 ***	31.90	0.0000	0.00004 ***	13.50	0.0000	0.00007 ***	30.34	0.0000
sta	0.000005 ***	20.11	0.0000	0.000002 ***	5.15	0.0000	0.000002 ***	5.92	0.0000
wcta	0.00002 ***	36.12	0.0000	0.00002 ***	10.94	0.0000	0.00003 ***	19.77	0.0000
const	−0.00337 ***	−0.0001	0.0000	−0.00337 ***	−4030.59	0.0000	−0.00337 ***	−4809.04	0.0000
LR chi2		2477.79			815.74			1272.57	
prob chi2		0.0000			0.0000			0.0000	

SK = Slovakia			
Indep.	Coef	t	p > t
ebitta	0.00010 ***	3.40	0.0010
sta	−0.000002	−0.53	0.5970
wcta	0.00006 ***	4.65	0.0000
const	−0.00336 ***	−539.59	0.0000
LR chi2		52.95	
prob chi2		0.0000	

Source. Performed by the authors based on data provided by Amadeus database. Note: *, **, *** statistically significant at 10%, 5% and 1%, respectively. Ebitta = earnings before interest and taxes (ebit)/total assets; sta = sales/total assets; wcta = working capital/total assets.

5. Conclusions

The purpose of this paper was to improve the knowledge of bankruptcy prediction of companies and to analyse the predictive capacity of factor analysis based over discriminant analysis using five models for assessing bankruptcy risk well-known in the literature: Altman, Conan and Holder, Tafler, Springate and Zmijewski. We used data for non-financial large companies from Europe for the period 2006–2015. In order to analyse the effects of risk scores over firm performance, we applied a dynamic panel-data estimation model, with GMM estimators to regress firm performance indicator over risk by year and we used Tobit models to infer about the influence of company performance measures over general bankruptcy risk scores by country. In summary, results evidence that PCA used to build a bankruptcy risk scored based on discriminant analysis indices is effective for determining the influence of corporate performance over risk.

Results reveal a negative influence of risk scores over firm performance in the financial crisis years of 2009–2011. However, bankruptcy risk scores increase performance (as measured through the ratio Earnings before Interest and Taxes over Total Assets) in the upcoming years of recovery, especially from 2014 onwards. These results were obtained by applying dynamic panel data estimations. Afterwards, using Tobit estimations we analyze the influence of performance measures over risk score (the variable risk was censored between three, negative and positive, inclusively). The higher the performance the higher the risk score, meaning the lower the bankruptcy risk probability. The scoring methodology through PCA applied to discriminant analysis of bankruptcy risk indicators used to obtain the bankruptcy risk scores by year and country highlight that higher performance is the solution to decrease bankruptcy risk.

Therefore, and provided that bankruptcy can be caused by poor management, improper sales forecasting, inexperienced management, rapid technological advances, preference changes, and inability of the firm to follow as a leader in these changes, our sample of large companies in Europe and results obtained lead us to conclude that firms' strategy is vital in terms of market survival. The literature already points that better corporate governance simultaneously improve firm performance and reduce firm risk, especially during crisis (Wang et al. 2019). Our results seem to highlight the importance of good corporate governance as a key indicator for firm performance and lower bankruptcy risk, with clear differences among European countries. In future works we intend to use other scoring techniques to predict bankruptcy risk like data envelopment analysis in order to be able to understand differences among countries and years, and to test the performance of bankruptcy models using different risk build scores.

Author Contributions: Conceptualization, N.B.-M. and M.M.; methodology, N.B.-M. and M.M.; results and discussions, N.B.-M. and M.M.; formal analysis, N.B.-M.; resources, N.B.-M. and M.M.; data curation, M.M..; writing— N.B.-M. and M.M.; writing—review and editing, N.B.-M. and M.M. All authors have read and agreed to the published version of the manuscript.

Acknowledgments: This work was supported by the SOP IEC, under Grant SMIS-CNSR 815-48745, no. 622/2014. This work was in part financially supported by the research unit on Governance, Competitiveness and Public Policy (UID/CPO/04058/2019), funded by national funds through FCT—Fundação para a Ciência e a Tecnologia.

Appendix A

Table A1. Pearson Correlation values.

Variable	wcta	reta	ebitta	bvebvtd	sta	rza	ebitcliabil	ppi	curnt	fs	pexpenditura	zcc	wcta_1
wcta	1												
reta	-0.256 ***	1											
ebitta	-0.3086 ***	0.4387 ***	1										
bvebvtd	0.006 **	0.002	-0.002	1									
sta	-0.658 ***	0.394 ***	0.404 ***	-0.004	1								
rza	-0.029 ***	0.040 ***	0.034 ***	0.998 ***	0.055 ***	1							
ebitcliabil	-0.000	0.001	0.000	0.002	-0.001	0.001	1						
ppi	0.008 ***	0.002	-0.002	1.000 ***	-0.004	0.998 ***	0.002	1					
curnt	0.008 ***	0.001	-0.002	0.778 ***	-0.003	0.777 ***	-0.001	0.778 ***	1				
fs	-0.002	-0.003	-0.005 *	0.019 ***	-0.004	0.007 ***	0.000	0.019 ***	0.013 ***	1			
pexpenditura	0.002	-0.004	-0.011 ***	-0.004	0.003	-0.001	-0.000	-0.004	-0.002	-0.002	1		
zcc	-0.000	0.001	0.000	0.005 *	-0.001	0.001	1.000 ***	0.005 *	-0.001	-0.000	-0.000	1	
wcta_1	1.000 ***	-0.256 ***	-0.309 ***	0.006 **	-0.658 ***	-0.029 ***	-0.000	0.008 ***	0.008 ***	-0.002	0.002	-0.000	1
ebitta_1	-0.309 ***	0.439 ***	1.000 ***	-0.002	0.404 ***	0.034 ***	-0.000	0.008 ***	-0.002	-0.005 *	-0.011 ***	0.000	-0.309 ***
ebtcl	-0.000	0.001	0.000	0.002	-0.001	0.001	0.998 ***	0.002	-0.001	0.000	-0.000	0.998 ***	-0.000
sta_1	-0.658 ***	0.394 ***	0.404 ***	-0.004	1.000 ***	0.055 ***	-0.001	0.002	-0.003	-0.004	0.003	-0.001	-0.658 ***
zs	-0.000	0.001	0.000	0.002	-0.001	0.001	0.998 ***	0.002	-0.001	0.000	-0.000	0.998 ***	-0.000
pbtcl	-0.000	0.001	0.000	0.002	-0.001	0.001	0.998 ***	0.002	-0.001	0.000	-0.000	0.998 ***	-0.000
cat	0.008 ***	0.001	-0.002	0.821 ***	-0.003	0.819 ***	-0.000	0.821 ***	0.996 ***	0.008 ***	-0.002	-0.000	0.008 ***
clt	-0.928 ***	0.246 ***	0.350 ***	-0.006 **	0.715 ***	0.033 ***	-0.001	-0.009 ***	-0.005 **	-0.003	0.002	-0.001	-0.928 ***
qaclspbtd	0.000	-0.002	-0.012 ***	-0.008 ***	0.000	-0.005 *	0.000	-0.009 ***	0.000	0.000	0.000	0.000 ***	0.000
ztta	0.000	-0.002	-0.012 ***	-0.008 ***	0.000	-0.005 *	0.000	-0.009 ***	0.000	0.000	0.000	0.998 ***	0.000
nincomt	0.012 ***	0.354 ***	0.658 ***	-0.000	-0.030 ***	0.010 ***	0.001	-0.000	-0.001	-0.011 ***	-0.009 ***	0.002	0.012 ***
tliat	-0.741 ***	0.341 ***	0.495 ***	-0.006 **	0.824 ***	0.042 ***	-0.001	-0.006 **	-0.005 **	0.000	0.002	-0.001	-0.741 ***
cac	-0.002	0.001	0.001	0.001	-0.000	0.000	0.337 ***	0.001	0.000	0.000	-0.000	0.337 ***	-0.002
zzzmij	-0.005 *	0.002	0.002	0.001	0.003	0.003	0.337 ***	0.001	0.000	0.000	-0.000	0.337 ***	-0.005 *

Source. Performed by the authors based on data provided by Amadeus database. Note: *, **, *** represent statistically significant at 10%, 5% and 1% respectively.

Table A2. Pearson Correlation values.

Variable	ebitta_1	ebtcl	sta_1	zs	pbtcl	cat	clt	qaclspbtd	ztta	nincomt	tliat	cac	zzzmij
wcta													
reta													
ebitta													
bvebvtd													
sta													
rza													
ebitcliabil													
ppi													
curnt													
fs													
pexpenditura													
zcc													
wcta_1													
ebitta_1	1												
ebtcl	0.000	1											
sta_1	0.404 ***	−0.001	1										
zs	0.000	1.000 ***	−0.001	1									
pbtcl	0.000	1.000 ***	−0.001	1.000 ***	1								
cat	−0.002	−0.000	−0.003	−0.000	−0.000	1							
clt	0.350 ***	−0.001	0.715 ***	−0.001	−0.001	−0.005 *	1						
qaclspbtd	−0.012 ***	0.000	0.000	0.000	0.000	0.001	0.002	1					
ztta	−0.012 ***	0.000	0.000	0.000	0.000	0.001	0.002	1.000 ***	1				
nincomt	0.658 ***	0.001	−0.030 ***	0.001	0.001	−0.001	0.012 ***	−0.016 ***	−0.016 ***	1			
tliat	0.495 ***	−0.001	0.824 ***	−0.001	−0.001	−0.005 **	0.727 ***	0.001	0.001	0.019 ***	1		
cac	0.001	0.363 ***	−0.000	0.363 ***	0.363 ***	0.000	0.001	0.000 ***	0.000 ***	0.001	0.001	1	
zzzmij	0.002	0.363 ***	0.003	0.363 ***	0.363 ***	0.000	0.004	0.000	0.000	0.001	0.003	1.000 ***	1

Source. Performed by the authors based on data provided by Amadeus database. Note: $*$, $**$, $***$ represent statistically significant at 10%, 5% and 1% respectively.

References

Adalessossi, Kokou. 2015. Prediction of Corporate Bankruptcy: Evidence from West African's SMEs. *Journal of Economics, Finance and Accounting* 2: 331–52. [CrossRef]

Agarwal, Vineet, and Richard J. Taffler. 2007. Twenty-Five Years of the Taffler Z-Score Model: Does It Really Have Predictive Ability? *Accounting and Business Research* 37: 285–300. [CrossRef]

Aleksanyan, Lilia, and Jean-Pierre Huiban. 2016. Economic and Financial Determinants of Firm Bankruptcy: Evidence from the French Food Industry. *Review of Agricultural, Food and Environmental Studies* 97: 89–108. [CrossRef]

Alkhatib, Khalid, and Ahmad Eqab Al Bzour. 2011. Predicting corporate bankruptcy of Jordanian listed companies: Using Altman and Kida Models. *International Journal of Business and Management* 6: 208–15. [CrossRef]

Altman, Edward I. 1968. Financial ratios, discriminant analysis and the prediction of corporate bankruptcy. *The Journal of Finance* XXIII: 589–609.

Altman, Edward I., John Hartzell, and Matthew Peck. 1998. Emerging Markets Corporate Bonds: A Scoring System. In *Emerging Market Capital Flows*. Part of the The New York University Salomon Center Series on Financial Markets and Institutions Book Series (SALO, Volume 2); Boston: Springer, pp. 391–400.

Altman, Edward I. 2000. Predicting Financial Distress of Companies: Revisiting the Z-Score and Zeta ® Models. New York University. Available online: http://pages.stern.nyu.edu/~{}ealtman/Zscores.pdf (accessed on 10 October 2019).

Altman, Edward I. 2002. Revisiting Credit Scoring Models in a Basel II Environment. In *Credit Rating: Methodologies, Rationale, and Default Risk*. Edited by Michael K. Ong. London: Risk Books, Available online: https://pdfs.semanticscholar.org/9899/c671599ca41a1310d9b5e0ed5a3953c930f0.pdf (accessed on 10 October 2019).

Altman, Edward, Malgorzata Iwanicz-Drozdowska, Erkki Laitinen, and Arto Suvas. 2017. Financial Distress Prediction in an International Context: A Review and Empirical Analysis of Altman's Z-Score Model. *Journal of International Financial Managament & Accounting* 28: 131–71.

Armeanu, Stefan Daniel, Georgeta Vintila, Maricica Moscalu, Maria-Oana Filipescu, and Paula Lazar. 2012. Using quantitative data analysis techniques for bankruptcy risk estimation for corporations. *Theoretical and Applied Economics* XIX: 97–112.

Armeanu, Stefan Daniel, and Sorin Iulian Cioaca. 2015. An assessment of the bankruptcy risk on the Romanian capital market. *Procedia Social and Behavioral Sciences* 182: 535–42. [CrossRef]

Arroyave, Jackson. 2018. A comparative analysis of the effectiveness of corporate bankruptcy prediction models based on financial ratios: Evidence from Colombia. *Journal of International Studies* 11: 273–87. [CrossRef]

Ashraf, Sumaira, Elisabete G. S. Félix, and Zélia Serrasqueiro. 2019. Do Traditional Financial Distress Prediction Models Predict the Early Warning Signs of Financial Distress? *Journal of Risk and Financial Management* 12: 55. [CrossRef]

Avenhuis, Jeroen O. 2013. Testing the generalizability of the bankruptcy prediction models of Altman, Ohlson and Zmijewski for Dutch listed and large non-listed firms. Master's Thesis, The School of Management and Governance, University of Twente, Enschede, The Netherlands, November 13. Available online: https://essay.utwente.nl/64326/1/MSc_Oude%20Avenhuis.pdf (accessed on 25 November 2019).

Aziz, M.A., and H.A. Dar. 2006. Predicting corporate bankruptcy: Where we stand? *Corporate Governance* 6: 18–33. [CrossRef]

Bărbuţă-Mişu, Nicoleta. 2009. Modelling the financial performance of the building sector enterprises—Case of Romania. *Romanian Journal of Economic Forecasting* 4: 195–212.

Bărbuţă-Mişu, Nicoleta. 2017. Assessing the Risk of Bankruptcy. Case Study on a European Manufacturing Company. In *Understanding Bankruptcy: Global Issues, Perspectives and Challenges*. Chapter 4. Edited by Ignatius Ekanem. Hauppauge: Nova Science Publishers, Inc.

Bărbuţă-Mişu, Nicoleta, and Radu Stroe. 2010. The adjustment of the Conan & Holder model to the specificity of Romanian enterprises—A local study for building sector. *Economic Computation and Economic Cybernetics Studies and Research* 44: 123–40.

Bărbuţă-Mişu, Nicoleta, and Elena-Silvia Codreanu. 2014. Analysis and Prediction of the Bankruptcy Risk in Romanian Building Sector Companies. *Ekonomika* 93: 131–46. [CrossRef]

Beaver, William H. 1966. Financial Ratios as Predictors of Failure. *Journal of Accounting Research* 4: 71–111. [CrossRef]

Beaver, William H. 1968. Alternative Accounting Measures as Predictors of Failure. *The Accounting Review* 43: 113–22.

Belyaeva, Elena. 2014. On a New Logistic Regression Model for Bankruptcy Prediction in the IT Branch. U.U.D.M. Project Report. p. 35. Available online: https://uu.diva-portal.org/smash/get/diva2:785084/FULLTEXT01.pdf (accessed on 15 October 2019).

Brédart, Xavier. 2014. Bankruptcy prediction model: The case of the United States. *International Journal of Economics and Finance* 6: 1–7. [CrossRef]

Burns, John, and Gudrun Balvinsdottir. 2005. An institutional perspective of accountants' new roles—The interplay of contradictions and praxis. *European Accounting Review* 14: 725–57. [CrossRef]

Cielen, Anja, Ludo Peeters, and Koen Vanhoof. 2004. Bankruptcy prediction using a data envelopment analysis. *European Journal of Operational Research* 154: 526–32. [CrossRef]

Conan, Joel, and Michael Holder. 1979. *Variables explicatives de performances et controle de gestion dans les P.M.I. Universite Paris Dauphine [Explanatory Variables of Performance and Management Control in the SMEs]*. Paris: Paris Dauphine University.

Cultrera, Loredana, Melanie Croquet, and Jeremy Jospin. 2017. Predicting bankruptcy of Belgian SMEs: A hybrid approach based on factorial analysis. *International Business Research* 10: 33–41. [CrossRef]

Chaitanya, Krishna. 2005. Measuring Financial Distress of IDBI Using Altman Z-Score Model. *The IUP Journal of Bank Management* 4: 7–17.

Chung, Kim-Choy, Shin Shin Tan, and David K. Holdsworth. 2008. Insolvency prediction model using multivariate discriminant analysis and artificial neural network for the finance industry in New Zealand. *International Journal of Business and Management* 3: 19–29.

Dakovic, Rada, Claudia Czado, and Daniel Berg. 2010. Bankruptcy prediction in Norway: A comparison study. *Applied Economics Letters* 17: 1739–46. [CrossRef]

De, Ranabir. 2014. *Principal Component Analysis and General Regression Auto Associative Neural Network Hybrid as One-Class Classifier*. Kanpur: Indian Institute of Technology, Available online: https://www.idrbt.ac.in/assets/alumni/PT-2014/Ranabir%20De_Principal%20Component%20Analysis%20and%20General.pdf (accessed on 5 January 2020).

Diakomihalis, Mihail. 2012. The accuracy of Altman's models in predicting hotel bankruptcy. *International Journal of Accounting and Financial Reporting* 2: 96–113. [CrossRef]

Dun & Bradstreet. 2019. Global Bankruptcy Report 2019, Dun & Bradstreet Worldwide Network. Available online: https://www.bisnode.se/globalassets/global-bankruptcy-report-2019.pdf (accessed on 21 December 2019).

Elviani, Sri, Ramadona Simbolon, Zenni Riana, Farida Khairani, Sri Puspa Dewi, and Fauzi Fauzi. 2020. The Accuracy of the Altman, Ohlson, Springate and Zmejewski Models in Bankruptcy Predicting Trade Sector Companies in Indonesia. *Budapest International Research and Critics Institute (BIRCI-Journal)* 3: 334–47. [CrossRef]

European Commission. 2003. Commission Recommendation of 6 May 2003 Concerning the Definition of Micro, Small and Medium-Sized Enterprises. Available online: http://eur-lex.europa.eu/eli/reco/2003/361/oj (accessed on 18 December 2019).

Euler Hermes Economic Research. 2019. The View Economic Research. Available online: https://www.eulerhermes.com/content/dam/onemarketing/euh/eulerhermes_com/erd/publications/pdf/Global-Insolvencies-Jan19.pdf (accessed on 21 December 2019).

Fulmer, John G., Jr., James E. Moon, Thomas A. Gavin, and Michael J. Erwin. 1984. A Bankruptcy Classification Model for Small Firms. *Journal of Commercial Bank Lending* 66: 25–37.

Heffernan, Shelagh. 2005. *Modern Banking*. Chichester: John Wiley & Sons Ltd.

Hillegeist, Stephen A., Elizabeth K. Keating, Donald P. Cram, and Kyle G. Lundstedt. 2004. Assessing the probability of bankruptcy. *Review of Accounting Studies* 9: 5–34. [CrossRef]

Jouzbarkand, Mohammad, Farshad S. Keivani, Mohsen Khodadadi, and Seyed R.S.N. Fahim. 2013. Bankruptcy prediction model by Ohlson and Shirata models in Tehran Stock Exchange. *World Applied Sciences Journal* 21: 152–56.

Karels, Gordon V., and Arun J. Prakash. 1987. Multivariate normality and forecasting for business bankruptcy. *Journal of Business Finance & Accounting* 14: 573–93.

Kim, Myoung-Jong, and Ingoo Han. 2003. The discovery of experts' decision rules from qualitative bankruptcy data using genetic algorithms. *Expert Systems with Applications* 25: 637–46. [CrossRef]

Koh, Hian Chye, and Sen Suan Tan. 1999. A neural network approach to the prediction of going concern status. *Accounting and Business Research* 29: 211–16. [CrossRef]

Král', Pavol, Milos Fleischer, Maria Stachová, Gabriela Nedelová, and Lukas Sobíšek. 2016. Corporate financial distress prediction of Slovak companies: Z-score models vs. alternatives. Paper presented at the 9th Applications of Mathematics and Statistics in Economics—AMSE 2016, Banská Štiavnica, Slovakia, August 31–September 4.

Li, Hui, and Jie Sun. 2011. Predicting business failure using forward ranking-order case-based reasoning. *Expert Systems with Applications* 38: 3075–84. [CrossRef]

Mousavi, Mohammad Mahdi, Jamal Ouenniche, and Kaoru Tone. 2019. A comparative analysis of two-stage distress prediction models. *Expert Systems with Applications* 119: 322–41. [CrossRef]

Ohlson, James A. 1980. Financial Ratios and the Probabilistic Prediction of Bankruptcy. *Journal of Accounting Research* 18: 109–31. [CrossRef]

Onofrei, Mihaela, and Dan Lupu. 2014. *The Modelling of Forecasting the Bankruptcy in Romania.* MPRA Paper 95511. Munich: University Library of Munich.

Ouenniche, Jamal, and Kaoru Tone. 2017. An out-of-sample evaluation framework for DEA with application in bankruptcy prediction. *Annals of Operations Research* 254: 235–50. [CrossRef]

Paradi, Joseph C., Mette Asmild, and Paul C. Simak. 2004. Using DEA and worst practice DEA in credit risk evaluation. *Journal of Productivity Analysis* 21: 153–65. [CrossRef]

Prusak, Blazej. 2018. Review of research into enterprise bankruptcy prediction in selected Central and Eastern European countries. *International Journal of Financial Studies* 6: 60. [CrossRef]

Ryu, Kisang, and Soocheong Jang. 2004. Performance Measurements through Cash Flow Ratios and Traditional Ratios: A Comparison of Commercial and Casino Hotel Companies. *Journal of Hospitality Financial Management* 12: 15–25. [CrossRef]

Scapens, Robert W. 2006. Understanding Management Accounting Practices: A personal journey. *British Accounting Review* 38: 1–30. [CrossRef]

Shetty, Udaya, T. P. M. Pakkala, and T. Mallikarjunappa. 2012. A modified directional distance formulation of DEA to assess bankruptcy: An application to IT/ITES companies in India. *Expert Systems with Applications* 39: 1988–97. [CrossRef]

Shin, Kyung-Shik, Taik Soo Lee, and Hyun-Jung Kim. 2005. An application of support vector machines in bankruptcy prediction model. *Expert Systems with Applications* 28: 127–35. [CrossRef]

Shirata, Cindy Yoshiko. 1995. Read the Sign of Business Failure. *Journal of Risk and Management* 23: 117–38.

Shumway, Tyler. 2001. Forecasting bankruptcy more accurately: A simple hazard model. *Journal of Business* 74: 101–24. [CrossRef]

Sigrist, Fabio, and Christoph Hirnschall. 2019. Grabit: Gradient tree-boosted Tobit models for default prediction. *Journal of Banking & Finance* 102: 177–92.

Springate, Gordon. 1978. Predicting the possibility of failure in a Canadian firm. Master's Thesis, Simon Fraser University, Burnaby, BC, Canada.

Taffler, Richard J. 1982. Forecasting company failure in the UK using discriminant analysis and financial ratio data. *Journal of Royal Statistical Society Series A* 145: 342–58. [CrossRef]

Taffler, Richard J. 1983. The assessment of company solvency and performance using a statistical model. *Accounting and Business Research* 15: 295–307. [CrossRef]

Taffler, Richard J. 1984. Empirical models for the monitoring of UK corporations. *Journal of Banking & Finance* 8: 199–227.

Tam, Kar Yan. 1991. Neural Network Models and the Prediction of Bank Bankruptcy. *Omega* 19: 429–45. [CrossRef]

Theodossiou, Panayiotis. 1991. Alternative models for assessing the financial condition of business in Greece. *Journal of Business Finance & Accounting* 18: 697–720.

Xu, Ming, and Chu Zhang. 2009. Bankruptcy prediction: The case of Japanese listed companies. *Review of Accounting Studies* 14: 534–58. [CrossRef]

Zavgren, Christine V. 1985. Assessing the vulnerability to failure of American industrial firms: A logistic analysis. *Journal of Business Finance & Accounting* 12: 19–45.

Zhang, Guoqiang, Michael Y. Hu, Eddy B. Patuwo, and Daniel C. Indro. 1999. Artificial neural networks in bankruptcy prediction: General framework and cross-validation analysis. *European Journal of Operational Research* 116: 16–32. [CrossRef]

Zmijewski, Mark E. 1984. Methodological issues relating to the estimation of financial distress prediction models. *Journal of Accounting Research* 22: 59–82. [CrossRef]

Wang, Jo-Yu, Juo-Lien Wang, and Hui-Yu Liao. 2019. Does Corporate Governance Enhance Firm Performance and Reduce Firm Risk? Evidence from Taiwanese Listed Companies. *Journal of Economics and Management* 15: 61–91.

Woods, Margare, and Kevin Dowd. 2008. *Financial Risk Management for Management Accountants, Management Accounting Guideline.* Toronto: The Society of Management Accountants of Canada (CMA Canada), Durham: The American Institute of Certified Public Accountants, Inc. (AICPA), London: The Chartered Institute of Management Accountants (CIMA), Available online: https://www.cimaglobal.com/Documents/ImportedDocuments/cid_mag_financial_risk_jan09.pdf (accessed on 25 November 2019).

Wu, Yanhui, C. Gaunt, and S. Gray. 2010. A Comparison of Alternative Bankruptcy Prediction Models. *Journal of Contemporary Accounting and Economics* 6: 34–45. [CrossRef]

Permissions

List of Contributors

Błażej Prusak
Faculty of Management and Economics, Gdańsk University of Technology, 80-233 Gdańsk, Poland

Minhas Akbar and Hafiz Muhammad Arshad
Department of Management Sciences, COMSATS University Islamabad (Sahiwal Campus), Sahiwal 57000, Pakistan

Ahsan Akbar and Minghui Yang
International Business School, Guangzhou College of South China University of Technology, Guangzhou 510080, China

Petra Maresova
Department of Economy, Faculty of Informatics and Management, University of Hradec Kralove, Rokitanskeho 62/26, 500 03 Hradec Kralove, Czech Republic

Mehreen Mehreen, Maran Marimuthu and Amin Jan
Department of Management and Humanities, Universiti Teknologi PETRONAS, Bandar Seri Iskandar, Seri Iskandar 32610, Perak, Malaysia

Samsul Ariffin Abdul Karim
Fundamental and Applied Sciences Department and Centre for Smart Grid Energy Research (CSMER), Institute of Autonomous System, Universiti Teknologi PETRONAS, Bandar Seri Iskandar, Seri Iskandar 32610, Perak Darul Ridzuan, Malaysia

Tomasz Korol
Faculty of Management and Economics, Gdansk University of Technology, Narutowicza 11/12, 80-233 Gdansk, Poland

Tamás Kristóf and Miklós Virág
Department of Enterprises Finances, Corvinus University of Budapest, Fővám tér 8, 1093 Budapest, Hungary

Jakub Horak, Jaromir Vrbka and Petr Suler
School of Expertness and Valuation, Institute of Technology and Business in Ceske Budejovice, Okruzni 517/10, 37001 Ceske Budejovice, Czech Republic

Tomasz Iwanowicz and Bartłomiej Iwanowicz
Department of Accounting, Akademia Leona Koźmińskiego, Jagiellońska 57/59, 03-301 Warsaw, Poland

Dagmar Camska and Jiri Klecka
Department of Economics and Management, University of Chemistry and Technology Prague, Technická 5, 166 28 Prague 6, Czech Republic

Tomasz Pisula
Department of Quantitative Methods, Faculty of Management, Rzeszow University of Technology, al. Powstancow W-wy 10, 35-959 Rzeszow, Poland

Oliver Lukason and Art Andresson
Faculty of Economics and Business Administration, University of Tartu, Liivi 4, 50409 Tartu, Estonia

Nicoleta Bărbuţă-Mişu
Department of Business Administration, "Dunarea de Jos" University of Galati, 800008 Galati, Romania

Mara Madaleno
GOVCOPP — Research Unit in Governance, Competitiveness and Public Policy, Department of Economics, Management, Industrial Engineering and Tourism (DEGEIT), University of Aveiro, 3810-193 Aveiro, Portugal

Index

Printed in the USA
CPSIA information can be obtained
at www.ICGtesting.com
JSHW051626061123
51533JS00005B/119